ARMS CONTROL AND TECHNOLOGICAL INNOVATION

Edited by

DAVID CARLTON and CARLO SCHAERF

A HALSTED PRESS BOOK

JOHN WILEY & SONS

NEW YORK   TORONTO

© International School on Disarmament and Research on Conflicts Sixth Course

Published in the USA, Canada and Latin America by Halsted Press,
a Division of John Wiley & Sons, Inc., New York.

Library of Congress Cataloging in Publication Data

International School on Disarmament and Research on Conflicts, 6th, Nemi,
Italy, 1976.
Arms control and technological innovation.

"A Halsted Press book."
1. Military art and science – Addresses, essays,
lectures. 2. Weapons systems – Addresses, essays,
lectures. 3. Disarmament – Addresses, essays,
lectures. I. Carlton, David, 1938-
II. Schaerf, Carlo. III. Title.
U104.155 1976   327′.174   77-8790
ISBN 0-470-99274-3

Printed and bound in Great Britain

CONTENTS

Preface

Glossary of Acronyms

1. Summary of Proceedings *Herbert M. Levine* 11

2. New Technologies and New Weapons Systems
    Kosta Tsipis 36

3. Can Conventional New Technologies and New Tactics
    Replace Tactical Nuclear Weapons in Europe?
    Jorma K. Miettinen 52

4. The International Political Economy of Proliferation
    Steven J. Baker 70

5. Arms Limitation and Security Policies Required to
    Minimise the Proliferation of Nuclear Weapons
    Enid C.B. Schoettle 102

6. The Anglo-American Nuclear Relationship: Proliferatory
    or Anti-Proliferatory? *David Carlton* 132

7. Proliferation: Sophisticated Weapons and Revolutionary
    Options — The Sub-State Perspective *J. Bowyer Bell* 146

8. Arms and Politics: Old Issues, New Perceptions 161
    Michael Nacht

9. A Different Approach to Arms Control — Recirprocal
    Unilateral Restraint *Herbert Scoville, Jr.* 170

10. A New Approach to Strategic Arms Limitation and
     Reduction *William Epstein* 176

11. Strategic Arms Limitation and Military Strategic Concepts
     M.A. Milstein 198

12. Nuclear Testing — No End in Sight? *Thomas A. Halsted* 210

13. Reconnaissance Satellites and the Arms Race
     Herbert F. York 224

14. The Realities of Arms Control: The Cruise Missile Case
     Robert A. Nalewajek 232

15. The Diffusion of Economic and Military Power and its
     Impact on the Middle East Conflict *Mario'n Mushkat* 247

16. The Fallacy of Thinking Conventionally about Nuclear   255
    Weapons   *Hans J. Morgenthau*
17. All at Sea? A Critique of the American Strategic Force
    Structure   *Peter King*   265
18. The Function of Military Power   *B.V.A. Röling*   288
19. 116 Wars in 30 Years   *István Kende*   303
20. The Role of Arms in Capitalist Economies: the Process
    of Overdevelopment and Underdevelopment
    Mary Kaldor   322
21. Economic and Technological Prerequisites for
    Achieving Political and Military Stability
    Tom Stonier   342

    Contributors   358

    List of Course Participants   362

PREFACE

The papers in this volume were presented to the Sixth Course of the International School on Disarmament and Research on Conflicts, held in Nemi, Italy, from 21 June to 5 July 1976.

The organisation of the course was made possible by the generous collaboration and financial contributions of different organisations and individuals.

For their financial contributions we wish to express our gratitude to:

The Ford Foundation, in particular Michael Nacht;
The Italian Ministry of Public Education;
The Italian Ministry of Foreign Affairs;
For hospitality in Nemi we are indebted to the Collegio Missionari Verbiti;
Fernando Pacciani collaborated in the preparatory work in Frascati.

We also wish to acknowledge the dedicated collaboration of Viviana Panaccia, Virginia Valore, Maurella |della Seta and Maria Rosi.

We are grateful to James Digby and to the International Institute for Strategic Studies for granting permission to Jorma Miettinen to reproduce a table first published in an *Adelphi Paper*. Thanks are also due to the Stockholm International Peace Research Institute for allowing Enid Schoettle to use material from her forthcoming book which is to be published under its auspices.

All opinions expressed during the formal lectures as well as during the ensuing discussions are of a purely private nature and do not necessarily represent the official opinion either of the organisers of the School or of the organisations to which the speakers belong.

GLOSSARY OF ACRONYMS

ABM	Anti-Ballistic Missiles
ACDA	Area Control and Disarmament Agency (United States)
AEC	Atomic Energy Commission (United States)
ALCM	Air Launched Cruise Missile
ASW	Anti-Submarine Warfare
CCD	Committee on Disarmament (Geneva)
CEP	Circular Error Probable
CLGP	Cannon Launched Guided Projectile
CPSU	Communist Party of the Soviet Union
CTB	Comprehensive Test Ban
EEC	European Economic Community
ERDA	Energy Research and Development Administration (United States)
FOBS	Fractional Orbital Ballistic Missile System
GCD	General and Complete Disarmament
GE	General Electric
GNP	Gross National Product
IAEA	International Atomic Energy Authority
ICBM	Inter-Continental Ballistic Missile
IISS	International Institute for Strategic Studies
IRA	Irish Republican Army
IRBM	Intermediate Range Ballistic Missile
LDC	Less Developed Countries
LWR	Light Water Reactor
MARV	Manoeuvrable Re-entry Vehicle
MBFR	Mutual Balanced Force Reductions
MIRV	Multiple Independently-Targetable Re-entry Vehicle
MIT	Massachusetts Institute of Technology
MPLA	Movimento Popular de Libertação de Angola
MRBM	Medium Range Ballistic Missile
MT	Megaton
MWe	Megawatts electric
NATO	North Atlantic Treaty Organisation
NNWS	Non-Nuclear-Weapons State
NPT	Non-Proliferation Treaty
NWS	Nuclear Weapons State

OECD	Organization for Economic Co-operation and Development
OPEC	Organization of Petroleum Exporting Countries
PGM	Precision-Guided Munition
PNE	Peaceful Nuclear Explosions
R and D	Research and Development
RPV	Remotely Piloted Vehicle
RV	Re-entry Vehicle
SAC	Strategic Air Command (United States)
SALT	Strategic Arms Limitation Talks
SCAD	Subsonic Cruise Armed Decoy
SIOP	Single Integrated Operational Plan
SIPRI	Stockholm International Peace Research Institute
SLBM	Submarine Launched Ballistic Missile
SLCM	Submarine/Ship/Sea Launched Cruise Missile
SRAM	Short Range Attack Missile
SS-BN	Nuclear Ballistic Missile-Firing Submarine
SWU	Separation Work Units
TNW	Tactical Nuclear Weapon
TTBT	Threshold Test Ban Treaty
VLF	Very Low Frequency
WDC	World Disarmament Conference

1 SUMMARY OF PROCEEDINGS

Herbert M. Levine

Introduction

The Sixth Course of the International School on Disarmament and Research on Conflicts (ISODARCO) took place in Nemi, Italy, between 22 June and 7 July 1976. It was primarily concerned with three subjects: the causes of the arms race; the consequences of the arms race to the world; and the control of the arms race.

The principal problem of the arms race, according to several lecturers, is that weapons and delivery-systems technology have developed so much as to threaten the survival of civilisation itself. The pace of technological change is proceeding more rapidly today than ever before, and there is serious doubt whether political institutions are adapting to this change in time to avoid devastating consequences to the world.

The present technology was described. The most powerful weapons belong to the United States and the Soviet Union with strategic arsenals composed of nuclear explosives and delivery systems. Weapons with explosives measured in kilotons and megatons have been produced. Delivery systems — composed of bombers, inter-continental ballistic missiles (ICBMs), and submarine-launched ballistic missiles (SLBMs) — are poised for instant use on command. Defence systems exist — particularly in the Soviet Union — but these are regarded as likely to be ineffective in an all-out war.

New military systems for use both in nuclear and conventional wars were described. Among the most significant of these systems are precision-guided munitions (PGMs), cruise missiles, remotely-piloted vehicles (RPVs), electronic warfare and anti-submarine warfare (ASW) devices, advanced ballistic missiles and anti-ballistic missiles (ABMs). Although each system has different features, the major consequences for nuclear war are that they improve weapon accuracy and threaten to make existing systems obsolete.

In conventional war the new technology is being applied to ground-forces combat. Principally, accuracy and intelligence-gathering have improved, although electronic warfare achieved mixed results in the Vietnam War and in the Yom Kippur War. Weapons for conventional wars, moreover, are being transferred to Third World countries from

11

states with vast armaments industries, and the consequence of this weapons transfer is to make wars potentially more devastating. The conventional arms build-up in the Middle East was cited by one lecturer as being the most dangerous in the world.

The Causes of the Arms Race

The causes of the arms race were explained in terms of international political, military, economic, bureaucratic and domestic political and evolutionary factors.

1. International Political Factors

From the international political point of view the state system produces insecurity which leads to a search for armaments. The Soviet Union, viewing the United States as a threat to its security, sees American bases, high defence budgets and interventionism as dangerous. The United States, observing the Soviet Union as a threat to its security, sees Soviet bases, high defence budgets and interventionism as dangerous. There was considerable discussion concerning these perceptions, with participants differing about the realistic bases of the fears.

One commentator argued that the Soviet Union was responsible for the tensions which produce arms build-ups. Soviet involvements in Vietnam, Angola and the Middle East were cited as a specific examples of the Soviet lack of sincerity in *détente*. The subject of the denial of human rights in the Soviet Union was given as another illustration of Soviet irresponsibility.

Another lecturer blamed the West — and particularly the United States — for precipitating and promoting conventional wars around the world from 1945 to 1974. He defined a war as any armed conflict characterised by regular armed forces used by at least one side, a degree of organised fighting by both sides, and continuity of armed clashes. In the thirty-year period examined there were 116 wars fought in 69 countries involving 81 regular armies and about 25 million deaths. There were only 26 days without war. The 116 wars represented about 350 years of war if the time period of each war is included in the calculations.

Data was presented which led to the following conclusions: the trend of war was sharply increasing until 1967, when it began to decline; wars after World War Two were fought mainly in Third World countries; about 80 per cent of the time spent in war was devoted to *anti-régime* wars (involving the overthrow of existing governments) rather than *tribal* wars (fought between parts of a country or between religious, national or ethnic groups) or *border* wars (wars between nation-states on borders of states); most of the wars involved foreign forces, and foreign participation makes wars more intensive and longer; the United States has used its forces in more wars than any other nation; and the United States was followed by Great Britain, France and Portugal in such intervention.

In the discussion it was argued that it is often difficult to decide at what point incidents constitute a war. It is also not easy to classify a war as anti-régime, tribal or border since a war often has more than one of these features. It was further argued that a different criterion — such as military aid, rather than the use of foreign troops — might lead to assessments which would give prominence to countries other than the United States and its allies. Moreover, the inclusion of Vietnam in calculations relating to the total time spent in war was bound to produce a distorted picture.

In reply it was argued that opinions may vary in characterising a war as anti-régime, tribal or border, but each war possesses a dominant feature. It is true that different criteria might lead to different results, but the researcher must decide what to examine. Vietnam, moreover, should be included in any evaluation because of its extreme importance. Even if Vietnam were excluded, however, the results would be much the same.

2. Military Factors

Several speakers pointed to the military establishments of the United States and the Soviet Union as being responsible for the arms race. The military leaders are charged with the primary responsibility for the security of their countries. They will be blamed if any weaknesses appear. They fear constantly the military capabilities and intentions of their major adversaries. The argument was put forward that military claims are self-serving. Military leaders seek to expand their influence through demands for larger budgets. The military leaders always plan for new weapons acquisition. If left uncontrolled, the military would never be satisfied.

It was asserted by one speaker that arms control arrangements are prevented by militarist circles in the United States and by those who have vested interests in the arms race. There is no Soviet threat. Fictions concerning the 'Soviet menace' have become part and parcel of American politics. Another participant claimed, however, that there are militarists in the Soviet Union, too. The problem is that more is known about Western nations than about Communist countries, since

the Western Nations are open societies. Certainly less information
appears publicly from Soviet sources. Attention was drawn to the
so-called military-industrial complex in the Soviet Union. But other
participants maintained that there are no contradictions between
military and political representatives in the Soviet Union and that
there are no groups in that country which are for the arms race.

The influence of the American military establishment in developing
the cruise missile was cited as an example of the power of the military
bureaucracy. It was asserted that when Secretary of Defense Melvin
Laird introduced the submarine-launched cruise missile (SLCM) in
1972, there was no tangible need for the development of this weapon
as a response to Soviet initiatives. The same could be said about the
air-launched cruise missile (ALCM). It was further argued that the
continuing rivalry over future missions and roles of the United States
Air Force and Navy may have been a motivating factor in cruise
missile development. The Air Force insisted that its bombers were the
only component of the strategic nuclear triad which was capable of
both a nuclear and conventional role. The B-52 is a vehicle not only
usable in nuclear war, but one which has already been employed in the
conventional, non-nuclear war of Vietnam. On the other hand, the
development and deployment of SLCMs will provide the Navy with
dual capability, a factor which may have been one reason for Navy
interest in this system. In addition, the military looked upon the cruise
missile as a system which could circumvent Strategic Arms Limitation
Talks (SALT) I agreements. Admiral Elmo Zumwalt was quoted as
saying that 'as a result of the SALT agreements and the resulting
constraints on our sea-based ballistic missile system, the cruise missile
remains the only viable concept by which we can strengthen and
diversify our sea-based deterrent'.

Another lecturer presented the view that to understand why arms
races occur, one must first identify the central factors which the
strategist must consider. These factors were described as technology,
leadership, strategic theories and theorists, service interests and
doctrines, budgets, domestic politics and alliance politics. The problem
with this analysis, one observer noted, was that it provided no way to
give weight to each determinant. Moreover, other factors, such as
foreign policy, perceptions of the adversary and economics, should also
be included.

The role of the military in institutionalising a weapon was regarded
as a major cause of the arms race. It is not technological innovation
which is crucial, one speaker noted, but rather the manner in which it

is exploited. There is always a long time gap between an invention and its acceptance by armed forces. Gunpowder was developed in the thirteenth century, but it took four hundred years before it was assimilated. Agreements on arms control must therefore precede assimilation. If constraints are to be imposed, the factors which determine the assimilation process must be understood.

It was argued that chemical and biological weapons in the twentieth century had not been assimilated thus far into military units. There was considerable discussion as to whether or not|such weapons were not used because of lack of assimilation or because of lack of utility. It was asserted, for example, that the reason why the United States withdrew from the biological war business in 1969 was that biological weapons were ineffficient, not that they were not assimilated.

One participant contended that chemical weapons were not much used in World War Two for political and military reasons. President Franklin D. Roosevelt was opposed to their use. Chemical weapons, moreover, had hardly any effect on Germany, although they may have had an effect on Japan. Germany did not use her chemical stocks at the beginning of the war because she did not need to do so; and she could not do so during the Normandy invasion since it would have been disastrous to her own troops.

3. Economic Factors

The economic causes of the arms race were also considered. It was asserted that various industrial and financial interests in the United States encourage the arms race. The view was also presented that there are economic interests in the Soviet Union which gain from continuing the arms race.

The link between economic forces and arms transfers was considered. One lecturer described the relationship of arms to the world economy — with particular attention to the Western industrialised nations. The thesis was advanced that the United States economy is on the decline and that arms both reflect and reinforce this process. The thesis rested on three propositions: the secular increase in the procurement of arms reflects the process of decline; the procurement of arms acquires a momentum of its own stemming from the momentum of the arms industry; and increases in the procurement of arms and/or military spending accelerate economic decline, a process which occurs because resources are diverted into declining industries.

In discussion the view that increased spending on military budgets is related to technological decay was challenged. The United States, for example, is spending a large share of its defence budget on manpower costs rather than on hardware since it has moved from a conscript to a volunteer army. Another question arose concerning the importance of economic factors. If the United States were going to experience technological decline after the Second World War, why did she place Federal Germany and Japan under her security umbrella and allow those two countries to gain advantages through technological competition? The inevitability of the decline of technologies was also disputed. Some institutions, such as the multinational corporations, for example, have adapted quite well to change.

Attention was also directed to the relationship between increased use of nuclear energy and the proliferation of nuclear weapons. As private corporations and national governments build new nuclear capability, economic pressures are exerted to export nuclear technologies to other nations. The effect of competition in the nuclear energy field makes it increasingly possible for more nations to develop nuclear weapons capabilities. A view was expressed, however, that it is by no means certain that Third World countries will move rapidly to build nuclear facilities, since these are capital-intensive.

4. Bureaucratic and Domestic Political Factors

Bureaucratic and domestic political factors were analysed. The internal debate within each country is time-consuming. It may take years before the different agencies of a government agree on a negotiating position. Unless there is strong leadership at the top to move the bureaucracy, it was argued, technological changes may encourage the arms race.

The case of SALT was used as an example. Negotiations proceeded for several years before some agreements were concluded. In the meantime technological developments in new weapons were taking place. It was asserted that a contributing factor to the success of SALT was the leadership of President Richard Nixon and Secretary of State Henry Kissinger, who dominated the United States SALT strategy. Even with strong leadership, however, progress was slow.

5. Evolutionary Factors

Finally, the arms race was explained in terms of the evolution of humanity. One lecturer presented a theory to explain the interrelated phenomena of war and the arms race: War can be explained in the context of social and economic forces of a global nature which are part of unfolding evolutionary-historical processes. From the point of

view of macro-history, the world has moved from an agrarian society
to a mechanical society and is now entering a communicative era. The
mechanical society was characterised by industrialisation. A principal
cause of the abolition of slavery was that as the mechanical age
developed, the need for coerced labour was obviated. As society moves
from the mechanical to the communicative age, the need for war also
diminishes. The primary social motivation for war, it was asserted, is
the quest for resources. This primary motivation has now been replaced
by a new force, namely technological innovation, which lays the
foundation for the demise of war as an institution. The new age is
characterised by an enormous increase in productivity in technologically
advanced nations, an improvement in transnational co-operation
coupled with economic, technical and cultural interdependence (as, for
example, in the European Economic Community), and the ascendancy
of industrial-economic power over military power (as in Japan). Most
of the world is only now moving from an agrarian to a mechanical
society. Wars will be eliminated as the world evolves to the new age:
Policies should be directed towards increasing economic, technical and
cultural independence and encouraging global productivity. Arms
control advocates should continue their work since history is on their
side. The arms race is but a reflection of cultural lag and will end when
the world moves to a new stage.

This evolutionary view was challenged on factual grounds. One
participant argued that the new international institutions – such as
the multinational corporations – are not necessarily the bearers of
peace. It was also asserted that nationalism remains a strong force in
the advanced societies, as may be seen, for example, in Canada and
Belgium.

There was considerable discussion about whether reality changes
technology or technology changes reality. The view was presented that
the Aztecs never applied the invention of the wheel and the Chinese
did not apply gunpowder to war. The rejoinder was offered that there
were draught animals in Aztec civilisation, and it was easier to roll
stones on barges; and that the Chinese did not need gunpowder. It
was also argued that a view of war based exclusively on technological
motivations does not adequately describe the complex and varied
causes of war.

The Consequences of the Arms Race to the World

Lecturers described the consequences of the arms race to the world.
Attention was directed primarily to military, international political,

domestic political and economic factors.

1. Military Factors

The effects of the arms race on strategy, tactics, national and international security and nuclear proliferation were considered. Some lecturers contended that for the superpowers the main purpose of the arms race is to keep parity, to prevent any one side from possessing first-strike capability. Strategic policy has emphasised deterrence rather than defence. Deterrence, it is believed, is credible if no country achieves a first-strike capability. The superpowers desire to preserve this situation. Thus new weapons are viewed as stabilising or destabilising, depending on the degree to which they increase the prospects of a state acquiring a first-strike capability. In this connection special attention was given to the American cruise missile because of the possibility that this weapon may be viewed as destroying parity.

The technical characteristics of the cruise missile were described. It is being developed for use from sea, air and land platforms. It is small — about the size of a torpedo. It has a range of up to 2,000 nautical miles and can be launched from outside Soviet air-defence systems. It can fly at low altitudes and, consequently, avoid radar. It is difficult, and sometimes impossible, to detect the existence of a cruise missile by national means of verification. Even if it is detected, it is almost impossible to determine if it has strategic or tactical capabilities.

Two important points were made about this new weapon. First, the development and production of strategic cruise missiles may negate the SALT accords which were based on national technical means of verification. Second, it may be possible for Third World countries ultimately to develop strategic capabilities with cruise missiles. The costs are relatively low — at least less expensive than the current systems of ICBMs, bombers and SLBMs. Thus a cheap proliferation potential exists.

Much attention was given to the presence of tactical nuclear weapons in Europe. Both NATO and Warsaw Pact countries have thousands of these weapons in place. They vary in size from less than one kiloton to one megaton. There was much discussion about the feasibility of removing them from Europe.

Several arguments were advanced in favour of keeping these tactical nuclear weapons at least in Western Europe:

1. They contribute to deterrence since the Soviet Union may be tempted to plan a major land attack if it believes that NATO does

not have or is not willing to use these weapons in response to a Soviet conventional or nuclear attack.

2. It would be politically unwise to reduce or eliminate tactical nuclear weapons in the expectation that European NATO members would then re-arm with conventional weapons. The removal of tactical nuclear weapons might instead lead each European NATO country to make whatever deal it could with the Warsaw Pact powers – a process of 'Finlandisation'.

3. Federal Germany would object to removal of these weapons. The result might be West German neutrality or even a decision to make independent West German nuclear weapons.

Several arguments were advanced, however, in favour of removing these weapons from Western Europe.

1. There is no real distinction between tactical and strategic nuclear weapons. The tactical nuclear weapons currently deployed in Europe have explosive power more devastating than the atomic bombs detonated at Hiroshima and Nagasaki. It is foolish to think that there is an inherent distinction.

2. The new technology in conventional military weapons – particularly those relying on PGMs – will give advantages to the defensive and can serve as suitable substitutes for tactical nuclear weapons.

3. There is no way of preventing total nuclear war once tactical nuclear weapons are used.

4. Tactical nuclear weapons in forward-based positions may be captured in case of a surprise attack. At least, they should be removed several hundred miles back from the possible initial battlefield.

5. The destruction of Europe would be assured by the use of these weapons.

6. A balance of military power already exists in Europe even without these weapons.

Participants also gave attention to the use of reconnaissance satellites. From the outset their purpose has been the gathering of intelligence, and recently they have been used as a basis for national technical means of verification of strategic forces included in the SALT agreements. It was argued that these satellites had a 'benign purpose' in controlling the arms race. On the other hand, there has been a tendency for these instruments to be used in battlefield situations, for example in the Bangladesh crisis and in the Yom Kippur War. Thus reconnaissance satellites may increasingly help to undermine rather than strengthen security.

The role of the arms race in promoting national and international security was considered. The thesis was put forward that there is an inverse relationship between strategic nuclear weapons and national security because of (1) the danger of accidents; (2) the possibility of accidental war; (3) the difficulty of maintaining proper inventory control; and (4) the gap between the effectiveness of defensive and offensive nuclear weapons.

1. Accidents. There are thousands of nuclear weapons deployed around the world. Accidental nuclear explosions are possible. Fissionable material which is toxic could be dispersed causing immediate or delayed deaths.

2. Accidental war. Wars may occur because a nuclear accident is viewed as a belligerent move, or because there is a failure of command, control and communication, or because there is a major international crisis which may be combined with accidents or failures of command, control and communication.

3. Inventory control. It is impossible to design an inventory control system which is one hundred per cent accurate. It is reasonable to believe that non-state actors will eventually gain access to some of these weapons because of the difficulty in protecting such a large number of weapons.

4. Gap between the effectiveness of defensive and offensive nuclear weapons. There is no feasible passive defence from nuclear weapons. Nor is there a feasible active defence: a pre-emptive attack will not work because the entire force of the other side must be destroyed.

It was pointed out that although the conclusion that there is an inverse relationship between strategic nuclear weapons and security is true, the real problem is how to make arms control politically negotiable. Merely stressing the so-called inverse relationship takes us no further. Again, should we not continue to try to improve safeguards? Just saying that accidents are possible, *ergo,* we should disarm, does not solve the problem. The view was also expressed that accidental war is not really very likely because of the existence of hot lines, which link the communication networks of the political leaders of the superpowers.

Another lecturer described the dangers of nuclear proliferation in terms of its destabilising potential: (1) even primitive weapons could cause accidents, and terrorists could get control of these with devastating consequences; (2) local wars will become nuclear; (3) there is an increased possibility of the superpowers getting involved in local nuclear wars, and this involvement can lead to nuclear escalation; (4) the danger of catalytic war rises with an increasing number of nuclear states; (5) nuclear weapons might fall into the hands of so-called 'crazy states'; (6) as each nation is added to the nuclear club, a domino effect would result; (7) all successive régimes will have access to nuclear weapons so that nations which had been ruled by responsible leaders could eventually institute irresponsible policies; (8) as more nations get nuclear weapons, the chances of their use increase, and any such future use of nuclear weapons would of course breach the valuable post-1945 taboo; (9) further proliferation justifies a continued arms race between the superpowers; and (10) it would confuse arms control negotiations by making them more complex.

Participants differed as to whether nuclear proliferation would automatically occur. One commentator discussed why proliferation had been so slow after the Chinese detonation of its nuclear weapon in 1964, an event which might have influenced many other nations to obtain nuclear weapons. The following reasons were given: (1) the United States had given security guarantees which constrained some states; (2) domestic opposition to nuclear proliferation was strong; (3) the economic and technological costs of going nuclear were high; (4) there was in many cases no perception of threats; (5) there was not enough enriched uranium and plutonium; and (6) the prestige of going nuclear was not high. It was argued that many of these considerations have altered recently.

There was considerable discussion about whether proliferation can be halted or only delayed. The view was advanced that states may seek nuclear weapons for different reasons. Some may need them for security (Israel, Taiwan and South Korea); some may seem them for status (France, Iran, Brazil and Argentina); and some ('crazy states') may want them for 'irrational' purposes (Libya and Uganda). Many states which fall into these categories cannot be much influenced by the present nuclear weapons states. It was argued, however, that many states do not fall into these categories and hence they can be influenced by non-proliferatory policies by the existing nuclear weapons states.

A participant commented that the decision to go nuclear will rarely be taken at a time when a state does not have either a programme for the development of nuclear energy for peaceful purposes or the embryo of a nuclear weapons establishment. Decisions to build nuclear weapons will more usually be taken after a long series of non-military or preliminary military moves has been made. The experience of India and France illustrates this point. India had a large nuclear establishment involved in peaceful nuclear development. The decision to build a nuclear weapon may thus have been taken because India already had a nuclear establishment and a nuclear capability. In the case of France there were several turning-points: (1) Dien Bien Phu in 1954 — when it was decided to increase plutonium production; (2) the Suez Crisis in 1956 — when France announced the intention to separate uranium isotopes; and (3) finally one Prime Minister took out options on testing; and another Prime Minister ordered the actual tests.

2. International Political Factors

The international political consequences of the arms race were also considered. The superpower rivalry, it was argued, is not limited in its effects to the two countries and their power blocs. Since the results of nuclear war between the superpowers would produce radioactive fall-out and possibly attacks on neutrals, there have been numerous wider international attempts to control the arms race. Small powers have played a role in negotiating the Limited Test Ban Treaty and the Non-Proliferation Treaty (NPT). They have, moreover, advocated nuclear-free zones and general disarmament conferences. Another consequence of the arms race is that small powers must consider adopting nuclear weapons of their own. India tested a nuclear device while contending that it was not for military purposes. It is widely believed that Israel already possesses nuclear weapons although they have never been tested. The arms race has also directed attention to nuclear energy with consequences for war and peace. Small powers seek nuclear reactors for peaceful purposes which, however, can produce the fissionable materials needed for military weapons. Again as a result of the superpower arms race, it was argued, small powers have tended to become distrustful of large powers. Some of the Third World countries look upon the United States-Soviet Union arms control arrangements as devices to control the world.

3. Domestic Political Factors

The arms race produces internal political effects. Several participants mentioned how arms control issues can be injected into political campaigns. In the United States, for example, Ronald Reagan criticised

President Ford for the SALT accords, and this criticism may have had an adverse impact on the pace of SALT negotiations. Also emphasised was the importance of political leadership at the executive level in promoting arms control. In the United States, for example, Nixon and Kissinger, who sometimes worked without the approval of the SALT negotiating team, dominated the United States position in the SALT talks. When Nixon's position was weakened because of Watergate, so too was his ability to enter into arms control agreements with the Soviet Union.

The impact of nuclear weapons on the behaviour of sub-state actors in the international arena was discussed. The question was asked whether a group could seize control of a nuclear weapon and hold a city to ransom. The argument was put forward that terrorist groups lack the expertise to deal with these weapons. The experience of the Irish Republican Army, guerrilla groups in Angola, and guerrilla groups in Israel before national independence illustrates a lack of expertise in the use of sophisticated weapons. Unless there is support from a foreign nation which can provide the necessary scientific and military skills, it was argued, it is doubtful whether terrorist groups represent a nuclear danger.

The consequences to democracy of great-power arms transfers to the Third World were discussed. The argument was advanced that the role of the United States in furnishing vast amounts of military aid to Pakistan was detrimental to democratic development there. The United States had supported the professional military at the expense of Pakistani political leaders and had contributed to the military *coup* in 1958. How much the superpowers were responsible for the decline of democracy and how much Third World countries bear the principal responsibility for this phenomenon were subjects which were also considered.

4. Economic Factors

The consequences of the arms race to the economies of the superpowers and other countries were examined in some detail. One lecturer asserted that the view that military spending is economically beneficial is, in fact, a myth. The United States' economy has deteriorated in the past thirty years. Military spending has produced inflation and unemployment because of the economic nature of military goods and because of the effect of military production on technological progress. From the point of view of economics, it was argued, military goods do not contribute to the present or future standard of living. Military goods absorb resources. The cost-plus method of contracting puts no necessity on a corporation to be efficient. The economy, moreover, is distorted. In 1967, for example, one-third of all engineers and scientists in the United States were engaged in defence and space work. This military emphasis served to pre-empt critical resources. The stationing of forces abroad, moreover, had an adverse effect on the United States' balance of payments position. Military spending has also had an unfavourable effect on technological progress. Defence industries attract the most talented people, so that less talented people are directed to more productive industries. United States technology, consequently, is declining now in leadership as may be seen in machine tools, chemicals, shipbuilding and steel manufacturing. Engineering training, moreover, is distorted, so that new engineers are not being trained for more productive ventures.

In the discussion a comment was made that in some areas technological advantage was the result of military spending. In response it was argued that the advantage was temporary. A criticism was made that this kind of investigation is difficult to quantify when one looks at cross-national analyses. It was also mentioned that the support of a large number of engineers would not have happened without defence paranoia. The GI Bill in the United States indirectly contributed to economic development by providing for the education of scientists. The emphasis on science which appears in part from a military motivation also contributes to economic development.

A participant challenged the proposition that defence expenditures hurt the economy, and argued that the United States has one of the strongest economies in the world. The economic decay argument is exaggerated; defence expenditure on hardware represents less than 2 per cent of the United States' gross national product, hardly a share which can have such devastating consequences.

The view was presented that other factors should also be taken into account in analysing reasons for technological decline — factors such as the effect of trade unions in the United States, the emergence of the European Economic Community and Japan, and anti-trust prosecutions. It is essential to compare other countries which have similar problems.

The relationship between arms expenditures and economics was explored by another lecturer. Three broad theories about the relationship were explained: orthodox development, modernising and Marxist. The orthodox development theorists assert that arms are bad for development because they lead to war. Moreover, war absorbs resources which could be used for development. The modernising school advocates say that arms are good because they create stability (good for aid and investment); induce modern attitudes; require an industrial infrastructure; and tend to exist with a more relaxed fiscal policy which leads to bigger markets and investment. The Marxists argue that arms maintain an unequal social structure and lead to foreign investment.

The evidence is scant for all three theories. Libya, Brazil, Turkey and Iran have high military expenditures and high growth. Cuba and Southern Yemen have low growth and low military expenditures. Cambodia has high military spending and low growth.

A participant argued that military leaders do not understand the necessity of improving agricultural production which must be done in most developing countries. These leaders emphasise industrial production geared to military purposes, rather than more economically beneficial agricultural production.

The Control of the Arms Race

Participants offered numerous proposals for controlling the arms race. We may conveniently summarise the discussion by considering the following five different approaches to arms control: (1) multilateral, bilateral and unilateral; (2) comprehensive and incremental; (3) horizontal and vertical; (4) legal; and (5) substantive and procedural.

1. Multilateral, Bilateral and Unilateral

Although limiting negotiations to the superpowers had the support of some participants, the argument was put forward that the multilateral approach offered a distinct advantage. Small and non-aligned powers should be included in arms talks because some outside input from other countries is needed. Such countries have in the past had a positive impact on arms control negotiations. In 1962, for example, eight non-aligned countries introduced a plan which promoted the partial test ban; and small powers contributed to the Non-Proliferation Treaty. Again, multilateral discussions attract the attention of public opinion, which, it was argued, is necessary for pressure to be put on governments to enter into arms agreements. It was conceded, however, that multilateral negotiations take a long period of time to conclude. Also, technological innovation appears to be evolving more rapidly than the multilateral institutions capable of dealing with it.

Some participants argued that a way to control the arms race was to strengthen the social responsibility of scientists across international lines. Scientists should monitor work to promote peace by placing limits on scientific research. Attention was directed to the dangerous military implications of advances in new technologies – solid state materials, electronics, computers, lasers, small jet engines and sensors. It was argued that research in these areas should be stopped. But in reply it was contended that it is impossible for psychological, economic and political reasons adequately to limit research merely by appealing to the consciences of scientists and by-passing governments. Moreover, much research work is applicable to many fields, and it is difficult to distinguish between military and civilian uses of the new technologies.

The problem of the effectiveness of ensuring international safeguards on nuclear weapons and materials was considered. It was argued that there are no new safeguards. Improvements may be made here and there, yet they remain within the framework of an unreliable system. Before 1964 there was little risk. Since 1968, however, there has been a change, because plutonium and enriched uranium make a black market possible.

The safeguard measures of the European Community were described. In 1968 the number of safeguard personnel was increased to 140 inspectors; sophisticated instruments were provided; and unlike the practice of the International Atomic Energy Agency (IAEA), the European Community inspectors were given power to enter territories of states, to investigate practices in factories, and even to close companies.

The question was asked if a black market of nuclear material does exist. The reply was that the economic motivation for one does. It was noted that one kilogram of plutonium could command a price of between $60,000 and $1 million. It is also possible to cheat safeguards by circumventing physical controls and accountability and diverting to other countries.

The point was made that International Atomic Energy Agency safeguards were designed to deter proliferation but not to give firm guarantees that would prevent it from occurring. One participant commented that safeguards were *not* meant to prevent a country from going nuclear. They were designed to sound a warning which would make it difficult for a country to go nuclear in a clandestine manner. In effect, safeguards serve as an alarm system. Viewed from this perspective, the present system is basically efficient. The early French nuclear decision would now be impossible to keep secret.

It was noted that, recently, there have been instances of the acquisition of sensitive elements by non-nuclear weapons states. The following events have directed attention to the problem: the Indian test in May 1974 of a nuclear device developed from a Canadian-supplied reactor; the announcement in May 1975 of a Federal German-Brazilian deal to supply Brazil with an entire fuel cycle; United States' offers in 1974 of large reactors to Israel and Egypt, neither of whom are parties to the Non-Proliferation Treaty; French sales of reprocessing plants, particularly to South Korea and Pakistan, although South Korea withdrew after pressure from the United States; and general concern expressed at the NPT Review Conference about tightening safeguards.

The focus of attention has been on new mechanisms for better management and control: a suppliers' club and multinational regional centres. Suppliers have met, but they express much disagreement because of different perceptions and competitive commercial interests. Under the multinational regional centre idea, many states would invest their funds in their own reactor programmes but would go to a 'supermarket' for the rest. The facilities would be run by international agencies. Countries would get for a lower cost an assured amount of nuclear fuels.

It was argued that the regional centre idea assumed that nuclear power development is inevitable. One participant contended that this is not so. It is technically and economically not necessary, although politically it may be so.

The view was presented that the multinational regional centre idea should be buried. Instead, efforts should be directed towards getting an international agreement on a moratorium on reprocessing plant sales. No sales of fuel or facilities should be made to states unwilling to accept IAEA safeguards on all their nuclear programmes. The United States and other powerful states should concentrate more on incentive problems and dismantle symbols of reverence for nuclear weapons.

It was argued that there was no way to stop nuclear power development. Reasons given were the advanced status of nuclear technology and the tremendous political and economic power of nuclear energy industries, making alternatives to nuclear energy sources difficult to promote. Unless industry runs into high capital expenditure difficulties, or there is a major accident or a technological fix, the world will have nuclear power. If this premiss is correct, then attention focuses on political strategy. One participant asked if arms control supporters should fight public reliance on nuclear energy. It was argued that rather than oppose nuclear energy, critics should wage a fight for conservation and solar energy.

The bilateral approach involving the United States and the Soviet

Union offers the advantage of limiting discussion to the nations with
the most power and responsibility for the use of nuclear weapons. It
was argued, however, that agreements take a long time to negotiate
and are often superseded by rapid technological change, as is the case
with multilateral negotiations. Even when agreements are concluded, the
superpowers carry on the nuclear struggle in other ways. For example,
underground nuclear tests actually increased in number after the Limited
Test Ban Treaty was ratified. Another example was that the quantitative
limits on strategic weapons agreed upon at SALT resulted in a qualitative
struggle, particularly in multiple independently targetable re-entry vehicles
(MIRVs). The bilateral approach also leads to a search for 'bargaining
chips' (for example, cruise missiles and backfire bombers) which the
military leaders in each country are not willing to give up. In effect, the
bilateral approach may thus even serve to speed up the arms race.

The argument was made that the various SALT accords are
significant. They demonstrated that the United States and the Soviet
Union – two countries divided by ideology, historical traditions and
contradictory interests – could enter into important arms control
agreements. *Détente* between the superpowers had thereby been
strengthened. Peaceful coexistence might otherwise have been replaced
by a return to the Cold War. Moreover, the arms control limitations
will stop the race in the development of strategic offensive arms.

The advantages and disadvantages of the unilateral approach to arms
control were considered. The major advantages are speed, flexibility
and low cost. The major disadvantage is that the response may be of
minimal significance. One lecturer advocated a programme of Reciprocal
Unilateral Restraint (RUR). Under this plan each side cuts back on any
military component it chooses without waiting for an international
agreement. Each side could decide for itself which forces or weapons it
wished to reduce or phase out. The adversary, it was argued, would take
similar steps since it would view the initial move as sign of genuine
willingness to bring effective arms control. The approach is flexible in
that it could be reversed if no response came from the other side.
Examples which led to satisfactory treaties were the unilateral test
ban by President John Kennedy and the ban on biological weapons
by President Nixon. Arguments were presented against the plan.
A unilateral step would not necessarily be viewed by an adversary
as a real measure in arms control. If the United States removed its
Pershing tactical nuclear weapons from West Europe, for example, the
Soviet Union might see this move not as a sign of arms control, but
rather a move by the United States to get rid of an outmoded weapons

system. Indeed, the United States is already reputed to have reduced its tactical nuclear weapons in Western Europe by 3,500 without a reciprocal response from the Soviet Union. It was also argued that RUR might play into the hands of the hawks since it may create expectations which — if not realised — may lead to a stepping up of the arms race.

Another unilateral line to be recommended was that the United States should eliminate its ICBMs and long-range bombers, and rely exclusively on the sea-based deterrent. Weapons above a few kilotons, moreover, should be excluded from the inventories so that there would be no capability to destroy cities by the use of individual weapons. The advantage of these moves, it was argued, was that the continental United States would be a less desirable target for a nuclear attack. Lives and property would be saved.

Criticisms were directed at this proposal. The feasibility of the plan was questioned. Such a step might be destabilising to the nuclear balance since the advantages of bombers and ICBMs would be lost. Even putting forces to sea would not limit the arms race. The arms race would, instead, be continued in other areas such as ASW and submarine deployment. It was further argued that the plan was asymmetrical. It does not have equal attraction to both sides. It would be more to the Soviet than Western advantage, since the Western interest is to be able to keep limits on nuclear war by in the last resort merely taking out silos rather than destroying cities. The Soviets, however, may prefer to exchange cities since they may have less of a problem with domestic public opinion in continuing such a war.

Another unilateral approach recommended a military policy of defensive deterrence. The suggestion was made that a military force be created which was capable of defending a country rather than conquering other nations. The defence structures of Switzerland and Sweden were used as illustrations. It was argued in reply that no superpower could adopt such a policy. Again, there is no objective criterion for determining what is defensive and what is offensive.

Some participants concluded from the foregoing analysis that multilateral, bilateral and unilateral approaches all have weaknesses. But there was support for the idea that each approach be tried on a pragmatic basis so long as it appears to be leading towards effective control of armaments.

2. Comprehensive and Incremental

Another area of discussion concerned the relative merits of the comprehensive versus the incremental or step-by-step approach to disarmament. A comprehensive package was presented by one lecturer. It included an underground test ban; cessation of the production of fissionable material for weapons purposes; the reduction and phasing out of all land-based ICBMs and strategic bombers; the reduction of SLBMs; a ban on the testing, manufacture and deployment of new strategic weapons and delivery systems; a ban on new tactical nuclear weapons and mininukes; superpower acceptance of all regional treaties creating nuclear-free zones or peace zones; new draft treaties for General and Complete Disarmament (GCD); freeze and then reduction of conventional armaments; and reduction of sales and transfers of arms to Third World countries. It was argued that this kind of comprehensive approach deals with nearly all of the problems. The incremental approach has been tried, and it has not worked. Even if the comprehensive approach does not work, it is at least good peace propaganda to the extent that it attracts the attention of world public opinion. In reply it was argued that such a programme is unrealistic and impractical. But this raised the issue of who is to decide that a programme is unrealistic. The Partial Test Ban Treaty seemed unrealistic until it was signed.

One participant maintained that the major problem of disarmament is trust. But world disarmament conferences would tend to produce only propaganda; whereas bilateral incremental agreements could produce real trust. This thesis was disputed. It was also argued that in any case the world cannot wait for trust slowly to be built up. Some participants remained convinced, however, that the incremental approach represented the best way to produce arms control. Nations will not accept grandiose designs for bringing about disarmament. Accordingly, much attention was given to the specific steps which might promote further progress, in particular with regard to SALT, test ban and nuclear-free zones.

3. Horizontal and Vertical

A further way of seeing the problems of the arms race is to focus on the relationship between the nuclear posture of the superpowers and the prospects of nuclear proliferation to other states. This is usually referred to as the relationship between vertical and horizontal proliferation.

It was argued that there is some causal relationship between the arms and security policies of the nuclear weapons states (NWS) and the subsequent decisions by relevant non-nuclear-weapons states (NNWS) about whether or not to develop, acquire and deploy a particular nuclear force structure at a particular rate. Accordingly, NNWS policy objectives with regard to military security and political prestige were considered. It was then asked what kind of posture by the superpowers would best minimise nuclear proliferation by the NNWS. Three doctrines were considered: High Posture, Extreme Low Posture and Modified Low Posture.

In the High Posture Doctrine, the Soviet Union and the United States maximise the gap between their own nuclear weapons capabilities and those of minor NWS and NNWS by keeping a large inventory of nuclear weapons. By threatening the use of such nuclear weapons in a wide range of diplomatic and military contingencies, the superpowers may in these circumstances be able to make security guarantees to other states relatively credible and thus reduce incentives to such states to obtain their own nuclear weapons. In the Extreme Low Posture Doctrine, the Soviet Union and the United States minimise the gap between their own nuclear weapons capabilities and those of minor NWS and NNWS by maintaining a small inventory of nuclear weapons, constraining the rate of qualitative development of nuclear weapons, and relying upon the use and threatened use of nuclear weapons in only a very limited range of diplomatic and military contingencies. Nuclear security guarantees to other states would not be given and the superpowers would both give pledges not to be the first to use nuclear weapons. Such weapons would thus cease to be as important as at present and might not therefore seem to be as attractive to those contemplating acquiring them.

It was argued that concentration on the alleged vertical/horizontal link ignores the wider issues. Regional and local political and economic issues may be more important to the proliferation of nuclear weapons than anything the superpowers may do. This is particularly likely to be the case with Third World countries like Iran, Brazil and Taiwan.

The case of Great Britain was examined as an individual case study in proliferation. At first, during World War Two, the United States co-operated with Great Britain to build the bomb. After the war, however, there were varying periods of co-operation and non-co-operation. Did non-co-operation in the immediate post-war years raise the possibility that the British would in turn act as proliferators by giving serious thought to co-operating instead with her Dominions or with France? Did the renewed co-operation between the Americans and the British, which reached a new peak in 1962 with the Nassau Agreement, encourage France to press on with her own independent nuclear weapons programme when otherwise she might have allowed it to decline? Faced with these questions most participants appeared to be undecided as to whether American aid to Great Britain had on balance promoted or retarded a wider proliferation.

A recommendation was made that the Middle East should become a nuclear-free zone. It was further pointed out that the superpowers have poured enormous amounts of weapons into the region. Indeed, the pace of conventional military build-up in the area is faster than that between NATO and the Warsaw Pact. Now the spread of nuclear weapons to this region seems probable unless there is some form of local disarmament or arms control. There was considerable discussion as to the kinds of policies that would work in the Middle East and whether or not any agreement would be possible.

The view was expressed that perhaps too much responsibility for the evils of the world is being attributed to the superpowers. For the use of force has never been a monopoly of great powers. In the nineteenth century, for example, small wars often occurred that did not involve the great European powers of the day.

4. Legal

Consideration was given to the role of international law with respect to arms control. International law is designed to prevent violent conflicts, solve conflicts and impose sanctions. To prevent conflict, international law provides a world structure and rules of conduct. Rules of conduct concerning arms, peaceful coexistence, human rights, population, pollution and scarcity are established. To solve conflicts, international law helps to promote peaceful settlement of disputes on a voluntary basis. It also provides in varying degrees for collective action. Could international law not play a larger part in the future in the arms control arena? It was argued that states are relying more and more on international law, and there is no reason to believe that international law cannot help with arms control — provided that states have the political will. Some participants were extremely doubtful, however, about the wisdom of approaching the quest for arms control with too much emphasis on the international legal aspect. A discussion then arose as to whether international law is not really Western law and, consequently, discriminatory against Third World countries. Some participants pointed out, however, that in the West the view is often advanced that in recent times the United Nations has had a tendency to use international law to the advantage of Third World countries rather than Western states.

5. Substantive and Procedural

The distinctions between substantive and procedural approaches to controlling the arms race were considered. Substantive was defined as referring to detailed treaty provisions about specific weapons systems, and procedural was defined as providing merely a general method of approach. Various test ban agreements were given as examples of the substantive approach. An example of the procedural approach might be a flexible plan for an overall cut in budgets by a given percentage over a period of years. Perhaps more important than the provisions of the agreement would be the general improvement in the international atmosphere which such a flexible agreement would symbolise. The motivation behind the SALT agreements may be to some extent a combination of the two approaches. According to one participant, the United States at least believed that a SALT agreement would create a political climate which would improve Soviet-American relations. In turn, this would lead to the economic development of the Soviet Union, the modernisation of Soviet life, consumerism and a consequent curbing of any aggressive tendencies. The Soviet Union, for its part, may have had several objectives. First, it wanted to stop the growth of certain American weapons systems and to avoid a technological race with the United States because the United States is technologically superior. It may have seen the anti-ballistic missile (ABM) as dangerous and may have begun to doubt the effectiveness of its own ABM. Second, the Soviet Union may have wanted a formal statement that parity had been reached. Third, the Soviets are interested in obtaining help with advanced computers in the field of management skills and in the development of the vast resources in Siberia. They may, therefore, have hoped that the agreements on armaments might secure these objectives. Fourth, the Soviets probably sought to make certain that the United States would not reach a fundamental understanding with the People's Republic of China.

More traditional substantive arms control efforts were the various test ban treaties. One lecturer described their history. He compared the attempt to reach significant test ban agreements since 1945 to 'the search for the Holy Grail'. Although the United States and the Soviet Union placed moratoria on testing from 1958 to 1961, it was not until 1963 that a Limited Test Ban Treaty was concluded. This was described by one participant as an environmental, rather than an arms control, accord. A Threshold Test Ban Treaty (TTBT) was signed in 1974. Under the terms of the treaty, both the Soviet Union and the United

States agreed to stop underground testing of nuclear weapons which were larger than 150 kilotons after 31 March 1976. A Treaty on Underground Nuclear Explosions for Peaceful Purposes (PNE) was concluded in May 1976. This treaty allows nuclear explosives to be used for peaceful purposes provided there is some on-site inspection and limitations.

The TTB and PNE treaties were criticised as being more harmful to arms control than would have been the case if no treaties had been concluded. The following arguments were made:

1. The 150-kiloton limit of the TTB was described as the minimum that the hawks are willing to accept. Under PNE, moreover, group explosions (which may have yields as high as 1½ megatons for peaceful purposes) are legal.
2. Peaceful nuclear explosions have been given a new respectability. PNEs have been legitimised, which no document has ever done before. In fact, the stage may have been set for a new PNE lobby in the United States at a time when it seemed that there was only limited support for the use of nuclear explosives for peaceful purposes.
3. These treaties will put a freeze on the future limitation of testing. Peaceful tests, as legitimised by the new treaty, will serve as obstacles to a comprehensive test ban.
4. The fact that on-site inspectors are now permitted is not the breakthrough that treaty advocates are claiming. Observers are permitted at pre-announced sites provided notice is given long in advance. There is nothing in the agreements which deals with inspectors who can do what they want and go where they want.
5. The new agreements show a total disregard for progress in controlling superpower appetites in arms races, which they were pledged to under the NPT. Hence many nations view these new test ban treaties as a fraud.

It was argued that a comprehensive test ban treaty would better serve the interests of both the United States and the Soviet Union. Such an agreement would have two principal military implications. First, the reliability of weapons will be downgraded but this could mean more stability. Second, future destabilising options would also to a great extent be foreclosed for both superpowers. Each side will thus have to consider whether the benefits of ending testing are more important than the risks of continuing.

In discussion some participants argued that the CTB is not a panacea. The arms race would continue, although CTB would be a step in the right direction.

A procedural alternative to the substantive agreements like SALT and the test bans was recommended by one lecturer. Instead of dealing with specific reciprocal specifications, SALT negotiators should set up, for example, a system based on a plan of mutual reduction of 5 per cent annually over a ten-year period. Such a programme would be more flexible and would to some extent avoid the internal governmental clashes which are possibly more serious than the external governmental differences. |In discussion the feasibility of achieving much progress along these lines was questioned. The United States, it was argued, likes specificity; the Soviet Union prefers generality in arms control programmes. This approach also has the weakness that it takes no account of the increase in armed might on the part of other countries not party to any agreement.

Conclusion

Although the participants shared the view that continuing technological innovation and the proliferation of weapons — particularly nuclear weapons — were grave dangers facing the world, they expressed different views about the consequences, control, and causes of the arms race. There was wide agreement, however, that the very act of studying the arms race is a demonstration of concern and this in turn may contribute to a feeling of hope that solutions to this major problem of our time will be found.

2 NEW TECHNOLOGIES AND NEW WEAPONS SYSTEMS

Kosta Tsipis

Some New Technologies Applicable to Weapons Systems

Of a group of half a dozen or so technologies (such as electronics, sensor, computer, laser, electromagnetic waves and small turbojet engines) with direct impact on the development of weapons systems it will be possible here to examine in detail only one: computers. But first it is necessary to examine the state of the science, or the art, of solid-state materials that form the base of most of these new technologies. For the entire revolution in new electronic technologies and in new weapons is based on these types of materials and their properties. Developments in solid-state physics and the understanding of phenomena that relate to the behaviour of crystalline matter at the atomic and sometimes even nuclear level have presented us with opportunities to build what is known as 'microelectronics' — first the transistor and now large-scale integrated electronics — that have made micro-miniaturisation of electronic circuits possible; which in turn has made the new technologies, both of weapons and computers, practical.

There are several materials that are of interest. First are the so-called *optically active materials*. These are crystals which, if an electric field is applied to them, react; for example, they emit light. Light-emitting diodes are a practical example: they have found uses not only in modern digital watches, but in many other things; they are finding extensive uses in weapons. So optically active materials are very interesting objects for weapons designers.

Another type is made up of materials that display *large electro-optical effects*. These are crystals that, if a field is applied to them, drastically a magnetic but mainly an electric field, change drastically their index of refraction. They are transparent in one state and opaque in the other state and therefore one can create essentially optical logic with them. Instead of having electronic logic with little transistors and diodes and resistors and capacitors, one has entire circuits that perform logical operations that are exclusively based on light and optics. They are based on the fact that a beam of light can go in and can be routed to go right or left at a junction; one may do binary logic that way, logic circuits may be constructed from that and then entire machines can be organised that work on light rather than on electric current. The basis of these devices, which are only now appearing in an experimental stage, is the large electro-optical effect materials. There is a large variety of such crystals and there is very little known about them at the present time; at the same time, there is active research and therefore it is a field that is going to grow very rapidly — as also will its weapons applications.

Another interesting application of such material is *the solid state laser*. These are essentially little sources of coherent light that are miniature, and which correspond to the source of charges in the electric circuits. Only instead of electrons they provide photons. The solid-state lasers can be used to provide the light for all kinds of optical logic circuits mentioned previously. They are extremely important because another application of solid-state lasers is in devices which are called *electro-optical devices,* namely devices that have a laser beam going through a special crystal which the physicists call a Bragg cell, and by means of which one may do all kinds of fantastic kinds of frequency modulation (or detection of the frequencies of electromagnetic waves out in space). Therefore small lasers coupled to acousto-optical cyrstals are going to be applied increasingly in what we call monitoring or electronic intelligence in such missions as trying to find out what an adversary is doing with the electromagnetic spectrum. So, although at the present time they seem to be far away from any kind of military applications, there is a clear-cut indication that eventually these solid-state lasers will find increasing use, not necessarily in weapons but in monitoring, intelligence-gathering, decoding systems and other such applications.

In addition, there are not new but increasingly important examples of what we call *magnetically active materials*. These are materials whose magnetisation state may be changed by the application of an external magnetic field on them. They have found initial use in the memories of computers but now they are becoming increasingly important in actually devising some logic circuits that have magnetic properties. In addition, they are very important because, if developed properly, they can provide the kinds of computer memories that will allow very large amounts of information to be stored in very small space and be read out easily. Then even a small missile will be able to carry a very sophisticated memory with a capacity to store large amounts of information; one could store the world's map in digital form on it if magnetically active materials were used successfully. Such applications could cut the cost of missile guidance schemes drastically and make missiles quite flexible in their missions.

These acousto-optical materials, in conjunction with the solid-state lasers, provide the base for monitoring and intelligence equipment with many future uses. What one has is a very effective light-modulating system: either a laser beam passing through a piece of electro-optical material is modulated by pulsing the material through which it goes with an electric field, or inversely, one can have the laser beam going through the material and one can have essentially a little antenna that receives waves from the electromagnetic spectrum coupled to the crystal. These waves pulse the material and again modulate the laser beam. The time modulations of the beam can then be detected with, for example, photo-diodes. So, although these new materials are deeply buried in the heart of new devices, they are the basis of new technologies in monitoring and intelligence, new technologies in optical logic and optical circuits, and new technologies in the parsimonious storage of information.

Finally, mention must be made of *photo-piezo-electric effect material.* This is a very new material which may have applications in anti-submarine warfare. As one bends it, its surface changes optical properties completely. In addition, if light is shone on it, it bends so it can be used both as a detector and as a source of acoustical energy, of vibrations. If light is shone on it, it vibrates, or inversely, when mechanically vibrated while one shines light on it, the light changes characteristics. Now, the properties of this specific material, which is still in the experimental stage, are such as to make it an ideal device for sonars; it just happens to have the right kind of properties. Fortunately, it was developed by a Greek and a Pole in a laboratory at the Massachusetts Institute of Technology, and hence it is out in the open in the literature and accordingly it is not something that can be used by one side and not the other.

There are other new types of materials emerging which will also account for profound changes in the technologies of new weapons. I will mention here three types of materials that are in the pipeline, but have not yet seen extensive application. The first is *infra-red substrates.* These are materials sensitive to infra-red light. For example, silicone, which is the substrate on which we make the microminiaturised logic circuits, can under certain conditions be used in what we call charged-coupled devices that can detect visible light. Charged-coupled devices can be used in the following way: one makes an array of these very small electronic objects and then one shines light on it, and if one shines light through the proper optics, namely the optics of a telescope, one gets a picture of what this telescope sees focused on this array. The picture can be decomposed into dark spots, light spots, or grey spots. Charged-coupled devices change this difference in light value at each point on the array into differences in the amount of charge stored in each device. An array like this could be installed on a satellite; the camera on the satellite could take a picture of whatever is under it; a charged-coupled device could transform light values into amounts of charge that could be read out and transmitted directly and in real time (immediately) from the satellite down to earth, where the electronic signals could be reconstituted into light values, that is a picture. Thus one does not have to wait to take a picture with film, then drop the film, pick it up, develop it and examine it. Charged-coupled devices used in an optical mode can and probably do now provide intelligence agencies in the United States with detailed, very clear, high-resolution pictures in real time. These devices now work in the optical part of the spectrum – they see what we see. But if, instead of silicone, one used a substrate in the charged-coupled devices which is sensitive to infra-red, then one can take the same picture with the same accuracy also in real time but in the infra-red part of the spectrum. Therefore, pictures may be taken at night. And this increases manyfold the ability of satellites to monitor what is going on because it looks at a different part of the electromagnetic spectrum. It could tell, for example, whether a cruise missile in flight is powered by a turbojet or a turbofan engine. These infra-red-sensitive devices are a little bit harder to build for two reasons. First the material that is sensitive to infra-red is much more fragile. Secondly, to make infra-red substrates and to transform them into charged-coupled devices takes more processing; the number of layers of the stuff one has to put on the substrate is increased from nine, which is normal, to 14 or 15; therefore, since every time one does something one has a chance of breaking the device, the chance of successfully making an intact charged-coupled device with infra-red substrate is much less, the probability of getting an integral device out is much smaller and the yield of the process is much smaller. Thus far, therefore, those engaged in this field have not been able to produce devices of that type at any reasonable rate. But the technology is there.

Another future family of solid state materials is *liquid crystals*. Liquid crystals are crystals that exhibit properties of a solid in one direction but of a liquid in another direction. They have great properties for displays. For example, there are some watches now that have liquid crystals. They are supposed to be a very interesting class of future materials.

The most important class, however, is *organic crystals*. Organic materials have not been extensively crystallised, but chemists and solid-state physicists have found that in crystalline form they have remarkable properties. There are hundreds of thousands of organic materials that remain to be crystallised, and hence, since their properties are so interesting one can reasonably expect that as we crystallise more and more and study their properties, new phenomena, new areas of application will be discovered. So this is the one type of research that is now being pursued most eagerly in the United States — crystallisation and characterisation of organic macromolecules. Many of those that have been studied have exhibited useful properties. Usually they are highly assymetric in electro-optical ways, and because they are non-linear, they can be used in a large variety of ways.

There are three reasons why we may confidently predict that the field of solid-state physics and new technologies deriving from new materials will keep on developing into the indefinite future. First, the field is very new; we have been studying these materials for 25 years now, and we do not even know very well yet how silicone works. Therefore, there is every reason to believe that as more and more people study these materials, new properties will be developed, and then from the new properties and the new phenomena, new applications will be found, and from the new applications new systems will be built. Therefore, there is no reason to believe that we have reached anywhere near the limit of solid-state development, and anywhere near the limit of solid-state development, and anywhere near the limit of the kinds of applications and systems that we have seen coming to fruition during the last five or ten years, literally revolutionising both peaceful and non-peaceful processes and systems. Secondly, the organic crystals field is completely virgin in a sense, and therefore there is no doubt that there will be breakthroughs and surprises in it. We cannot predict what is going to happen in this field precisely because it is so new. Thirdly, and most interestingly, are the prospects likely to arise out of space-processes crystals. In order to grow a pure regular crystal of a material on earth, one melts the material in a vessel and then starts pulling at one point on the surface of the melt. As the material is removed from the hot pool it solidifies into the desired crystalline form. Pulling at a fixed rate causes the solid crystal to grow. But because of gravity there are little convection currents at the interface of the formed crystal and the hot pool. These little currents agitate the melt and therefore the crystal is not completely uniform. Also, to grow a crystal, one puts the melt in a vessel which is made of some other material. Some of the molecules of the material from the vessel come into the crystal and contaminate it. Therefore crystals that grow on this planet are neither uniform nor pure. Out in space, however, there is no gravity and hence there are no convection currents; so the crystals grown in outer space are absolutely uniform. And since a vessel to hold the material in space is not necessary, it can just be confined without a vessel so that it is absolutely pure. Such crystals have been manufactured and are now on earth being researched. Nor is there any reason to believe that this process cannot be reproduced on a large scale. So limitations in properties of crystals that are now caused by their impurity or their non-uniformity will disappear as larger and larger quantities of crystals are grown in space. For example, Federal Germany is interested in building a satellite that will be in outer space as a processing plant for the sole purpose of growing crystals. They will send a shuttle up once a year, or once every two years, to harvest the crystals. So there is clearly an enormous amount of new opportunities for new applications that may be expected to arise out of these new space-processed crystals.

All these improved properties — the fact that they will be more pure, the fact that they will be more uniform — will tend to continue the technological trend that started out with vacuum tubes, continued with transistors and integrated circuits, and now with charged coupled devices; namely, that a simple switching operation, a simple logical operation, involves fewer and fewer charges. In a vacuum tube the difference between the 'on' state and the 'off' state was the difference between 10^{14} electrons and 10^7 electrons flowing through. The transistor reduced this amount of charge by three orders of magnitude and the integrated circuits took it down three more orders of magnitude. Charged couples perform all logical operations by transporting a few thousand electrons and probably this number will be reduced down to a few hundred. What does that mean? By switching less and less current we have less and less heat dissipation. Hence we can make circuits smaller and smaller. The number of charges involved in existing devices is reasonably large, namely a few thousand, precisely because the impurities and inhomogeneties compelled circuits to function out at that level of charge. But with very pure crystals the number of charges being switched can be reduced, minimising the amount of power being dissipated in the circuit. Hence the circuit can be made even smaller because the minimum circuit element size is determined by the amount of power it must dissipate.

We may therefore conclude that a survey of the field of materials shows no indication that the present technological trend is going to be arrested in the near future. On the contrary, it seems to be a wide open field that is going to surprise us again and again during the next two decades.

Finally, let us give special consideration to computers, the devices that manage complex processes by breaking them down into single procedural steps. A computer has three basic elements: the processor, that essentially does the actual logic; the memory, where the information is stored; and the input-output devices. The characteristics that are required in a computer are speed, reliability, minimum size and weight for a given processing capability and memory size, least amount of power dissipated, and low cost. The physical limits imposed on the computer elements by the present technology, which involves micro-circuits, micro-miniaturised integrated curcuits or large-scale arrays, form the ultimate boundaries of computer technology. First, the size of a single logic element (the logic element means just switching diodes) can be as small as 10 Å in principle. That is determined by the dynamics of dissipating power. But because of manufacturing vicissitudes the smallest element that can be made is about 10 times bigger, 100 Å. The switching speed, the speed with which a logical process can be achieved, is 10^{-10} to 10^{-11} seconds, which means ten millionths of a millionth of a second. One can say 'yes-no', a binary kind of operation that underlies computer logic, with that speed. This is a practical limit that assumes a lot of power consumption. An operation is not a single logic step and an instruction takes 10^{-9} seconds because an instruction involves a lot of logical operations. The reliability for a single element is a million million seconds between failures (10^{+13} seconds between failures of a single element) but a computer has 10^8 elements and therefore the overall reliability of the computer is much lower, say 10^5 seconds. These physical limits will be reached within ten to 15 years.

In the large-scale integrated circuits technology, the yield of the manufacturing process of the kinds of curcuits that are used in a computer is improving by 30 per cent a year. So the density of individual logic circuits on large-scale arrays is being improved by the same amount. Therefore the price per logic curcuit drops by about 30 per cent a year precisely because more and more elements can be put on a single array. The limits of these parameters will be reached in about a decade.

Consider a computer with one processor only. By 1980 this

computer will be able to perform 50 million operations per second, 50 MIPS. And by 1990 it will perform 300 MIPS. This applies to command and control computers that are used on planes, missiles and for general military applications – by 1980 such a computer will have 10,000 logic gates, will have a 100,000-word memory, will weigh 10 kilograms and it will be 5,000 cubic centimetres, which is a cube 13 cm on a side. That computer will be able to perform all foreseeable operations needed for a plane or a missile. So that is the state of computer technology that will be applied and used in weapons systems. The computers that are now in weapons systems incorporate technology which is a decade old, a different generation entirely. Very few computers now in weapons systems use large-scale integrated electronics. So there is a lot of improvement possible there, and there is nothing to stop weapons becoming more and more sophisticated in the next fifteen, twenty or twenty-five years.

New Weapons Systems

We shall now outline the properties of some of the weapons that have been developed from these new technologies. These are: precision guided munitions (PGMs), cruise missiles, remotely piloted vehicles (RPVs), satellite monitoring, electronic warfare and counter-measures, advanced ballistic missiles, anti-submarine warfare (ASW) and anti-ballistic missiles (ABMs).

Before discussing PGMs a general comment about weapons may be useful. For a given target, a weapon has a given kill radius, which is defined by saying that if the target lies within the kill radius it will be destroyed, while if the target is outside the kill radius it will remain intact. Clearly, the kill radius of a weapon depends on its explosive power and the strength of the target. Therefore, the measure of the effectiveness of a weapon against a target is its kill radius (r_k). Another measure of effectiveness is the accuracy of delivery. The way we measure accuracy is by the error radius (r_e) or the circular error probability (CEP). CEP is defined as the radius of a circle with the target at the centre within which the weapon would land 50 per cent of the occasions on which it was launched against the target. this is the definition of CEP or r_e. Now, if r_k of a weapon is smaller than r_e, it follows that most of the times the weapon would fall too far from the target to destroy it. If, however, r_k is larger than r_e, it means that the weapon will probably land close enough to kill the target. In the case of nuclear weapons, for example, the kill radius is very large against most targets so they do not have to be very accurate. There was a tendency in the past, since the weapons were inaccurate, to make them more and more powerful, thereby increasing the probability that once launched against a target they would destroy it. Another approach in the case of inaccurate weapons is to launch a large number against a target in order to increase the probability of a hit. Neither measure is necessary for weapons with small r_e.

Let us now examine *precision guided munitions* (PGMs). In the case of PGMs, r_e, the error radius of the weapon, is much smaller than r_k. It means the chance that the weapon will land so far away from the target that it will not destroy it is small. The working definition of a PGM is that if one sees a target and one shoots a PGM at it there is a better than 50 per cent chance that one is going to hit it. Another property is that the cost of one round of PGM is usually much less than the cost of the target it can destroy. For example, an anti-tank missile that can destroy a tank with more than 50 per cent probability costs a few thousand dollars while a tank costs one million dollars. A surface-to-air missile that may cost $150,000 can shoot down a plane with a very high probability which cost four or five million dollars. So the cost of PGMs not only is a very important factor in itself, but it becomes even more important if it is compared with the cost of the targets which PGMs have a better than 50 per cent chance of destroying. A third property of PGMs is that they are easy to carry and use. One does not need to be highly trained to launch a PGM and sometimes even a vehicle is not needed to carry these munitions.

PGMs have a number of important operational implications. First, the defence is favoured over the offence. With PGM, if a target is sighted, it can usually be destroyed and therefore visibility is a disadvantage. But while defensive positions can be prepared, camouflaged or concealed, an offensive force must move into new open territory. Hence the offence is more vulnerable in general than the defence if both sides have PGMs.

A second implication of PGMs is that they reduce the problems of battlefield logistics. For example, to destroy a bridge with ordinary gravity bombs one might send against it five planes with four bombs each; they go over, drop the bombs, usually they fail to hit the bridge, they return and one sends five more planes, and so on. On average one may need 100 such bombs to destroy the bridge. Thus 100 bombs would have to be taken to the landing strip of the planes; fuel for these planes must also be available; the planes have to be maintained; personnel for all this is needed; food for the personnel has to be transported; and so on. Hence a large logistic train is necessary to support these five planes using iron bombs. On the other hand, one or at most two PGMs would probably be needed to destroy the bridge. Moreover, if instead of planes cruise missiles with proper range are used, planes are not needed at all — one would just launch the precision-guided cruise missile that goes and finds its target. So there is a drastic reduction of the support and logistic train implied by a switch to inexpensive dispensable munitions. That has profound military and economic implications.

A third implication of PGMs is that they deepen the battlefield. The accuracy of PGMs is more or less independent of their range, for a PGM has 50 per cent probability of hitting its intended target one, five, ten or more miles away if it is designed to do that. This means that the battlefield can be not one but 30 miles on either side of the forward edge of the battle. So the battlefield becomes much deeper and that leads into the next implication of PGMs, namely that they increase the rate of violence among combatants. For if 100 PGMs instead of 100 gravity bombs are launched, many more tanks will be destroyed and many more combatants will be killed. The level of violence does not take place on a strip a mile on each side, but takes place on a strip 40, 50 or 60 miles wide.

Finally, it is necessary to stress that high-value vehicles, such as planes, tanks and ships, are becoming increasingly vulnerable to inexpensive, light munitions. If four or five million dollars is spent on a plane and then it is shot down with a missile that cost a mere 100,000 dollars, planners will tend to think twice before buying a plane. This is in fact something that is being now seriously considered in many countries. Indeed, James Digby of the Rand Corporation claims that armies are going to end up with little jeeps with PGM launchers on them and will do away with tanks and planes. Perhaps nothing so drastic as that will occur, but clearly there will be an effort to move away from very expensive vehicles that can be destroyed very easily.

Next we must consider the *cruise missile*. There is in one sense nothing new about cruise missiles. For example, the V-1 of World War Two was a cruise missile. Moeover, the Soviet Union has for many years had cruise missiles deployed on naval vessels. But interest in cruise missiles has been recently re-awakened because the United States has decided to develop a class of cruise missiles that have some extraordinary properties. Their range will be about 2,000 nautical miles, which is more than 3,000 km. It has already been demonstrated that they can fly as fast as 800 km per hour at altitudes anywhere from 10,000 metres down to 50 metres. Their expected accuracy is 70 metres

CEP, meaning that if one of these objects is directed to a target 3,000 km away, 50 per cent of the time it will land within 70 metres of that target. The cost of each of these missiles will probably be about one million dollars.

The extraordinary accuracy of these new cruise missiles is achieved by an interesting guidance system. It is basically an inertical guidance system (just like the one that ballistic missiles have), with a drift rate of about 1,000 metres an hour off the intended course. This could lead to large inaccuracies, but in addition cruise missiles can update their location fix by means of a digital map of the terrain over which they are supposed to fly, which they carry in the memory of an on-board computer. The map is an elevation map that shows the altitude of every point in their flight path. How dense these points are is not public knowledge but it is of the order of 100 metres from each other in two dimensions. The missile also has a little radar altimeter that looks down and finds out what the altitude is over the terrain over which it is flying. By comparing this stream of information provided by the radar altimeter with the information from the map, the computer can determine where the missile actually is and thereby correct any errors caused by the drift of the inertial guidance system.

Because of their accuracy, their range and their cost, these cruise missiles are potentially attractive to the military establishments of a large number of countries. The technology which they now employ is already surpassed by better guidance systems. Hence, before long, there may be temptations to export. If weapons like this became widely spread there would be a vast proliferation of strategic means of delivery with ranges of 3,000 km or more. Then the difficulties that we are now encountering in SALT because of this weapon will be augmented by the proliferating number of countries that will have such strategic delivery vehicles, and therefore will be tempted to acquire nuclear warheads for them.

But not all cruise missiles are dangerous. Short-range versions suitable for tactical missions have no unfavourable arms control implication. Consider, for example, the American naval cruise missile 'Harpoon'. Its guidance consists mainly of a seeker radar and a radar altimeter that keeps it a few metres above the waves. It promises to fulfil the expectation that cruise missiles are more efficient and accurate delivery vehicles than ballistic missiles for ranges over 10 km and under 5,000 km. It carries a high explosives charge — some 150 kgr — and in 32 tries it has hit the target 29 times at operational ranges.

Let us now briefly consider *remotely piloted vehicles* (RPVs). These are little planes without pilots. Their advantage is that they can be very cheaply built; they can carry weapons or intelligence-gathering equipment; or they can be designators for laser-guided weapons. They can even act like flying mines. Consider, for example, an RPV with a large explosive charge in it and a little receiver that detects radar emissions. The RPV just flies around over the battlefield and the moment an enemy radar goes on it homes on to the radar and destroys it — it is thus just like a mine in the air. RPVs have a lot of uses and the interest in them is that they are manless; therefore, by employing them in large numbers we are moving one step closer to the automated battlefield. This creates both problems and opportunities.

Another important field is that of *electronic warfare and counter-measures*. Efforts may be directed, for example, at trying to avoid being hit by a PGM or at finding out what an adversary's radar frequencies are. Essentially, the microminiaturisation of electronic circuits has opened up opportunities for electronic warfare that are now being exploited. The main focus is to counter the effectiveness of PGMs against aircraft, PGMs having a very high accuracy. Electronic counter-measures try somehow to confuse and frustrate the guidance of PGMs, and apparently the competition now is not only about which country is going to get the smarter PGM but which is going to get an even more sophisticated electronic countermeasure to frustrate the smarter PGM. So there is an enormous amount of qualitative competition going on, spurred by fears in air forces that the manned aircraft is becoming vulnerable.

Satellite monitoring is also making great progress. Formerly we had satellites which looked down, took pictures, then released the film which had to be developed and scanned to discern activity. This process might take as long as a month. To avoid this delay the equivalent of a television camera began to be used. This looks down and sends in real-time streams of information. But that is not very efficient because the amount of unprocessed information the data link must transmit is very large. Hence the capability of the data link between the satellite and the ground must be enormous. So the trend now is to process the data on the satellite. Since computers are very small, a computer may be put on a satellite and ordered to discriminate for specific events, for example at infra-red plumes or specific shapes. Then the computer scans the output of the optical system, chooses those shapes or events that it has been programmed to recognise, follows them, monitors them and then if they are significant sends the data down to the ground. So we now have selective information-processing on the satellite and transmission to the ground in real time. This is currently in the experimental stage in the United States and will probably be fully operational in a few years.

The infra-red counterpart of this will probably be operational in ten years. What can apparently be done already in to characterise completely, not necessarily from a satellite, a jet engine in flight. By looking at the jet engine output of a plane from a great distance one may tell whether it is, say, a Pratt-Whitney or a Rolls Royce and what its thrust is. And a sort of a picture gallery of their infra-red signatures may be built up, thereby also aiding identification from a distance. With sufficient money and effort satellites could be used for these purposes but so far this has not yet been done in practice. For example, given the money, the technology exists to identify the difference between turbofan and turbojet engines that have 600 lb thrust. It is of course a 600 lb thrust engine that powers most cruise missiles. So detection systems could be built to enable one to tell whether something that is flying around deep in the atmosphere is a cruise missile with a turbojet engine and therefore capable of short-range tactical missions only or whether it is a turbofan and therefore a strategic missile.

Monitoring systems can also monitor ballistic missile tests. But they cannot tell whether or not the test is of a manoeuvrable re-entry vehicle (MARV) warhead if the country carrying out the test makes an effort at concealment. (A MARV warhead is a warhead that manoeuvres at the end of its trajectory in order to hit its target.) Because of this problem of verification we should not, therefore, expect to see international agreements that specifically ban tests of MARV warheads.

We must next review current developments of *ballistic missiles,* particularly in the case of the United States. There are several programmes in being. First there is the MX programme which is to design a large missile, 210 centimetres in diameter, to be deployed in a canister. This could be placed either in existing silos; or used as an air-mobile missile (that is, it can be dropped from a plane); or as a land-mobile system. This is a cold-launch missile, which means that the missile just pops out from the silo and hence it is not necessary to leave room around the missile in the silo for the gases to come out when its engine ignites in the silo. It is a system first developed by the Soviet Union. The throw-weight of the MX will be four times greater than the Minuteman III. It will contain ten warheads which are called 'precision-guided re-entry vehicles': that is, they will be terminally guided. Moreover there are many, many ways in which they may be guided. One may do area correlation pattern recognition, which means that the missile guidance computer has a map of the area, not necessarily of the target, but of the area near the target; the computer knows where the target is with respect to, say, a crossroads or a railway track or to something clearly discernible. So, the computer figures out where the target is once it finds these bench-marks and guides the re-entry vehicle towards the target. The warheads could be guided by the 'global positioning satellite' system which is a series of 24 satellites at 18,000 mile orbits around the earth so that any point of the earth can be seen by four satellites. These satellites emit signals simultaneously which arrive at different times at a point near the earth's surface, since the distance of a warhead from the four satellites is different. From these time differences of arrival and additional information the satellites beam down. The computer inside the warhead can determine the position of the warhead to ten metres in three dimensions. Using that location information the warhead can guide itself on to the target. Probably this system will not be used, however, to guide ballistically re-entering vehicles because the satellites are vulnerable to attack. Hence guidance probably will not be based on global-positioning-satellites, but on something else — Tercom, for example, which is the system that the cruise missiles use. Even use of a very sophisticated kind of pattern recognition system is possible in which a picture of the target area is made in one part of the e.m. spectrum, say the infra-red or the microwave, and then the computer inside the warhead recognises the same terrestrial features in a different part of the spectrum. For example, one gives it an optical map and it recognises the same features in the microwave region of the spectrum. It is thus a sophisticated system that is now being developed. Moreover, the MX could be deployed in the same silos as the Minuteman missiles, or in shelter complexes interconnected with tunnels, or in some other facility.

There is another re-entry vehicle being tried in the United States called the 'large advanced ballistic re-entry vehicle', which contains a one megaton weapon. It is being prepared as an alternative to the ten warheads for the MX. Finally, another weapon that is now being actively developed and may be deployed in the United States is the MARK 12A warhead. This has a CEP of 700 feet and a yield of 0.4 megatons (that is just double the Minuteman III yield). It fits in exactly the same re-entry vehicle that the Minuteman III have now, but it has just double the yield and the CEP is better. The radius of the crater that this device will open is about 160 metres or about 500 feet (given that the soil is standard soil). Of course, if a silo is within the crater that a weapon opens when it explodes, then the silo is destroyed. Hence the MARK 12A is not very far from being a warhead that can destroy with reasonable certainty a silo with a single shot.

Now for some good news: there is no breakthrough in anti-submarine warfare (ASW). The progress in ASW is very slow. But we may note that there have been a few small advances. First, better sonars are being developed. Second, the layers of the thermocline can be predicted a little more easily. Third, the United States has a system that can pull information from all ASW platforms — from underwater sonar devices, from monitoring aeroplanes, from ships, and feed everything into a very large computer, which is called ILIAC-4. That computer makes predictions not about where the submarines are, but where the submarines could hide. Finally, another very interesting ASW weapon is being developed by the United States which is called the CAPTOR mine. The CAPTOR is a torpedo that goes to sleep at the bottom of the ocean until a submarine passes over it. Then it is awakened, follows the acoustical signature of the submarine, hits it and sinks it. The effective radius of the CAPTOR is about one nautical mile. So if the CAPTOR mines are spread in the ocean with the proper surface density they can deny that portion of the ocean to submarines. The CAPTOR has the capability of recognising submarine signatures. Whether it is deployed or not is something that is not in the public domain. The CAPTOR is not very popular in the American Navy but it is a very effective weapon. But in conclusion, it is necessary again to stress that a destablishing breakthrough in the ASW field is nowhere in sight.

Finally, reference must be made to ideas that have been developed with reference to anti-ballistic missiles (ABMs). They are mainly the work of Richard Garwin and are designed to protect silos, but would be inadequate for defending cities. An incoming missile, Garwin reasons, would probably be exploded above the ground to avoid dust and débris that are generated by an explosion on the ground. But to explode a warhead above the ground requires a radar altimeter, because any other kind of altimeter is not accurate enough. A radar jammer on the silo, then, designed to jam the radar altimeter, Garwin argues, would cause the weapon to explode at the wrong altitude and therefore probably overfly the silo. Another scheme is based on the fact that missiles approach the earth's surface at a very low angle. Hence if a picket fence consisting of 11-foot high steel rods half an inch in diameter are planted close enough so that the warhead cannot go through, it will disintegrate on impact on them and never explode. Such picket fences spread out in an east-west direction north of the silo bases in Montana and in North Dakota would be inexpensive and effective. A third approach is to deploy a little radar above the silo that detects the incoming warhead. North of the silo one constructs a trough with some explosives in it and a lot of gravel on top. As the warhead comes in the radar signals detonate the explosives and the gravel comes up in the air and destroys the re-entry vehicle by impact. Again, this is a fairly good way of preventing the re-entry vehicle from hitting the silo. There is logic in this because all one has to do is to make the outcome of an attack against silos less predictable. An attack against silos is uncertain enough as it is. If the outcome is made even less predictable by such ABM measures the political leadership of a country will be less inclined to attempt an attack. Therefore, although Garwin's defences may not be very sophisticated or very effective, in the sense that they might not destroy all the incoming missiles, they increase the uncertainty of a counter-silo attack which clearly increases the probability that the counter-silo attack will never be tried. So there is much to be said in favour of Garwin's suggestions.

3 CAN CONVENTIONAL NEW TECHNOLOGIES AND NEW TACTICS REPLACE TACTICAL NUCLEAR WEAPONS IN EUROPE?

Jorma K. Miettinen

Introduction

Military technology and military tactics are closely interdependent. The four main elements of combat, command, reconnaissance, movement and firepower are all affected by military technology, which is constantly evolving. Improvements in firepower demand greater dispersal. Dispersal involves greater distances and this requires long-range indirect fire. This also presupposes target-acquisition and reconnaissance to greater depth. Faster movement and deeper combat areas also necessitate faster and better means of command, control and communication.

Steady improvement of military technology is usually relatively easily adapted to the existing military doctrine. But sometimes such qualitative leaps occur in weapons technology that their effects upon tactics are not immediately understood. They may require great changes in tactical doctrine.

Examples of Revolutionary Leaps in Military Technology

A few modern examples of revolutionary leaps in military technology may be cited. Some derive from World War One, when the use of machine-guns and massive artillery barrage fire in land combat and the use of submarines against commercial shipping caused millions of casualties and millions of tons of sunken ships, respectively, before the necessary changes were made to the tactics of land combat and to naval tactics.[1] At sea this took the form of convoy. On land, stalemate was reached in trench warfare; firepower, combined with protection of trenches and field fortifications, made defence temporarily superior to offence, which lacked mobility. The Germans tried to break the stalemate with the use of gas warfare, and the British, at Cambrai in 1917, by concentrating 400 tanks in an offensive.[2] Both did, indeed, achieve a local breakthrough but were then unable to take decisive advantage of either case, because of insufficient motorisation of infantry and artillery. Moreover, the new armoured technology was still in its infancy, the tanks of 1917, for example, being slow, clumsy, unreliable and rather vulnerable.

World War Two is no less revealing. Germany understood the value of armoured vehicles, and in the inter-war period General Heinz Guderian developed the tactics of 'Blitzkrieg' — the use of armoured divisions and mechanised infantry in large tank armies, together with the firepower of strike aircraft, the 'Stukas', for carrying out deep operations at a stunning speed.[3] The French relied on defensive tactics, symbolised above all by the Maginot Line, and were taken by surprise through the back door. Again, the German 'Wolfpack' tactics, namely simultaneous, co-ordinated attacks by a great number of submarines upon a convoy were also developed, and at first proved very successful. Eventually, however, the Allies gained superiority by skilful use of anti-submarine warfare techniques, in particular radar and sonar and air reconnaissance, which put an effective end to the German threat by destroying tens of submarines per month.[4]

Recent Developments

Since the end of World War Two, tremendous developments have taken place in military technology. The greatest potential change has been caused by nuclear weapons. But they are highly political weapons. Their use as a real fighting weapon in land combat would be so disastrous that no nuclear weapon state will resort to them, unless its whole existence is at stake. Nevertheless, the possibility that such a situation eventually may arise has compelled the great powers to increase mobility, dispersal and the protection of their troops. This has involved the almost complete mechanisation of their armies and corresponding changes in their military doctrines.[5]

Nuclear weapons have, however, never been tested in land battle. Therefore we have no experience as to how successful the present tactics would be in a limited nuclear war. Indeed there must be grave doubts about the rationality of their use on the battlefield at all.

The development of conventional military technology has also been very rapid and continues at an increasing pace. The deployment of missiles has greatly extended the range of indirect fire, while the large-scale introduction of helicopters has added a new dimension to the mobility of ground troops. These factors have tended to change tactics in much the same direction as the possible use of nuclear weapons, namely by increasing the importance of dispersal, camouflage and surprise.[6]

Experience from the Vietnam and Near East Wars

The Vietnam War and the two Near East Wars, particularly the latter, have given us some evidence of the capability of existing conventional technology and make possible some predictions about the future development of tactics, although the Near East wars were desert wars, and one must therefore exercise great caution in assuming that any lessons automatically apply in other circumstances.[7] Perhaps the most interesting lesson from the war of October 1973 was that the use of a wide range of anti-tank weapons (from bazookas to sophisticated missiles, highly accurate up to 3,000 to 4,000 m), if available in sufficient numbers, may make the massive use of tanks too costly.[8] Thus, they may make defence superior to offence, at least temporarily, until a new generation of tanks with an armour impenetrable at least to bazookas and hand-held rockets has been developed or until tactics are devised to deal with the new problems.

A second important conclusion concerns the effectiveness of air defence. By the combined use of high-, medium- and low-range missiles and automatic, radar-controlled action weapons, Egypt gained local air superiority at the Suez bridgehead without fighter aircraft for several days. A third surprising feature was the importance of electronic counter-measures. Israel's air force was unable to fulfil its tasks until it obtained improved means of electronic warfare from the United States.[9]

Impact of New Technology

What, then, will be the impact of the 'new technology' which is still under development during the next ten to fifteen years? Since the lead time for a modern weapon is normally about a decade from the demonstration of the idea or the prototype of the weapon through research, development, engineering development, production, initial development and large-scale deployment, and since most new inventions have an important effect on tactics only when deployed on a sufficiently large scale, there is a broad pattern for forecasting future weapon deployment during the next ten to fifteen years. It is impossible of course in this context to cover in any comprehensive way the impact of the whole spectrum of conventional new technologies, as will be obvious if it is appreciated that the American code name list of new electronic warfare alone comprises 420 items.[10] Table 3.1, while not exhaustive, lists some of the principal items which may have an important effect on land combat. But here it will only be possible to

Table 3.1:   Some New Military Technologies with Eventual Effects
             on Tactics

---

1. Precision guided munitions (PGM)
2. Remotely piloted vehicles (RPV)
3. Precision positioning (NAVSTAR)
4. Correlation guidance: Cruise missile (tactical versions)
5. Munition novelties:
   - 'tailoring' of munitions
   - fragmentation munitions
   - cluster bomblet units
   - terminally guided submunitions
   - air scatterable minelets (GATOR)
   - fuel air explosives

6. Target acquisition:
   - optical sensors; television
   - radar
   - microwave radiometry
   - infra-red from hot metal or plume; night vision devices
   - any of above carried by RPV or satellite
   - seismic, acoustic and other sensors

7. C^3 : Command, control, communication:
   - real-time view of theatre using computer-processing
   - immediate counterfire by on-line computers
   - automated tactical systems
   - laser communication over optic fibre
   - tactical satellite communication system

---

deal in detail with the first item, precision-guided munitions (PGMs)
and to a lesser extent with remotely-piloted vehicles (RPVs). These are,
however, the new technologies which are likely to have the greatest
impact on tactics.

1. Precision-Guided Munitions

The deployment of PGMs is expected to have a revolutionary effect
on future land combat.[11] Although there exists no agreed definition
of PGMs, one suggestion which may be as good as any is: 'a PGM is a
guided munition whose probability of making a direct hit on its target
at full range — when unopposed — is greater than a half.'[12] In combat
the hit probabilities would certainly be much smaller than a half, since
peacetime test conditions are always less severe than real battlefield
conditions.

Anti-tank weapons,[13] various gliding bombs provided with homing

devices and small air-defence missiles are typical PGMs. Quite a number
of different methods have been developed for guiding these weapons,
but one can broadly divide them into three groups.

First, we may note the group guided by manual line of sight, usually
obtained via a wire (a radio link would be jammable). Utilising this method,
the gunner must follow the movements of the target and the missile and
correctly estimate the crossing point of their vectors. To reach a 50 per
cent kill-probability requires much training and special skill.
Furthermore, the gunner has to remain visible and thus vulnerable
throughout the flight — which can be as long as 20 to 30 seconds.

The second group consists of semi-automatic line-of-sight guidance
weapons such as HOT, Milan and TOW (see Table 3.2). In the TOW system,
the gunner has a 13-power telescope. He only needs to keep the target in the
crosshair during the flight of the missile. An infra-red tracker mounted
in the launcher sees a modulated infra-red source in the missile tail. As
the missile flies, control wires attached to the launcher unwind from
two bobbins in the missile. The tracker measures automatically the
angle between the lines of sight from the missile and from the target to
the tracker and sends steering commands which move the aerodynamic
fins, steering the missile along the line-of-sight from launcher to target.
Tracking is easy but the gunner is vulnerable during the flight of up to
15 seconds.

The third group covers methods of automatic homing. These are
used particularly during the last part of the trajectory. The projectile
has a seeker, a receiver with sensors which receives some kind of
radiation coming from the target; it can be visible, infra-red, laser or
microwave radiation. Aircraft, ships, tanks and motor vehicles send
infra-red radiation from their hot motors or exhaust gas. An electro-
optical contrast seeker differentiates aircraft and ships easily against
the featureless background of the sky or sea. The target can be designated,
for example by radar, during flight, using signals from the seeker
which can be in the front of the missile. An imaging infra-red seeker
(IIS) for use at night is under development for use in the Maverick
air-to-surface AT missile's optical versions carried on the US F-4, A-7
and A-10 aircraft and helicopters.[14] Infra-red guidance can be also used
for homing cruise missiles and kamikaze RPVs.[15]

The battlefield missile has to fulfil a great number of requirements
before it may be used in practice. Accuracy and reaction speed are
perhaps the most important ones. Because a tank's gun or a fighter's
rocket can react within a second or two, the first shot ought to be a hit.
The missile's gunner requires steady nerves to continue careful tracing

Designation	Developed by	Min./max. range (m)	Weight of round (kg)	Guidance	Comments
ENTAC	France	400/2,000	12	Manual command	Production complete, 13,000 produced
SS-11/AS-11	France	350/3,000	29.9	Manual command	Anti-submarine version for helicopters, 160,000 produced
SS-12/AS-12	France	800/6,000	76	Semi-automatic	Anti-submarine version for helicopters 8,000m max. range
HOT	France/ Germany	75/4,000	22	Semi-automatic command	May be used in Bö-105 light helicopter
Cobra	Germany	400/2,000	10.3	Manual command	No connection with the American AH-1Q Cobra helicopter
Milan	France/ Germany	25/2,000	6.7	Semi-automatic command	Two-man crew
Swingfire	Britain	<150/4,000	34	Manual command + aids	Operator can be offset 100m, vehicle in defilade
Shillelagh MGM-51C	USA	(?)	27	Semi-automatic command infra-red link	Fired from 152mm gun mounted on the M-551 Sheridan or M-60A2 medium tank
TOW BGM-71A	USA	65/3,750	19	Semi-automatic command	Many carriers, but M-113 APC and AH-1Q Cobra predominate in US Army. (See note under Cobra above.)
Dragon M-47	USA	?/1,000	6.35	Semi-automatic command	Man-portable
Snapper AT-1	USSR	500/2,300	22	Manual command	Used in several Pact armies. Mounts on BRDM armoured reconnaissance vehicle
Swatter AT-2	USSR	(?)	about 20	Manual command, infra-red terminal guidance	Mounts on APC and BRDM reconnaissance vehicle
Sagger AT-3	USSR	500/3,000	11	Manual command	Mounts on APC and BRDM reconnaissance vehicle (which carries 6 under a retractable plate).

Sources: *Flight International*, 14 March 1974; *Jane's Weapon Systems, 1973-1974*. Reproduced from James Digby, *Precision-Guided Weapons* (International Institute for Strategic Studies, Adelphi Paper, No.118, London, 1975).

if he himself becomes the target of counter-fire. Therefore, it is helpful for the tracking device to be separate from the launcher, particularly if the missile leaves a noticeable signature.

The Vietnam War proved that total automation is often erroneous, unreliable and expensive. Terminal guidance is better. Only after the target has been selected by the gunner, the missile sighted, released, and perhaps tracked half-way, may the final homing be taken care of automatically. Furthermore, the system ought to be new — otherwise the enemy may have developed counter-methods. Also it ought to be simple, cheap and easy to repair in the field. Cheapness is relative, however. The missile can also be quite expensive if its kill probability is high and the target very valuable. In the war of October 1973 Israel used 58 Maverick missiles (each $10,000) which destroyed 52 tanks (each around $500,000).[16]

One promising short-range guidance system at this moment is laser designation and semi-active homing.[17] In this system the target is illuminated or designated from either a ground position, a helicopter, an aircraft or an RPV by a laser gun sending an invisible laser beam of a few centimetres diameter to the target during the last few seconds of the flight of the projectile. The missile can be released from behind a hill in the approximate direction of the target. The laser light is reflected from the target into the laser seeker in the missile which homes into the target steered by small auxiliary rockets or aerodynamic fins. The system works equally well at night if the laser gun is provided with a night telescope. A number of American laser-guided projectiles are listed in Table 3.3. Today most of these are bombs, but many more missiles will be produced in due course. At present these are all using the Nd-YAG laser, wavelength 1.06 μm (Figure 3.1). The far-infra-red lasers, for example the CO_2 laser, wavelength 10.6 μm, would be more powerful and would penetrate the atmosphere better, but at present sensors for them are more complicated and expensive than the diodes for the near infra-red. But new sensors are already being developed for the 10 μm-region. The longer wavelength has the drawback that the beam is more strongly dispersed (Figure 3.2), but this is more than compensated for by about a 50 times better haze-penetration than with the near infra-red (see Figure 3.3).[18] Tables 3.4 and 3.5 list a few American laser designators in use or under development.[19] The US Army lightweight laser designator still under development weighs around 7 kg and is highly accurate to at least 4 km.[20] The cannon-launched guided projectile (CLGP) merits special mention.[21] This project has run into technical difficulties. An artillery projectile has in

Table 3.3: Laser-guided American Projectiles

Bombs	Missiles (developmental)	Projectiles
Paveway	Maverick (aircraft)	CLGP (Cannon-launched guided projectile)
Pave Strike	Hellfire (helicopter)	
Pave Storm	Bulldog (naval vessels)	
Rockeye	Stinger (army; troops)	
MK 82-LGB		
MK 84-LGB		

Source: K.E. Verble and C.J. Malven, 'Precision Laser Target Designation — a Breakthrough in Guided Weapons Employment', *International Defense Review*, VII (1974), pp.204-9.

a cannon tube acceleration of around 16.000 G. Hence a 2.5 kg sensor system has to stand a force of 40 tons. And it also spins fast. Hence it has to be very sturdy. At last, however, the problems have been overcome and this artillery projectile will come into service in 1978. It will be quite expensive. The forces of inertia would be much smaller in a rocket, but the United States does not have a 4-inch rocket, and the 2.75 inch one is too small to penetrate the armours of the 1980s. The Americans also contend that the gun is the cheapest way to send a 50-kg to a 30 km distance with a relatively high accuracy (CEP/200m). In tests at White Sands the new rounds have scored direct hits on moving tanks at illumination range of 2-4 km and shooting range of 8-12 km. Finally, the value of a weapon system depends on many things, including counter-measures. Some counter-measures for PGMs are listed in Table 3.6.[22] Smoke and optical jamming are efficient against a semi-active laser system. The United States is currently devoting over $100 million per year to testing about 90 different counter-measures. Some of the tests performed are listed in Table 3.7. One can, for example, provide the tank with a stronger Nd-YAG laser at the top of a flagpole which automatically starts to radiate when the tank is illuminated, drawing the missile over the tank. The laser system has several great merits:

(1) very high accuracy, CEP $\sim$1m;
(2) cheapness;

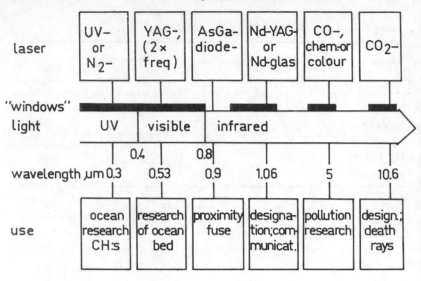

Figure 3.1:   Laser types, light penetrability in the atmosphere and use of the
laser.

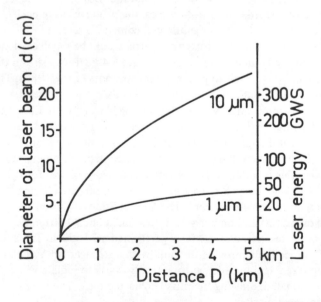

Figure 3.2:   Minimal laser diameter d and laser energy E for a 1 μ sec. laser
pulse for penetration of 1 cm thick material with direct hit without focusing,
as function of distance D (km), for two wavelengths. Stray laser of higher
order not reckoned with. From F. Handlos *et al.*, 'Laser als Waffe',
Wehrkunde, XXIV (1975), No.2.

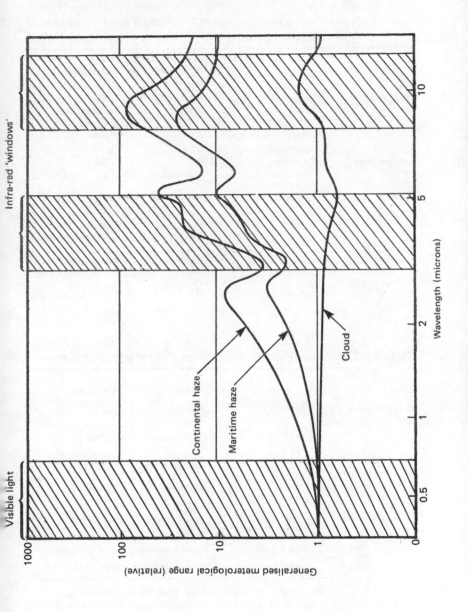

Figure 3.3:   Relationship between range performance and wavelength. From
James Digby, *Precision-Guided Weapons* (International Institute for Strategic
Studies, Adelphi Paper No.118, London, 1975).

Table 3.4:   American Laser Designators for Aircraft and Helicopter-Carried Weapon Systems

Type	System	Application	Contraction
High performance aircraft	Paveway	F-4	Martin
	Pave Knife	F-4D; A-6	Philco-Ford
	Pave Spike	F-4D	Westinghouse
	Long Knife	F-4D	Philco-Ford
	TRAM	A-6E	Hughes
Low performance aircraft	Pave Spot	0-2A	Varo
	Pave Nail	OV-10	LTVE
	Pave Spectre	AC-130E	LTV
	Pave Pronto		
	Marine Gunship	YOV-10	Hughes
Helicopter Systems	SMAL	Helicopter	Philco-Ford
	SPAL	Helicopter	Northrop
	ALLD	AH-16; AAH	Philco-Ford; Bell

Source: K.E. Verble and C.J. Malven, 'Precision Laser Target Designation — a Breakthrough in Guided Weapons Employment', *International Defense Review*, VII (1974), pp.204-9.

Table 3.5:   American Laser Designators for Ground and RPV Systems

Type	System	Application	Contractor
Ground systems	LWLD	Hand or tripod	ILS
	PERLI	Test mounts	MICOM
	GLLD	Ground mount	ILS/Philco-Ford Hughes
RPV systems	Strike drone	BGM-34B	Philco-Ford
Mini-RPV-systems	Praeire	Miniature-RPV	Philco-Ford
	Calere	Miniature-RPV	Philco-Ford
	RPAODS	Miniature-RPV	To be determined
	Acequare	Miniature-RPV	Lockheed

Source: K.E. Verble and C.J. Malven, 'Precision Laser Target Designation — a Breakthrough in Guided Weapons Employment', *International Defense Review*, VII (1974), pp.204-9.

Table 3.6: Potential PGM Counter-Measures

Weapon	Guidance	Potential Counter-Measures
1. Anti-tank Weapons		
AT-3, SS-11[+]	wire; manual	smoke
TOW, Dragon, Milan[+]	IR tracking; automatic	smoke and IR jamming
Shillelagh	IR-link; automatic tracking	the same
Hellfire	semi-active laser homing	smoke and optical jamming
2. Small SAMS		
Redeye, SA-7	IR (hot metal)	flare, IR-jamming
Stinger	IR (plume)	flare, IR-jamming
Roland[+], Crotale[+], Rapier	command guidance radio-link + optical automatic	radio link jamming and optical jamming
RB-70 (Sweden)	laser beam rider	optical jamming

[+]French

Source: P.E. Wilson, 'Battlefield Guided Weapons: The Big Equalizer', US Naval Institute Proceedings, February 1975, pp.19-25.

Table 3.7: US Laser Guided Weapons Counter-Measures Tests Performed

(a)   Passive devices, including reflectors, aerosols, and chaff.

(b)   Military inventory equipment employed in unique modes.

(c)   Laser devices having millijoule output energies, fixed or random pulse rates, and various beam divergences.

(d)   Solid state EO sources capable of any modulation waveforms.

(e)   Pulsed light sources providing up to megawatt peak output powers, fixed or random pulse rates, pulse widths from nano-seconds to milliseconds, and various beam divergences.

(f)   Continuous wave (CW) light sources providing kilowatt out-put powers, various output spectra, and several beam divergences.

(g)   Electro-optical detectors having a composite capability of up to hemispherical surveillance with various wavelength detection ranges and direction-finding resolutions.

Source: *Electronic Warfare*, VII (1975).

(3)   ease of operation;
(4)   short duration of designation — 2 to 3 seconds;
(5)   designator can be located far from the launcher;
(6)   launcher can be behind a hill;
(7)   it is impossible, so far, to locate the origin of the laser beam from outside the beam because of the small amount of stray radiation caused by the atmosphere.

Thus the designator is safe if he is well camouflaged. But laser warning and locating receivers based on the charge-coupled device technology are already under development.[23]

2. Remotely-Piloted Vehicles

These are small pilotless aircraft, propeller or jet-driven, which can be used for reconnaissance, target acquisition, target designation, strike and electronic warfare.[24] In their target designation role they form a part of the laser PGM-system. They are much smaller than aircraft. They are also almost without radar signature and therefore difficult to detect. They are much cheaper too, and do not put the life of a pilot at risk. This is important today when air defence is becoming increasingly murderous to aircraft.

The precision guidance makes high accuracy at great range possible, but this presupposes target acquisition and designation at great range. Hence, full benefit from the former (precision guidance) cannot be attained without the latter. Since designation distances seem to be limited to a few kilometres because of the properties of the atmosphere, the designator must be sent within such a distance of the target. This can be done with RPVs and this may become one of their most important roles.

3. Precision positioning

The US Global Positioning System NAVSTAR is said to be under advanced engineering development. Within a few years it will, for example, enable missile launchers to reach, anywhere on the globe, to an accuracy of about 10m. Three rings of eight satellites on 12-hour orbits will ensure at least four well-located satellites in view any time anywhere in the world.[25]

4. Correlation Guidance

This will be used in cruise missiles and will soon allow an accuracy of about 10m at long distances. Present accuracy is said to be CEP =

20m (70 feet). Both this and the previous system are probably more important for strategic than battlefield weapons, but they may play a role in long-range interdiction, even on the conventional level, particularly initially, before eventual escalation to the nuclear level.[26]

5. New Conventional Munitions

New explosives and designs of munitions have greatly increased weapon effects. There is now a 'choice of custom-tailored' munitions:

(1) fragmentation munitions against personnel;
(2) cluster bomblet units against troop concentrations;
(3) penetrative munitions against hard points;
(4) fuel air explosives for area effect;
(5) terminally guided sub-munitions for the same purpose;
(6) air-scatterable mines for area effect against tanks which they can immobilise.

Many of these developments necessitate better protection — for instance use of fast armoured personnel carriers. All increase the rate of attrition, which is very high in modern land battles. In the October 1973 war, for example, both Israel and Egypt plus Syria lost about half of their heavy weapons within two weeks. The total losses in this war were 2,700 tanks and 555 aircraft in 18 days.[27] Between 15 October and 15 November, the United States provided to Israel 52,000 tons, while the Soviet Union sent to Egypt an estimated 100,000 tons of supplies, mostly ammunition and equipment.

6. New Methods of Target Acquisition and Identification

These are needed because of the increased dispersal and mobility and extended range of fire. Microwave radiation and infra-red radiation from hot metals or plumes can be used for target acquisition and identification as well as for homing of projectiles. Remotely piloted vehicles, airborne radars (AWACS)[28] and even satellites[29] are the best possibilities for acquisition in great depth. Sensors, the 'electronic battlefield', have already been tested in Vietnam but with contradictory results. Such sensors were evidently often dropped rather randomly from aircraft into the area of the enemy, for instance onto the Ho Chi Minh Trail. Evidently, they quite often did not work properly, or were too easily detected and removed, or were foiled by the enemy. If they were to be used in a different manner, for example manually put into place by commando troops and carefully hidden, they could extend surveillance capability considerably.[30]

More important on the battlefield may be the new devices which allow night vision, such as thermal imagers and image intensifiers, because movement must take place much more than previously at night, any movement in daytime simply being too dangerous. This depends of course on the terrain and on the target acquisition and on the capability for high-precision fire at long range by the enemy.

7. Command, Control and Communication (C^3)

In the near future commanders will have a theatre-wide view of the battlefield on a TV-screen.[31] Small, dispersed units will be able to stay under constant contact, not only with their higher and lower command, but even with bordering units and supporting forces, such as the air force.

8. Battlefield Computers

Wisely used computers can greatly facilitate and speed up command and thus increase the tempo of the combat. On-line computers will make possible, for example, immediate counter-artillery fire, response being so fast that counter-fire will commence before the primary salvo has arrived at its target.[32]

Impact of PGMs and RPVs on Tactics

The advocates of PGMs say that any weapon which has a close to 100 per cent kill probability for tanks and aircraft *must* have a great effect upon tactics. Valuable weapons or vehicles can become too vulnerable. Tanks can be destroyed at distances of 3 to 4 km. Because of RPV reconnaissance and designation, camouflage is essential even far in the rear. Movement is possible safely only in a dense forest or at night. A squad or half-squad can have very high fire-power if it has PGMs provided with different munitions. It might even carry air-defence weapons. It may not need even to carry the munitions, since these can be air- or ground-launched from far in the rear. Highly accurate PGMs provide less collateral damage and reduce drastically logistic needs. This may be very important, as an armoured division requires daily thousands of tons of supplies, mainly ammunition and fuel. Much of the fuel is consumed in transporting ammunition.

The advocates of PGMs also maintain that they can prevent the attacker from massing his forces, especially tanks and armoured vehicles. PGMs can thus make defence at least temporarily superior to offence and, therefore, have a stabilising effect. But there are others who say that the attacker can concentrate area fire to suppress the designators, or use of foot infantry ahead of tanks, since PGMs effective against dispersed troops have not been developed, so far, and would probably prove too expensive. The attacker may also use smoke, dust, aerosols, chaff, dummy units, jamming or other counter-measures against the PGM-systems. New types of armour which have a layer of rubber-cement or ceramics between two layers of armour are already evolving. These will be impenetrable to the smaller shaped-charge warheads. Attrition may be high but massing may still be worthwhile in order to gain an initiative through a breakthrough. Thus, although the development of PGMs and RPVs will certainly require some modification of tactics, their impact upon land combat may be, after all, smaller than that predicted by their most optimistic advocates.

Can PGMs Replace the Tacnukes?

Perhaps the most interesting question is whether the application of new weapons and tactics can possibly obviate the need to maintain the tactical nuclear weapons (TNWs) in their present role in Europe. Several reasons can be advanced to support an affirmative response. First, most of the tasks of small TNWs can be performed more cheaply by large conventional explosives, if these can be delivered at an accuracy of, say 1 m. Second, since RPVs and satellite surveillance will probably require underground protection even in the rear, the effect of nuclear fire will be drastically reduced. Third, the main reason for maintaining first strike readiness for the TNWs may be that, if the enemy achieves a breakthrough for an armoured spearhead, the only means by which it may be halted may be nuclear strikes. If PGMs can do this, it is a much safer and preferable way to do it.

It is not easy for anybody devoted to disarmament to recommend wide-scale application of a destructive new technology and I am *not* recommending it as an addition to the existing systems, and I am particularly not urging their linkage to nuclear weapons, for example to the so-called mininukes. But as a *replacement* for TNWs, PGMs have several great virtues: they are clearly defence-favouring since the defender can camouflage himself while the attacker must be mobile and thus visible; they do not cause any such collateral damage as nuclear weapons; they are not escalatory; their use is not politically restricted; and their wide-range application would reduce logistical needs and the size of the military apparatus.

If both military alliances in Europe really are purely defensive, as they both claim, and if the new technology can be used to reinforce the defence against the offence, then both sides should agree to the non-first-use of TNWs and to their withdrawal to second-line weapons as chemical weapons now are. Even some military experts agree that Europe cannot be defended by TNWs, but only destroyed.[33] The present arsenals are so destructive and the doctrines so asymmetric that even a limited nuclear war would mean *finis* to Europe. The European people should therefore take a hard look at the present plans for the use of TNWs. They would discover that they are not reasonable weapons of war, particularly not weapons for defence, but only the highly political tools of a dangerous, confusing gamble. Moreover, many studies have proved that TNWs do not save manpower or reinforce defence. On the contrary, they are manpower-consuming, and, eventually, favour the offence. They should not be maintained in Europe because of their questionable deterrent effect on the tactical level or because of their supposed psychological linking effect to the strategic level. Real battlefield use would lead to chaos, huge losses and the utilisation of untrained reservists. Real defence would be much better served if TNWs were removed and defence reinforced by wide application of the new technology, which is not politically restricted and therefore dependable, non-escalatory, cheap, favours the defence, limits collateral damage, and reduces logistical costs. The superpowers may wish to maintain TNWs in their present role because they guarantee the leadership of their alliances. But in the final analysis even they would gain if the TNWs were removed because they cannot guarantee a victory, only increase the losses. Europeans, in particular, should fight against any plans to miniaturise and modernise TNWs and to make them more flexible and usable in real combat. Otherwise we shall never get rid of them from Europe.

Notes

1. See, for example, J. Ellis, *The Social History of the Machine Gun* (New York, 1976); D. Chandler, *The Art of Warfare on Land* (London, 1974), pp.194-214; and E. Horton, *The Illustrated History of the Submarine* (London, 1974).
2. L. Thompson, 'The Beginnings of Tank Warfare', *Armies and Weapons,* IV (1975), pp.63-9.
3. Chandler, *The Art of Warfare on Land,* pp.215-20.
4. M. Stark, *Allmän sjökrighistoria, 1930-1945* (Stockholm, 1972), pp.174-7.
5. F. Wiener, *Die Armeen der NATO Staaten* (Munich, 1970); and W.G. Resnitschenko (ed.), *Taktik des allgemeinen Gefechts im Kernwaffenkrieg* (Berlin, 1971).
6. Resnitzchenko (ed.), *Taktik des allgemeinen Gefechts im Kernwaffenkrieg.*
7. C. Herzog, *Entscheidung in der Wüste:/ Die Lehren des Jom Kippur-Krieges*

(Berlin, 1975).

8. J.D. Glassman, *Arms for the Arabs* (Baltimore, 1975).

9. R.N. El-Rayyes and D. Nahas (eds.), *The October War* (Beirut, 1973).

10. Electronic Warfare Magazine, *International Countermeasures Handbook* (1975), pp.67-74.

11. James Digby, *Precision-Guided Weapons* (International Institute for Strategic Studies, Adelphi Paper no.118, London, 1975); J.T. Burke, 'Smart Weapons: A Coming Revolution in Tactics', *Army*, XXIII (1973), no.2, pp.14-20; J.T. Burke, 'Precision Weaponry: The Changing Nature of Modern Warfare', *Army*, XXIV (1974), no.3, pp.12-16; and S.D. Fair, 'Precision Weaponry in the Defence of Europe', *NATO's Fifteen Nations,* August-September 1975.

12. Digby, *Precision-Guided Weapons*, p.1.

13. Anon., 'Anti-tank Weapons', *Armies and Weapons,* IV (1975), no.20, pp.45-54.

14. Ibid.

15. M. Hewish, 'Guided Missiles First Principles no.2: Infrared Guidance', *Flight International,* CIX (1976), p.884.

16. W. Schütze, 'Les nouvelles armes guidées avec précision et leurs conséquences militaires et politiques', *Défense Nationale,* XXXII (1976), pp.69-86.

17. Ibid.; and Digby, *Precision-Guided Weapons*.

18. Digby, *Precision-Guided Weapons*.

19. K.E. Verble and C.J. Malven, 'Precision Laser Target Designation – a Breakthrough in Guided Weapons Employment', *International Defense Review,* VII (1974), pp.204-9.

20. J.S. Phillip, 'True Magic for Artillerymen', *Aerospace International,* XII (1976), no.1, pp.22-4.

21. Ibid. and R.D.M. Furlong, 'The US Cannon Launched Guided Projectile', *International Defense Review,* IX (1976), pp.117-19.

22. P.E. Wilson, 'Battlefield Guided Weapons: The Big Equalizer', *US Naval Institute Proceedings,* February 1975, pp.19-25.

23. F. Handlos, H. Hora, G. Langguth and K. Oettle, 'Laser als Waffe', *Wehrkunde,* XXIV (1975), no.2, pp.77-82.

24. H. Sadowski, 'CCD: A Candidate Technology in Electro-Optical Countermeasures', *Electronic Warfare,* VIII (1976), no.1, pp.65-74; and R. Boehe, 'RPV als Seekriegsmittel?', *Marineforum,* LI (1976), no.1/2, pp.19-20.

25. Digby, *Precision-Guided Weapons*.

26. Kosta Tsipis, 'The Long-Range Cruise Missile', *The Bulletin of the Atomic Scientists,* XXXI (1975), no.4, pp.15-26.

27. SIPRI, *World Armaments and Disarmament: SIPRI Yearbook, 1974* (Stockholm, 1974), pp.5-8.

28. E. Ulsamer, 'Military Electronics', *Air Force Magazine,* July 1975, p.44.

29. J.M. Kuhn, 'Tactical Satellite Communication Systems', *Signal,* March 1976, pp.29-31.

30. Ibid.

31. G.-A. Weidemann, 'Unterstützung der Führung in Gefecht mit Hilfe der Fernsehtechnik', *Soldat und Teknik,* December 1975, pp.618-24.

32. A.B. Crawford, 'Future Trends in the Army', *Signal,* March 1975, pp.54-9.

33. H. Trettner, 'Atomare Gefechtsfeldwaffen für Mitteleuropa?', *Allgemeine Militärrundschau,* February 1971, pp.199-208.

4 THE INTERNATIONAL POLITICAL ECONOMY OF PROLIFERATION

Steven J. Baker

Up to 1973 there were two statuses relevant to the problem of nuclear proliferation — nuclear weapons states (NWS) and non-nuclear weapons states (NNWS). Each of these statuses was in turn divided into two subgroups: superpowers and minor nuclear weapons states; threshold non-nuclear weapons states and others. On the basis of this relatively simple international structure, an international non-proliferation régime was constructed in the late 1960s, a régime of which the nuclear Non-Proliferation Treaty (NPT) was the capstone.

The mutual interest of the superpowers in limiting the spread of nuclear weapons led to intense co-operation between them to impose a non-proliferation régime. The compatibility of the interests of minor nuclear weapons states with those of the superpowers was much less clear; thus Great Britain chose to co-operate in establishing the NPT system while France and China abstained. But while rejecting the NPT system in principle, the interests of the French and Chinese in the existence of such a system led them to do little to undermine it in practice.

The objects of the co-operation among NWS were the second-status, nuclear threshold nations, especially the major industrial nations of the non-Communist world, and in particular Federal Germany and Japan. Their integration into the non-proliferation régime was part of a broader pattern of political and economic interdependence among members of the US bloc. Of a dozen or so threshold nations, only three or four were Third World nations, with India at the head of the list.[1] Because these Third World nations were less integrated into the broader political and economic system, they were difficult to incorporate in the non-proliferation régime. But as long as they were few in number and geographically peripheral to the major NWS, the threshold countries of the Third World seemed to pose less of a threat to the international régime than the industrialised threshold nations.

This rather neatly structured situation has begun to change rapidly, and for the sake of convenience the Middle East conflict and subsequent oil crisis may be seen as a turning-point. The emergence of two additional 'nuclear states' in the period since 1973 is one indication of a much more complicated international system, one in which there has been a proliferation of nuclear statuses. The 'firebreak' between NWS has gone. It seems doubtful that an international non-proliferation régime based on a simpler international structure can survive these kinds of changes.

It is convenient to date Israel's emergence as a nuclear state from the 1973 war. Although Israel is not a nuclear weapons state in the terms of the NPT, namely one that has detonated a nuclear device, there is a growing consensus that Israel has indeed fabricated a number of nuclear weapons. Recently rumours that Israel has nuclear weapons 'available for use' have become increasingly concrete. A *Boston Globe* report estimated that there were 'at least 10' such weapons, the CIA leaked an estimate of 10 to 20, and *Time Magazine* (12 April 1976) gave the number as 13. Even those who are not convinced that Israel actually possesses nuclear weapons seem ready to concede that she is but a few hours (12 to 48) away. The closer one gets to actual fabrication, the less meaningful the distinction between nuclear weapons state and non-nuclear weapons state becomes. Israel's strategy has long been to keep its nuclear status sufficiently ambiguous to receive the benefits of a nuclear deterrent while being free from the political costs of going nuclear. This ambiguity has been reduced to the point where Israel must be considered a nuclear nation: certainly, Israel's neighbours cannot afford to treat Israel as anything but a nuclear nation. This gives Israel the status of a non-demonstrated, militarily nuclear nation.

The Indian nuclear test of May 1974 adds another nuclear status, that of a non-military but demonstrated nuclear nation. Although a nuclear weapons programme will probably emerge around 1980 as India's delivery system programmes mature, as yet the Indian explosion is an isolated event without much short-term military significance, but of greater political consequence. Despite any ambiguity about Indian military intentions, India is clearly a nuclear nation.

As nuclear energy continues to spread in the wake of the oil crisis, and as delivery systems adaptable to nuclear weapons continue to be merchandised as part of the traffic in conventional arms, subgroups of several nuclear statuses will become relevant. The number of days or months a nation is considered to be from fabricating nuclear devices may be as important as having demonstrated a nuclear explosion in the calculations of other nations.[2] Indeed, a nation thought to be a few hours from assembling a nuclear weapon which also possesses means of delivery will be considered more dangerous than a nation which has demonstrated a Peaceful Nuclear Explosive (PNE) but has only very crude, limited-range delivery systems. Important distinctions will be made among nations whose delivery systems give them at best a symbolic nuclear threat, or a more substantial regional capability, or one with extra-regional, strategic dimensions.

The disappearance of the 'firebreak' between threshold states and nuclear weapons states is of fundamental importance to non-proliferation policies. Past policies have been predicated to some extent on rewarding nations for voluntarily refusing to cross the nuclear threshold: implicit has been the threat of sanctions to be imposed on those which did cross the threshold. These policies have always had in them the inherent contradiction that the closer one came to the nuclear threshold, the better one's claim to special rewards. In the past this has meant proposals to accord nations with high nuclear capabilities such as Japan the prestige and consideration usually reserved for NWS, such as a permanent seat on the United Nations Security Council. Secretary of State Henry Kissinger's trip to Brazil and the proclamation of a 'special relationship' between the United States and Brazil closely followed the latter's negotiation of the nuclear agreement with Germany which will make her in five to ten years a first-rank nuclear nation, thus anticipating and rewarding her approach to her new nuclear status.

But the same kinds of rewards have been held out to those nations which have crossed the threshold. Kissinger also moved rapidly to improve relations with India following the nuclear test of May 1974. And the conviction that Israel is no more than a few hours from having nuclear bombs will make many in Washington more inclined to supply Israel with conventional weapons lest the Israelis be faced with a situation in which they are forced actually to use their nuclear capability. With the blurring of the distinction between the threshold and nuclear nations, it becomes difficult to decide whether nations are being rewarded for refusing to go nuclear or because they are thought to have already done so. The whole calculus of rewards and potential sanctions depends on the existence of a standard, nuclear weapons states as distinct from non-nuclear weapons states, which is fast disappearing.

Not everyone agrees that the emergence of two additional nuclear states in the last three years means that the spread of nuclear weapons cannot be limited.[3] The very special circumstances in which Israel and India find themselves are often cited as evidence that their behaviour does not necessarily set a precedent for other nations. A variant of this argument is that if non-proliferation policies are to be successful, they must be country-specific, dealing not in a universally applicable policy but approaching proliferation on a case-by-case basis.[4] Non-proliferation policies tailored to each of these special cases, it is argued, can limit the spread of nuclear weapons in the future.

The requirements for formulating and executing non-proliferation policies on a case-by-case basis seem formidable. Early American non-proliferation initiatives were essentially case-by-case and were vitiated by the inconsistencies of a policy that favoured aiding British nuclear weapons programmes, vacillated over aiding the French but in the end chose to oppose their nuclear programme, and steadily opposed the nuclear ambitions of Germany, Japan and Italy. Even more subtle distinctions would have to be made on policies towards present threshold states; why should Iran or Brazil be considered less of a 'special case' than Israel or India? The proliferation of nuclear statuses makes a universal approach, based on a neat distinction between NWS and NNWS, impossible. And the requirements of reconciling the various domestic points of view and co-ordinating national policies with those of other governments suggest that a case-by-case approach will very likely be a euphemism for having no non-proliferation policy at all. As a result, there is every reason to believe that as time goes on the costs of going nuclear — political, technical and economic — will continue to decrease while the difficulty of maintaining a non-proliferation régime will increase.

Going nuclear requires a political decision to transform technical capabilities into military reality. Since the target nations of non-proliferation policies have been by definition those with the capability to go nuclear, that is threshold nations, the primary emphasis of past non-proliferation policies has been to reduce the political incentives to go nuclear. Alliance systems and bilateral security arrangements have been maintained in part because of their function of reducing nuclear incentives. A secondary emphasis has been to place political restraints on civil nuclear technology to impede its weapons use. Bilateral inspections of nuclear exports and international inspections of civil nuclear industries under the International Atomic Energy Agency (IAEA) and the NPT were designed to circumscribe the freedom of threshold countries to use their technology for weapons. In the political context of the mid-1960s superpower co-operation was sufficient to maintain this kind of international non-proliferation régime.

The present shift of emphasis of non-proliferation policies from incentives to capabilities reflects a redefinition of the target nations. With the projected rapid expansion of nuclear energy in the Third World, arms control advocates have begun to focus on the problem of nuclear weapons capabilities as the most dynamic factor in proliferation today. The most worrisome nations are those only now beginning to acquire nuclear weapons capabilities, especially the Third World nations.[5] The superpowers are unwilling to extend security guarantees to these nations, nor would such guarantees be welcome or credible in most cases. And there seems to be less confidence that political restrictions placed on nuclear energy development in the Third World will be as effective as they have proven to be among the industrialised nations in preventing proliferation.

While it is possible to imagine non-proliferation policies that would restrict the availability of technology beyond simply placing political restrictions on the uses to which the technology might be put, these measures could not be imposed by the superpowers alone. Restriction of capabilities would involve the co-operation of the several nuclear suppliers of the developed world, Communist and non-Communist, as well as a few nations like India and South Africa that would be hard to absorb for political reasons. But more importantly, non-proliferation measures affecting capabilities involve the interests of a broad range of actors even within the advanced industrial nations, not only the diplomatic and military establishments, but scientific communities, bureaucracies in the nuclear energy and commerce fields, industrial and financial interests, as well as domestic political groups. The task of either formulating or implementing a policy of restricting capabilities is much more difficult than was the case with past non-proliferation objectives.

The lack of consensus on non-proliferation policies, either within individual nations or among relevant groups of nations, combined with the international economic, technical and political interests favouring the increased reliance on nuclear energy, suggest that nuclear capabilities will continue to spread. These capabilities will result in nuclear statuses of various kinds, some of which will have a political impact irrespective of the presence of conscious military motivation. The incentives to go nuclear have not declined over the last decade, although it is arguable whether they have remained constant or increased.[6] It seems likely, however, that the spread of capabilities will increase the incentive to go nuclear if only because it will reduce the difficulty and cost of doing so.

There are two general paths for approaching and crossing the nuclear threshold, each of which might have several variants.[7] The two most recent nuclear nations, Israel and India, are fair approximations of these different paths, though neither is a perfect example. The first is the most direct, cheapest, and possibly technically least demanding path. Israel's nuclear option was based on a small plutonium production reactor, not subject to international safeguards. Plutonium has apparently been separated in a small fuel-reprocessing facility and secretly fabricated into nuclear devices. There has been no demonstration of a nuclear capability – only information leaked abroad of sufficient credibility to convince many observers that Israel does have nuclear weapons. This route involves minimal vulnerability to nuclear-related sanctions from outside: having broken no international commitments, and having no nuclear power industry open to technology embargoes or fuel cut-offs, Israel has preserved her freedom of action in the nuclear field.

The second path is less direct, more expensive, and technically more challenging. India's nuclear option was spun off from an ambitious nuclear energy programme, based partly on indigenous and partly on imported facilities. All aspects of the programme were open except the device fabrication and test phases; and even these were the subject of considerable advance speculation in the Indian press. And, of course, the programme culminated in a highly publicised nuclear demonstration. Parts of the programme are under international inspections of various sorts, although India was able to claim to have broken no international agreement in the manner in which the test was carried out. This kind of programme trades off the benefits of outside technical assistance and material support against the risks of outside vulnerability to sanctions at the moment of going nuclear.

The advantages of the first path are obvious and this model will probably be followed by a few nations bent on acquiring a small nuclear weapons force in as short a time as possible. Given the widespread availability of nuclear technology, technical expertise[8] and the circulation of nuclear materials, the obstacles to going nuclear in this fashion may be relatively few. But the costs in terms of international isolation are great. The second path seems to be the model that will be preferred by a larger group of nations aiming only at the acquisition of a *nuclear option,* with the question of actually going nuclear a bridge to be crossed at some undetermined future point. Even for nations with no present nuclear weapons aspirations, a nuclear option for the future would be foolish to forgo, especially as it is afforded in the course of pursuing national energy and technical development priorities. Moreover, it will probably be easier to build and maintain a domestic basis of support among diverse groups — political, bureaucratic and economic — for a multipurpose nuclear energy programme than for an exclusively military programme. Certainly, it will be easier to get technology imports, materials and technical assistance for a nuclear energy programme than for a nuclear weapons programme. Incrementalism favours the nuclear energy path to nuclear weapons; it is procedurally easier to provide a government with options than it is to commit the government to specific programmes that require fundamental political choices.

Domestic nuclear energy programmes usually come with international strings attached — IAEA inspections, dependence on imported technology and foreign licences, imported materials and fuels, foreign capital and outside assistance. Few nations can aspire to a completely autonomous nuclear energy programme. In particular, nuclear energy programmes in the Third World may be the source of new kinds of dependency relationships. The ways in which these relationships might be used for non-proliferation purposes may be important. But the Indian case suggests that the potential vulnerability of technological dependence may in fact not result in the imposition of heavy costs or sanctions on nations choosing to go nuclear. Nuclear suppliers have to have the political will to exercise the leverage their technological superiority gives them. The failure to do so in the case of the Indian nuclear detonation establishes a presumption against imposing sanctions in the future. With non-proliferation barriers dependent on a concerted political will among several nations which has proved to be lacking recently, proliferation becomes increasingly likely as nuclear capabilities continue to evolve.

The projected increased dependence of the advanced industrial nations on nuclear energy in the wake of the 1973-4 oil crisis implies the vertical proliferation of nuclear weapons capabilities. Most of the advanced industrial nations already have a scientific and industrial nuclear capability of some kind; accelerating nuclear programmes in these nations will have the effect of improving their weapons potential further. A greater need will be created for nuclear fuel facilities, which will give them direct access to potentially weapons-grade nuclear materials. Furthermore, larger domestic nuclear power programmes will lead to the creation of productive capacity for power reactors, fuel facilities and components for domestic markets, which can then be exported to other nations, thus contributing to both vertical and horizontal proliferation. The growth of nuclear power in the advanced industrial nations will, in the broadest sense, reinforce the image of dependence on nuclear energy as the wave of the future, encouraging emulation in circumstances where nuclear energy may objectively may be unsuited.

By 1973, there were about 115 power reactors ' in commercial operation' in 16 countries, 14 of which were nations of the industrial world; the total generating capacity of these reactors was about 85 GWe. The nations were Canada, Czechoslovakia, France, the German Democratic Republic, Federal Germany, Great Britain, India, Italy, Japan, the Netherlands, Pakistan, Spain, Sweden, Switzerland, the United States and the Soviet Union. The seven major nuclear supplier nations – the United States, the Soviet Union, Great Britain, France, Federal Germany, Canada and Japan – accounted for 95 reactors.[9] Power reactor construction was at an advanced stage in an additional ten nations, five of them in Europe, namely Argentina, Austria, Belgium, Brazil, Bulgaria, Finland, South Korea, Mexico, Taiwan and Yugoslavia.[10] The dramatic rise in the price of oil led most advanced industrial nations to project increased dependence on nuclear power. The countries of the European Economic Community (EEC) nearly doubled their projected dependence on nuclear energy for 1985;[11] the Organization for Economic and Commercial Development (OECD) as a whole estimated that pre-crisis projections of 846 GWe for 1985, which up to 1973 had proved to be too optimistic, would be realised as a result of the oil crisis.[12]

But by late 1974 these projected increases were proving to be too optimistic. Besides making nuclear energy more economically attractive, the rise in oil prices helped to reduce demand for electrical energy and contributed to conditions that made capital-intensive nuclear energy hard to finance. This was accompanied by a continuing escalation in the cost of nuclear plants. The impact of these conditions was such that in the United States there was an overall reduction of about 20 in electric installations in 1974-5. Because of the higher capital costs and longer lead times required of nuclear plants, the cut-back was two to one at the expense of nuclear over fossil fuel plants.[13] Other major OECD nations had similar financial problems. France and Italy committed themselves to essentially all-nuclear power programmes from 1974, but soon found it difficult to finance these ambitious programmes. Federal Germany and Japan have yet to experience serious financial constraints on their nuclear energy programmes, but public opposition, particularly concerning environmental and public health and safety concerns, is growing in these countries and could in the near future pose serious obstacles to expanding nuclear programmes.[14]

The financial problems of the nuclear industry are serious and a major source of uncertainty about the future of nuclear energy. World-wide capital expenditure in nuclear-generating plants between 1971 and 1985 has been estimated at $250 billion, with an additional $45 billion estimated to be expended on the fuel cycle.[15] Raising the capital to finance this kind of effort could prove to be very difficult. Increased dependence on nuclear energy is deemed desirable by governments hoping to limit their dependence on the politically unreliable Organization of Petroleum Exporting Countries (OPEC). In those nations where the government is also the utility customer — like France and Italy — one can expect a maximum effort to maintain the expanding nuclear programmes. But in countries like the United States and Federal Germany, private utilities may well opt for the short-term economically attractive fossil fuel plants in spite of the longer-term economic advantages of nuclear energy — and despite the international political implications of such a choice.

Regarding the other major source of uncertainty in nuclear energy's future, public acceptability, little can be said definitely. The nuclear debate has long been joined in the United States and in Japan. In Western Europe public attention has been drawn to the broader implications of dependence on nuclear energy only in the last few years. Until recently, nuclear energy policy in Europe has been the exclusive province of bureaucrats, scientists and industrial interests in the nuclear field; the impact of broad public pressure is only beginning to be felt now, with signs of public opposition to nuclear power growing. The recent defeat of the California referendum which would have limited nuclear power expansion in the state suggests that the public can be persuaded of the necessity of nuclear energy. In nations which have fewer energy alternatives than the United States the economic and social dislocation of energy shortages could in time incline public opinion in favour of heavily increased dependence on nuclear power. On the other hand, a major nuclear accident or terrorist incident anywhere in the world might result in the imposition of severe limits on nuclear energy. In both its economic dimensions and in terms of public acceptability, uncertainty seems to be the principle characteristic of the future of nuclear energy in the industrialised nations.

The more rapid the growth of nuclear-generating capacity, the faster demand will grow for fuel cycle facilities and services. Since the fuel cycle is the principal cross-over point between a weapons programme and a nuclear energy programme, the number, size and location of fuel facilities is a crucial determinant in the proliferation of weapons capabilities. The two types of facilities of particular relevance to the production of weapons-grade fissile material are uranium enrichment plants and spent fuel reprocessing facilities.

In addition to the nuclear weapons states only a few nations have enrichment facilities in operation or under construction: The Netherlands has two small centrifuge plants built under the auspices of the Urenco consortium; one of these is in fact a Federal German plant built across the border in Almelo as a matter of political convenience. South Africa has a small enrichment plant under construction, reputedly based on the German nozzle separation process. Other nations that have advanced enrichment programmes are Australia, Israel, Italy and Sweden (see Table 4.1). Brazil has negotiated the eventual purchase of an enrichment plant based on the nozzle process from Federal German industries. Belgium, Spain, Italy and Iran are partners along with France in the Eurodif enrichment consortium, but little or no technology-sharing is involved — essentially these other nations have agreed to help finance the construction of a French plant in return for an option on the plant's output.

Enrichment is technically very complex and enormously capital-intensive. The cost of a 10,000,000 Separative Work Units (SWU)/year capacity plant is estimated at over $3,000,000,000, whether it be a gaseous diffusion or centrifuge plant.[16] On a rough calculation based on an estimated 120,000 SWU/year/1000 megawatts electric (MWe) light water reactor (LWR) plant capacity factor of 75 per cent, such a plant could serve about eighty 1000 MWe LWR a year.[17] Gaseous diffusion plants much smaller than this are thought to be uneconomical but small-scale centrifuge plants are economically feasible, and could be scaled down to meet the needs of just a few reactors. A laser isotope separation facility might be even more economically attractive on a small scale but it will not be commercially feasible for a decade or more.

These latter, small-scale kinds of enrichment technologies are the main concern from a proliferation standpoint, and are the technologies being most widely studied around the world. Of the existing enrichment processes, gaseous diffusion and centrifuge technologies have been subject to military classification; but the nozzle process has never been classified, which explains why it was available for export to Brazil and, perhaps, to South Africa. Yet despite national security

Table 4.1:   Planned and Projected Research and Development
             Programmes

Country and/or Organisation	Location	Process	Comment
Urenco (UK, FRG, Neth.)	Capenhurst (UK) & Almelo (Neth.)	Gas Centrifuge	Additions projected by Urenco leading to 2 million SWU/yr by 1982 and 10 million SWU/yr by 1985.
Eurodif (France, Belgium, Spain, Italy)	Tricastin (France)	Gaseous Diffusion	Plant under construction projected at 4.7 million SWU/yr by 1978 and 10.7 million SWU/yr by 1983.
South Africa	Not chosen		Announced objective is 5 million SWU/yr plant for the early 1980s.
FRG	Karlsruhe	Jet Nozzle	Small pilot plant built in 1967 at KfK.
Brazil	Not chosen	Jet Nozzle	Part of 1975 agreement with FRG, would be first production-scale plant and therefore very small but based on 5 million SWU/yr reference design by STEAG, AG.
Japan	Tokai-Mura	Gas Centrifuge	Growing research programme, experimental cascade operations involving several hundred machines under way: interested in 3-4 million SWU/yr.
Canada Zaire	Not chosen	Gaseous Diffusion	Studies have been undertaken on the advantages of siting in low-electric-power-cost areas.
Italy	Various	Gaseous Diffusion & Gas Centrifuge	Modest basic research programmes.
Australia	Lucas Heights	Gas Centrifuge	Small basic research programme since 1965.
UK USSR Israel FRG France Australia Sweden PRC		Processes utilising laser illumination	Various countries and groups are interested in laser isotope separation research.

Table 4.1 *(contd.)*

Country and/or Organisation	Location	Process	Comment
Sweden		Rotating Plasma	Small research programme.

US Energy Research and Development Administration. IAEA Branch. Office of International Program Implementation. 'Lists of US reactors exported and of reprocessing and enrichment facilities abroad', by Elizabeth T. McFadden, November 1975.
Source: 'US Nuclear Power Export Activities: Final Environmental Statement', ERDA-1542, vol.2, Appendix D-3, Table 5.

classification restrictions, enrichment technologies have been shared, and are increasingly being considered for export for commercial reasons. The Soviet Union transferred its enrichment technology to China in the late 1950s and early 1960s. The United States may have aided the British in enrichment technology in the late 1950s; and since 1971 the Americans have proposed to share enrichment technology with selected allies among the advanced industrial countries. Consideration of the export of Urenco and Eurodif technologies to countries like Canada and Australia has been reported in the press. As demands for enriched uranium grows and the smaller-scale technologies become perfected, the spread of enrichment facilities to more nations may be expected.

Countries interested in purely national facilities would be those with power programmes large enough to justify such a facility — a centrifuge plant of the size that Urenco projects in 1982 would be adequate for fifteen 1000 MWe LWRs and several nations will have an installed nuclear capacity of this size by 1990. These will certainly include the United States, the Soviet Union, Japan, Great Britain, France, Federal Germany and Italy, and perhaps some of the smaller European countries like the Netherlands; and also very likely India, Brazil and Mexico. But also nations with uranium deposits like Canada, Australia, South Africa and Nigeria may be interested in acquiring enrichment plants in order to export a finished product instead of a raw material. And, finally, nations more concerned about 'security of supply' than about the cost of enriched uranium might invest in very 'uncommercial' facilities. As with nuclear power in general, financing enrichment facilities could be a major obstacle to the international spread of these plants. One might

tentatively conclude that the financial difficulties of the nuclear power
industry which reduce the investment in nuclear power and reduce the
demand for enrichment capacity may have a positive non-proliferation
impact.

Reprocessing plants are the most proliferation-prone part of the fuel
cycle because they can be potentially used to separate plutonium from
the wastes of all reactor types — research and power, enriched
uranium-fuelled and natural uranium-fuelled reactors. Small-scale
facilities, costing from a few million to a few tens of millions of dollars
may be adequate to supply a small nuclear weapons programme.[18] And
the technology involved in unclassified, widely available, and within the
grasp of dozens of nations with some chemical and engineering
infrastructures. Besides the nuclear weapons states, Argentina, Belgium,
India, Japan, Spain, Taiwan and Federal Germany are known to have
experimental or small-scale reprocessing facilities (see Table 4.2). Most
were constructed indigenously, although there has been some
international trade in plant components; for example, French parts
have been supplied to Japanese and American plants.

Commercial reprocessing is not now being done anywhere in the
world. In the United States two reprocessing facilities have been closed
down for economic and technical reasons; one of these never went into
operation because of technical defects. The new, large Barnwell, South
Carolina plant is now awaiting its operating licence; but action on this
will be withheld until an environmental impact statement on the
implications of plutonium (Pu) recycle is filed, which will require at
least a year. Even then, ancillary facilities costing tens of millions of
dollars will be necessary to allow the plutonium separated from other
waste products to be refabricated into fuel elements. Abroad, several
nations are evaluating the experience of small pilot facilities to gauge
the feasibility of larger, industrial-scale operations. The multinational
Eurochemic plant in Mol, Belgium, has been shut down. The
governments and industries of Britain, France and Federal Germany
have formed the United Reprocessors consortium, a sort of market-
sharing arrangement that will in the future provide reprocessing
capacity as necessary not only to their own national nuclear power
industries but also to other nations like Japan.

The economic feasibility of plutonium fuel recycle in LWR has yet
to be clearly established. It is uncertain how high the cost of uranium
ore and enrichment charges must go before it is economically justified
to substitute plutonium containing fuel elements (mixed oxide fuels)
for uranium fuel elements. The decision to recycle will also be

affected by the timing of the eventual commercial operation of breeder reactors, although here there is a sort of 'catch 22' for those who, because of fears of proliferation, seek to postpone the emergence of a 'plutonium economy': the longer it takes to bring breeders on line, the more incentive there will be to recycle plutonium in LWRs. But most important, it should be emphasised that under the best of circumstances, the contribution of plutonium recycle in LWRs to nuclear energy will be limited: with full recycle, mixed oxide fuels will only extend uranium supplies 20-30 per cent,[19] and only effect the cost of nuclear-generated electricity 1-2 per cent. It is as yet an open question whether nations will be willing to cope with the wide range of problems inherent in recycling plutonium in order to realise these limited advantages.

Nevertheless, even 'uneconomic' reprocessing facilities may have a role in expanding nuclear energy programmes. While reprocessing is not presently considered economically justified, it is widely assumed that it will be so in a decade, and plutonium will be essential to the breeder reactor that is expected to replace present reactor types. Therefore, nations wanting to get on the learning curve today may be justified in investing in a pilot facility for a few million dollars. Compared to the cost of nuclear power plants, such costs are marginal. This investment, justified in terms of national economic and technical development, will incidentally give nations ready access to potentially weapons grade plutonium.

The degree to which the growth of nuclear power in the developed countries leads to improved nuclear weapons capabilities in each of these nations depends on the pattern of development of the nuclear industry, whether it tends towards international interdependence or national autonomy. For example, there is presently a high degree of industrial interpenetration among the nuclear reactor suppliers of the industrial world. Westinghouse and General Electric (GE) have licensing agreements with industries in most of the nuclear supplier nations (see Table 4.3). American companies even supply up to 30 per cent of the components for the Candu reactor which is the product of Canadian technology.[20] This degree of interpenetration suggests that any nation breaking faith with its partners by, for example, exploding a nuclear device, might face high costs in terms of disrupted economic and technical relations. It also suggests that particular governments, principally that of the United States, may have significant leverage over the nuclear activities of other industrial countries. But the commercialisation of nuclear energy has been predicated on making

Table 4.2: Nuclear Fuel Reprocessing Plants

Country	Type of Fuel	Start of Operation	Feed Capacity (Tonne U/yr)	Pu Product/yr[a] at Capacity (kg)	Comments
Argentina[1]			200 kg/yr	—	
Belgium (Mol)[4]	Metal/LWR	1968[5]	80	516 (1077)[c]	167 tonnes U have been processed
Eurochemic	MTR[b]	1966	40	—	Eurochemic is not expected to process any more fuel
France[4]					
Marcoule	Metal	1958	500	2150	French military and civilian reactors
La Hague	LWR	1975/78	400	2580	Will increase production gradually until 1978
Germany[4]					
WAK, Karlsruhe	LWR	Sept. 1971	36	232 (206)	32 tonnes U have been processed
KEWA	LWR	1983/84	1400	9030	
India[1]					
Trombay	HWR	1967	100	230	
Tarapur	HWR & LWR		150	968	Assume all LWR fuel
Italy[4]					
Eurex 1	MTR	1970	5	—	
	LWR	1975	10	64	
Japan[2]					
Tokai-Mura	LWR & Nat U	1976	200	1290	Assume all LWR fuel
Spain[1]					
Moncla					
Taiwan[3]	MTR		100 kg/yr	—	Small pilot plant

Table 4.2 (contd.)

United Kingdom[4]					
Windscale 1	Metal Nat U	1964	2500	10,750	
Windscale 2	LWR	1970 (76)	400	2580 (645)	Shut down 1973 after processing 100 Te/yr and 1977 400 Te/yr.
Dounreay[1]	Highly Enriched U and Pu	1982	400	2580	
			1	—	

a. For LWR fuel we use an average production rate between PWR and BWR fuel. We assume a mature fuel cycle which produces 6.45 kg of fissile plutonium per tonne of uranium reprocessed. Heavy Water Reactor (HWR) fuel is assumed to have an average recovery of 2.3 kg Pu/TeU. Metal Fuelled Reactors (that are used for power production) are assumed to produce 4.3 kg of fissile Pu per tonne of uranium.

b. MTR – Materials Test Reactor uranium aluminium alloy fuel. Usually enriched to 20 per cent or higher in ^{235}U, normally produces very little Pu.

c. Assumes all 167 tonnes of uranium that have been processed were LWR fuel.

Reprocessing References
1. *The Nuclear Industry*, 1970, p.264.
2. *Nuclear Engineering International*, February 1955, p.82, World Digest.
3. William Epstein, 'The Proliferation of Nuclear Weapons', *Scientific American*, vol.CCXXXII no.4, April 1975, p.18.
4. Walter Schuller, 'Reprocessing in Europe', ANS/CNA Joint Topical Meeting on Commercial Nuclear Fuel Technology Today, 28-30 April 1975, Toronto, Canada.
5. *Science*, vol.CLXXXIV, no.4144, p.1315, 28 June 1974.

Source: David E. Rundquist, Tashai Gozani and Glenn M. Reynolds, 'Technology for Nuclear Weapons Capability', *Science Applications*, July 1975, pp.84-5.

international nuclear exchanges like other commercial exchanges, with initiative increasingly left to private industrial interests. This pattern militates against using ties in the nuclear energy field for political purposes except within very narrow limits.

Genuinely multinational industrial arrangements may have a more effective non-proliferation impact; for example, the German Urenco plant built in the Netherlands will not be available for a German nuclear weapons programme under any conceivable circumstances. The development of multinational fuel storage and/or reprocessing facilities might reduce the national incentives even for small, pilot reprocessing facilities. The nuclear fuel cycle may be one area in which national economic interests and international security are compatible.

Table 4.3: Westinghouse Nuclear Licensees, 1957

Belgium:	Cockerill-Ougree-Providence et Esperance-Londoz Société Franco-Belge de Fabrication de Combustibles — minority ownership Ateliers de Constructions Electriques de Charleroi — majority ownership
Finland:	Oy Wartsila/AB
France:	Eurofuel-Société Européene de Fabrication de Combustibles à Base d'Uranium Pour Reacteurs a Eau Légere — minority ownership Société Franco-Américaine de Constructions Atomiques — minority ownership
Italy:	Fiat, S.p.A. Breda Termomeccanica S.p.A. Sopren S.p.A.
Japan:	Mitsubishi Heavy Industries, Ltd. Mitsubishi Nuclear Fuel Company, Ltd. — minority ownership
Spain:	Empresa Nacional del Uranio, S.A. Equipos Nucleares S.A. — in negotiation
Sweden:	Steam Generator AB
Federal Germany:	Nuklearbrentstoff GmbH — minority ownership

Source: private correspondence with representatives of Westinghouse Electric Corporation.

But, on balance, neither economic nor technical criteria seem clearly to favour large-scale, multinational fuel cycle ventures, and, as time goes on, will favour them even less. Politico-economic concerns like 'security of supply' may well incline governments to national autonomy and the development of national fuel cycle capabilities. Improved industrial capabilities have already made Federal Germany's *Kraftwerkunion* (KWU) largely independent of American licensed technology; France's *Framatome* is clearly moving in the same direction,[21] and other advanced industrial nations can be expected to do likewise. This pattern of national self-sufficiency will make it considerably easier for several governments to go nuclear in a military sense.

The link between the development of nuclear weapons capabilities in the developed countries and those in the less developed countries is closer than the linkage between vertical and horizontal proliferation; in other words, capabilities are more interrelated than incentives to go nuclear. In an increasingly diverse international system, the threshold states' primary preoccupations — security, prestige and economic well-being — are likely to be perceived in terms of local and regional considerations and less in terms of the global East-West confrontation that has dominated in the past. Therefore, it is difficult to believe that even substantial Soviet-American disarmament moves would have much positive non-proliferation impact on the nuclear weapons decisions of nations like Iran, Brazil, Taiwan and other Third World countries. These decisions will be based on more local and regional kinds of concerns.

But the vertical proliferation of nuclear weapons capabilities is likely to have a direct impact on the horizontal spread of nuclear capabilities. Increased dependence on nuclear energy in the developed countries reinforces the image of the desirability of nuclear energy and its contribution to national development. In less developed countries (LDCs) nuclear reactors could assume the symbolic importance that steel mills enjoyed in the 1960s, with even more questionable relevance to national needs. The development of a large productive capacity for nuclear hardware in the developed countries leads to irresistible pressures to export any excess capacity. These kinds of high-technology exports are the developed countries' principal comparative economic advantage, and developing markets for them is an important economic policy goal.[22] This leads to an observation that contradicts the tentative conclusion advanced above, and results in a genuine dilemma. While it was suggested that a slow-down in the nuclear industry might have a positive non-proliferation impact, it might be argued that a healthy, booming nuclear energy economy in the industrial nations might be necessary to reduce the dangers of horizontal spread of nuclear capabilities; this would commit productive capacity exclusively to meeting the energy needs of the industrial world. The dilemma is how to meet the expanding nuclear power needs of the industrialised world, which will inevitably contribute to the vertical proliferation of capabilities, without at the same time encouraging the Third World to emulate dependence on nuclear energy and thus contribute to horizontal proliferation as well.

The projected horizontal spread of nuclear weapons capabilities to a large number of Third World nations with little or no present nuclear capability is the most troublesome factor in the proliferation situation today. But the size and kind of emerging nuclear energy programmes might make possible the exercise of political leverage on behalf of non-proliferation. The role of the IAEA in promoting nuclear power in the Third World deserves close examination in terms of its impact on the evolution of capabilities. Commercial competition among suppliers, and in particular the financing of nuclear exports, will also be important determinants in the spread of nuclear weapons options.

It can be argued that the improved nuclear weapons capabilities of many of the advanced industrial countries are not likely to result in more proliferation of nuclear weapons, these nations are only marginally more likely to do in the future what they have been capable of doing for the last several years and have chosen not to do. But it is more problematic to anticipate what a whole range of additional nations of the Third World will do as they rapidly acquire nuclear weapons potential.

Third World nations are generally less restrained by political and military ties to the superpowers than near-nuclear nations of the industrialised world. Their domestic political processes are often less open to influence of public or world opinion, but very subject to frequent, extra-legal changes of government and régime. The practical ability of the IAEA to carry out its safeguards responsibilities is increasingly open to question in the face of expanding power programmes in the industrial nations. But in coping with the spread of nuclear energy to the nations of the Third World, the IAEA is faced with political as well as practical problems. The Agency must maintain its political acceptability in a period in which UN bodies are increasingly politicised, and in the face of domestic political changes in Third World nations which can be mercurial. These general conditions make the

Third World more proliferation-prone than the advanced industrial countries.

An IAEA market survey of 14 LDCs, published in September 1973, estimated that 60,000 MWe of nuclear power could be installed in the period 1980-9.[23] This was to be in units over 600 MWe. But with the oil price rises of the winter of 1973-4, the IAEA revised its projections. Assuming that oil prices would remain above $6 per barrel, the IAEA estimated a total market for all LDCs of 200,000 MWe.[24] All plant sizes 100 MWe and above were said to be economically competitive with fossil fuels. And the total value of this market for nuclear plants was estimated at $75,000,000,000. While the bulk of nuclear capacity would be installed in five or six nations, the number of LDCs installing at least one nuclear power plant in this period rose from 9 to 43 (see Table 4.4).

These sharply increased projections have not gone unchallenged. In particular, a report prepared for the US Energy Research and Development Administration (ERDA) by a private research firm, commonly referred to as the Barber report, has raised fundamental questions about the IAEA's method of projecting energy demand, the way in which the relative costs of nuclear versus fossil fuel plants were calculated, and concluded *inter alia* that the market for nuclear power in LDCs is certainly less than that projected by the IAEA and subject to multiple uncertainties.[25]

The difference between these sets of estimates is important, because both the number and identity of nations expected to invest in nuclear energy programmes are crucial to future proliferation. The different estimates also raise the question of the IAEA's balance between its regulatory and promotional functions. Both the 1974 IAEA study and the Barber revisions of those estimates agree that the same small group of LDCs can be expected to have substantial nuclear energy programmes by 1990. These are the nations that may have an economic justification for fuel facilities that will give them a ready nuclear option. Some of these nations — notably India and Brazil — are clearly moving towards domestic self-sufficiency in the nuclear field. The others seem likely to be dependent to a considerable degree on suppliers for nuclear power plants, fuels and financing of nuclear power.

A large nuclear power programme, dependent on outside supplies, is obviously politically vulnerable. It is argued, for example, that a nation like Iran would not be likely to jeopardise its nuclear power programme by going nuclear and thereby risking such blows as fuel cut-offs and suspension of technical assistance. The implication is that large nuclear

Table 4.4:   IAEA Projection of Nuclear Plants Installed in LDCs
             Between 1981 and 1990 by Size of Unit

Capacity, MW	150	200	250	300	400	500	600	800	1000	1200	1500	Total
India								4	6	15		27.2
Brazil								2	2	6		10.8
Mexico							1	4	6	8	1	20.9
Argentina							2	3	3			6.6
Iran							3	4	5			10.0
Taiwan							7	4				7.4
Venezuela							6	1				4.4
Korea							5	2	4			8.6
Turkey							3	4				5.0
Colombia						1	2					1.7
Pakistan							8					4.8
Egypt							7	1				5.0
Thailand		1		1	1	2	3					3.7
Peru				2	1							1.3
Philippines							2	2	2			4.8
Hong Kong			2	4	2							3.2
Chile				3	2							1.7
Cuba			2	4	1							2.1
Singapore			5	6			1					4.3
Malaysia		3	1	3								1.7
Indonesia		4		3								1.7
Rep. Vietnam	1	4										1.0
Bangladesh		2	2		2	1	3					4.0
Uruguay	1	2	2									1.1
Kuwait	2	4	1									1.4
Iraq	2	4										1.1
Jamaica	5	2		2								1.7
Ghana	2											0.3
Morocco		2										0.4
Nigeria	2	1										0.5
Algeria	3											0.45
Lebanon	0											0.0
Syria	3											0.45
Cameroon	0											0.0
Costa Rica												0.3
Dominican Rep.	1											.15
Ecuador	1											.15
Panama	1											.15
Uganda	1											.15
Tunisia	1											.15
Bolivia	1											.15
Zambia	1											.15
Saudi Arabia	1											.15
Guatemala	1											.15
Liberia	1											.15
El Salvador	1											.15
Sudan	0											0.0
Number of Units	32	29	13	18	18	7	53	31	28	29	1	261
Total Capacity	5.1	5.8	3.3	5.4	7.2	3.5	31.8	24.8	28.0	34.8	1.5	151.40

Source: Richard J. Barber Associates, Inc., 'LDC Nuclear Power Prospects,
1975-1990', ERDA-52, UC-2, 1975, Figure II-17.)

power programmes may be safer from a proliferation standpoint than small programmes. And this may lead to the conclusion that promoting heavy dependence on nuclear energy is an anti-proliferation measure.[26] But this argument is subject to several qualifications. It assumes that suppliers would have the political will to impose these kinds of sanctions if such a nation were to go nuclear; the Indian case is ambiguous in this regard, since Canada suspended its nuclear assistance but the United States maintained its nuclear agreement and continues to supply fuels for the Tarapur reactors. Reluctance to offend oil-rich Iran would be even greater than reluctance to offend India.

Tnis proposition also assumes that sanctions would be effective — namely that all suppliers would agree and act in concert, and that their actions would have the intended effect; This is far from clear. Could the French suspend fuel deliveries to Iran from a Eurodif plant owned in part by Iran? Would the French government do it even if it could? If Iran had stockpiled fuels and/or had the capacity to separate and recycle plutonium it could extend its nuclear power operations for some time after sanctions were imposed, depriving fuel cut-offs from having their intended effect, at least immediately. While the potential leverage of nuclear suppliers over a large, dependent nuclear energy programme is considerable, the actual leverage in any particular case might be very small and subject to multiple conditions.

The smaller nuclear programmes projected to begin in the 1980s will presumably be completely dependent on suppliers for reactors. A few LDCs with uranium ore deposits might have an independent fuel supply, especially if they should choose the *Candu* reactor type (perhaps in a small version marketed in the 1980s by the Indians?) And some of these countries, especially the oil-rich ones, might be free of foreign financial dependence, increasing their freedom of action. But in general, it is precisely the small size of these nuclear programmes which make them dangerous and least susceptible to outside influence despite their technical dependence. One or two small reactors are unlikely to supply more than a fraction of a nation's electric capacity; the disruption attendant upon shutting down these reactors, for example as a result of a fuel cut-off, is likely to be rather limited. Thus, were such sanctions to be imposed by suppliers, their impact would be marginal. This knowledge makes it less likely that in the event any sanctions would be imposed. Small nuclear energy programmes may be only marginal in terms of meeting an LDC's energy problems, but could be quite adequate for a limited nuclear weapons programme. In this small kind of nuclear power programme the two paths to weapons proliferation outlined above converge.

The primary difference between the IAEA's 1974 estimate and the Barber report estimate results from the latter's insistence that no plants less than 600 MWe are economically attractive. In part this is due to the contention that costs cannot be scaled down along with plant capacity past a certain point — very small power reactors turn out to be disproportionately expensive.[27] Cynics might observe that it is not coincidental that the Barber report chooses as a cut-off point the smallest power plant that American industries are presently prepared to export. But it is also true that no other major nuclear suppliers are currently producing power plants much smaller than 600 MWe since, like their American counterparts, they are exporting the excess capacity created to serve their domestic market's needs. Whatever their relevance to the needs of the Third World, power reactors smaller than 600 MWe are not thought to be economical in the developed countries. The IAEA 1974 study notes that given the size of the market for small power reactors, capacity to supply this demand should be created. And more recently, the IAEA has apparently succeeded in convincing three European firms to offer small-scale nuclear reactors for the Third World market.[28]

The fact that the IAEA should seek to promote nuclear energy in developing nations — first by conducting economic and technical studies to demonstrate nuclear energy's viability, and then by urging nuclear firms in the industrial countries to invest in productive capacity to meet the demand projected in IAEA market estimates — raises the question of the Agency's priorities. Out of a total yearly budget of around $36 million, about $6 million is allocated to IAEA safeguard activities, the Agency's major regulatory function.[29] Other Agency activities may total more than three times the safeguards budget.[30] The IAEA promotional activities have one important effect: they skew the energy policies of LDCs in favour of nuclear power, with a broad range of technical, economic and political implications.

There are several reasons for this apparent imbalance in the Agency's activities. For the nations of the developed world, the Agency's principal value is as a regulator of the international nuclear industry, especially under the provisions of the Non-Proliferation Treaty. But in order to gain and maintain the support of the Third World, the IAEA must deliver positively valued things — technical aid and, in some cases, actually serving as the conduit for reactor transfers and fuel supplies.[31] This support is crucial to the Agency's acceptability in its safeguard functions, and the mutual reinforcement of these roles is used as an argument to oppose any division of functions such as that which followed the break-up of the United States Atomic Energy Commission (USAEC). But it is curious that while the Agency has been eager to expand its role in promoting nuclear energy, it has often been reluctant to assume additional safeguard responsibilities. The Agency's institutional tendency to 'accentuate the positive' is comprehensible; but it inspires little confidence regarding the effectiveness of the Agency in performing its regulatory role.

In the most general sense, the relevance of nuclear energy to the needs of most Third World countries must be questioned. These nations are typically capital-scarce with large labour surpluses; nuclear energy is capital-intensive but not labour-intensive, and is therefore the opposite of the kind of technology the Third World needs. Oil and coal at any price are more easily absorbed into developing economies than nuclear power. And the costs of reliance on nuclear energy do not end with the importation of generating equipment and fuel supplies — LDCs will be encouraged to invest in nuclear research centres and to develop manpower trained in nuclear sciences either at local universities or through sending students abroad, all of which represents a distortion in the allocation of the limited resources these nations have. Encouraging LDCs to invest in nuclear energy does more for the balance of payments of the nuclear exporter nations than it does to improve the technical and economic infrastructures of Third World nations.

Financing is the key variable in the spread of nuclear energy in the Third World. More than any other single factor, the availability and terms of capital for nuclear power plant and fuel facility construction will determine the breadth of nuclear energy's spread. In the past, nuclear exports have been financed largely by supplier nations, and usually on very favourable terms. The terms offered by Federal German banks to Brazil — including low-interest loans and repayment deferred until the reactors begin operating — were similar to the concessionary terms under which the United States sold power reactors to India.[32] Competition among nuclear suppliers has been less among differentiated products — there have been only two major reactor types (light and heavy water reactors) on the market at any given time — than in terms of financing, operating experience and fuel supplies. Each of these factors has up to now favoured American reactor vendors over European and Canadian competitors, and up to 1974 the United States had 80 per cent of the international reactor market. But other nations are now supporting their nuclear exports with interest rates and financing terms as good or better than those offered by the Americans.[33] German,

French and Canadian manufacturers are establishing reputations for
dependability. And the diversification of fuel suppliers has reduced the
American vendors' competitive edge. In the period 1974-5, the
American share of the reactor export market slipped to about 50 per
cent.[34]

A recent study suggests that there should be no difficulty in
financing nuclear exports to LDCs through established export finance
channels like the Exim Bank:[35] the ability of LDCs to pay off these
loans in the future seems open to more question. Greater product
differentiation (for example European-exported plants without the
expensive modifications necessary for American environmental
protection standards) or technical packages to accompany reactor sales
(like Federal Germany's willingness to include reprocessing and
enrichment facilities in the Brazil deal) could be added to financing as
important dimensions of international competition for the LDC market
in the future.

It remains to be seen whether co-operation among nucelar suppliers
can reduce some of the obvious proliferation dangers in the present
pattern of competition to export nuclear energy to the Third World.
The 1975 London suppliers talks made a step in the right direction —
an agreement to impose IAEA safeguards on all nuclear exports.[36] But
far more is needed to make a meaningful non-proliferation contribution.
Market-sharing arrangements of various sorts are possible,[37] but not
very likely. The problem is that the suppliers have a differential interest
in exports in general and nuclear exports in particular: half of KWU's
capacity of 6 reactors per year must be exported given the present
demand in the domestic market; Westinghouse and GE can have a
much smaller proportion of their capacity devoted to exports, while
the capacity of Atomic Energy of Canada, Ltd (AECL) seems essentially
committed to filling domestic and already contracted foreign orders.[38]
While, in general, European and Japanese economies are much more
export-dependent than the American economy, and although nuclear
exports still count for only a small fraction of total exports, none of
the major nuclear suppliers seems willing to forgo the possibility of
future major nuclear contracts by adopting serious export restrictions.
The suppliers' national economic interests seem likely to continue to
predominate over their collective security interests; supplier commercial
competition seems likely to be a major contributor to the horizontal
spread of nuclear weapons capabilities.

Capabilities continue to set the parameters within which political decisions, like that required to go nuclear, take place. We have already suggested that the evolution of technical capabilities is important enough as a determinant in proliferation to be considered separately from political incentives to go nuclear; changes in the evolution of capabilities can affect the number and identity of nations able to go nuclear, the timing of the process, and the kind of nuclear forces that will result. Given the doubts about the efficacy of political restraints on the uses of nuclear technology, in many respects restrictions on the spread of nuclear technology seem to be the most promising non-proliferation strategy.[39]

These considerations lead to a set of interrelated propositions that link capabilities and incentives, and which, should they prove to be true, are likely to favour the emergence of many more nuclear nations as time passes.

(1) The possession of a nuclear capability may create an interest in going nuclear where little or none existed before. It has usually been assumed that intent to go nuclear precedes and motivates the acquisition of the technical capability to go nuclear. Therefore, if intent is judged to be low or absent, and/or if political commitments to non-proliferation like NPT membership have been assumed, a given nation's technical capabilities can be safely improved without increasing the threat of proliferation. But options resulting from nuclear energy programmes may not reflect prior weapons intent. And capability may be transformed into a weapons programme in a wide range of situations that may be difficult to predict or influence from the outside. Very modest shifts in the international milieu could trigger a decision to go nuclear — and such shifts need not necessarily be negative, that is need not appear to threaten the physical security of the nation in question. Furthermore, domestic political conditions may be more important determinants of a decision to go nuclear than changes in the international milieu — changes of government, bureaucratic in-fighting and domestic political intrigue may all contribute to a decision to use the technical capability at hand to fashion nuclear weapons, irrespective of the international milieu.

The Indian decision to test a nuclear devices appears to reflect these kinds of considerations. While weapons intent was undoubtedly present to some degree in the Indian nuclear energy programme from the beginning, the maturing of India's nuclear capability made it feasible for the government to decide in 1971 and 1972 to go ahead with a nuclear demonstration; the technical capability to separate plutonium had been in place since 1964 — but only by the early 1970s was the

Indian nuclear energy programme far enough along to withstand the threat of sanctions in the form of technology or fuel supply cut-offs. The initial decision seems to have been made before the war with Pakistan over Bangladesh in 1971, and was persisted in after Pakistan's dismemberment: in other words, India went nuclear at a point when its strategic position on the subcontinent was better than ever before. That going nuclear was expected to be politically popular with the masses must have strengthened the hands of those in the Atomic Energy Department and the armed forces who had long argued in favour of a nuclear demonstration. Nations like the United States and Canada which had aided the development of Indian nuclear technology under 'peaceful uses' agreements did not anticipate this sequence of events and were unable or unwilling to persuade the Indian government not to make the test.

(2) The acquisition of nuclear weapons does not dramatically transform a nation's relations with all other nations. One of the major restraints against acquiring nuclear weapons has been the anticipated impact of such a move on friends and potential foes. The transformation from the status of a threshold nation to that of a nuclear weapons state has been supposed to have implications going far beyond the change in military capability, affecting a nation's international political influence and status: the most commonly assumed effects are that such a move would weaken the commitment of allies, while provoking adversaries quickly to follow suit. Obviously, there are many factors that would influence the reaction of other members of the international community as a result of the identity of the country going nuclear, and the mode followed such as whether international agreements are broken or not. The number of precedents to draw on is very limited. But based on the limited experience to date, the general proposition advanced above seems to be true. The international position of India and Israel has not been dramatically transformed as a result of their going nuclear, either positively nor negatively. Neither has been abandoned by allies — indeed, there is some tendency towards improved relations with major powers in each case. Whatever advantages they have achieved *vis-à-vis* regional adversaries are limited. The only obvious political cost either has paid as yet is the Pakistani decision to buy a small reprocessing plant from France. But even here, it could be argued that the Indian nuclear test made such a purchase more rather than less difficult by giving it the unmistakable imprint of a weapons-related move. (There may be significant advantages to being the first to go nuclear in a given region, with the knowledge that as a result international pressures and

restraints are likely to be imposed on neighbours.)

While the realisation that going nuclear does not change one's ties with all other nations may lead some to eschew nuclear weapons because their possession results in at best limited accretions of power and influence, on the whole this is likely to weigh in favour of going nuclear rather than against it. Governments are likely to be tempted by what is perceived as a marginal step, one that may improve the nation's standing in a particular political context but which will not necessarily threaten established friendships. The more routine a decision to go nuclear, the less dramatic the consequences for relations with other nations, the more likely proliferation becomes. The accession of India and Israel to the status of nucelar nations has not changed dramatically their relations with all other nations, either for better or worse. But their going nuclear has made it more likely that additional nations will inch their way across the difficult-to-discern nuclear threshold.

(3) An economical nuclear energy programme may be necessary to justify the cost of creating a nuclear weapons option. If a nuclear option were necessary to confront an overwhelming threat to national security, if it were a 'high politics' kind of necessity, then considerations of cost would be secondary. But if a nuclear option is being pursued with no immediate intent to transform it into a nuclear weapons force, and this option is to be spun off from a civil nuclear energy programme, then the evolution of nuclear options may be sensitive to cost considerations. For example, the less economically viable national plutonium reprocessing or uranium enrichment facilities are, the less proliferation potential. This represents an inversion of the logic of present nuclear weapons states for whom nuclear energy programmes have been high-cost spin-offs from military programmes.

India is the first example of this second kind of option. The costs of a nuclear weapons programme were long an argument of Indian opponents of nuclear weapons, especially among the military, who feared that acquiring a nuclear force would drain funds away from their conventional armaments programmes. Factors reducing the economic attractiveness of nuclear energy will raise the costs of acquiring a nuclear weapons capability, and may require in turn a higher level of political determination to achieve a ready weapons option.

This suggests that manipulation of the economics of nuclear power could have substantial non-proliferation benefits; however, such manipulation would be difficult to balance so as to have the intended effects. Nuclear suppliers might remove subsidies that make nuclear energy more attractive than it would otherwise be, and in particular limit the availability of capital for financing nuclear energy and nuclear exports, while stiffening the terms of such financing. The export of fuel facilities might be eliminated altogether, or subject to various criteria such as 'only when justified by economic and technical criteria' or 'only to multinational ventures'. At the same time the ability of present nuclear suppliers to guarantee future fuel needs of other nations should be assured by increasing enrichment capacity, and perhaps through political pricing of fuels that would make national fuel facilities economically unattractive. The balance between promotion and restriction here would be very delicate. Less delicate is the present imbalance between promotion and regulation in the IAEA, which is obviously weighted in favour of promotion and should be redressed.

(4) The definition of the problem of proliferation as a function of technical and economic considerations makes it more difficult to cope with on both international and domestic levels. As long as proliferation was clearly defined as a national security issue, the national security bureaucracies of the relevant governments could negotiate a common approach on handling the issue; the imperative of national security gave agreements like the NPT a high probability of being accepted by domestic political and public opinion in many of the most relevant countries. But proliferation as a technical and economic problem involves more and more diverse kinds of states at the international level, and many more actors and interests at the domestic level. These considerations make it a more difficult kind of problem to handle.

Given the nature of the problem, non-proliferation measures are likely to be marginal and incremental: export limits on particular facilities, financing restrictions, multinational fuel facilities, and fuel-pricing policies are measures with very limited non-proliferation implications. The marginality of these non-proliferation measures has two interrelated effects: fewer people can get interested in such piecemeal approaches — at the mass public level, these counter-measures have not the appeal of the categorical 'ban the bomb'; and at the professional level, there are likely to be many such anti-proliferation measures, each pushed by a coterie of supporters but none drawing the interest or support of a sufficient number to be adopted as policy. And finally, the practical question arises as to whether such admittedly marginal gains can be justified in terms of the political exertions needed to achieve them, in the face of possible economic costs.

In recent months, non-proliferation measures like the creation of regional, multinational nuclear fuel centres, the formation of a nuclear fuel suppliers cartel, a market-sharing arrangement among reactor vendors and a plutonium bank have joined the established list of non-proliferation measures like reductions in superpower arms stocks, a comprehensive test ban, and a 'no first use' pledge; each of these newer proposals seeks to limit the spread of capabilities, but there is little prospect of any one of them attracting enough interest to be realised. The cumulative impact of these considerations is that nuclear capabilities will continue to grow while the inhibitions against using these capabilities to go nuclear are at best steady. The result seems likely to be a pattern of future proliferation that is disjunctive and difficult to predict or restrain in particular cases, but generally even wider than usually feared.

Notes

1. See, for example, George Questor, *Politics of Nuclear Proliferation* (Baltimore, 1973). His list of threshold countries includes four Third World nations — India, Brazil, Argentina and Chile.
2. Thomas C. Schelling, 'Who Will Have the Bomb?' *International Security,* I (1976).
3. See, for example, George Questor, 'What's New on Nuclear Proliferation?' a paper prepared for the 1975 Aspen Workshop on Arms Control.
4. See, for example, James E. Dougherty, 'Nuclear Proliferation in Asia', *Orbis,* XIX (1975).
5. See, for example, William Epstein, 'Nuclear Proliferation in the Third World', *Journal of International Affairs,* XXIX (1975).
6. See Enid C.B. Schoettle, 'Arms Limitation and Security Policies required to Minimise Future Proliferation of Nuclear Weapons', below, pp.102-31.
7. George Rathjens and Albert Carnesale, in 'The Nuclear Fuel Cycle and Nuclear Proliferation', a paper prepared for a Pugwash Symposium on International Arrangements for the Nuclear Fuel Cycle, Racine, Wisconsin, 24-27 May 1976, distinguish four paths to acquiring nuclear weapons, three of which are variants of the two general methods outlined here and the fourth of which involves the theft of nuclear weapons from another state.
8. Lewis Dunn, in 'Nuclear Gray-Marketeering', Hudson Institute, HI-2384-P, 20 January 1976, has demonstrated the likelihood that in the near future international scientific mercenaries will be available for work on clandestine bomb projects.
9. 'The World List of Nuclear Power Plants', *Nuclear News Buyers Guide, 1976.*
10. Ibid.
11. 'Energy Policies in the European Community', ERDA-51, February 1976, Tables 3-6, p.60.
12. OECD Nuclear Energy Agency, *Annual Report, 1974,* Table 1, p.12.
13. Jerome S. Katzin, 'Effects of Inflation and Recession on Nuclear Project Financing in the U.S.A.', *Nuclear Engineering International,* March 1975, pp.184-6.
14. For an optimistic industry survey see 'Reports on Nuclear Programmes Around the World', *Nuclear News Buyers Guide, 1976,* pp.47-51; for other views see R.A. Black, Jr., 'Energy Policies in the Nine', and K.R. Stunkel, 'Energy Policy and Alternatives in Japan', papers prepared for delivery at the

International Studies Association Annual Meeting, Toronto, Canada, 25-29 February 1976.

15. Denis M. Slavich and Charles W. Synder, 'Meeting the Financial Needs of the Nuclear Power Industry', *Nuclear Engineering International*, March 1975.
16. David Smith, 'What Price Commercial Enrichment?', *Nuclear Engineering International*, July 1974, p.577.
17. Manson Benedict, 'Fuel Cycles for Nuclear Reactors: Uranium Enrichment and Reprocessing', a paper prepared for the International Conference on Nuclear Power, Technology, Economics, Taipei, Republic of China, January 1975, p.136.
18. David E. Rundquist, Tsahi Gozani and Glenn M. Reynolds, 'Technology for Nuclear Weapons Capability', *Science Applications*, July 1975, pp.43-60.
19. Rathjens and Carnesale, loc.cit.
20. Richard J. Barber Associates, Inc., 'LDC Nuclear Power Prospects; 1975-1990', ERDA-52, UC-2, 1975, p.C-10.
21. The French Government is buying-out Westinghouse's share of Framatome by 1982 in order to become an independent reactor manufacturer for the home and overseas markets. French Embassy Press and Information Division, Washington, D.C., February 1976.
22. In 1972, the then Atomic Energy Commission head, James R. Schlesinger, projected a cumulative total of $40,000,000,000 for American nuclear exports by 1985, and compared this to the much lower projections for high-technology exports like jet aircraft and electronics, which in the past provided major American balance of payments advantages. 'AEC Authorizing Legislation', Fiscal Year 1973, Hearings before the Joint Committee on Atomic Energy, 92nd Congress, 1st Session, 7, 8 and 9 March 1972, Part 4, pp.2337-8. More recently, Henry Kissinger estimated American nuclear exports from 1975 to 2000 at $140,000,000,000. *Nuclear News,* March 1976, p.17.
23. 'Market Survey for Nuclear Power in Developing Countries', *General Report,* IAEA, September 1973, Table II-3, p.5.
24. James, A. Lane, 'The Impact of Oil Price Increases on the Market for Nuclear Power in Developing Countries', *Bulletin of the International Atomic Energy Agency,* XVI (1974).
25. Barber Report, loc.cit., p.II-53-5.
26. For example, the Federal German Government has argued that its agreement with Brazil, the cornerstone of an ambitious Brazilian nuclear programme, extends IAEA safeguards more stringent than those under the NPT to non-signatory Brazil. *German International,* August 1975, p.22.
27. Barber Report, loc.cit., p.II-11.
28. 'Three Organizations (Techniatome, France; Interatom, Federal Germany; and UKEA and/or Fairey Engineering of Great Britain) which have designs for plants in the size range 92-345 MWe have informed the IAEA that they would respond reasonably promptly to a bid invitation.' André Jacques Polliart and Eli Goodman, 'Prospects for Utilization of Nuclear Power in Africa', *IAEA Bulletin,* XVIII (1976).
29. 'The Agency's Program for 1977-82 and Budget for 1977', IAEA Board of Governors, Gov/1780, 2 April 1976, Table 5.
30. For an example of IAEA activities in Africa where there are as yet no nuclear power plants see Polliart and Goodman, loc.cit.
31. For example, despite the absence of a bilateral agreement for co-operation in nuclear energy between the United States and Mexico, General Electric is supplying Mexico with power reactors and ERDA will supply fuel for them with the IAEA as intermediary. 'Exports of Nuclear Materials and Technology', Hearings before the Subcommittee on International Finance, before Senate

Committee on Banking, Housing and Urban Affairs, 93rd Congress, 2nd Session, 12 and 15 July 1974.

32. Norman Gall, 'Atoms for Brazil, Dangers for All', *Foreign Policy*, no.23, Summer 1976.

33. Barber Report, loc.cit., p.IV-39, figure IV-6.

34. Tom Alexander, 'Our Costly Losing Battle Against Nuclear Proliferation', *Fortune*, December 1976, p.145.

35. Efraim Friedmann, 'Financing of Power Expansion for Developing Countries', *IAEA Bulletin*, XVII (1975).

36. See the statement of ACDA Director Fred Iklé before the Subcommittee on Arms Control, International Organizations and Security Arrangements, Senate Committee on Foreign Relations, 23 February 1976.

37. See, for example, Senator Abraham A. Ribicoff, 'A Market-Sharing Approach to the Nuclear Sales Problem', *Foreign Affairs*, LIV (1975-6).

38. Barber Report, loc.cit., Chapter IV and Appendix C.

39. This is the opposite of the conventional wisdom that since the spread of nuclear technology is inevitable, non-proliferation policy can only seek to impose political restraints on the uses of nuclear technology.

5 ARMS LIMITATION AND SECURITY POLICIES REQUIRED TO MINIMISE THE PROLIFERATION OF NUCLEAR WEAPONS

Enid C.B. Schoettle

Introduction

This paper is based on two assumptions. First, we shall assume that minimising the future proliferation of nuclear weapons to the governments and potential governments of relevant non-nuclear-weapons states (NNWS) is a crucial international policy objective because such proliferation may have a variety of destabilising and high-risk effects. Some analysts dispute this view, holding that in certain strategic situations, the acquisition of nuclear weapons by one or more adversary states might actually contribute to a relationship of stable, mutual deterrence, much as the development of invulnerable, second-strike nuclear weapons capabilities have arguably stabilised relations between the United States and the Soviet Union.[1] Such analysts conclude that in these instances nuclear proliferation is either positively beneficial for, or at least not detrimental to, the stability of the international security system. Despite the superficial plausibility of this analogical reasoning, we reject this argument, since the possible risks inherent in the future proliferation of nuclear weapons are several. We shall note ten of these risks, which are widely referred to in the strategic literature on nuclear proliferation.

First, as a threshold condition, a domino effect may operate in which proliferation to a seventh or eighth nuclear weapons state (NWS) may encourage several more relevant NNWS to acquire a nuclear weapons capability. As we shall note below, this is particularly true given the linkages between specific regional adversaries or competitors.

Second, with further proliferation of nuclear weapons, particularly the proliferation of primitive capabilities without reliable command and control procedures, the probabilities of accidental or unauthorised use of these weapons may increase.

Third, with further proliferation, future local wars between two middle or small powers may become nuclear wars. This is particularly true in the immediate post-proliferation transition period. In these early stages, the nuclear capabilities of one new NWS are in their most primitive state and thus are most vulnerable to nuclear or conventional attack either by the existing NWS or by regional NNWS adversaries. Alternatively, if two states which are regional adversaries each acquire primitive and vulnerable first-strike nuclear capabilities and each become fearful of surprise attack, they may each be tempted to pre-empt.

Fourth, further proliferation may increase over time the probability of major nuclear war, in that it may recouple local wars, in which nuclear weapons are first used, to nuclear intervention and escalation by major NWS.

Fifth, further proliferation may increase the probabilities of catalytic war.

Sixth, any future use of nuclear weapons may, by breaching the post-war taboo against their use, render this firebreak a less effective deterrent against any subsequent use.

Seventh, further nuclear proliferation may provoke a continued arms race between the major NWS, since each might augment its own deterrent capability in order to be able to retaliate against attacks by all other NWS. More generally, it would make more difficult all future negotiations on arms limitation.

Eighth, further proliferation may extend to states, or counter-élites which are potential governments in states, which|Yehezkel Dror has pungently characterised as 'crazy'. Such 'crazy states', or crazy counter-élites within states, may be tempted to use nuclear weapons in non-normal, non-routine situations and in particularly nasty fashions. Such crazy states must be of serious concern, since they are increasingly likely in a world in which many states or counter-élites within them have failed to achieve minimal aspirations levels, have intense feelings of deprivation, repression and injustice, and are disillusioned with contemporary values.[2]

Ninth, while there are great difficulties in assessing the significance and likelihood of any of the above-mentioned risks, it is responsible to adopt 'worst plausible case assumptions' concerning the intentions of present and future decision-makers in relevant NNWS. Analysts should be particularly careful in assessing the risks of proliferation in the long-term future. To say that we do not feel particularly threatened if State X acquires a nuclear weapons capability now is to make an optimistic prognosis about all potential governments and competitive counter-élites in State X which might inherit an organisationally established and, hence, probably irreversible nuclear weapons capability. Given the strands of militancy and xenophobia and the important national-liberation or separatist movements which exist in many contemporary political cultures, such a prognosis may well be unwarranted.

Tenth and last, one may argue about the significance and likelihood of any one of the foregoing risks of proliferation, and even assert that in particular cases nuclear proliferation may not be destabilising. The composite list of risks, however, is necessarily worrisome because the proliferation of nuclear weapons will complicate international politics. If, in particular, several new NWS were to emerge in quick succession, the international security system might simply be swamped by the new level of complexity in international politics.

Our second assumption is that the proliferation to many NNWS of fissile materials and sensitive nuclear fuel cycle facilities, and thus the capability to produce nuclear weapons, cannot over time be denied. Fissionable materials are becoming widely available as a by-product of the world's increasing reliance upon nuclear energy to generate electric power. Assuming that alternative energy sources will not be widely exploited, the shift to nuclear energy for electric power generation will result in an annual world plutonium output from nuclear-power reactors which may reach millions of kilograms by the year 2000. Sensitive nuclear fuel cycle facilities for uranium enrichment, fuel fabrication and chemical reprocessing are still quite concentrated in states with large nuclear power industries. However, such fuel cycle facilities are now being constructed more widely and technological innovations providing much lower-cost processes will spur this trend.[3]

Thus, as NNWS acquire a nuclear power industry, they move out along what George Questor has called the 'innocent progress toward the bomb' curve, in which the time lag between the innocent progress in the development of a nuclear power industry and a crash programme to produce nuclear weapons sinks asymptotically to a very short time period required for residual efforts to fabricate at least a few crude nuclear weapons.[4] In effect, any NNWS which has a small nuclear power industry, the sophisticated industrial infrastructure and technical manpower which are the preconditions of a nuclear power industry, or the political will to divert the resources necessary to create such an industry regardless of high opportunity costs, has the potential capability to become a NWS by the year 2000. Furthermore, we can envisage no politically realistic safeguards system which could prevent the government or potential government of such a NNWS from exploiting these capabilities and diverting nuclear materials for weapons purposes if it chose to do so.

Certainly, varying international export policies and international safeguard systems can impose differential constraints upon the capabilities of various NNWS. Indeed, these are important policy instruments and are the focus of much current attention.[5] This is due in large measure to the growing interest expressed in nuclear energy for electric power generation by various NNWS in the developing world since the Middle East war of October 1973 and the ensuing energy crisis. Many of these developing states are only now beginning to acquire nuclear energy capabilities. Thus, the rate and conditions of their acquisition of such capabilities can be controlled and regulated if the industrial states which are the major suppliers of fissile materials and sensitive nuclear fuel cycle facilities can agree upon appropriate export policy mechanisms.

It is important to note, however, that while the spread of nuclear energy capabilities can be regulated and perhaps slowed, it cannot be stopped, given the increasing reliance throughout the world on nuclear energy to generate electric power. Over time, nuclear energy capabilities will gradually spread and policy constraints on such capabilities will be of dwindling efficacy. Thus there are no long-term means of denying such NNWS the capabilities to acquire nuclear weapons if they choose to do so.

Therefore, if by assumption, access to the requisite physical capabilities to develop nuclear weapons cannot over time be denied and at the same time proliferation of nuclear weapons is to be minimised, the only recourse is to influence the intentions of NNWS with respect to their acquisition of independent nuclear weapons capabilities. If, as we shall argue below, the Non-Proliferation Treaty (NPT) and the comprehensive international security régime in which it is currently embedded cannot effectively minimise the future proliferation of nuclear weapons, we must propose additional, mutually compatible arms acquisition, arms limitation, and broader security policies for the major states in the international political system, particularly the NWS, which largely determine the régime. A comprehensive anti-proliferation régime must be designed which can buttress and amplify the NPT so as to satisfy the security and political objectives of various NNWS which might, alternatively, be satisfied by their acquisition of independent nuclear weapons capabilities. Otherwise, the NPT will be degraded and, much more importantly, the proliferation of nuclear weapons will proceed.

Policy Objectives of Relevant NNWS

As noted above, it is widely projected that from thirty to forty NNWS have or will have by the year 2000 a nuclear power industry or industrial base and thus the technological capability to exercise a nuclear weapons option should they purposefully choose to do so. Such states may choose to exercise this nuclear weapons option in order to enhance their military security and/or their political prestige relative to other important referent states. Thus, in order to minimise future nuclear proliferation, a comprehensive anti-proliferation régime must include mutually compatible arms limitation and security policies which will satisfy the objectives of various classes of NNWS as or more effectively than would their acquisition of independent nuclear weapons capabilities.

We shall identify eight specific military security and political presitge objectives of NNWS which such policies must satisfy if they are to minimise the future proliferation of nuclear weapons. A given NNWS might have several such objectives which varying arms limitation and security policies must satisfy if the state is to continue to forgo the acquisition of an independent nuclear weapons capability. We can also identify seven geopolitical regions in which nuclear weapons might proliferate by the year 2000: South Asia, the Middle East, East Asia, Australasia, Southern Africa, Latin America and Europe.[6] For each type of objective under consideration we shall attempt to identify all plausible examples of NNWS which might choose to acquire nuclear weapons in order to achieve the given objective. A summary is given in Table 5.1. It should be noted that some of these examples may now appear to be extremely low probability contingencies. But they may become more likely or even materialise by the year 2000.

It should also be noted that various coalitions of domestic political and bureaucratic-organisational interests might account for the decision of any given NNWS to acquire nuclear weapons. Some component of the military and technical communities must favour exercising the nuclear weapons option for it to go forward, but the bureaucracy and the wider political system are not likely to be uniformly favourable to the acquisition of nuclear weapons. Thus possibilities exist for outside manipulation of the internal decision processes concerning nuclear weapons acquisition. These internal decision processes must be analysed on a case-by case basis and we cannot discuss them here. However, in discussing the policy objectives of NNWS as if they were unitary actors, it is important to recall that in fact various arms limitation and security policies are likely to be differentially influential with important bureaucratic and political actors in any given NNWS.[7]

1. The Objective of Military Security

First, NNWS may seek to enhance their military security through the acquisition of nuclear weapons. With the exception of the Sino-Soviet fighting on Chen Pao/Damansky Island in March 1969, no NWS has ever had its homeland placed under any form of attack by any nation-state adversary after having acquired nuclear weapons. Historically, nuclear weapons have thus appeared to be an effective military deterrent. If a NNWS has a pressing concern for its military security, acquiring nuclear weapons clearly becomes a salient policy option.

We can identify four specific military security objectives – which we shall denominate objectives 1.A, 1.B, 1.C and 1.D – for which the acquisition of nuclear weapons might seem an appropriate option: first: deterrence of, defence against and/or retaliation for a nuclear or conventional attack or nuclear blackmail by a superpower NWS; second: deterrence of, defence against and/or retaliation for a nuclear or conventional attack or nuclear blackmail by a minor NWS; third: deterrence of, defence against and/or retaliation for conventional attack by a hostile local or regional NNWS or group of NNWS or domination of such NNWS adversaries; and fourth: anticipatory reaction to the prospective acquisition of nuclear weapons by a local or regional NNWS adversary in order to deter or dominate such an adversary.

1.A. Deterrence of, Defence against and/or Retaliation for a Nuclear or Conventional Attack or Nuclear Blackmail by a Superpower NWS. The Soviet Union, Great Britain, France and China have already acquired substantial strategic nuclear weapons in order, among other reasons, to deter nuclear attack or blackmail by a superpower. Furthermore, Great Britain, France and NATO, according to the doctrine of flexible response, rely upon a policy of possible first use of nuclear weapons in order to deter or defend against a possibly superior conventional attack by the Soviet Union and its Warsaw Pact allies.[8]

The force structures which NNWS might acquire in order to achieve this objective will vary with the state's size and wealth, as measured in terms of some combination of population and gross national product (GNP). Regardless of the particular force structure, all such states can be viewed as attempting some form of 'proportional deterrence' by threatening the superpower adversary with an unacceptably high risk of damage to its population or industrial base as compared with the strategic value to the superpower of the state in question.

A great power might attempt to develop a second-strike force sufficiently large and invulnerable to deter strategic attack or blackmail by its superpower adversary. It might in addition attempt to develop tactical nuclear weapons in order to deter or defend against conventional attack by the superpower adversary. NNWS which might acquire such strategic and/or tactical capabilities in order to achieve this objective include: Federal Germany, Japan, and a future Western European Community, should one come into existence, against the Soviet Union and its Warsaw Pact allies.

A middle or small power might attempt to develop a tactical nuclear weapons force sufficient to deny its superpower adversary military victory at an acceptable level of costs and risk. NNWS which might acquire tactical nuclear weapons in order thus to deter or defend against a nuclear or conventional attack by a superpower adversary include: Austria, Belgium, Finland, Greece, Iran, Italy, the Netherlands, Romania, Sweden, Switzerland, Turkey and Yugoslavia against the Soviet Union and its Warsaw Pact allies;[9] and Bulgaria, Czechoslovakia, Hungary, the German Democratic Republic and Poland against the United States and its NATO allies.

Finally, a middle or small power might acquire a small, vulnerable, pre-emptive first-strike force in order to make suicidal deterrent threats and thereby create uncertainties for a hostile superpower or, *in extremis,* actually to retaliate against a superpower adversary's threatening or mounting a conventional attack. Such capabilities would imply that the country, faced with immediate destruction, would prefer 'suicide at a high cost to the adversary to loss of the conflict'.[10] NNWS which might acquire such nuclear weapons in order to deter or retaliate against such a conventional attack by a superpower adversary include Israel, Romania and Yugoslavia against the Soviet Union, and Cuba and conceivably Libya and Saudi Arabia against the United States.

Many of these NNWS, including great, middle and small states, now depend on fairly stable, explicit or tacit positive security guarantees from one of the superpowers in order to meet the objective of deterring or defending against nuclear or conventional attack by the other. Such NNWS might consider exercising their nuclear weapons option should such positive security guarantees lose their credibility and should no alternative security policies be forthcoming which would provide effective substitutes for such positive security guarantees.

1.B. Deterrence of, Defence against and/or Retaliation for a Nuclear or Conventional Attack or Nuclear Blackmail by a Minor NWS. India may be developing such forces in order, among other reasons, to achieve this objective against China. This objective might be sought by great, middle and small states utilising a variety of nuclear force structures including an invulnerable second-strike force, a tactical nuclear weapons force, or a small vulnerable pre-emptive first-strike force. NNWS which might acquire nuclear weapons in order to achieve this objective include: Japan and Taiwan against China; Pakistan and Iran against India; and Australia and Indonesia against China and/or India. Of these states, Taiwan — increasingly an international pariah state — and potentially Pakistan face particularly difficult regional conflict situations and may feel their very survival depends upon the acquisition of nuclear weapons.

Such contingencies clearly cluster into specific local or regional pairs or groupings. Thus the acquisition of nuclear weapons by China and India may involve a local or regional 'domino effect' or 'chain reaction' in South Asia, East Asia and Australasia, whereby the relevant NNWS adversaries and competitors of China and India may proceed to acquire nuclear weapons. Some of these states have not received sufficiently credible positive security guarantees from one or more NWS and do not enjoy any alternative policies which would provide effective substitutes for such positive security guarantees. Such NNWS thus have a strong incentive to acquire at least a tactical nuclear weapons force or a small strategic nuclear force, since, without any nuclear weapons, they are peculiarly vulnerable to nuclear or conventional attack or nuclear blackmail by their local or regional NWS adversary.

1.C. Deterrence of, Defence against and/or Retaliation for Conventional Attack by a Hostile or Regional NNWS, or Group of NNWS, or Domination of such NNWS Adversaries. There are no current NWS which acquired nuclear weapons in order to achieve this objective. It might, however, be achieved by nuclear force structures ranging from a tactical nuclear weapons force, a small vulnerable pre-emptive first-strike force, or an ostensibly peaceful nuclear explosive capability. It is particularly likely in the case where a NNWS faces hostile local or regional NNWS enjoying an existing or potential advantage in conventional military capabilities which, by dint of population size, natural resources, and/or potential industrialisation, is both overwhelming and irreversible. NNWS which might acquire nuclear weapons in order to achieve this objective include: Israel against a group of non-nuclear Arab states; South Korea against a non-nuclear North Korea; South Africa against a group of non-nuclear black African states, possibly supported by coercive states elsewhere; Iran against a non-nuclear Iraq; and Australia against a non-nuclear Indonesia.

Most of these states have, in the past, received fairly credible American guarantees of ongoing conventional arms supplies or promised military intervention should a conventional attack occur. But their faith in the future reliability of such American guarantees is declining and they may feel that the acquisition of an independent nuclear weapons capability might strengthen the superpower guarantor's commitment to defend its client, lest an unprotected client feel impelled to use its nuclear weapons. Of these states, Israel, South Korea, and potentially South Africa — increasingly viewed as international pariahs — face particularly difficult regional conflict situations and may feel that their very survival depends upon the acquisition of nuclear weapons. 'Crazy states' might pursue this objective as well. It should be noted that such decisions to exercise a nuclear weapons option may well generate the local or regional domino effect discussed in 1.B, whereby the NNWS adversary is subsequently under enhanced pressure to acquire nuclear weapons. Case 1.C can also merge into 1.D.

1.D. Anticipatory Reaction to Prospective Acquisition of Nuclear Weapons by a Local or Regional NNWS Adversary in order to Deter or Dominate such an Adversary. As in the previous case, there are no current NNWS which acquired nuclear weapons in order to achieve this objective. This objective might be achieved by a tactical nuclear weapons force, a small, vulnerable, pre-emptive first-strike force, or an ostensibly peaceful nuclear explosive capability. There are several local or regional pairs or groupings of NNWS adversaries, any one of which might acquire nuclear weapons as an anticipatory reaction to their prospective acquisition by its adversary in order to deter or dominate it. Such an action may well generate a counter-action by its adversary which would then, as in cases 1.B and 1.C, feel increasingly threatened by the new NWS and thus be under enhanced pressure to acquire nuclear weapons. A local or regional nuclear arms race might then ensue, evincing the same local or regional domino effect discussed in 1.B and 1.C. Should both states acquire small, vulnerable, pre-emptive first-strike forces, such an arms race would be quite destabilising. Clusters of regional NNWS adversaries which might acquire nuclear weapons in order to achieve this objective include: North Korea and South Korea against each other; Greece and Turkey against each other; Nigeria and Zaire against South Africa; Egypt, Iraq, Libya, Saudi Arabia and Syria against Israel, or Iran, or against each other, should any one of them appear to be acquiring nuclear weapons; Australia, Indonesia, the Philippines and Thailand against Japan or against each other, should any one of them appear to be acquiring nuclear weapons; Australia, Indonesia, the Philippines and Thailand against Japan or against each other, should any one of them appear to be acquiring nuclear weapons; and Argentina, Brazil, Chile, Cuba and Mexico against each other, should any one of them appear to be acquiring nuclear weapons. 'Crazy states' might pursue this objective as well.

2. Political Prestige

In addition to, or in some instances in place of, such military security objectives, NNWS may seek to enhance their political status and prestige through the acquisition of nuclear weapons. Enhancing political prestige is a serious objective for any state, since such increased status represents potential political power and influence which is fungible in many international situations.

Many NNWS have observed that nuclear weapons have served important symbolic functions since the onset of the nuclear age. Like the classic role of gold in the international monetary system, nuclear weapons constitute perhaps the quintessential attribute of prestige and determinant of status in the international political hierarchy.[11] Nuclear weapons symbolise a state's modernity, scientific prowess and technological dynamism, and thus clearly possess political as well as military utility. Whether out of perceived domestic or international political needs, should the government of a NNWS have a pressing concern for enhancing its political prestige, acquiring nuclear weapons is a salient policy option.

Again, we can identify four specific political prestige objectives — which we shall denominate objectives 2.A, 2.B, 2.C and 2.D — for which the acquisition of nuclear weapons might seem an appropriate option: first: enhanced political prestige with reference to the great powers in the post-war international political hierarchy; second: enhanced political prestige with reference to existing military alliances; third: second-order power status and/or enhanced political prestige with reference to a particular local or regional grouping of states or transregional status cohort in the international political hierarchy; and fourth: enhanced political prestige in order to change the existing distribution of status and power in the international political hierarchy.

2.A. Enhanced Political Prestige with Reference to the Great Powers in the Post-war International Political Hierarchy. Some NNWS may seek to acquire nuclear weapons in order to achieve great-power status — the highest status cohort in the existing international political hierarchy as measured by some combination of population, wealth and historical-cultural tradition, in addition to military power. A nuclear weapons capability has, since the onset of the nuclear age, constituted an explicit component of great power status. Indeed, until India tested its nuclear explosive in May 1974, the five NWS were the only states with permanent membership in the UN Security Council, another explicit indicator of post-war great power status. The nuclear weapons capabilities of the United States, the Soviet Union and Great Britain were derived from programmes originating in World War Two and directed against the Axis Powers. France, China and India — as well as Great Britain — more recently initiated nuclear weapons programmes in order, among other reasons, to lay claim to the manifest status of a great power and thus to join the 'top table' in the post-war international political hierarchy.[12] Certain NNWS such as Federal Germany, Japan, Brazil, Iran, South Africa and a future Western European Community, should one come into existence, might plausibly lay claim to such great-power status in the existing international political hierarchy. Such a NNWS might acquire nuclear weapons in order to rectify its perceived status inconsistency by conforming its military capabilities to its other components of great-power status.[13]

2.B. Enhanced Political Prestige with Reference to Existing Military Alliances. In addition to seeking great power status in the international political hierarchy as in 2.A, France and China acquired nuclear weapons in order to achieve more political independence and higher political status in relation to their respective NWS allies. France and China each sought to transform their political alliances into less hegemonic relationships by, respectively, challenging the supremacy of the United States and Great Britain within NATO, and the Soviet Union within the Sino-Soviet Treaty and Agreement of 1950.[14]

India, in pursuit of a related objective, may be developing a nuclear weapons capability in order, among other reasons, to assert its disinterest in joining any tacit military alliance with or receiving any positive security guarantees from existing NWS. India thus emphasises its commitment to a non-aligned political status independent of existing military alliances.

Certain NNWS such as Federal Germany, Japan and a future Western European Community, should one come into existence, might acquire nuclear weapons in order to gain enhanced political prestige with reference to the United States — the dominant NWS ally in these cases. Other NNWS, such as Brazil or Iran, might acquire nuclear weapons in order to assert their non-aligned political status independent of existing military alliances.

2.C. Second-order Power Status and/or Enhanced Political Prestige with Reference to a Particular Local or Regional Grouping of States or Transregional Status Cohort in the International Political Hierarchy. Apart from, or in addition to, seeking manifest status as a great power or enhanced status with reference to military alliances, some NNWS may acquire nuclear weapons in order to gain or reinforce what S.B. Cohen has termed 'second-order power status', and hence symbolic leadership with reference to a particular local or regional grouping of states or transregional status cohort in the international political hierarchy.[15] India may be developing a nuclear weapons capability in order, among other reasons, to achieve this composite objective. India has reason to expect that a nuclear capability will buttress its status and leadership claims in the local subcontinent and broader Indian Ocean region and in the Third World — the more general status cohort which India has, at times, aspired to lead.

Now that India has exploded a nuclear device, another NNWS in the same region or status cohort may experience some relative status loss. Should such a NNWS perceive that its local, regional or transregional competitor, such as India, achieves second-order power status by exploding a nuclear device or acquiring nuclear weapons, it may be tempted to follow suit and an arms race for political prestige may ensue. Thus, the pursuit of this composite objective may result in the type of pre-emptive regional nuclear arms races discussed in 1.D since, clearly, acquiring nuclear explosive capabilities or nuclear weapons in anticipation of a competitor's doing so may be justified on the grounds of political prestige as well as military security.

The NNWS which might over time seek to achieve this composite objective include: Algeria, Argentina, Australia, Brazil, Chile, Cuba, Egypt, Greece, Indonesia, Iran, Iraq, Italy, Libya, Mexico, Nigeria, North Korea, the Philippines, Saudi Arabia, South Africa, Spain, Syria, Taiwan, Thailand, Turkey, Venezuela and Zaire. Many of the foregoing states are in the developing world and may have relatively few economic and political resources with which to gain political status. Such states, with few alternative sources of political prestige, may be under particular pressure to acquire or at least to threaten to acquire nuclear weapons so as to maximise their otherwise low levels of potential political influence and gain political and economic benefits *vis-à-vis* their local or regional status cohort. 'Crazy states' might pursue this objective as well. It should be noted that such competition for prestige and leadership, by definition, falls into specific local, regional or transregional clusters. Thus, if some nuclear proliferation occurs among such a group, the remaining NNWS may feel relative status loss and move to acquire nuclear weapons. In this way, the pursuit of objective 2.C threatens to bring about the same domino effects discussed above in 1.B, 1.C and 1.D.

2.D. Enhanced Political Prestige in order to Change the Existing Distribution of Status and Power in the Internaional Political Hierarchy. Rather than raising their particular status in the existing international political hierarchy, some NNWS may seek instead to alter the hierarchy itself in the direction of greater equality among states. Should the proliferation of nuclear weapons become fashionable and its momentum build to such a point that a large number of middle and small powers acquire nuclear weapons, nuclear weapons capabilities will obviously cease to connote automatic great power or even second-order power status. Thus, if several middle and small powers perceive nuclear weapons as a 'great equaliser' and expect that by acquiring them they can collectively change the existing distribution of power and status in the international political hierarchy, they may have an added incentive to exercise their nuclear weapons options.

Many states in the Third World perceive the current international political hierarchy as inherently discriminatory in favour of the great powers and other industrialised states and against their own interests. Such a discriminatory world order is rapidly becoming less viable. Dependence upon great powers is increasingly unacceptable to many states and demands for more equal status among states are voiced in many issue areas and institutions in contemporary international politics.[16] The issue area of nuclear proliferation is no exception. The widespread criticism by many NNWS of the discriminatory nature of the NPT, of its associated international safeguards, and of various nuclear suppliers' policies, and the positive reception given to the first nuclear explosions of China in 1964 and India in 1974 by many countries in the Third World attest to these anti-hegemonic attitudes towards the nuclear superpowers and other traditional great powers. This reaction suggests that for many NNWS which advocate a redistribution of power and status in the international political hierarchy, including most of those which might pursue objective 2.C, the acquisition of nuclear weapons may appear to be a salient means of achieving this objective.[17] Moreover, once nuclear proliferation becomes widespread, NNWS with no particular drive to change the existing international political hierarchy, such as middle or small industrial powers, may feel impelled to acquire nuclear weapons merely in order to keep pace with the many other states which have already done so.

In summary, there are many possible policy objectives of various NNWS which might be achieved by the acquisition of an independent nuclear weapons capability. As noted in Table 5.1, the most common categories are objectives 1.A — deterrence of superpower attack, 1.D — anticipatory reaction to a regional adversary's acquiring nuclear weapons, 2.C — enhancing regional political prestige and achieving second-order power status, and 2.D — changing the existing international political hierarchy.

Most NNWS interested in achieving objective 1.A are the industrialised European states which have for some years been the recipients of fairly stable and hence credible positive security guarantees from one superpower guarantor against the other superpower. These states, and the satisfaction of their military security objectives, were the original targets of the anti-proliferation régime which evolved in the early and middle 1960s and culminated in the NPT.

In the past decade, numerous NNWS have emerged which are interested in achieving objectives 1.D, 2.C and 2.D. These states are, by contrast, primarily developing states in the Third World which have not received, or do not want to receive, positive security guarantees from the NWS. In the past, most of these states have lacked the capabilities to exercise an independent nuclear weapons option. However, such technical constraints are diminishing as nuclear energy capabilities become more widespread. Thus, the requirements for designing a comprehensive anti-proliferation régime which will minimise the intentions of such states to acquire nuclear weapons by the year 2000 are becoming increasingly demanding.

Alternative Arms Limitation and Security Strategies of the NWS which might Satisfy Policy Objectives of Relevant NNWS

If the proliferation of nuclear weapons is to be minimised, a comprehensive anti-proliferation régime must include various mutually compatible arms limiation and security policies which can to some degree satisfy the eight specific military security and political prestige

Table 5.1: Policy Objectives of Relevant NNWS

1.A	1.B	1.C	1.D	2.A	2.B	2.C	2.D
Austria						Algeria	
Belgium	Australia	Australia	Argentina			Argentina	
			Australia			Australia	
Bulgaria			Brazil	Brazil	Brazil	Brazil	
Canada							
Cuba			Chile			Chile	
Czechoslovakia						Cuba	
German Democratic Republic			Egypt			Egypt	
Federal Germany				Federal Germany	Federal Germany		
Finland							
Greece			Greece			Greece	
Hungary	Indonesia		Indonesia			Indonesia	
Iran	Iran	Iran	Iran	Iran	Iran	Iran	
			Iraq			Iraq	
Israel		Israel	Israel				
Italy						Italy	

Table 5.1 (contd.)

1.A	1.B	1.C	1.D	2.A	2.B	2.C	2.D
Japan	Japan			Japan	Japan		Many NNWS including most of the aforementioned states in the Third World
Libya			Libya			Libya	
			Mexico			Mexico	
Netherlands							
	Pakistan		Nigeria			Nigeria	
			North Korea			North Korea	
			Philippines			Philippines	
Poland							
Romania							
Saudi Arabia		South Africa	Saudi Arabia			Saudi Arabia	
		South Korea	South Africa	South Africa		South Africa	
			South Korea				
						Spain	
Sweden							
Switzerland	Taiwan						
			Syria			Syria	
						Taiwan	
Turkey			Thailand			Thailand	
Future W. Europe Community			Turkey	Future W. Europe Community	Future W. Europe Community	Turkey	
						Venezuela	
Yugoslavia			Zaire			Zaire	

objectives of various NNWS enumerated above. Such policies affect
the entire international security system but are largely subject to
control and manipulation by the NWS and, in particular, by the two
superpowers. Thus, we assume that some causal relationship exists
between the arms limitation and security policies of the NWS and
subsequent decisions by NNWS whether or not to develop, acquire and
deploy a particular nuclear force structure at a particular rate.[18]

This relationship between the arms limitation and security policies
of the NWS and the decisions of NNWS whether or not to acquire
nuclear weapons exists primarily because the NWS, and particularly the
two superpowers, currently occupy the dominant positions of power
and status in the international security system. In general, NWS now
serve as the major custodians of world order and their behaviour in the
international security system is an important determinant of the policy
choices of other nation-states. Thus, by their ongoing choices regarding
such controllable policy variables as the size and quality of their own
nuclear weapons inventories, the deployment of their nuclear weapons
inventories, the permissible contingencies in which these capabilities
might be used, the political utility of nuclear weapons in their conduct
of foreign policy, and their broader security policies towards NNWS,
the NWS largely construct and manage the international order and
climate within which given NNWS must choose whether or not to
acquire nuclear weapons. There may be a few instances in which the
decisions of particular NNWS to acquire nuclear weapons are insensitive
to such policy choices of the NWS. Over time, however, the NWS can
and do 'influence perceptions about the utility and centrality of
nuclear weaponry in the relations of states' and thus substantially
influence the extent of nuclear proliferation.[19]

Given this assumption that the arms limitation and security policies
of the NWS concerning the development, acquisition, deployment,
contingent uses and political utility of their own nuclear weapons
capabilities will determine to an important degree future nuclear
proliferation, what is the form of this relationship? In a seminal article
published in 1967, Hedley Bull outlined two alternative, hypothetical,
grossly linear relationships between the arms limitation and security
policies of the NWS, as the independent variable, and future nuclear
proliferation by various NNWS as the dependent variable.[20] Bull termed
these two alternative models of NWS behaviour — each a strategy
designed, among other objectives, to minimise nuclear proliferation —
as the doctrines of 'High Posture' and 'Low Posture' respectively. The
High Posture Doctrine and the Low Posture Doctrine each constitutes a

comprehensive arms limitation and security régime in that each attempts to regulate and manage the security environment of the NNWS systematically rather than to influence each particular NNWS episodically and differentially on a case-by-case basis.

These two hypothetical postures are also relatively polar models of possible NWS arms limitation and security policies and, as such, clearly illuminate the possible relationships between the arms limitation and security policies of the NWS and future nuclear proliferation. They fall towards opposite ends of a continuous variable which is a composite of the size of the nuclear weapons inventories of the NWS, the rate of qualitative development of their nuclear weapons, and their strategic doctrines governing the diplomatic and military contingencies in which the deployment, use or threatened use of nuclear weapons is contemplated. These three components of the composite variable are assumed to move together. The variable can thus be viewed as a composite measure of a NWS's overall investment in and political utilisation of nuclear weapons. Given their adversary relationship, Bull assumes that the superpowers will pursue the same doctrine at any given point in time.

These two postures differ in various respects: in their major policy prescriptions; in their assumptions about the amount of change in the international security system which is required in order to minimise nuclear proliferation by the year 2000; and in their objective functions.

In the High Posture Doctrine, the two superpowers maximise the gap between their own nuclear weapons capabilities and those of minor NWS and NNWS by maintaining a large inventory of nuclear weapons, sustaining a rapid rate of qualitative development of nuclear weapons, and relying upon the development and threatened use of nuclear weapons in a wide range of diplomatic and military contingencies. In the High Posture Doctrine, the superpowers rely on threats of nuclear or conventional force as the major policy instruments with which to deter other NWS from using and NNWS from acquiring nuclear weapons.[21] Its advocates differ somewhat on the form such threats should take and the range of contingencies in which they should be used. In general, however, the High Posture Doctrine projects much of the existing international security system into the year 2000 and rejects substantial changes in existing arms limitation and security policies. Finally, while designed, among other objectives, to minimise future nuclear proliferation, the High Posture Doctrine weights maintaining the American-Soviet strategic balance at a high level and the cohesion of American alliances with NATO and Japan above the minimisation of nuclear proliferation, should these priority objectives be seen as coming into conflict.

In the Low Posture Doctrine, conversely, the two superpowers minimise the gap between their own nuclear weapons capabilities and those of minor NWS and NNWS by maintaining a small inventory of nuclear weapons, constraining the rate of qualitative development of nuclear weapons, and relying upon the development and threatened use of nuclear weapons in only a very limited range of diplomatic and military contingencies. In the Low Posture Doctrine the NWS adopt a comprehensive range of new arms limitations and security obligations such as non-deployment zones, negative security guarantees, nuclear-free zones, non-first use undertakings, and, in the modified version, positive security guarantees, in order to deter NNWS from acquiring nuclear weapons. The Low Posture Doctrine also attempts to deligitimise nuclear weapons and to encourage alternative non-nuclear and non-military sources of international participation and prestige. The Low Posture Doctrine thus combines multiple policy instruments into a long-term anti-proliferation strategy which would significantly alter the international security system by the year 2000 and require major shifts in existing arms limitation and security policies. Finally, while the Low Posture Doctrine is designed, among other objectives, to minimise future nuclear proliferation, its advocates disagree as to whether reducing the American-Soviet strategic balance to a low level and minimising the use or threatened use of nuclear weapons should be weighted more highly than the minimisation of nuclear proliferation, should these priority objectives be seen as coming into conflict. Advocates of what we shall call a modified Low Posture Doctrine, such as Leonard Beaton, John Maddox, Max Singer and Ian Smart, support a floor for nuclear arms limitation and disarmament in order to provide unilateral, residual positive security guarantees for major allies and a co-operative positive security guarantee to other NNWS subject to actual or threatened nuclear attack, and thus give maximum weight to the objective of minimising future nuclear proliferation. Advocates of what we shall call an extreme Low Posture Doctrine, such as Hedley Bull and Richard Falk, reject all positive security guarantees to allies or non-aligned NNWS, thus weighting the reduction of nuclear weapons inventories and the non-use of nuclear weapons above the minimisation of nuclear proliferation, should these priority objectives be seen as coming into conflict.

Arms Limitation and Security Policies for Minimising the Future Proliferation of Nuclear Weapons

In this final section we shall make summary assessments of the High Posture Doctrine and the Low Posture Doctrine, respectively. We shall conclude that the adoption of a modified Low Posture Doctrine by the NWS would best satisfy most of the various policy objectives of the NNWS, thus amplifying the NPT and minimising future nuclear proliferation.

A summary assessment of the High Posture Doctrine as an anti-proliferation strategy must give it a mixed but potentially fairly low rating. The primary policy instrument which the High Posture Doctrine offers is the extension by the superpowers of unilateral or co-operative positive security guarantees to NNWS. This policy instrument is, however, an increasingly ineffectual and possibly counter-productive anti-proliferation strategy as positive security guarantees suffer an irreversible decline in credibility and acceptability. Given the state of mutual deterrence and *détente* existing between the two superpowers, unilateral positive security guarantees are a depreciating asset for NNWS.[22] At least in the United States since the end of the war in Indochina, such international commitments may be suffering a long-term erosion of domestic political support. Indeed, given their declining credibility, the emphasis placed on them in the High Posture Doctrine as the primary policy instrument by which proliferation is to be contained may become counter-productive, if NNWS are reminded too frequently of their relative inefficacy. Moreover, the value of co-operative positive security guarantees in the relatively few contingencies in which American-Soviet co-operation would be credible under the High Posture Doctrine is depreciating as opposition to superpower hegemony renders them politically less acceptable. Thus, inevitably, 'guarantor's stock is going down, fledgling nuclear stock up on the international power exchange'.[23].

The rate of this depreciation in credibility will vary. With respect to deterring nuclear or conventional attack or nuclear blackmail by the other superpower against major NNWS allies, the centrality of the security interests at stake and the availability of limited nuclear response options combine to provide unilateral positive security guarantees of substantial, although declining, credibility. The High Posture Doctrine also raises the costs for such NNWS of acquiring nuclear weapons to be directed against a potentially hostile superpower. It thus serves as a reasonably effective alternative means of satisfying and deterring NNWS which are contemplating the acquisition of an independent nuclear weapons capability in order to achieve objective 1.A. This is the primary anti-proliferation objective of the High Posture Doctrine since the cohesion of American alliances with NATO and Japan and, necessarily, the cohesion of the Warsaw Pact are thought to be of higher priority than the overall minimisation of future nuclear proliferation. Thus it is objective 1.A which the High Posture Doctrine achieves most effectively.

With respect to deterring nuclear or conventional attacks by local or regional adversaries — either minor NWS or other NNWS — the High Posture Doctrine provides NNWS with fairly credible positive security guarantees or commitments to intervene with conventional forces only if the security interest of one superpower is sufficiently unimportant to the other so that it tacitly tolerates intervention by the interested superpower, or if important security interests of both superpowers converge, enabling them to intervene jointly in a local or regional crisis. In these contingencies, the High Posture Doctrine can provide NNWS with reasonably effective alternative means of achieving objectives 1.B, 1.C and 1.D. However, there is rising opposition to superpower dominance in the international security system. Thus the hegemonic character of such co-operative superpower guarantees — whether direct or indirect — and conventional commitments may render them politically unacceptable over time, even in these contingencies. Furthermore, the High Posture Doctrine acknowledges that positive security guarantees and commitments to intervene with conventional forces may not be credible in a local or regional crisis if the superpowers are either disinterested or at odds. To the degree that the American-Soviet strategic balance is maintained at a high level in order to ensure credible unilateral positive security guarantees to their respective major allies, political tension between the two superpowers is likely to continue under the High Posture Doctrine and the likelihood of their joining in co-operative positive security guarantees or conventional commitments to other NNWS may remain low. In such contingencies, the High Posture Doctrine will fail to provide NNWS with an alternative means of achieving objectives 1.B, 1.C and 1.D.

Furthermore, with respect to the political prestige objectives of NNWS, the High Posture Doctrine is counter-productive as an anti-proliferation strategy in that it explicitly encourages NNWS to acquire nuclear weapons in order to achieve objectives 2.A, 2.B, 2.C and 2.D. This result is inescapable since the High Posture Doctrine contains a trade-off: the strategic superiority and extended deterrent posture which it prescribes in order to fulfil the military security objectives of certain NNWS focuses attention upon nuclear weapons and encourages other NNWS to acquire independent nuclear weapons capabilities in order to enhance their political prestige objectives.

Thus, while providing certain major NNWS allies with a reasonably credible alternative means of achieving objective 1.A, the High Posture Doctrine leads to a fairly high probability of future nuclear proliferation by a significant number of NNWS pursuing the other seven objectives. Specifically, NNWS for which the credibility of the superpowers' positive security guarantees or conventional commitments in local or regional crises depreciates too much over time and NNWS pursuing enhanced political prestige may choose to exercise their nuclear weapons option. Indeed, eventually even the credibility of unilateral positive security guarantees extended to major NNWS allies in the event of nuclear or conventional attack or nuclear blackmail by the other superpower may depreciate as well.

The High Posture Doctrine tolerates this prospect of substantially increased future nuclear proliferation by assuming that the risks of nuclear proliferation will fall on the NNWS involved in local or regional conflicts. Conversely, it assumes that the costs to the superpowers will be acceptable as long as they maintain their vantage point of strategic superiority over all minor NWS. To quote James Schlesinger writing in 1967 on this point:

> In the absence of major investments or extraordinary outside assistance the only option open to most nuclear aspirants is the aerial delivery of rather crude nuclear weapons. Though such capabilities can, of course, dramatically transform a regional balance of power (provided that the superpowers remain aloof), the superpowers themselves will remain more or less immune to nuclear threats emanating from countries other than the principal opponent.[24]

Assuming that the type of nuclear capabilities acquired by NNWS involved in local or regional conflicts or arms races cannot directly threaten the superpowers, the High Posture Doctrine concludes that such increased nuclear proliferation is preferable to the superpowers substantially reducing their strategic capabilities and thus putting at risk either their own security *vis-à-vis* the other or the security of their closest and most central military allies. Consequently, the High Posture Doctrine further concludes that the superpowers should not undertake

substantial changes in their own arms acquisition, arms limitation or
security policies in order to minimise the proliferation of nuclear
weapons.[25]

A summary assessment of the Low Posture Doctrine as an anti-
proliferation strategy must give it a mixed but potentially fairly high
rating, particularly in the case of the modified Low Posture Doctrine.
In contrast with the limited scope of the High Posture Doctrine, the
Low Posture Doctrine propounds a comprehensive range of major,
mutually compatible policy instruments as means of satisfying the
various military security and political prestige objectives of NNWS.
Chief among these are the limitation and reduction of existing nuclear
weapons inventories, particularly those of the two superpowers;
constraints upon the permissible deployment and uses of the remaining
nuclear weapons inventories; primary reliance upon various non-nuclear
and non-military policy instruments for resolving conflicts and
attributing status in the international security system; and, finally, in
the modified version of the Low Posture Doctrine, ultimate reliance in
certain hard residual cases upon the provision of unilateral or
co-operative positive security guarantees to deter or retaliate against
nuclear attack on certain NNWS. Advocates of the Low Posture
Doctrine thus seek to buttress the existing NPT with a combination of
collateral arms limitation and security measures, each of which, by
providing alternative means of achieving various military security and/or
political prestige objectives, may induce one or more NNWS to forgo
the acquisition of nuclear weapons. Thus it is the cumulative impact
of the multiple policy instruments advocated in the Low Posture
Doctrine that may minimise nuclear proliferation.

The combination of arms limitation and security measures included
in the Low Posture Doctrine vary in the degree to which they
effectively achieve the different military security and political prestige
objectives of the NNWS. With respect to deterring nuclear attacks
upon NNWS by either a hostile superpower or minor NWS, the Low
Posture Doctrine initially attempts to limit the nuclear capabilities of
the NWS and to constrain their rights to deploy and initiate the use
of nuclear weapons. These restrictions, if adhered to, would absolutely
reduce the threat of nuclear attack or blackmail against NNWS.

In the extreme version of the Low Posture Doctrine, which permits
a NWS to use nuclear weapons only in response to nuclear attack
against its own homeland, these arms limitation and use constraints
constitute the sole means by which NNWS can achieve the nuclear
components of objectives 1.A and 1.B. In this instance, a NNWS would

have no recourse should an actual or threatened nuclear attack materialise. Perceiving a realistic threat of nuclear attack from a hostile NWS, despite ongoing use constraints, a NNWS might thus be tempted to acquire an independent nuclear weapons capability in order to achieve the nuclear component of objectives 1.A or 1.B.

In the modified version of the Low Posture Doctrine, the NWS can extend unilateral or co-operative positive security guarantees to certain NNWS subject to actual or threatened nuclear attack by either a hostile superpower or a minor NWS, when all other policy instruments appear to have failed. Given the state of mutual deterrence and *détente* which would exist between the two superpowers under a Low Posture Doctrine, unilateral positive security guarantees to NNWS allies subject to nuclear attack by a hostile superpower could never be completely credible. Indeed, as noted in connection with our assessment of the High Posture Doctrine, their value is depreciating. But the modified Low Posture Doctrine, offering unilateral positive security guarantees to major NNWS allies as a last resort, and thereby expressing a willingness to use nuclear weapons on their behalf in certain nuclear contingencies, is in marked contrast to the broad direction of the doctrine which otherwise emphasises explicit constraints upon the permissible uses of nuclear weapons. Thus, such specific guarantees emphasise the exceptional character of the security interests at stake and, in this way, provide NNWS with a reasonably credible additional means of achieving the nuclear component of objective 1.A.

Furthermore, the extension of co-operative positive security guarantees to certain NNWS as a last resort in order to deter or retaliate against nuclear attack by a minor NWS would be more binding upon the superpowers and perhaps other NWS under the modified Low Posture Doctrine than Security Council Resolution 255 currently is. Given the state of *détente* existing between the two superpowers under the Low Posture Doctrine, such so-operative guarantees are more credible than under the High Posture Doctrine. Moreover, since such guarantees are, according to the modified Low Posture Doctrine, merely one of several explicit counter-discriminatory obligations to be undertaken by the NWS on behalf of the NNWS, they also appear less hegemonic and more politically acceptable to NNWS than is the explicit superpower hegemony advocated by the High Posture Doctrine. Thus, these guarantees may provide NNWS with a reasonably credible and acceptable additional means of achieving the nuclear component of objective 1.B.

With respect to deterring or defending against conventional attacks by either a hostile superpower or a minor NWS, both variants of the Low Posture Doctrine are of mixed effectiveness. Since all NWS should be party to a no-first-use agreement, positive security guarantees cannot be extended to NNWS so threatened. The Low Posture Doctrine does create expectations that any new NWS would immediately become subject to existing no-first-use undertakings. Such an ongoing use constraint is designed to deter NNWS from acquiring nuclear weapons in order to achieve the conventional components of Objectives 1.A and 1.B. The Low Posture Doctrine also advocates a variety of non-nuclear and non-military policy instruments, ranging from improved institutions for the peaceful resolution of disputes to conventional intervention by military allies, in order to provide NNWS with alternative means of achieving the conventional components of objectives 1.A and 1.B. Only if a NNWS perceived a realistic and irreversible conventional threat from a hostile NWS and found the alternative non-nuclear instruments insufficient might it have no other recourse than to acquire an independent nuclear weapons capability, despite ongoing use constraints, as a means of achieving the conventional component of objectives 1.A or 1.B. This might be likely if such a NNWS — as in the cases of Federal Germany confronting the Soviet Union or Pakistan confronting India — had a substantially smaller population and/or GNP than its NWS opponent and thus no reasonable expectation of being able, over time, to mount an effective conventional defence.

In the case of objective 1.C, both variants of the Low Posture Doctrine create expectations that any new NWS would immediately become subject to existing deployment and use constraints with respect to remaining NNWS. Such ongoing constraints are designed to deter NNWS from acquiring nuclear weapons in order to achieve objective 1.C. The Low Posture Doctrine also advocates various non-nuclear policy instruments as alternative means of achieving objective 1.C. Only if a NNWS perceived a realistic and irreversible threat from local or regional NNWS adversaries and found the alternative non-nuclear instruments insufficient might it have no other recourse than to acquire an independent nuclear weapons capability, despite ongoing use constraints, as a means of achieving objective 1.C. This might be likely, however, if such a NNWS, as in the case of Israel confronting several Arab states, had a substantially smaller population and/or GNP than its local or regional NNWS opponents and thus no reasonable expectation of being able, over time, to mount an effective conventional defence.

With respect to objective 1.D, both variants of the Low Posture

Doctrine advocate the establishment of nuclear-free zones in substantial regions of the world both as a long-term means of effectively deterring NNWS from entering into a local or regional arms race and as a means of protecting them from such actions by hostile neighbouring states. As in the case of 1.C, it also creates expectations that any new NWS would immediately become subject to other existing deployment and use constraints with respect both to remaining NNWS and to other NWS. Such ongoing constraints are designed to deter NNWS from acquiring nuclear weapons in order to achieve objective 1.D. Finally, the Low Posture Doctrine advocates various non-military policy instruments as means of maintaining peaceful relations among adversary states should such an incipient arms race actually materialise. Only if a NNWS perceived a realistic threat of prospective acquisition of nuclear weapons by a local or regional NNWS adversary and found the alternative non-military instruments insufficient might it have no other recourse than to acquire an independent nuclear weapons capability, despite ongoing use constraints, as a means of achieving objective 1.D.

Finally, with respect to the various political prestige objectives of NNWS, the Low Posture Doctrine in both variants minimise future nuclear proliferation in two ways. First, it explicitly attempts to stigmatise nuclear weapons, thereby minimising their utility for enhancing political prestige. Second, it attempts to provide NNWS with alternative means of achieving objectives 2.A, 2.B, 2.C and 2.D.

Thus, the modified Low Posture Doctrine in particular can lead to a fairly low incidence of future nuclear proliferation. Under this variant, it is only when various arms limitation and use constraints fail to reduce the threats facing NNWS and non-nuclear policy instruments and residual positive security guarantees appear insufficient to protect NNWS facing nuclear or non-nuclear threats that a NNWS will have no recourse but to acquire an independent nuclear weapons capability in order to achieve its military security objectives. Furtnermore, the modified Low Posture Doctrine — like the extreme version — minimises the number of additional NNWS which will seek to acquire nuclear weapons in order to gain enhanced political prestige.

As depicted in Table 5.2 the modified Low Posture Doctrine dominates both the High Posture Doctrine and the extreme Low Posture Doctrine in the degree to which it satisfies the various policy objectives of the NNWS. It fulfils more effectively than does the High Posture Doctrine the regional military security objectives and the political prestige objectives of the NNWS. And it deters more

effectively than does the extreme Low Posture Doctrine nuclear attacks
on NNWS by existing NWS. It is thereby the comprehensive anti-
proliferation régime which most effectively amplifies the NPT and
promises to minimise future nuclear proliferation.

As we have argued throughout, the objective of a comprehensive
anti-proliferation régime can only be to minimise future nuclear
proliferation, not to stop it. There are likely to be certain hard, residual
cases in which the modified Low Posture Doctrine will also be
ineffective in preventing a NNWS from acquiring nuclear weapons:
either by deterring it or by providing it with alternative means by which
to achieve its various military security and/or political prestige
objectives.

The modified Low Posture Doctrine is, however, very much worth
pursuing for three important reasons. First, it may well be a necessary
if not sufficient condition of minimising future nuclear proliferation.
Under the High Posture Doctrine, as we have argued, substantial nuclear
proliferation is likely to occur. Unless the arms limitation and security
policies incorporated in the modified Low Posture Doctrine are adopted,
there will be no chance of minimising future nuclear proliferation. In
short, failure to pursue a modified Low Posture Doctrine means
acceptance of a high probability of substantial nuclear proliferation in
the future. Second, the modified Low Posture Doctrine would
substantially raise both the domestic and international costs for NNWS
of exercising their nuclear weapons option. By imposing constraints
upon the existing NWS in the development, production, deployment
and use of nuclear weapons, the modified Low Posture Doctrine
deprives NNWS of easy and currently available excuses to acquire
nuclear weapons of their own. It also places them in some military and
political jeopardy if they do proceed to acquire nuclear weapons.
Finally, the modified Low Posture Doctrine would create a
comprehensive arms limitation and security régime which substantially
constrains the role of nuclear weapons in the international security
system. Should future nuclear proliferation materialise even after the
modified Low Posture Doctrine is in place, its constraints would
insulate the behaviour of any new NWS which did appear. Thus it
would make a proliferated world safer than otherwise would have been
the case under the High Posture Doctrine.

The modified Low Posture Doctrine would, as we have noted,
introduce a comprehensive range of new arms limitation and security
policies. What is required primarily of the NWS in accepting these
policies is the undertaking of substantial new obligations in the

Table 5.2:   Effectiveness of Alternative Postures to Satisfy Various
            Objectives of Relevant NNWS and thus Minimise
            Proliferation

	High Posture Doctrine	Modified Low Posture Doctrine	Extreme Low Posture Doctrine
1.A*			
Against nuclear attack	effective	effective	ineffective
Against conventional attack	effective	mixed	mixed
1.B			
Against nuclear attack	mixed	effective	ineffective
Against conventional attack	mixed	mixed	mixed
1.C	mixed	effective	effective
1.D*	mixed	effective	effective
2.A	ineffective	effective	effective
2.B	ineffective	effective	effective
2.C*	ineffective	effective	effective
2.D*	ineffective	effective	effective

* Most common objectives of relevant NNWS.

international security system: obligations necessitating hard choices, the
adoption of new norms of international behaviour, and the acceptance
of reduced freedom of action. Many NNWS have been urging the NWS
to undertake such obligations since negotiations began on the NPT in
1965. If the NWS, as the major powers in the current international
security system, are serious about the objective of minimising future
nuclear proliferation, they must be prepared to undertake such
obligations and bear their costs. Conversely, continued adherence by
the NWS to some approximation of the High Posture Doctrine will
indicate that the NWS are not truly serious about minimising future
nuclear proliferation. To quote Leonard Beaton on this final point:

> The future is therefore one of political choice, not of technical
> capacity. If the major powers choose to create a structure which will
> effectively prevent proliferation over a long period of time, they
> must in the process change the facts of power. Weapons of mass
> destruction which seem to give their sovereign independence a secure
> future will force them to sink that independence in wider

arrangements. If they choose to do nothing and leave others to take what decisions they must, the world around them will steadily become much less tolerable. Those who control the decisive weapons would obviously like to go on as we now are; but that is the one choice which is not open to them.[26]

Notes

1. See Uri Ra'anan, 'Some Political Perspectives concerning the US-Soviet Strategic Balance', in Geoffrey Kemp, Robert Pfaltzgraff Jr. and Uri Ra'anan (eds.), *The Superpowers in a Multinuclear World* (Lexington, Mass., 1974); Steven J. Rosen, 'Nuclearization and Stability in the Middle East', unpublished research paper, Brandeis University, 1975; Robert R. Sandoval, 'Consider the Porcupine: Another View of Nuclear Proliferation', *Bulletin of Atomic Scientists,* XXXII (1976).
2. Yehezkel Dror, *Crazy States* (Lexington, Mass.); and Yehezkel Dror, 'Small Powers' Nuclear Policy: Research Methodology and Exploratory Analysis', *The Jerusalem Journal of International Relations,* 1 (1975). See also speech by Yasser Arafat, *New York Times,* 14 November 1974.
3. For a review of the developing technology see Theodore B. Taylor and Mason Willrich, *Nuclear Theft: Risks and Safeguards* (Cambridge, Mass., 1974), pp.59-76.
4. George Questor, 'Some Conceptual Problems in Nuclear Proliferation', *American Political Science Review,* LVI (1972), p.491.
5. See Steven J. Baker, 'The International Political Economy of Proliferation', above, pp.70-701; Steven J. Baker, 'Monopoly or Cartel?', *Foreign Policy,* no.23, Summer 1976, pp.202-20; Benjamin Sanders, *Safeguards against Nuclear Proliferation* (Stockholm, 1975); Taylor and Willrich (eds.), *Nuclear Theft.*
6. See Ian Smart, 'Non-Proliferation Treaty: Status and Prospects', in Anne Marks (ed.), *NPT: Paradoxes and Problems* (Arms Control Association, Washington, D.C., 1975), p.26.
7. See Graham Allison, *Essence of Decision* (Boston, Mass., 1971).
8. See Johan Jorgen Holst, 'Perspectives on Post-NPT Proliferation Issues: An Introduction' and K. Subrahmanyam, 'The Role of Nuclear Weapons: An Indian Perspective', in Johan Jorgen Holst (ed.), *Security, Order and the Bomb* (Oslo, 1972), pp.12, 134; and US Department of Defense, *FY 1976 and 197T Annual Defense Department Report,* ch.III, p.2.
9. See Geoffrey Kemp, *Nuclear Forces for Medium Powers* (International Institute for Strategic Studies, Adelphi Papers nos. 106 and 107, London, 1974). But see David Vital, *The Inequality of States* (Oxford, 1967), ch.9.
10. Dror, 'Small Powers'Nuclear Policy', loc.cit., p.39. See also p.45.
11. See Uwe Nerlich, 'Nuclear Weapons and European Politics: Some Structural Independencies', in Holst (ed.), *Security, Order and the Bomb,* pp.78-83.
12. See ibid., p.75.
13. See Robert W. Cox and Harold K. Jacobsen, *The Anatomy of Influence* (New Haven, Conn.,1973), Appendix A.
14. See Nerlich, 'Nuclear Weapons and European Politics', in Holst (ed.), *Security, Order and the Bomb,* p.74.
15. Saul B. Cohen, 'The Emergence of a New Second Order of Powers in the International System', in Onkar Marwah and Ann Schulz (eds.), *Nuclear*

Proliferation and the Near-Nuclear Countries (Cambridge, Mass., 1975), p.19. See also John Maddox, *Prospects for Nuclear Proliferation* (International Institute for Strategic Studies, Adelphi Paper no.113, London, 1975), pp.19-20.

16. See Lincoln Bloomfield, 'Nuclear Spread and World Order', *Foreign Affairs,* LIII (1974-5); R.P. Dore, 'The Prestige Factor in International Affairs', *International Affairs,* LI (1975), p.202; Harold Isaacs, 'Nationality: "The End of the Road"?', *Foreign Affairs,* LIII (1974-5); Maddox, *Prospects for Nuclear Proliferation.* But see Stockholm International Peace Research Institute, *The Near-Nuclear Countries and the Non-Proliferation Treaty* (Stockholm, 1972), p.76.

17. See Hedley Bull, 'Rethinking Non-Proliferation', *International Affairs,* LI (1975), pp.175, 177, 179.

18. See Hedley Bull, 'The Role of Nuclear Powers in the Management of Nuclear Proliferation' and James Schlesinger, 'The Strategic Consequences of Nuclear Proliferation', in James Dougherty and J.F. Lehman (eds.), *Arms Control for the Late Sixties* (Princeton, New Jersey, 1967), pp.143, 175, 183; Max Singer, 'A Non-Utopian, Non-Nuclear World', *Arms Control and Disarmament,* 1 (1968).

19. Nerlich, 'Nuclear Weapons and European Politics', in Holst (ed.), *Security, Order and the Bomb,* p.91.

20. See Bull, 'The Role of Nuclear Powers', in Dougherty and Lehman (eds.), *Arms Control for the Late Sixties, passim.*

21. See Leonard Beaton, *Must the Bomb Spread?* (London, 1966), p.129.

22. See Richard Rosecrance, 'Introduction', in Richard Rosecrance (ed.), *The Future of the International Strategic System* (San Francisco, 1972), p.4. See also Bull, 'Rethinking Non-Proliferation', loc.cit., p.176.

23. Rosecrance in Rosecrance (ed.), *The Future of the International Strategic System.* See also Walter Hahn, 'Nuclear Proliferation', *Strategic Review,* III (1975), p.22.

24. Schlesinger, 'The Strategic Consequences of Nuclear Proliferation', in Dougherty and Lehman (eds.), *Arms Control for the Late Sixties,* p.179. See also Bull, 'The Role of Nuclear Powers', in ibid., p.149 and Malcolm Hoag, 'Superpower Strategic Postures for a Multipolar World', in Rosecrance (ed.), *The Future of the International Strategic System,* pp.42, 48.

25. See ibid. and Schlesinger, 'The Strategic Consequences of Nuclear Proliferation', in Dougherty and Lehman (eds.), *Arms Control for the Late Sixties,* p.175.

26. See Beaton, *Must the Bomb Spread?,* pp.132-3.

6 THE ANGLO-AMERICAN NUCLEAR RELATIONSHIP: PROLIFERATORY OR ANTI-PROLIFERATORY?

David Carlton

There has been much academic speculation in recent years about the factors which lead states to acquire nuclear weapons.[1] In particular, there has been a debate about the relative significance of various kinds of perceptions in near-nuclear-weapons states relating to other states already possessing nuclear weapons. The most obvious and uncontroversial factor is fear. Thus we may presume that India's explosion of a nuclear device in 1974 was much influenced by the knowledge that the Chinese, who had attacked her territory in 1962, had acquired nuclear weapons in 1964. But it is sometimes contended that the behaviour and declarations of friendly nuclear weapons states can be no less influential than fear of potential enemies. Thus some analysts would argue that the Indians were much encouraged to become a nuclear weapons state by the United States and the Soviet Union, with both of whom New Delhi has long had quite amiable relations. But such analysts are not invariably in agreement about the reasons for this. Some stress that adequate nuclear guarantees of Indian security were not, and perhaps could not, be offered by the superpowers in sufficiently clear terms to carry credibility, notwithstanding the language used at the time of the signing of the Non-Proliferation Treaty in 1968. Others maintain that, on the contrary, the Americans and the Soviets have given nuclear weapons too high a declaratory emphasis and that it was probably in essence this which has tempted India— and others — to place a significant military and prestige value on joining the nuclear club.

It is in fact too early to form precise judgements about the factors which counted for most in the Indian case. But it is possible that lessons may be learnt by considering the example of Great Britain. For she became a nuclear weapons state in the more distant past and hence more evidence of motive is available. Official Histories, based on governmental archives, cover the period from 1939 to 1952; and much is known from unofficial sources about what occurred during the following decade.[2] It is also possible to analyse in this case how shifting American attitudes influenced thinking in the capital of a friendly state.

The case of Great Britain is in one respect unique. For almost from the outset the development of her nuclear capability was entwined to a greater or lesser degree with that of the Americans. Some analysts of proliferation may therefore contend that no conclusions of general applicability can be derived from such an example. On the other hand, both the Americans and the British always had the option to terminate their co-operation. And if that had occurred, it seems likely that the British would in any case have remained determined to be a nuclear weapons state. Thus the fact of a degree of interdependence arguably does not in itself render invalid all lessons to be gleaned from a study of the British case.

We shall now trace in brief outline the story of the British experience with nuclear weapons in order to focus on the following questions:

First, why did Great Britain originally become a nuclear weapons state and how, if at all, could the Americans have prevented it?

Secondly, why has Great Britain not ceased to be a nuclear weapons state and how far is this due to American action and inaction?

Thirdly, has Great Britain's conduct served as an incentive to other states to acquire nuclear weapons?

Fourthly, if denied a special nuclear relationship with the United States, would Great Britain have sought co-operation with other non-nuclear-weapons states and thus possibly promoted further proliferation?

There is a sense in which Great Britain has been involved in the business of becoming a nuclear weapons state since 1939 and thus on one interpretation she is a founder member of the club to whom proliferation analysis is inapplicable. For she was one of five countries which all simultaneously, separately and in no sense as a reaction to one another's efforts, began to explore the military implications of the atom on the eve of World War Two. The others were the United States, the Soviet Union, France and Germany. But it is more useful to regard Great Britain as having definitely decided to become a nuclear weapons power only in 1947-8 and as having achieved a tested capability in 1952. For if one chooses to stress the continuity of research back to 1939, much the same case can be made for France, both countries having had their citizens at work in North America on the programme that culminated in the bombing of Hiroshima and Nagasaki in 1945. One might even perversely argue, carrying this logic a little further, that if either German state today announced that she possessed nuclear weapons this would not be proliferatory in a strict sense, as Germany had become a founder member of the nuclear weapons research club in 1939. But common sense suggests that for purposes of analysis we should treat the United States as the first nuclear weapons state (1945) and consider all others as examples of proliferation. The Soviet Union was the first such case, testing an atomic bomb in 1949. This may be easily explained in terms of her adversary relationship with the United States. The third and fourth examples – Great Britain (1952) and France (1960) – are, however, more complicated, since both may be described as having been in the American sphere of influence and thus arguably in less obvious need of a nuclear capability than the Soviet Union. The British case is perhaps the more instructive of the two in that she was the first and in that she had begun to boast of having a special relationship with Washington long before her first nuclear test was held and was thus arguably even less in need of her own nuclear weapons than France.

Great Britain's decision to become a nuclear weapons state was taken by Clement Attlee's Labour Government during 1947-8. The matter was never debated in full Cabinet. And the manner in which the decision was made public was extraordinary. On 12 May 1948 a backbench Labour MP, George Jeger, was put up to ask the Minister of Defence, A.V. Alexander, an apparently innocuous question about whether he was satisfied that adequate progress was being made in the development of the most modern types of weapons. Alexander said:

> Yes, Sir. As was made clear in the Statement relating to Defence 1948 (Command 7327), research and development continue to receive the highest priority in the defence field, and all types of weapons, including atomic weapons, are being developed.

Jeger then asked whether the Minister could give any further information on the development of atomic weapons. Alexander replied: 'No. I do not think it would be in the public interest to do that.'[3] There was no further public notice given of the government's intentions and no pressure group arose to query it. This may have owed much to the consensus between the major political parties that the decision was justified. But it is also possible to argue that the decision and announcement of 1947-8 were not seen as a major turning-point. Those who hold this opinion argue, with Herbert York, that wartime collaboration with the United States meant that what was done in 1947-8 'could be seen as a small detail about how to continue rather than as a major decision about how to start'.[4] Let us, therefore, consider the earlier phase and attempt to assess whether York is correct and whether, if so, the Americans could have done more to alter the British attitude in 1947-8.

During the early part of the war when the potential importance of nuclear weapons was recognised, the relevant British and Free French research teams were transferred to Canada. Subsequently, in August 1943 at Quebec, Winston Churchill and President Franklin D. Roosevelt agreed that part of the British team should be further transferred to the United States to work there in collaboration with their American counterparts. The two leaders also agreed to share relevant raw materials in short supply. Meeting a year later at Hyde Park, they reached a further agreement whose character has been a subject of some dispute. Roosevelt's record of what occurred was apparently treated as such an important secret that the only signed copy was placed in the President's personal files under the code-name 'Tube Alloys'. After his death in April 1945 nobody recalled its location and it was only discovered many years later. Accordingly, Harry S. Truman's Administration may have been genuinely unaware of the extent to which Roosevelt had undertaken to engage in post-war co-operation with the British in this field. But what was the extent of the undertaking? On the one hand Margaret Gowing, the official British historian, has argued that the Hyde Park Agreement was unambiguous and far-reaching. On the other hand, Lord Sherfield, who as Roger Makins was much involved in the post-war negotiations on the subject, has asserted not entirely persuasively that the wartime agreements were'. . .on a strict interpretation valid for the war period only and thus provided a rather weak basis for the claim that collaboration and exchange of information should be continued in time of peace'.[5]

Whatever we may think of the merits of this dispute, it is undeniable that in the post-war era both the Americans and the British placed an extremely limited construction on the Roosevelt-Churchill Agreements. This may have been mainly due to ignorance of the true facts on both sides. For not only had Truman replaced Roosevelt but in the British general election of July 1945 Attlee defeated Churchill, who appears to have neglected to give advice to his successor on this vital subject. The two new leaders thus met in November 1945 with at best an incomplete picture of what had gone before. They did, it is true, reach a vague agreement about the desirability of continued collaboration and a combined Policy

Committee was invited to regulate the detailed terms. This Committee failed to arrive at a mutually satisfactory agreement. Incidentally, this has been seen by Gowing as further proof of American bad faith, while by contrast Sherfield's reference to the matter reveals no similar sense of outrage.[6]

The way was now open for the American Congress to pass the McMahon Act of 1946, which appeared to close the door to American co-operation in nuclear matters with Great Britain or any other foreign state. No doubt support for this measure was much reinforced by high-minded American calls for the internationalisation of nuclear energy led by Bernard Baruch. The passing of the McMahon Act did not, however, deter the British from going ahead with the attempt to become a nuclear weapons state. The decision was formally made in January 1947 by a meeting of a Cabinet Committee known as Gen 163 — its members being Attlee, Alexander, Ernest Bevin (Foreign Secretary), Hugh Dalton (Chancellor of the Exchequer), Herbert Morrison (Lord President), Lord Addison (Dominions) and John Wilmot (Supply). The decision was made public, as we have seen, on 12 May 1948, in a reply to an obscure Parliamentary question.

The questions with which we are here concerned relate to the American influence on the British decision. Certainly the Americans were not by early 1947 giving the British overt encouragement, as the passing of the McMahon Act testifies. Indeed, not until January 1948 did the United States Government contrive to find a way round the McMahon Act and offer even a small concession to the British desire for collaboration in the form of the so-called *modus vivendi* involving mutual assistance in the matters of raw materials and intelligence. Nor can it be claimed that the Americans were strongly emphasising their belief in the diplomatic or strategic worth of nuclear weapons. For in the immediate post-war era they did not seek to exploit their monopoly to overwhelm or even to wring concessions from other states; and they generously offered, under the Baruch Plan, to permit the internationalisation of their own nuclear energy. It may of course be objected that this whole stance was insincere. To this a powerful rejoinder is to ask whether it can safely be assumed that Joseph Stalin would have made no more use than the Americans of such a monopolistic position if he had been the first to obtain it. Superficially, therefore, the timing of the British decision — January 1947 — would appear to suggest that an American policy of discouragement both by denying assistance and by playing down the worth of nuclear weapons made no impression on London. This does not lend much support to the advocates of what Hedley Bull has called the 'Low Posture' doctrine for combating proliferation.[7]

Supporters of the alternative 'High Posture' doctrine, such as James Schlesinger, may, however, choose to draw some comfort from the British decision, for they believe that credible guarantees of non-nuclear states in a threatening environment are a disincentive to proliferation.[8] Plainly, the British decision was taken at a time when the extent of the Sovietisation of Eastern Europe was becoming apparent and when the Americans seemed set on gradually withdrawing from active involvement in Europe. For example, March 1946 had seen Churchill's famous anti-Soviet Fulton speech. And by May 1946 Bevin felt obliged to warn his Cabinet colleagues that 'the danger of Russia has become certainly as great as, and possibly even greater than, that of a revived Germany'.[9] At the same time American intentions were still unknown. The British decision to make the atomic bomb was made two months before the enunciation of the Truman Doctrine; five months before the Marshall Plan was launched; and more than two years before the formation of NATO. Is it possible that an earlier and more decisive American response to the emerging British fears about Soviet intentions would have made the British Cabinet question whether an independent nuclear capability was necessary? The best guess we can make is that while such an American attitude would have strengthened the arguments of such doubters within the British policy-making élite as P.M.S. Blackett and Henry Tizard, the decision would probably have been the same, though perhaps principally because of the special circumstance that the British in 1947 still saw themselves as a power of the first rank, as one of the Big Three in the world. It is probably in this sense that York is correct to discern a continuity in British nuclear policy that made 1947-8 something less than a perceived turning-point. While accepting that the British circumstances were uniquely conducive to seeking nuclear rank for reasons of prestige, we may, however, tentatively conclude that at least the near-unanimity of the British decision owed much to the absence of adequate American security guarantees in a threatening situation.

We must next consider in some detail the importance of the first post-war example of positive American aid to the British enterprise. This occurred, as already indicated, in January 1948 when a so-called *modus vivendi* was agreed. The wartime agreements, controversial in character and already nullified in practice by the McMahon Act, were formally ended by mutual consent. In particular, the British agreed to the American request that the reciprocal veto on the use of nuclear weapons contained in the Quebec Agreement be given up. In return extremely limited co-operation regarding raw materials and intelligence was resumed — an evasion of the spirit if not the letter of the McMahon Act. Conflicting evaluations of this *modus vivendi* have recently been seen in Great Britain. Gowing in her Official History was disapproving. She considered the surrender of the veto a major concession for which London got little in return. But Sherfield, who had a major responsibility for negotiating the *modus vivendi,* has contended that the veto had become 'unrealistic and unenforcible'. Moreover, basing himself particularly on John Cockroft's testimony, he has argued that the benefits to the British of resumed co-operation were 'not as valueless as Mrs. Gowing claims'.[10]

The present writer is unable to offer any evidence decisively to buttress either of these contending assessments. But the interesting case for those concerned with proliferation arises if Sherfield and Cockcroft are seen as correct. In that case the Americans contributed positively to Great Britain becoming a nuclear weapons state — or at least to her becoming one as early as 1952. In any event the *modus vivendi,* whether of short-term practical significance or not, kept alive the appearance of collaboration in the military applications of nuclear weapons. In the longer run this certainly did have practical importance. For the Skybolt and Polaris deals arranged by Harold Macmillan between 1957 and 1962 could otherwise scarcely have been practical politics in the United States. This would arguably have led to an early decline of Great Britain as a nuclear weapons state and perhaps in turn to a very different attitude by France in the early years of Charles de Gaulle's presidency.

It would, however, be an oversimplification to argue that the cause of non-proliferation would necessarily have been best served in 1948 by an American refusal to resume limited co-operation with the British. For it is clear that the British would in any case have pressed on in the late 1940s and early 1950s with their quest for nuclear weapons and would eventually have been successful but, in addition, there was a serious possibility that the British might have sought collaboration instead with European or Dominion allies. In such cases Great Britain would of course have been the senior partner. The result might have been that the various junior partners could have become in due time independent nuclear weapons states. Proliferation could thus in theory at least have been more, not less extensive, but for the reforging of an Anglo-American special nuclear relationship in 1948.

The quest for other partners is indeed the course for Great Britain which Gowing, with all the advantage of hindsight, would appear to regard as having been most advisable. For, as we have seen, she has judged that there was little advantage for Great Britain in the *modus vivendi*. The fact is, however, that the British were not seriously tempted to seek European and Dominion collaboration in the late 1940s. This owed a good deal no doubt to the American offer of aid which it was hoped, correctly as matters turned out, would in due time be increased. But it also owed something to the unattractiveness of the European and Dominion alternatives. None of the old white Dominions, not even Canada, was then enthusiastic about becoming a nuclear weapons state – perhaps a result of their geographical locations that rendered them immune to a sense of threat at the hands of any other nuclear weapons state. And France in the late 1940s, then the only conceivable European partner, was racked with instability and her own nuclear research, such as it was, was under the leadership of the Communist Frédéric Joliot-Curie. So, *because of these special circumstances,* it may well be that an American refusal to accept the *modus vivendi* would have been in practice anti-proliferatory in its long-term consequences. But obviously no lesson of general applicability can be derived from this. On the contrary, the evidence would suggest that American unwillingness to renew even a token special nuclear relationship would have led the British to incline on balance to seek collaboration with others if suitable partners had been available. Certainly an abrupt cancellation of American support for the British nuclear capability in the 1980s would be more likely to have a net proliferatory rather than anti-proliferatory consequence. For economic constraints make a go-it-alone course uninviting and there are now several European partners with whom the British might find it relatively easy to envisage co-operation.

The 1950s saw Great Britain actually become a nuclear weapons state; Her first atomic bomb was successfully tested in 1952; and her first hydrogen bomb five years later. At the same time domestic opposition to the possession of nuclear weapons became evident, in sharp contrast to the mood in the 1940s. The political parties, especially the Labour Party, were distracted by the issue at various points between 1955 and 1961; the Liberal Party even adopted as official policy the abandonment of British nuclear weapons while reaffirming loyalty to NATO; and the Campaign for Nuclear Disarmament, which eventually evolved in a neutralist direction, flourished between 1958 and 1962. Perhaps this increase in opposition to an independent nuclear deterrent was in part due to the actual testing of nuclear weapons as distinct from mere decisions in principle. But it is also possible that other factors were significant which may be of special interest to analysts of proliferation in general. The 1950s saw a reduction in East-West tension following the death of Stalin and the end of the wars in Korea and Indochina. Hence many in Great Britain may have had a reduced perception of an external threat. At the same time the United States was much more definitely committed to the defence of Western Europe in the 1950s than in the immediate post-war years.

We have seen how uncertain the future of American involvement was when the British Government decided to make atomic bombs in January 1947. By 1949, however, the situation was transformed by the formation of NATO. And in the immediately following years the United States showed reassuring resolution in resisting aggression in the Korean War. There then ensued the Republican Administration of Dwight D. Eisenhower. This provided evidence of a large degree of bipartisanship in American foreign and defence policy. Thus by the second half of the 1950s many in Great Britain, and not merely pacifists and anti-Americans, began to question whether the independent nuclear deterrent was not a useless duplication of effort. The resolve of the Americans to defend Western Europe, even to the point of nuclear war, seemed to many to be permanently assured. Indeed, some who favoured retaining British nuclear weapons began to deploy arguments that tacitly reflected this recognition. Some stressed the possession of nuclear weapons as a key to achieving multilateral disarmament: the supposedly matchless British experience of diplomacy would be at the service of mankind provided only that Great Britain remained qualified to sit at the 'Top Table' of disarmament negotiations. Incidentally, this kind of inverted jingoism, which seems rather amusing in retrospect, was matched on the unilateralist side of the argument by exaggerated expectations of overwhelming global gratitude, especially in the Third World, if Great Britain should adopt the supposedly uniquely noble policy of giving up her nuclear weapons. Another retentionist argument that was tacitly based on an expectation of continued American concern for the future of Western Europe was one that anticipated not so much American isolationism as American unwillingness to be quite as hawkish in a specific crisis as London might desire. Hence in such a case British nuclear weapons might be used in a catalytic fashion. The view that no American guarantee could be entirely adequate was expressed, for example, by Sir Alec Douglas-Home, Prime Minister in 1963-4. Labour's Denis Healey commented:

. . .so long as the Prime Minister insists that you cannot trust the
Americans to come to your help in a crisis and that therefore you
must have atomic weapons in order to trigger off the American
Strategic Air Command against the will of the American Government,
he is strengthening and accelerating that very trend in the United
States to reduce America's liabilities in Europe which is the excuse
for his position.[11]

No doubt many American internationalists had more sympathy on this
point with Healey than with Douglas-Home. And in Great Britain, too,
the growth of domestic opposition, particularly among the informed
élite who remained relatively immune to outright pacifist or neutralist
arguments, resulted at least in part from perceptions of American
security guarantees being so adequate as to make a British effort
superfluous or even potentially damaging to overall Western interests.

The fact is, however, that the opponents of British nuclear weapons
were ultimately defeated. The Conservative Governments of Macmillan
and Douglas-Home were to a great extent irrevocably committed to the
other point of view. But possibly of much greater importance in this
period were the actions of successive American administrations in giving
positive and vital aid to the British effort. First, Eisenhower agreed to
supply a modern delivery system – Skybolt – in what seems to have
been a tacit deal involving provision by the British of bases for the
vulnerable American Thor missiles when all other European allies
except for Italy and Turkey refused.[12] Later the British made the Holy
Loch facilities available for American Polaris submarines. The Skybolt
deal collapsed, however, when the Americans decided on cancellation
after receiving discouraging reports about its likely effectiveness.
Macmillan accordingly demanded a replacement, namely American
Polaris missiles for use in submarines to be built by the British. By now,
however, John F. Kennedy's dynamic administration was in office.
This resulted in there being important groups in Washington who were
more conscious than their counterparts under Eisenhower of the
implications of such a deal for arms control, for nuclear proliferation
and for relations with the French, who under de Gaulle were deeply
suspicious of the Anglo-American special relationship. In particular,
Robert McNamara, the Secretary of Defense, and George Ball, the
Under-Secretary at the State Department, objected to the United States
deliberately giving a new lease of life to the British independent
deterrent. But Kennedy was talked round by Macmillan at the famous
Nassau meeting in 1962. True, the British agreed to assign their nuclear

capability to NATO duties but, more important, they also reserved the right to withdraw it in the event of 'a supreme national emergency'. Significantly, after careful consideration in Washington, no precisely similar deal was offered to France.[13]

What the analyst of proliferation has to ask about these developments is whether an American refusal to offer Skybolt and/or Polaris would have been fatal for the British independent nuclear deterrent. The answer would appear to be that the British would not immediately have abandoned their stocks of V-bombers but that in the longer run they could scarcely have found the resources to retain nuclear status of the quality that exists today in the form of the British Polaris fleet. A further interesting question is whether such a gradual downgrading stopping short of outright renunciation would have had any effect on the French. One possibility might have been that the French would have sought collaboration with the British in the development of a first-rate delivery system. But Anglo-French differences on other matters in the 1960s were such that this might have proved difficult to arrange. Possibly the French, even under de Gaulle, would instead have been content, in company with the British, to maintain only a modest capability based on manned bombers rather than strive to achieve, at great cost, her present land-based and submarine-based nuclear missile forces. If so, the Americans must be judged to have a major responsibility, not perhaps for France being a nuclear weapons state at all, but for her being one with a serious potential to inflict unacceptable damage on a superpower. Hence some vertical if not horizontal proliferation among medium powers may be due to American policy between 1957 and 1962. Certainly most authorities on the development of the French nuclear capability place great stress on the influence of the British example and also on de Gaulle's extreme bitterness at the Nassau Agreement.[14] It should not, however, be supposed that American reluctance to provide a new generation of means of delivery to the British in the 1980s would be as anti-proliferatory as refusal to forge the Nassau Agreement might have been. For now Anglo-French relations are much improved and joint collaboration on the production of, say, cruise missiles cannot be ruled out; and if this proved extremely expensive Federal German funding might even be considered necessary. Thus American refusal to give exclusive help to the British might paradoxically be as proliferatory in the 1980s as the opposite course adopted in 1962 arguably was.

The most recent phase of the story of Great Britain as a nuclear weapons state is also not without interest. The most striking fact has perhaps been the diminution of support for the idea of the renunciation of the British independent capability. For example, the Labour Party in office between 1964 and 1970 took no serious steps to carry out the earlier pledge to renegotiate the Nassau Agreement and those responsible were subjected to surprisingly little criticism on this account. Again, the Labour Party in opposition between 1970 and 1974 showed minimal interest in the subject in striking contrast to the pre-1964 period of opposition. And on regaining office in 1974 the new Labour Government even felt able to arrange for underground nuclear tests to take place in the Nevada Desert. No doubt there are many reasons that may be adduced to explain this change – not least a belated recognition that British action in whatever direction would have little impact on the large majority of other states. But analysts of proliferation will perhaps see special significance in a worsening of the international atmosphere in the 1960s as compared with the late 1950s. The Cuban crisis, Vietnam and particularly the Soviet invasion of Czechoslovakia did much to change the climate of relative optimism about East-West relations that had prevailed at the time of, say, the inauguration of Kennedy. Paradoxically, however, apocalyptic assessments of the effects of nuclear testing or of the chances of accidental nuclear war simultaneously receded.

Again, analysts of proliferation may also see significance in growing doubts about the reliability of American pledges to defend Western Europe. The doubts now were not so much those expressed in an earlier phase by Douglas-Home but rather a more fundamental questioning of whether an era of American neo-isolationism might be becoming a serious possibility. Certainly at the time when the argument for renouncing nuclear weapons had stood high on the British political agenda, no American politician of note had expressed views of the kind held by such recent presidential aspirants as Eugene McCarthy and George McGovern. Nor did Congressional debates take place in the late 1950s comparable to those recently sponsored by Mike Mansfield on American force levels in Europe. Above all, the United States could never be accused of having betrayed pledges to Allied governments in the pre-Nixon era. Today, however, many of the friends of the United States in Cambodia and South Vietnam have been left to the mercy of their conquerors. Of course all confidence among Western Europeans in American guarantees has not as a result been totally destroyed, for corrupt Asian régimes are evidently not wholly comparable to the mature democracies of Western Europe. Nevertheless, there should be no surprise if events in South-East Asia and the growth of neo-isolationist voices in the United States have occasioned at least some growing doubt about the permanent reliability of the United States' remaining guarantees. This in turn may have served to reduce support for renunciation or downgrading of actual or potential independent nuclear options in Western Europe.

This brief survey of the British case has thus not provided much evidence that will give comfort to the advocates of a Low Profile Doctrine as a means of deterring proliferation – though some advocates of a so-called Modified Low Profile Doctrine might disagree.[15] On the other hand, there may be more grounds for contending that the United States by maintaining a High Profile – or rather a Higher Profile – could have encouraged more continuous resistance in Great Britain to nuclear weapons ambitions than has been the case. That is not to say that the British could have been persuaded to renounce nuclear weapons overnight, but that their involvement might have gradually taken a more modest form – with possible anti-proliferatory consequences elsewhere. Analysis is of course complicated by the fact that the present generation of British Polaris missiles was actually provided by the Americans. But, as has already been argued, merely blocking such deals will not necessarily have a net-anti-proliferatory result: much depends on the precise circumstances and alternative options. We may thus conclude that while the British case, like all others, is unique, there is perhaps some limited comfort to be derived from it by, say, Schlesinger, who both as an analyst and as a practioner at the US Department of Defense has espoused a variant of the High Posture Doctrine on the part of the superpowers.

Notes

1. See Enid C.B. Schoettle, 'Arms Limitation and Security Policies Required to Minimise the Proliferation of Nuclear Weapons', above, pp.102-31, and various works cited therein.
2. Margaret Gowing, *Britain and Atomic Energy, 1939-1945* (London, 1964); *Independence and Deterrence: Britain and Atomic Energy, 1945-1952* (2 vols., London, 1974). For a survey of unofficial studies of the period after 1952 see David Carlton, 'Great Britain and Nuclear Weapons: the Academic Inquest', *British Journal of International Studies,* II (1976), pp.164-72.
3. *House of Commons Debates,* vol.450, col.2117, 12 May 1948.
4. Herbert F. York, 'An Outline History of Nuclear Proliferation', in David Carlton and Carlo Schaerf (eds.), *International Terrorism and World Security* (London, 1975), p.114.

5. Gowing, *Independence and Deterrence,* I, p.7; Lord Sherfield, 'Britain's Nuclear Story, 1945-52: Politics and Technology', *Round Table,* no.258, April 1975, p.194.
6. Gowing, *Independence and Deterrence,* I, pp.99-104, 110-11; Sherfield, 'Britain's Nuclear Story', loc.cit., p.194.
7. Hedley Bull, 'The Role of Nuclear Powers in the Management of Proliferation', in James Dougherty and J.F. Lehman (eds.), *Arms Control for the Late Sixties* (Princeton, 1967), pp.143-50.
8. James Schlesinger, 'The Strategic Consequences of Nuclear Proliferation', in Dougherty and Lehman, *Arms Control for the Late Sixties,* pp.174-84.
9. Cabinet Memorandum, 3 May 1946, C.P. 186 (46), Cab.129/9, Public Record Office London, quoted by permission of the Controller of HM Stationery Office.
10. Gowing, *Independence and Deterrence,* I, pp.264-5; Sherfield, 'Britain's Nuclear Story', loc.cit., p.195.
11. Denis Healey, *A Labour Britain and the World* (Fabian Tract, no.352, London, 1964), pp.13-14.
12. See Andrew Pierre, *Nuclear Politics: the British Experience with an Independent Strategic Force, 1939-1970* (London, 1972), pp.140, 162.
13. See John Newhouse, *De Gaulle and the Anglo-Saxons* (London, 1970), pp.225-37; Richard E. Neustadt, *Alliance Politics* (New York, 1970), pp.54-5.
14. Lawrence Scheinman, *Atomic Energy in France under the Fourth Republic* (Princeton, New Jersey, 1965), p.119; Wolf Mendl, *Deterrence and Persuasion: French Nuclear Armament in the Context of National Policy* (London, 1970), pp.40-8; Wilfrid L. Kohl, *French Nuclear Diplomacy* (Princeton, New Jersey, 1971), *passim.*
15. For the Modified Low Profile Doctrine see Schoettle, 'Arms Limitation and Security Policies', above, pp.102-31.

7 PROLIFERATION: SOPHISTICATED WEAPONS AND REVOLUTIONARY OPTIONS — THE SUB-STATE PERSPECTIVE

J. Bowyer Bell

Introduction

In an uncertain world, one of the presently agreed verities is that revolutionary violence, terrorism and irregular war are growth areas. Efficient democratic states that can accommodate rational dissent and effective totalitarian régimes that can crush any open dissent may for the moment be immune to indigenous revolutionary violence, but vast areas — including several post-industrial states — may not be so fortunate. And any state, including and perhaps especially democratic ones, with an unresolved nationality problem cannot rest easy.

The most important factor, perhaps, is not the strategy and tactics of the various revolutionaries, whether they seek power or only through propaganda of the deed an audience to their despair, but rather the arrival of a patron and with a patron a new and deadly weapon. If a revolutionary can make an appropriate connection in Havana or Washington, with the Russians or the Libyans, his capacities are greatly increased, his prospects enhanced, and his challenge to order heightened. If the new patronage sparks a jealous response, what had been a small, tolerable armed struggle, waged in isolation, may become an area for the clash of major power ambitions quite removed from the parochial issues. Consequently, the aspirations, intentions and capacities of revolutionary organisations may suddenly matter a great deal. And one means to make them matter to advantage is to inject more and better weapons into the armed struggle. Some revolutionaries have to depend on their own resources, certainly at first; but most, sooner or later, make a connection.

Weapons procurement procedures for revolutionary organisations must take into account certain factors rarely of concern to conventional governments. Essentially the revolutionary spectrum of acquisition runs from scavenging, theft and construction on a local level to illicit shipments by agents, by friends or by patrons. Some groups begin with almost nothing. The Irgun Zvai Leumi in the Palestine Mandate did not even have an automatic weapon at the outset of their campaign against the British. The paucity of weapons was such that each was cherished,

never discarded even at the risk to the bearer. When the Stern
Group assassinated Lord Moyne in Cairo in November 1944, the
British authorities discovered that the Nagant revolver used had
been also used to kill a policeman in Jerusalem six weeks
before, a police inspector and constable in February 1944, a police
constable in March 1943, another constable in Tel Aviv
in May 1944, an Arab in Jerusalem as far back as November
1937, along with still another murder of an unknown date.
('You don't think we would be so silly as to throw it away when it
still worked?').

Other revolutionary groups have had the immediate support of
a patron eager to achieve influence or position by stocking the
revolutionary arsenal — in fact in some cases the revolutionary
organisation is little more than an agency of the patron — EOKA-B
in Cyprus, PORF in South Arabia and the present Polisario in the
former Spanish Sahara. (EOKA-B was controlled after General
George Grivas' death by the Greek Central Intelligence Agency
(KYP), PORF was in part staffed and fully controlled by an
the Egyptians, and Polisario is all but an agency of the Algerians.)

In any case most revolutionaries would like 'more', even if the new
weapons may create problems. These may include the following: the
necessary skills may not be available and technicians may thus have to
be imported; the new weapons may determine inappropriate tactics;
and the ease of acquisition may not inculcate effective revolutionary
habits of mind.

The acquisition of weapons by revolutionaries is a form of
technology transfer — proliferation to the fearful — that almost
inevitably presents the same difficulties as the conventional movement
of technology from the skilled to the unskilled. A weapon is not simply
a piece of hardware to be acquired and immediately used to effect —
a hat that fits any head. For revolutionaries are self-elected and
self-taught. In less developed countries they may represent a mix of
talent, including as leaders the Westernised, who often appear on
forums but not in the bush. The new revolutionary variant in
democratic or Western societies reflects a combination of intellectuals
and men of no property — few with real military experience. Most
revolutionaries learn their business on the job; the incompetent
guerrillas or bomb-makers have a high attrition rate. In the recent
campaign in Ulster, for example, nearly as many Irish Republican Army
(IRA) volunteers have been killed by their own bombs as by British
security forces. Other than carelessness that comes from familiarity and

limited original training, the necessity for speed and the quality of the materials are the major reasons for premature explosions.

Many members of the Basque ETA or the Provisional IRA have never fired a shot except in anger. In any conventional military terms they are badly trained — which is one of the reasons that revolutionaries prefer to rely on unconventional tactics. This level of competence severely limits what sort of weapon can be absorbed effectively just as does the terrain — an urban guerrilla not only cannot make use of a tank but also even a 30-calibre, air-cooled machine gun can prove no boon. Even in a rural guerrilla campaign with secure bases, the introduction of even relatively simple new weapons can cause difficulties. The Viet Cong rocket attacks on Saigon were effective simply because no one knew where they would land, least of all the Viet Cong; thus military targets were regularly missed and the entire civilian population intimidated.

Despite any difficulties in acquiring and effectively absorbing more sophisticated weapons, every revolutionary movement, almost without exception, avidly wants new, elegant weapons. And just as weapons systems have grown larger and more complex and more expensive — main battle tanks, huge nuclear submarines, computerised battlefields — so have systems grown smaller, but hardly any cheaper. Each new generation of precision-guided missiles includes, seemingly, still one more set, more accurate, easier to carry and more flexible than the last. One or two men with a slim metal tube and a bit of courage can destroy at distance an immeasurably more expensive and complex bit of equipment. There are tiny grenades no larger than a 35 mm film capsule, a sub-machine gun that is totally silent and fires 3-shot bursts, hand-held flame throwers, gas guns, cunningly miniaturised bombs to pop in the mail, even tactical nuclear weapons quite capable of being slipped into a camera case. And doubtless the ingenuity of those involved in weapons technology will contrive even more elegant devices. Not unreasonably a great many of the concerned have become alarmed that these new, deadly and sophisticated weapons — even a nuclear device — will, sooner or later, appear in the hands of the unauthorised. Somehow for many the idea of such weapons in the hands of those not legally authorised to kill by recognised governments strikes terror. And it is abundantly clear that in the immediate future the world will be filled with those engaged in armed struggles under an unrecognised flag for an alien cause. It seems equally clear that each new generation of light weapons will almost surely find its way into such hands. Certainly there is no doubt that frantic men will seek any and every means to advance their cause. If they cannot find patrons to donate the new weapons, they can depend on theft, extortion, the spin-off residue of bigger wars. Proliferation of the new light weapons is — seemingly — assured. Yet such arms procurement is not a simple conduit from patron to recipient. If a new weapon becomes available, there are three options: the device can be ignored or misused, volunteers can be despatched outside the area to acquire the needed skills, or instructors can be imported. In the first case the level of violence remains the same. In the second the returning members may introduce a variety of personal, political and ideological problems. And in the last case alien instructors guarantee less freedom of action, a greater dependency on the distant patron. Moreover, the new instructors almost always also guarantee an escalation in the conflict. They provide a more significant international component, as the patron becomes more visible, and perhaps inspire intervention by the friends of the threatened.

Northern Ireland

As an example of the difficulties and dangers for revolutionaries, the trials and tribulations of the Provisional IRA in Northern Ireland specifically reveal certain trends. In 1969 communal rioting in Northern Ireland necessitated the intervention of the British army. The other, secret army, the IRA, had been noticeable during the disturbances by its absence. The nationalist population had assumed that such a force existed and, in fact, so had many Irish Republicans; but for some years the IRA leadership had turned toward radical politics rather than military adventures. Some of the military men drifted away taking their weapons or their knowledge of dumps with them. Other weapons were lost or stolen or rusted away untended. The paucity of military supplies was a major factor in producing the split of the IRA into the Officials and Provisionals. For the latter the primary responsibility in 1970 was to organise and arm an underground army, especially in the areas of high nationalist vulnerability in Belfast and Derry.

The first major effort to arm the nationalist defenders involved members of the Fianna Fail Government in Dublin, who turned over funds to agents from Belfast and promised to arrange swift passage for the shipment when it arrived on the Dublin docks. The Provisionals had a patron. They purchased the arms but the scheme aborted. The arms dealer turned out to be untrustworthy, the Irish emissaries naïve, and the Fianna Fail Prime Minister Jack Lynch unwilling to ignore the operation. Subsequent Provisional efforts in Europe aborted as well. The failures meant that there were not going to be thousands of weapons to arm the nationalist population but rather only enough for a relatively small urban guerrilla force, adequate to defend pressure points and quite capable of waging a low-intensity campaign against the British army. Unless, of course, the Provisionals found another patron. The Provisionals, fluctuating in size from several hundred to several thousand volunteers, were armed largely by scavenging in Ireland and Europe, from the United States, and later with the help of the Libyan government — although the latter source was more visible than viable.

There has been in recent years a sporadic trickle into Ireland from these sources but never a flood. Even though the IRA has come into flush times with perhaps over a million dollars funelled in from the United States alone to the financial officers of the GHQ, the funds have not assured a constant source of weapon supply. The most notorious single attempt, however, cost the IRA little or nothing. Colonel Muammar Qaddafi of Libya, seeing the Provisionals as an anti-imperialist force, arranged for both arms and money to be handed over to appropriate representatives. Joe Cahill, the IRA Quartermaster, leased a vessel, the *Claudia,* picked up the arms and, carefully followed by the British, sailed off to be met in Irish waters by the Irish Navy. Consequently, the Provisional IRA has had to depend on the American connection to supply weapons as well as money. In the early days all sorts of weapons came into Ireland in coffins and golf bags, were shipped to England and back to Ireland, arrived in crates and disappeared from the docks, slipped by customs at Shannon airport.

The most effective weapons to arrive in Northern Ireland have been the civilian version of the M-16, the Colt AR-15, and the AR-180 Armalite, first manufactured in Japan for an American company — Armalite Corporation of Costa Mesa, California. (When the Japanese run was shut down, Armalite subcontracted another run of fifty thousand to Sterling — a British arms manufacturer, which must prove something about the British need for foreign exchange, since it is now well known where many Armalites end up.) Both the Colt AR-15 and the AR-180 Armalite may be purchased legally and openly in the United States. Incidentally, several Irish-Americans and Irish resident aliens in the United States have been arrested or are sought — usually for purchasing arms in quantities large enough to attract attention. Others have refused to answer grand jury questions and have consequently been interned.

For IRA purposes the weapons are ideal. Neither is automatic, which is a virtue in untrained hands, and in any conventional sense the IRA volunteer is badly trained. They are light. The AR-180 Armalite with a folding stock can be reduced to a two-foot length − 'Fits inside a cornflake box, it does' − and the high muzzle velocity (3,250 feet per second) permits the 223 bullets to penetrate standard issue British body armour and the armour of British personnel carriers. It has a very flat trajectory, and the rate of fire gives the inexpert marksman a chance of hitting the target. The two are in fact perfect urban guerrilla weapons. An Armalite, however, does not really give the IRA a greater capacity than would an M-1 rifle or even the old Lee-Enfield. The virtue is that it is easy to use. It must be stressed again that most urban guerrillas learn on the job. Very few have fired many shots in practice. Very few have had any formal military training. Very few handle weapons with special skill. And the Armalite, in particular, compensates for incompetence.

Once the level of weapon sophistication is increased this problem of competence becomes more serious. In the autumn of 1972 the IRA at last managed to get a shipment of arms into Ireland that included Soviet-made RPG-7 rocket-launchers. To anyone with an exposure to the military, a bazooka or a PIAT is quite a simple weapon used for obvious purposes. The IRA had never been trained to use a launcher. The GHQ was not about to practise with the few rockets available. Instead the RPG-7 was used for IRA purposes rather than in the way the maker had intended. Fired into military and police posts the armour-piercing rocket zapped in one side and out the other. Although the use of the RPG-7 intrigued the press, the entire exercise proved futile for the IRA. Some of the weapons were lost, others went into dumps, and the volunteers went back to rifles and infernal devices. Assuming that the IRA had persisted, the solution would have been to import skilled instructors − the obvious candidates being Irish-American veterans of Vietnam. This has almost always been the only option open to revolutionaries unless the opportunity occurs to send volunteers abroad for short courses. And such 'graduates' introduce problems along with the skills. There is, however, the possibility in certain areas of learning on the job.

The IRA explosive devices in 1971 were often crude, two decades behind the time, and a danger to transporter and detonator. As the supply of commercial explosives dried up, the IRA engineering officers had to become more ingenious − and the libraries supplied the first step. Although competence has improved, the mixtures of diesel oil, nitrobenzene, sodium chlorate, water oil, calcium carbonate and ammonium nitrate often leave something to be desired. But, again, they generally work well enough. For most urban guerrilla operations sophisticated weapons are not of any great help. A Browning 30-calibre machine gun may cause more problems than solutions. Once fighting has gone beyond incidents and operations to an irregular war, then heavier weapons — mortars, heavy machine guns, bazookas — are highly desirable. At that stage, however, the whole problem of revolutionary strategy has been transformed. Many revolutionary organisations, like the IRA, cannot aspire to fighting an irregular war. Most revolutionary organisations in advanced countries, the Basque ETA or the Argentinian ERP, can make do quite well with conventional infantry weapons, stolen, scrounged, even in some cases turned on lathes, coupled with home-made bombs and great ingenuity. Less is often more.

Palestine

In Palestine between 1944 and 1948, the Irgun Zvai Leumi ran a classic revolutionary insurgency. Starting in January 1944 without a single automatic weapon and with an arsenal little different from the IRA hodgepodge of 1969, the Irgun with the help of the tiny Stern Group, and at times the Haganah, ran a low-intensity campaign ona shoestring. In the autumn of 1947, when the United Nations partition resolution was passed, they still had arms for only seven hundred volunteers, although active service strength was several thousand. The Haganah, many times larger, faced a similar weapon problem. While the Irgun's campaign against the British exploiting less as more was most effective, by December 1947 it was clear that a real war was coming with Arab irregulars and probably the neighbouring Arab states. The Zionist underground was quite unprepared — with too few conventional light infantry weapons, a few machine guns, some home-made mortars, one or two derelict small-calibre artillery pieces, no armour, no real artillery, no air force, no sophisticated equipment of any sort and no way to acquire any legally. Both the Irgun and the Haganah had to create a real military force, first to defend the roads and settlements against Arab attacks and then to defend the new state against the Arab invasion. For this they had a variety of assets. There was a steady trickle back into Palestine of men who had served in the British army and had received conventional training. A whole array of agents and emissaries, many with important friends, most with adequate funds, zig-zagged across the world acquiring what they could find. In the meantime

Irgun-Haganah were left to fight with their limited supplies plus what
they could buy or steal from the British army.

In the five months before the proclamation of the state, only a few
tiny shipments came in but news of successful purchases, the
co-operation of various governments, and the *coups* of Zionist agents
indicated that help was on the way. On the eve of independence the
British released an Israeli arms vessel, ostensibly carrying a cargo of
onions, after a cursory inspection was inhibited by the onions' odour.
On 16 May 1948, two transports flew in arms purchased in
Czechoslovakia. And tnat was all. There were still almost no heavy arms
and the Israelis largely fought the four-week war with what they had on
hand. One exception was the arrival of four crated Messerschmitt 109s.
The pilots had been trained in the diaspora. Another was the arming of
new, untrained immigrants with arms that arrived in Tel Aviv on 25
May for an attack on Latrun. That attack and a second on 31 May were
disastrous. Arms most certainly did not make soldiers.

During the four-week United Nations truce that began on 11 June,
the military balance was completely transformed. Truce or no, a flood
of military supplies arrived in Israel, although fighting over the Irgun
arms ship *Altalena* saw much of that shipment destroyed off Tel Aviv.
The Israelis again had several major assets. If for no other reason than
the holocaust and/or self-interest, there were many states willing to
aid the Zionists. Some did so covertly, but others made little effort to
disguise their actions. Secondly, there was ample money and vast
amounts of World War Two equipment scattered about. Next, Israel
was a legal state, a fact that eased some consciences. Most important,
the new heavy arms could be effectively used without a lengthy process
of training because of the many skilled volunteers. B-17, four-engined
bombers were smuggled out of the United States and flown to an
Israel none of the American and Canadian crews had ever seen; they
were used to bomb Cairo on the way. Thus the haphazard weapons
mix posed few problems because of the variously trained volunteers.
There was hardly even a language problem because most of the skilled
spoke English as did most of the Israeli officers — many of the new
infantry recruits out of Europe knew little English and often less
Hebrew, a fact that did not ease their way at the battles of Latrun.
This availability of trained volunteers played a far more significant role
in the Israeli victories during the subsequent 1948 battles than popular
Zionist mythology would warrant. (Foreign volunteers — Mahal — came
from 52 countries and made up 18 per cent of Zahal.) Beyond their
specific military contribution, however, their presence made the

weapons technology transfer possible without the injection of alien skills with other loyalties. Although not every foreign volunteer stayed to become an Israeli, in 1948 they were most assuredly not seconded specialists or mercenaries.

Israeli experience, in weapons transfers like much else in the history of Zionism, was unique. Most revolutionaries face problems more like the IRA's than those of the Haganah. At the beginning most seek a friend, if not for arms and funds, at least for a certificate of revolutionary authenticity from a recognised centre — Havana or Peking or Moscow mostly. The most important prerequisite is to oppose an odious enemy — major candidates are colonial powers, rightist tyrannies, racist régimes, and all variants of imperialism. Those who have unfashionable opponents — any black African government or obscure indigenous régimes — may find difficulty in attracting an appropriate patron. Thus the Anyanya of the southern Sudan fought almost in isolation; the Kurds were manipulated by the Shah and the Americans. Few want to annoy the French on behalf of the Bretons, and fewer still would come to the aid of the Fascists in Italy.

Angola

A fairly typical last-decade revolutionary organisation is Movimento Popular de Libertação de Angola (MPLA), founded in December 1956. MPLA attracted largely the Kimbundu from north-central Angola. They first had a rival in the União das Populações de Angola (UPA) of Holden Roberto, which recruited largely from the Bakongo, and later, in March 1966, União Nacional para a Independência Total de Angola (UNITA), led by Jonas Savimbi and appealing to the third large tribal grouping to the south, the Ovimbundu. MPLA for a few years seemed to be preparing a campaign of subversion and conspiracy as hopes for a southern African non-violent strategy faded; but on 4 February 1961 several hundred Africans, including MPLA cadres, attacked Luanda's main political prison. In March, a widespread, ill-co-ordinated series of attacks on European settlers occurred almost simultaneously on the Congo border and further down in the Dembos region. Unexpectedly, the insurrection against Portuguese colonialism had begun. Over the next decade MPLA had several problems, often at times appearing insurmountable: first, to maintain the organisation and the armed struggle, second; to secure pride of place in contrast to the other two liberation movements and third, to escalate the international perception of the guerrilla war and MPLA's role. And MPLA had far fewer assets than the Haganah or the IRA. The MPLA tribulations were long and intricate. There were divisions within the movement, the rivalry of Holden's UPA, the complex problems of exile politics in the Congo, the physical difficulties of opposing the Portuguese presence, and there were few arms. MPLA collected some arms from the various forces in the Congo and managed to attract a little help from newly independent African countries, especially Ghana, Guinea and Algeria. There was some interest in Eastern Europe, particularly in the Soviet Union and Czechoslovakia; and a few MPLA cadres were sent out for training. As the years passed, MPLA gradually became the dominant Angolan liberation movement, certainly in the eyes of their Communist friends. An alliance was formed with similarly-minded anti-Portuguese liberation movements in Guinea-Bissau and Mozambique and then with other African liberation movements. Although the intimacy of the link varied, these organisations were the 'Russian' movements, in contrast to their various rivals who received aid from China. For MPLA the Soviet connection produced an erratic stream of infantry weapons in varying conditions, including Schmeisser sub-machine guns left over from World War Two, and odds and ends. Once the crates arrived on the docks of Dar-es-Salaam, the real obstacle was to move them half-way across Africa to the Angolan bush. By 1970 MPLA was still making do with hand-me-downs.

For the Soviet Union in 1970, the African liberation movements cost a tiny investment and paid comforting ideological benefits. The Soviets could counter the Chinese with future friends, challenge odious, colonial, racist régimes who would oppose Moscow in any case, and stand as a champion of the Third World. The bear's embrace was not all to MPLA advantage, for rivals claimed the movement was both Communist and a Soviet pawn. Efforts to slip out from under this image were difficult — after all the Soviet connection was vital. And so MPLA soldiered on. By 1972 the Portuguese were often sorely pressed, but sympathetic observers still assumed that the struggle would be protracted, that Lisbon would hold on.

As many had anticipated, the door to Angolan liberation opened in Lisbon, not the bush; but there in Africa the guerrilla presence had finally convinced the Portuguese army that they might not lose the war but could never win. In fact, the ideals and ideology of the MPLA, if imperfectly understood, had convinced many in the Portuguese army that there must be a new régime in Lisbon and an end to the anachronistic colonial wars. And so came the revolution of the carnations, in April 1974, a year of chaos, open Portuguese politics, and an end of empire. Yet Angola's future was unclear. The MPLA had the most talent, the most men under arms, and controlled the most territory, but Roberto and Savimbi had real assets. There appeared to be several alternatives. The Portuguese army might turn Angola over to MPLA, with whom they felt ideologically congenial, and MPLA either would or would not make a deal with the other two organisations. Outside Angola many hoped a guerrilla fusion would be possible, but there had been a decade of rivalry, often violent, and the persisting, if denied, tribal problems. If open conflict did come, as the pessimists anticipated, it seemed likely that the only hope for Roberto and Savimbi was a pact that might, more or less, put them on a par with MPLA.

It gradually became clear that there would be no fusion, that there would be no clear heir, that violence was likely, and the evacuation of most of the Portuguese population probable. To the north in the Congo, Joseph Mobutu, long anti-MPLA, feared the new government would control the vital rail lines that carried out Congo copper. In Zambia Kenneth Kaunda, oddly enough, seemed equally convinced that an MPLA victory would not be to Zambian advantage; and facing severe economic problems, he did not want MPLA with their Soviet friends as neighbours. The Americans were apparently willing to help out, and money and some arms began to flow to Roberto and Savimbi. Arms, however, as we have seen, do not make soldiers. As the Congo had indicated, a small well-trained commando force can dominate large, undisciplined, ill-trained forces. In southern Africa there was hardly time to bring together another mercenary force, although Roberto began to do so, hence the obvious candidate to thwart MPLA was South Africa. And Roberto and Savimbi felt, with Angola up for grabs and independence rapidly approaching, they only had a choice of acquiescing in South African intervention or watching MPLA take over.

As the South Africans began pushing columns north, MPLA resistance, tenuous at best, collapsed. With Roberto pushing in from the north and the South Africans and Savimbi from the south, MPLA would soon be isolated in Luanda. The trouble at this point was quite simply that while the Soviets were willing to give MPLA anything they wanted — no more used Schmeissers — this would not turn the tide. MPLA needed an army to face the South Africans and the mercenaries. And their friends supplied them with an instant army — enter the Cubans. Facing volleys of rockets and real amrour, Roberto's people withdrew. The South Africans discovered they were not holding the line for the West when the United States Congress refused to allow further American intervention. So Pretoria ordered the troops to pull back to the Cumene River hydro-electric complex. The Cubans and MPLA took over the visible parts of Angola. Savimbi went back into the bush. Roberto stayed in the Congo. The regular part of the Angolan war was over. And the MPLA, recognised by most nations, took over a country burdened or blessed with twelve thousand Cubans and five hundred Soviet advisers. Unlike the Israeli volunteers, these technicians and soldiers were alien, if welcome, would limit MPLA control, and would certainly engender external suspicion. It was, of course, not the first time that external intervention had tipped the military scales. General Francisco Franco would probably have lost without Italo-German aid and expeditions during the Spanish Civil War and the Republicans would at least not have resisted so long without the International Brigades and Soviet aid. In the Angola case, however, MPLA's inability to absorb sophisticated weapons escalated the war, provoked Cuban intervention, and indicated some of the prospects for the future.

Patterns of Future Military Activity

It appears that in the immediate future there are bound to be three general kinds of military activity: first, urban guerrilla terrorism, especially in countries with nationality problems or vulnerable, tyrannical governments; second, limited and irregular war, largely rural and occasionally between states; and third, conventional confrontations but probably not between two major powers. For the urban guerrilla, the terrorist, the assassin, while not adverse to trading up, all the new, elegant sophisticated weapons will not especially add to his capacity. It is easier to put an atmospheric pressure bomb on a jet airliner than go to the trouble of acquiring and using a missile launcher. Certainly the new weapons will dribble into the arsenals of the Basque, ETA and even the IRA, but such groups are seeking a victory over the will at the centre rather than in the field. This they can achieve with matches and knives if they can just persist until the shifting tides of history favour the cause, or the masses mobilise, or the tyrant flees.

The key moment in illicit and covert weapons acquisition comes when the struggle in the ghetto or the bush makes a quantum leap in capacity so that more elegant and lethal weapons can be deployed to effect. Then, as the guerrilla evolves into a soldier and the irregular war becomes more regular, the new skills can most swiftly, if speed is to be a factor, be supplied by a patron for a patron's purpose.

In this almost inevitable pattern of escalation and proliferation there has been increasing concern about the most elegant of all weapons — a nuclear device. It seems to be the case that the basis of an atomic weapon, plutonium, even if not weapons grade, might be available to the daring and determined. The necessary theoretical and technical information may be purchased at the United States Government Printing Office. The cost is not unreasonable and the material readily available. Even and, especially, if the level of scientific competence is not particulary high — a Massachusetts Institute of Technology (MIT) student has designed an effective bomb — then surely the ultimate weapon may be within the grasp of the dedicated and determined? Certainly for many academics the prospect is a real one — although from time to time for special purposes: those opposed to nuclear power are apt to create dread James Bond scenarios. In point of fact, few presently active revolutionary groups have the time, capacity or interest in 'going nuclear'. Fashioning bombs in an MIT laboratory is quite different from building them in Belfast or Beirut. Even the new breed of transnational terrorist is not really interested in killing people, especially large numbers of people, but rather attracting attention to a troubled cause. The nuclear option has long been that of the centres of imperialism. Ideologically, the prospect is not attractive. Strategically, it would absorb too many resources; warp existing strategy; alienate potential support. In most cases it appears an unattractive option. Conventional means will do as well, perhaps better. Perhaps, indeed almost certainly, some group will be attracted by the lure of a nuclear facility, but not to cause a melt-down, not even to steal plutonium but rather to stage one more dramatic terrorist spectacular, this time with a nuclear component. There is and will be serious, perhaps excessive, concern about this particular revolutionary option on the part of those with trained minds but little understanding of the nature of revolutionary options, revolutionary talents or even of the real world beyond the seminars and laboratories — a concern not necessarily misplaced but rather exaggerated. If there is to be a rational concern focused on nuclear proliferation, the weight of evidence would suggest that non-nuclear states should be a prime consideration rather than the harried and desperate revolutionaries — not that the world will, even if a revolutionary nuclear option is a relatively remote option, be a very comfortable place.

Over the next decade there seems every likelihood that there will be literally hundreds of revolutionary organisations — non-state actors — seeking the means to lever themselves into power — cross out the 'non' and act as a new state. If the scope of enquiry were limited, for example, simply to Western European democratic countries, the number of active or recently active indigenous groups almost boggles the imagination: various secret armies in Ireland, revolutionaries of all shades in Italy, nationalists in France, in Switzerland, again in Italy, bombs in Scotland and Wales. Certain of these organisations face obstacles so severe that the major impetus of their revolutionary strategy will be to seek prominence rather than power. As noted, these groups may opt, as have Black September and the Red Army, for spectacular transnational terrorism and might, therefore, like spectacular weapons. Yet it was quite possible to kidnap an entire international organisation — OPEC — with a handful of used weapons. Other organisations, like those based on frustrated nationalism — the IRA, or the Basque ETA - have not yet reached a level to absorb elegant weapons effectively. When they do — as the Kurds managed in part because of the terrain in northern Iraq — they will need a patron. Most organisations facing a vulnerable rightist tyranny, especially in Latin America, will find willing patrons to launch and fuel an armed campaign. Southern Asia is hardly a model of stability and is a focus of major power concern. And in Africa, Nigeria and the Congo are vulnerable — stable enough to resist a rebellion but not capable of crushing it quickly. The conservative Arab régimes are tempting targets to the ambitious, as is Iran. And the rumour of a new right to oppose the drift to the left, particularly in Europe, has proved real in Italy. Yet much of the violence will be on a lower level. The new weapons for a time will not be a serious component. The real danger for those in favour of an easy life will come when revolutionaries need steps beyond revolutionary capacity. Then an eye must be kept on new characters in the revolutionary drama — as small as the IRA arms ship *Claudia* or as large as the Cuban expeditionary force in Angola. Arms may not make the man or the soldier, but at that stage they are the foundation for escalation.

And, basically, it is escalation, not proliferation, that will threaten stability. Life may be made simpler for the assassin or the guerrilla with the injection of a new weapon, but order will not be unduly threatened. The danger or — more threatening — the opportunity comes not with the weapon but with revolutionary incapacity. Perhaps military technology will sooner or later devise still another generation of dreadful and elegant weapons especially for the untrained and incompetent, but until then the concern of academics and analysts may be excessive. In this one small area proliferation may not be a danger and in fact too elegant weapons in the hands of the untrained may be a blessing for those dedicated to peace and quiet. A revolutionary with an elderly pistol may be a greater danger than several men staggering under a portable precision-guided missile — cold comfort in a threatening world but some comfort nevertheless.

8 ARMS AND POLITICS: OLD ISSUES, NEW PERCEPTIONS

Michael Nacht

Introduction

Arms and politics and the relationships between them have always been crucial determinants of human affairs. Since the establishment of the system of nation-states, generally marked in the West by the Treaty of Westphalia in 1648, military force has been a tool of governments consistently relied upon to preserve and extend their influence over the affairs of men. With the dawn of the nuclear age, however, it was widely felt, at least in the United States, that two new considerations had been introduced: the capaicity of nuclear weapons to produce mass destruction made them virtually unusable, thereby shifting the attention of governments from the use of force to the threat of the use of force in order to achieve political objectives; and a non-linear relationship was created between the number of weapons and their military value, hence opening up the possibility of effecting arms control and disarmament measures that could bring some semblance of security and stability to the international system.

The history of the post-war period suggests that these premises were only partially correct. While the nuclear powers have not in fact used their weapons of mass destruction, they have failed to desist from engaging in conventional warfare. Nor has the possession of nuclear weapons by a handful of states prevented many other states from using military force both internally and externally, sometimes on a grand scale. Moreover, despite the plethora of arms control agreements fashioned since the end of World War Two, it is striking what little effect they have had in curbing either the quantitative growth or the qualitative improvement of the world's military arsenals.

Indeed, a fair summary of the contemporary period must necessarily stress the continued significance of military strength in international politics. The strategic arms competition and efforts to control it remain a central element of Soviet-American relations. The acquisition of sophisticated conventional weapons by a number of developing states highlights the great intensity of regional conflict situations. And the potential acquisition of nuclear weapons by many states, both developed and less developed, is at least in part an indication of the quest to effect a fundamental redistribution of global military, political and economic power.

To appreciate fully the role of force in international relations today and the ability of arms control and disarmament measures to diminish the likelihood of conflict among states requires that the characteristics of international society be perceived as they are rather than as we might wish them to be. It is the purpose of this essay to establish the nature of these characteristics; to set out the most pressing concerns in international security affairs, particularly from an American perspective; and to offer some tentative assessments of the role of arms control in alleviating these concerns.

Characteristics of International Society

International society is divided into roughly 150 states, entities that are best defined as sovereign, territorial, political units. Individuals are congregated into clearly defined physical segments. They are governed by ruling bodies of one form or another that exist in some cases with and in most cases without the consent of the governed. Their lives are most directly influenced by the rules or laws established by these governing bodies.

Four objectives have traditionally been at the core of most governments' activities. The first is to maintain the position of the régime in power. The second is to enhance the security of the state. The third is to stimulate domestic economic and, in some instances, social development. The fourth is to extend the influence and prestige of the state.

The interrelationships among these objectives are numerous and complex. Governments often confuse quite intentionally the first and second objectives, equating the two in order to obtain and then retain public support. Policies aimed at meeting the third objective are often orchestrated to maximise their impact in meeting the first objective. Since the third objective is intimately related to matters of foreign trade and investment, it can, if met successfully, contribute quite significantly to satisfying the fourth objective. And satisfying the fourth objective will, in turn, enhance support for the government at home — the objective of highest priority to the ruling régime.

These are but the most obvious linkages among the objectives of governments. What is glaringly evident, of course, is the central role military force plays in meeting these objectives. Sheer military might in many nations is all that keeps the ruling group in power. Armed strength is universally accepted as essential in order to preserve the security of the state. Use of military capabilities has often proved invaluable to secure the natural resources and to forge the political relationships necessary for the development of domestic economies. And classically it has been the military instrument that has been used most often and most successfully to extend the influence and prestige of the state.

In addition to these elementary truths, a number of additional factors tend to underscore the significance of military considerations in national and international affairs. An extreme maldistribution of resources and of wealth has been a permanent feature of the human existence. The few are rich and the many are poor: a recipe for conflict. In the less developed countries it is the army that is usually the most advanced in education and the most cohesive sociological unit within the society — hence the stress on the military instrument to achieve political goals and to resolve internal disputes. The élite structure in most nations is really quite tiny, far less than 0.1 per cent of the population. True democratic processes are evident in less than 20 per cent of the world's states. Consequently, in the absence of other forms of legitimation, ruling groups in the vast majority of states seize and maintain power principally through force of arms. And as a direct result of the enormous cultural, linguistic and religious heterogeneity among the world's people, nationalist feeling is pervasive and intense, providing a built-in ingredient for international conflict.

From these characteristics flow a number of conclusions. The struggle for political, economic and military power among and within the nations of the world is continuous and permanent. This situation is a reflection of the nature of man, of the human condition within the system of sovereign states, and of the relationships among these states. There is no reason to expect armed conflict to disappear unless and until there is a fundamental transformation in both the nature of man and his means of social organisation, a transformation whose occurrence is not supported by the slightest shred of evidence.[1] At the same time there is taking place today a significant diffusion of power on a global scale. This diffusion is unprecedented in scope and perhaps irreversible. It is, for example, very much at the core of the nuclear proliferation problem. But the powerful will not willingly relinquish power to the weak. The process of diffusion will not come easily or quickly.

If these conclusions are correct, substantial disarmament is a hopelessly Utopian goal. And arms control — the objectives of which have been defined as reducing the likelihood of war, limiting the damage should war come, and reducing the level of human and economic resources devoted to preparing for war — must be seen as an instrumentality of limited worth, aimed at producing a limited accommodation between adversaries within the context of the national security policies of these states. Expectations exceeding these seem, at this writing, to be wholly unwarranted.

American Perspectives on Current Security Problems

The debate in the United States on security and defence policy, the most open and comprehensive of its kind in the world, has traditionally involved three schools of thought which, at the risk of over-simplification, may be labelled the 'hawks', the 'doves', and the 'on the one hand — on the other hand' element. The hawks are dominated by their concern over the Soviet threat, and see American defence policy increasingly unresponsive to developing the capabilities needed to cope satisfactorily with this threat. The doves, alternatively, stress the enormous military power of the Americans, underscore the technological lead enjoyed by the United States *vis-à-vis* the Soviet Union, and seek to divert resources currently allocated for defence into American domestic programmes. The 'on the one hand — on the other hand' element sees the problems of defence policy in somewhat more complex terms than either the hawks or the doves. They are supportive of some weapon system developments and opposed to others, they endorse most but not all arms control agreements, and they generally tend to favour an incremental approach to international security affairs. The central objectives of this school of thought are to maintain a stable military balance between the United States and the Soviet Union, to encourage the implementation of a comprehensive nuclear non-proliferation policy, and to utilise arms control measures as a means to achieve these ends.

During the last few years the struggle over American defence policy has been fought primarily between the hawks and the on the one hand — on the other hand school, with a general shift toward the hawks' position and a decline in support for the policy of *détente* established dramatically in the Nixon-Ford years under the masterful guidance of Henry Kissinger. This shift has produced increased support for the development and deployment of a variety of strategic weapons systems and has stimulated a rethinking of the inadequacies of the North Atlantic Treaty Organization (NATO) defence posture. While it is certainly true that a number of regional conflict situations claim a great deal of attention in American policy-making circles — notably, of course, the Middle East and the Korean peninsula, and more recently the

Panama Canal Zone and Southern Africa — it remains the case that Soviet-American strategic relations and problems of the defence of Europe, in conjunction with concerns over the spread of nuclear weapons to other states, remain the highest priority matters from the perspective of American national security policy.

The reasons for the hardening of the American position *vis-à-vis* the Soviet Union are numerous. As is often stated by Soviet spokesmen, it is the 'correlation of forces' that influences policy, and this is the case as well with respect to American attitudes toward the Soviet Union. The deployment of four large land-based missile systems with a growing potential to acquire a first-strike capability against the United States Minuteman force; a re-examination of American estimates of Soviet defence spending that indicates the Soviet régime is allocating perhaps 13 per cent or more of its gross national product to military affairs; a major build-up of Soviet manpower and weaponry in the Western Soviet Union; the continuous effort to deploy a broad network of civil defence facilities for the protection of the political and military leadership, industrial facilities, skilled workers, food supplies and the population at large; uncertainty about Soviet motivations in light of their willingness to test the Strategic Arms Limitation Talks (SALT) Agreements of May 1972 to their limits and perhaps beyond; the emergence of a Soviet blue-water navy that has the potential to extend Soviet political influence beyond the Eurasian land mass for the first time in a truly significant fashion; the failure of Soviety policy to encourage peaceful settlement of the dispute in the Middle East or to assist the United States in extricating itself more easily from Vietnam; the disruptive role played by the Soviet Union in Portugal following the demise of the Salazar régime; Soviet military assistance in and co-operation with the Cuban intervention in the Angolan civil war; and the continued repression of human rights in the Soviet Union that constitutes a clear violation of the Helsinki Agreement of 1975 have, taken together, soured much of the American public on the ability of the United States and the Soviet Union to move from a relationship of confrontation to a relationship of co-operation.[2] Given the increased vulnerability of fixed-based systems and the introduction of new weapons whose numbers are enormously difficult to verify — the cruise missile is a prominent but not a sole example — it appears that technological developments as well as deep political differences will stand in the way of curbing Soviet-American military competition.

The problem of nuclear proliferation, while a matter of concern since 1945, has taken on new urgency in the last few years. After the

People's Republic of China exploded a nuclear device in October 1964, there was a similar sense of urgency which in retrospect was unwarranted. Why was this the case? It appears that a number of significant factors related to the spread of nuclear weapons were not well understood. Security guarantees helped to reassure some threshold countries and at the same time constrain their nuclear appetites. Domestic opposition to the nuclear option remained intense in a number of societies. The great economic and technological costs needed to launch a nuclear weapons programme were more than many nations could bear. The lack of a serious threat to the security of many states removed the necessity to acquire nuclear weapons. And, perhaps most importantly, the weapons-grade material required to manufacture nuclear bombs was simply unobtainable for many régimes that otherwise might have taken the nuclear option.

In recent years, however, the barriers provided by each of these factors have been lowered. Security guarantees, particularly those involving the United States, are, in the aftermath of the Vietnam War, less reassuring and less constraining than they were a decade ago. Domestic opposition in a number of threshold states has weakened; indeed, the acquisition of nuclear weapons is seen in many parts of the world as a highly prestigious development. Economic and technological costs, while still great, are more affordable, especially for the rich oil-exporting nations. Because military power continues to become more diffuse, nations in various regions see threats to their security where none existed before. And, with the likely spread of nuclear energy facilities for electrical power generation, stimulated by the availability of this technology and the 1973 Organization of Petroleum Exporting Countries (OPEC) oil embargo, the proliferation of enriched uranium and plutonium is bound to accelerate unless there is an embargo by the nuclear supplier states on the sale of uranium enrichment and spent fuel reprocessing plants.

The question has been raised, particularly in many of the less developed countries, whether so-called horizontal proliferation can be slowed in the absence of meaningful strategic arms control by the superpowers. There is no blanket solution to this question. For basically there are three types of states that might seek to acquire nuclear weapons: those fearful for their national security, such as Israel and South Africa; those seeking great power status, such as Iran and Brazil; and those states led by leaders who seek self-glorification through possession of nuclear weapons, such as Libya and Uganda. It is almost certainly correct that countries in the first group are virtually insensitive to superpower nuclear controls. They seek weapons of mass destruction to be used as a deterrent to prevent the demise of their national sovereignty, and this objective is totally divorced from any actions taken by the superpowers with respect to the management of their own strategic relationship. Because leaders of states in the third category function, at least in part, on the basis of highly personalised and perhaps non-rational considerations, this group of states is also unlikely to be affected by progress in SALT. It is possible, however, that the domestic debate in the governments of some of the states in the second category could be influenced by Soviet-American progress in nuclear arms control, at least to the extent of strengthening the arguments of those opposed to their nation acquiring nuclear weapons. Moreover, such progress will, at a minimum, strip away the argument of lack of progress in SALT which is used as an excuse by proponents of nuclear weapons acquisition within many of the threshold states. SALT progress, therefore, is a necessary but by no means a sufficient condition for nuclear proliferation to be held in check.

With respect to European security, the United States and the Soviet Union have had common and conflicting objectives. The United States seeks to maintain a stable military balance in Central Europe, one that will preserve the cohesiveness of the Atlantic Alliance and that will deter a westward invasion by the Warsaw Pact forces. But at the same time, it has been a central feature of American policy to keep the Federal Republic of Germany well ensconced within the Alliance, divided from the East, and shorn of an independent nuclear weapons capability. The Soviets, on the other hand, have sought the legitimisation of their sphere of influence in Eastern Europe, desire to maintain military superiority *vis-à-vis* NATO and hope to preserve a divided Germany. They may wish to exploit their military advantage over the West to gain economic and political concessions from the nations of Western Europe, to remove American presence from the Continent, and eventually to produce a Western Europe whose freedom of manoeuvre is constrained by the extent to which it conforms with Soviet policy.[3] The ability of the West to neutralise Soviet ambitions in Europe remains a permanent challenge.

The Role of Arms Control

Arms control has a role to play, although a limited one, in each of the areas touched upon in this brief paper. With respect to SALT, the highest-priority concern should be the elimination of a credible first-strike threat against land-based missiles. This involves a reduction in the number of high-accuracy ICBMs deployed with multiple independently targetable re-entry vehicles (MIRVs) as well as strict limitations on the number of full-range flight tests in order to reduce confidence in the reliability of those systems. (A far greater confidence is required for a first-strike against missile silos than for a retaliatory attack which might be launched not only at opposing forces but against high-value civil targets as well.) Limitations on other systems, such as cruise missiles, forward-based aircraft and other systems capable of delivering nuclear weapons to the homeland of the superpowers are desirable but far less crucial from the standpoint of strategic stability.[4]

Nuclear proliferation has at least a hope of being managed if a number of political-military and energy-related measures are adopted. These include the completion of a Soviet-American comprehensive test ban, a nuclear supplier's agreement to ban the exporting of uranium enrichment and reprocessing plants, the establishment of multinational fuel cycle facilities with arrangements to guarantee fuel supplies, the strengthening of the safeguards régime of the International Atomic Energy Agency, and possibly the forging of some no-first-use agreements that are constructed so as not to undermine Allied confidence in American security guarantees.[5] But it must be realised that some degree of nuclear proliferation is highly likely, given the objectives of many of the threshold states. With co-operation among these states, exclusive of supplier state involvement, leading inexorably to nuclear weapon development — for example, close linkages are already apparent among Iran, Brazil, South Africa and India — those opposed to nuclear proliferation have only limited means at their disposal to slow the process.

Prospects for arms control in Central Europe are not at all bright. The Mutual Balanced Force Reduction (MBFR) talks in Vienna have been deadlocked since they were initiated in 1973. They remain greatly dependent on progress at SALT, they involve on the Western side a complex web of domestic political and intra-Alliance problems and they are being held in a climate marked by a significant Soviet military build-up since the talks were initiated and an unexpected degree of ferment in Eastern Europe as a consequence of governments being held accountable for their actions by citizens who have chosen to interpret the signing of the Helsinki Agreement both literally and legally.

On balance the prospects for arms control are marginal rather than substantial. Particularly with respect to the Soviet Union, it must be remembered that military force is its principal — perhaps its only —

route to political influence. For the Soviet régime to permit itself to have nullified through arms control the one element of its strength is far beyond what we have any reason to expect.

Notes

1. This conclusion is, of course, not new. It is just frequently forgotten. A detailed analysis leading to similar findings is Kenneth Waltz, *Man, the State and War* (New York, 1959).
2. While the argument can be made that many of these developments are merely reactions to American initiatives, or are reflections of Russian tradition, bureaucratic rigidity or concern about the Chinese threat, many students of Soviet affairs are now less willing to assign weight to these factors than they are to the view that these actions reflect the Soviet leadership's malevolent intent towards the West.
3. At the same time much of Western Europe seeks to preserve the NATO tripwire defence that would trigger an American nuclear response in the event of Western Europe being invaded, while in the meantime reaping the economic benefits of American military presence on the Continent. The Eastern European states, meanwhile, hope in the short term to increase their room for manoeuvre *vis-à-vis* the Soviet Union, and in the long term to witness the removal of Soviet control over their territory. But by and large the aspirations of the Western and Eastern Europeans are dominated by the policies of the superpowers.
4. For a review of a number of proposals for the current and subsequent rounds of SALT see Paul Doty, Albert Carnesale and Michael Nacht, 'The Race to Control Nuclear Arms', *Foreign Affairs*, LV (1976–7), pp.119-32.
5. These strategies are elaborated in Michael Nacht, 'The United States in a World of Nuclear Powers', *The Annals of the American Academy of Political and Social Science*, March 1977, pp.162-174

9 A DIFFERENT APPROACH TO ARMS CONTROL –
RECIPROCAL UNILATERAL RESTRAINT

Herbert Scoville, Jr.

Formal arms control negotiations, such as the Strategic Arms Limitation Talks (SALT) and Mutual Balanced Force Reductions (MBFR) may have outlived their usefulness. At the very least they will have to be supplemented by other approaches if reasonable progress is to be made in controlling the armaments race. Such negotiations have proved too slow: SALT officially began in 1969 after several years of preliminary discussions and produced as the conclusion to Phase I, the Anti-Ballistic Missile (ABM) Treaty and the Interim Agreement on Offensive Weapons of May 1972. SALT II was even slower: in November 1974, the Vladivostok Accords established ceilings on strategic offensive delivery vehicles, but little progress has been made in the two years since then to put these into effect with formal agreements. The MBFR negotiations have been even less productive; no concrete results have been achieved in three years, and there is no expectation of early agreement in the future.

Meanshile, technical advances are clearly outpacing negotiations. Since SALT began the United States has completed the development of and has deployed two missile systems equipped with multiple independently targetable re-entry vehicles (MIRVs) – the Minuteman II and Poseidon. Since the 1972 Moscow Interim Agreement, the Soviet Union has begun testing and is now beginning deployment of four new inter-continental ballistic missile (ICBM) systems, three of which can deliver MIRVs and a new submarine-launched ballistic missile (SLBM). The United States, also since the Interim Agreement of 1972, has started developing and is now testing strategic cruise missiles, which can be launched from sea or air. These new strategic weapons have now become a major road-block to the translation of the Vladivostok Accords into treaty commitments. Similarly, NATO is reportedly deploying new types of nuclear weapons despite an offer, which has not been accepted in MBFR, to cut back on its tactical nuclear stockpiles if the Soviet Union would reduce some conventional forces.

Modern weapons technology is also becoming so complicated and also frequently has applications to so many types of weapons that it is often difficult to spell out in a formal agreement the limitations with sufficient detail to preclude evasion. In the case of SALT I Agreements, this has led to a number of accusations and counter-accusations of violations. Some of these are the inevitable result of attempts by opponents to discredit the arms control process, but others are the natural result of advancing weapons technology. The Standing Consultative Commission (SCC) established by the ABM Treaty has proved useful as a means of clarifying some of these legitimate misunderstandings. Actually the ABM Treaty is a good example of a well-drawn agreement which placed restrictions on technical advances as well as on the sizes of existing systems. However, it will be hard to duplicate this success in the offensive weapons area.

Furthermore, while the formal negotiations have been going on, they have frequently become the *raison d'être* for continuing arms development and procurement. Almost never has either nation stopped a programme in mid-stream during a negotiation because it anticipated the achievement of a future agreement. Instead, quite the contrary, continued procurement has been specifically justified to provide bargaining chips for the negotiating table. Unfortunately, these chips, once paid for, are almost never given up and only serve to force the negotiators to be satisfied with higher levels or even to forgo any agreement altogether. For example, in 1971, when procurement of MIRVs could no longer be justified on military grounds, because it became apparent that the Soviet Union was not deploying a large ABM system, they were justified as bargaining chips for SALT. The net result was that in the Vladivostock Accords the ceiling had to be set at a level of 1,320 MIRVed delivery vehicles, a level that allows both sides to have a counter-force capability against the ICBMs of the other. Secretary of State Henry Kissinger has confessed that he wished he had understood and addressed the MIRV problem in SALT I. Similarly, he approved starting a cruise missile programme in the summer of 1972 as a bargaining chip for SALT II, and now this has been the greatest stumbling block to achieving any SALT II Agreement. Likewise, the MBFR negotiations have prevented any early reductions in American forces in Europe. The pressures in Congress led by Senator Mike Mansfield to cut these back studdenly evaporated when MBFR began.

A basic criterion for arms control agreements between the East and the West has been that the forces of the two sides must have 'essential equivalence'. However, 'bargaining chips' and 'essential equivalence' are incompatible. Each side must seek to match the bragaining chips of the other, and this stimulates the arms race to ever-higher levels.

Even after arms control treaties have been formalised, they can become the excuse for new arms programmes. If a certain type of weapon is not included in the agreement or if an agreed ceiling has not yet been reached, then the treaties can become a justification for going ahead with programmes which may not be needed for security purposes. For example, the United States had less than 2,200 strategic delivery vehicles at the time when the Vladivostok Accord set the ceiling at 2,400. Secretary of Defense James Schlesinger then used this ceiling as an excuse for procuring additional delivery vehicles which had not previously been in the approved defence programme. Likewise, the American submarine-launched cruise missile programme was supported by American naval authorities because it was the only new development alternative left open to the Navy by the Moscow Interim Agreement. The Soviet Union, in turn, proceeded to develop and then deploy new larger ICBMs to replace those then in existence because the Interim Agreement prevented it from adding to the numbers of ICBMs but placed no firm restrictions on replacing old missiles by new ones.

A new approach to arms control, or at least a supplement to present ones, might be called Reciprocal Unilateral Restraint (RUR). One nation could announce that it was not going to proceed with a new weapons development or deployment provided that future events did not indicate that such restraint would prejudice its security. It could then watch the reaction of the other side which, in turn, might exercise reciprocal restraint either in the same or a related area. Force reductions could be made in the same manner; one side discarding a given number of its delivery vehicles or withdrawing a division from a certain theatre and then await the reaction of the other.

Such unilateral restraint can be exercised today without any adverse security consequences to either the United States or the Soviet Union. The thesis that there is a delicate balance of terror is a myth which has no doundation in fact. Both the superpowers have forces far in excess of those needed to deter an attack by the other. The Americans could suspend the procurement of the B-1 or the Trident submarines or a follow-on ICBM without any security risk regardless of any Soviet action that could be taken in the next five years. The Soviet Union, in turn, could halt the replacement of its existing ICBM by the newly tested models without any danger that the United States could take military or political advantage of this restraint. Arms control policies should take advantage of the extraordinary stability of the strategic balance today.

RUR would be a far more satisfactory and cheaper way of achieving arms control than buying bargaining chips and then having to develop some formal agreement to get rid of them. It would also be much safer; mutual security would have been enhanced if MIRVs had never been deployed. Now we have to build new generations to counter the MIRV threat.

Furthermore, it is an approach which has proved successful in the past. In 1969 President Richard Nixon made the unilateral decision that henceforth the United States would cease all research, development and procurement of biological weapons and toxins. Following this initiative, the Soviet Union indicated its willingness to negotiate a formal treaty banning all such offensive biological weapons (BW) programmes and the BW Convention incorporating such provisions was signed by 112 nations in 1972. Without such a unilateral American action, it is most unlikely that this success would have been achieved. Earlier, President John F. Kennedy used similar tactics in achieving the Limited Test Ban Treaty of 1963. In June of that year he announced that the United States would halt all further nuclear testing provided that the Soviet Union exercised similar restraint, and two months later the Limited Test Ban Treaty was signed in Moscow. Such rapid progress in arms control is rare indeed.

Furthermore, RUR has the great advantage of maintaining flexibility in the light of changes in the political climate or in the technical situation. Precise details need not be spelled out and new steps could be taken to assimilate technical advances as they occur. Verification would be simpler, since every detail in a formal agreement would not have to be carefully monitored to ensure that violations were not occurring. Thus, neither the Soviet failure to finish dismantling its old ICBM silos by the time its new submarines began sea trials nor the United States temporarily covering its new ICBM silos to allow concrete to harden, both technical SALT violations, could be ignored because they have no security significance. Instead, each nation could look for major developments that could affect the military balance. This would be a reversion to the type of verification which is used continuously in the absence of any arms control agreements. Intelligence sources are continuously employed to determine whether the other side's programme presents a significant threat to security.

If some major political event occurred or if one nation appeared to be taking advantage of restraint by the other, then the action could be reversed without creating a major international incident. The abrogation of treaties can in themselves create international crises. However, this flexibility is two-edged, since it has the disadvantage of making it easier for a nation to change its mind. The formality of a treaty makes it possible for a nation's leaders to resist opposition cries for a change in policy. Therefore, the idea of formal treaties should not be discarded entirely, and it may be that only the order of the procedures should be reversed. The nations could exercise restraint on their individual programmes and then these actions could be later formalised in an agreement, as was done in the case of the BW and the Limited Test Ban Treaties.

If the United States and the Soviet Union were to adopt the strategy of Reciprocal Unilateral Restraint, what types of actions they undertake? If this new posture is to be effective, the restraining actions must be meaningful. It would not be enough for a nation to forgo a weapons programme which it never had any intention of supporting. Thus, the removal from active forces of obsolete ineffective weapons would not serve the RUR objectives. For example, in the mid-1960s the United States offered to destroy its B-47 bomber fleet if the Soviets would reciprocate. Since it was well known that the United States could no longer afford to keep these old aeroplanes in operation anyway, this offer fell on deaf ears. Because of this offer, the B-47s were kept in the inventory at considerable expense several years longer than necessary.

In the strategic weapons area, restraint should be designed to increase stability and reduce incentives for any nation to initiate a nuclear strike. Vulnerable weapons systems could be phased out while simultaneously programmes could be carried out to enhance the invulnerability of those remaining. For example, the United States could halt its development and testing of its new ICBM (MX), maneouverable re-entry vehicles (MARVs), and the MK12A Minuteman warhead programmes, all of which are designed to improve its counter-force capabilities. The Soviet Union, in turn, might forgo further deployment of MIRVs on its heavy ICBMs which are viewed as a counter-force threat by American planners. The number of MIRVed ICBMs, which will inevitably be thought to be vulnerable in the distant future, could be cut back; thereby simultaneously reducing the number of provocative targets and the threat to destroy the other side's ICBM force.

The safety and control of nuclear weapons should, whenever possible, be enhanced so that the opportunities for launching nuclear weapons unnecessarily or by accident are circumscribed. Weapons programmes that widen the firebreak between conventional and nuclear conflicts should be supported while those that make the decision to use nuclear weapons easier, such as the tactical 'mini-nukes', should be forsworn. Precision-guided conventional munitions, which increase the effectiveness of defences and reduce the need to rely on nuclear weapons, are types whose development should be supported.

In the field of sea warfare, programmes which threaten the sea-based deterrent should be avoided, and attempts to improve tactical anti-submarine warfare should be directed towards methods which do not threaten ballistic-missile submarines. Naval mines with conventional explosives have tremendous potential in this respect. These could be used to create barriers closing off large portions of the ocean to submarines which might attack shipping. This would be a means of reducing the violence of the conflict at sea, and the need for large and expensive surface fleets without at the same time prejudicing the invulnerability of the ballisitc submarine deterrent. Surface or sub-surface vessels designed for continuous long-term tracking and destroying submarines, on the other hand, are destabilising and should not be procured.

In sum, the time is now ripe to alter our approach to arms control and review the order of current procedures. There are many areas where both the United States and the Soviet Union could exercise unilateral restraint which would enhance the security of both countries, decrease the risk of nuclear war, and save vast sums of money. Once some steps have been taken in this direction, it would be easier for others to follow. Formal treaty commitments emboyding the actions which had already been unilaterally taken could probably be effected more easily in such a climate than when both sides are racing to procure additional bargaining chips. RUR may be the only way to escape from the morass in which arms control negotiations are currently trapped.

10 A NEW APPROACH TO STRATEGIC ARMS LIMITATION AND REDUCTION

William Epstein

The Proliferation of Nuclear Weapons

More than thirty years have passed since Hiroshima and, indeed, since the Baruch plan was put forward in June 1946 as the first attempt to rid the world of the threat posed by nuclear weapons. During the intervening years, the world has witnessed an uprecedented and almost unimaginable escalation of the arms race. In particular, the nuclear arms race has led to a vastly greater accumulation in killing power than was ever dreamed of in the early post-war days. The amount of overkill that has been generated is, for any practical purpose, beyond the capability of the human mind to grasp.

In the past thirty years, in addition to the United States, the Soviet Union (in 1949), Great Britain (in 1952), France (in 1960) and China (in 1964) have become nuclear weapons powers. In 1974 India exploded a nuclear device for peaceful purposes. Since there is no essential technological difference between a device exploded for military or peaceful purposes, we must regard India as the sixth nuclear power.

While all the first five of the nuclear weapons powers have developed a spectrum of nuclear weapons ranging from tactical to strategic, the United States and the Soviet Union are each far ahead of the combined strength of the other three nuclear powers, and they are therefore regarded as superpowers. Appendix 1 sets forth the growth in the comparative strength of these superpowers in strategic nuclear arms up to 1975. It does not take into account the number or size of warheads or of nuclear bombs carried aboard bombers; nor does it indicate the types or numbers of intermediate-, medium- and short-range ballistic missiles or tactical nuclear weapons.

The Vladivostok Agreement of November 1974, the result of the Strategic Arms Limitation Talks (SALT) was hailed as a 'breakthrough' that put a 'cap' on the strategic arms race. It incorporated the previous Interim Agreement and fixed a ceiling on the number of all strategic nuclear weapons that the two superpowers can possess until 31 December 1985, on the basis of equality between them. Each side is permitted to have 2,400 strategic delivery vehicles, including land-based inter-continental ballistic missiles (ICBMs), submarine-launched ballistic missiles (SLBMs) and heavy bombers. Of that number, 1,320 missiles can be armed with multiple independently targetable re-entry vehicles (MIRVs). The agreement was said to establish ceilings well below the levels that otherwise could be expected to be operative in ten years. But the ceilings established are above the levels that each side had at the time, and are even higher than those envisaged for 1977 under the Interim Agreement. As regards the number of MIRVs permitted, the figure of 1,320 represents a considerable increase for both countries. The United States had previously announced that it would MIRV 550 land-based Minutemen and 496 SLBM Poseidon missiles, for a total of 1,046 MIRVed missiles. By 1975 it had MIRVed about 600 of the missiles. Thus the ceiling of 1,320 represents a considerably higher level than the United States had or planned to have. The Soviet Union has just begun to deploy MIRVs. It is developing several new MIRVed missiles, including the SS-17, the SS-18 (a replacement for the SS-9) and the SS-19 (a replacement for the SS-11), each with four to eight heavy warheads. It has not announced how many of its land or sea-based missiles it intended to MIRV, but 1,320 obviously represents a very high and costly ceiling that will take it several years to reach. The Vladivostok Agreement, moreover, put no limit on either the number of warheads that can be placed on each missile or the size of 'throw-weight' of the warheads. The agreement also puts no limitation on improvements or 'modernisation', of missiles by increasing their accuracy and manoeuvrability.

On 6 December 1974, the then Secretary of Defense, James Schlesinger, said that he foresaw a need for larger, restructured strategic forces for the United States as a result of the agreement, including 12 instead of ten of the monster Trident submarines (each having 24 missiles with 14 to 20 warheads, for a total of about 5,000 nuclear warheads), larger MIRVed ICBMs, and a new bomber. This programme, he said, would require 'some upward adjustment' in the strategic arms budget. It is thus clear that the 'limitation' envisaged by the Vladivostok Agreement, while it will put an eventual cap or ceiling on the number of strategic nuclear weapons, permits an expansion in both the quantitative and qualitative nuclear arms race. Since no limit is fixed on the number or size of warheads on the 1,320 MIRVed missiles or of nuclear arms carried in bombers, each of the two superpowers can build 20,000 or more strategic nuclear warheads under the agreement. For all practical purposes, both the United States and the Soviet Union are acquiring nuclear destructive capability approaching infinity.

In 1974, it was estimated by American government officials that the total strategic nuclear arsenal of the United States was sufficient to drop 36 bombs on each of the 218 Soviet cities with a population of 100,000 or more. The Soviet Union had 11 nuclear weapons for each comparably sized American city.

Despite the weird calculations of many nuclear-war strategists, there are not really a hundred targets for nuclear attack in either the Soviet Union or the United States, and only sick minds could think of destroying that many cities in either country. Each of the several thousand nuclear warheads on either side could obliterate a city much more thoroughly than Hiroshima and Nagasaki were destroyed. What purpose, then, can these weapons conceivably serve? If the purpose is to ensure mutual deterrence, this could equally well be achieved with no more than 50 to 100 submarine-launched ballistic missiles on each side. Yet the mad race goes on. And continuing vertical proliferation will of necessity breed further horizontal proliferation.

One of the reasons given for maintaining such an unconsciously high level of overkill capacity is the 'counter-force' argument. According to the counter-force theory, strategic nuclear arms should be used not for the hideous task of knocking out cities and their populations but rather against military targets such as missile silos, amunition dumps and nuclear bases, and for this purpose two or more warheads are needed for each target; in addition, sufficient arms must be kept in reserve for a second-strike capability against the enemy's cities if he launches a first strike against one's strategic nuclear sites. What this argument conveniently overlooks is that a nuclear exchange of such magnitude would poison most of the inhabitants of the northern hemisphere with radioactive fall-out and perhaps destroy much of the ozone layer of the earth's atmosphere, with all the unknown dangers that that might entail. In either case, whether the arms were used against cities or against nuclear targets, such an exchange would constitute a form of international insanity and suicide.

Apart from the MIRVs discussed, the United States is presently developing a new, more accurate manoeuvrable missile called manoeuvrable re-entry vehicles (MARV) and there is talk of the United States and the Soviet Union building mobile ICBMs, although the Americans announced at the time of the SALT 1 Agreements that they would regard the building of these as contrary to the spirit of those agreements. In addition, the United States is proceeding to develop a highly accurate long-range (up to 2,500 miles) nuclear cruise missile that could be launched from aircraft, submarines or surface vessels and land within about 10 metres of its target. As previously mentioned, it is also building a third generation of nuclear missile submarines (the Trident) and a new supersonic bomber (the B-1). The Soviet Union for its part is busy trying to catch up with the United States in nuclear weaponry and is still developing MIRVed missiles. It is also developing a new bomber (the Backfire). Current SALT negotiations are reported to have reached an impasse over whether the American cruise missile and the Soviet Backfire bombers are to be considered as strategic weapons (and therefore a proper subject for SALT) and, if so, whether and how there can be some trade-off between them.

At the other end of the nuclear spectrum, the Americans are continuing to develop and improve their tactical and battlefield nuclear weapons. While less is known about the Soviet Union's intention and programme one can expect that it too is developing new generations of tactical nuclear weapons or 'mini-nukes', which tend to blur the line of distinction between nuclear and conventional weapons.

The SALT agreements may have been a diplomatic success. They do tend to stabilise mutual deterrence between the two superpowers, at least for the present, on the basis of each side retaining a second-strike capability. They have also helped to promote the spirit of *détente*. But they have not served to achieve a cessation or any real limitation of the nuclear arms race, far less nuclear disarmament. In fact, many critics of SALT say that these negotiations have served only to replace the quantitative nuclear arms race with a more dangerous qualitative one, and that the action-reaction process that formerly fuelled the nuclear arms race has now been transformed into an internal domestic technological competition for the improvement — if that is the right word — of the accuracy, variety and lethality of weapons that proceeds by a dynamic of its own. It seems that the agreements already concluded, and indeed those now being negotiated, are designed not to halt or reverse the arms race but rather to institutionalise it and regulate it so that it may continue within each country on its own momentum and under conditions of relatively less instability and insecurity for the two great powers— in other words, a blueprint for the continuation of the arms race under agreed-upon terms and conditions.

During the past fifteen years or so, seven multilateral arms control treaties, including the Partial Test Ban Treaty of 1963 and the Non-Proliferation Treaty of 1968, and some ten bilateral American-Soviet treaties, including the SALT 1 agreements and the Vladivostok

Accord, have been concluded. (See Appendix 2 — Chronology of the Development of Nuclear Weapons and of Arms Control Measures.) Despite this abundance of arms control agreements, the arms race and in particular the nuclear arms race is proceeding apace. It has not been stopped or even slowed down. One measure of the escalation of the arms race is to be found in the shocking growth of military expenditure. Global military expenditure in 1960 totalled about $100,000,000,000 in 1975 was approaching $300,000,000,000. Making allowances for inflation, in terms of *constant* dollars there has been an increase of nearly 50 per cent. The disarmers appear to be losing the battle to control the arms race. Progress in military technology seems to have far outrun progress in arms control, not to speak of genuine disarmament. The 'incremental' or step-by-step approach which led to the conclusion of the multitude of arms control agreements seems, moreover, to have exhausted itself. The negotiations appear to have lost their momentum and to be reaching a stalemate. The small additional steps that are now being negotiated raise doubts as to whether they are more for 'cosmetic' purposes than for real arms control or disarmament. And there seems to be little likelihood in the near future of significant progress on even these small steps. What is most startling and depressing is that, if all the negotiations now proceeding at SALT II, at the Conference of the Committee on Disarmament (CCD) in Geneva and at the Force Reduction Talks in Vienna, were to succeed in their stated objectives, an eventuality much to be desired, the technological arms race and the massive military expenditures would continue to escalate.

Moreover, the continued vertical proliferation of nuclear weapons by the nuclear powers, and the failure of the nuclear powers to live up to their obligations under the Non-Proliferation Treaty can hardly fail to result in the horizontal proliferation of nuclear weapons to additional non-nuclear powers. The latter tend to regard the 1974 Threshold Test Ban Treaty and the 1976 Treaty on Peaceful Nuclear Explosives (which permit military and peaceful nuclear explosions up to a level of 150 kilotons — about ten times the size of the Hiroshima bombs) as evidence that the two superpowers are unable or unwilling to halt the nuclear arms race.

Both horizontal and vertical proliferation will lead to an increasing likelihood of non-governmental nuclear proliferation, that is the acquisition of nuclear weapons by terrorists and other politically or criminally motivated groups. The ongoing proliferation has changed many of the old rules and concepts. The likelihood is increasing that a nuclear war could occur as a result of accident, terrorism and blackmail. Some radical new approaches are thus necessary if the world is to avoid a nuclear disaster.

Proposals for a New Approach to Nuclear Disarmament

Very few people recall or know that six years ago the United Nations declared the decade of the 1970s as the Disarmament Decade and asked the CCD at Geneva to work out a comprehensive programme of disarmament to provide guidelines for future work. Unfortunately, due to the opposition of the two co-chairmen — the Soviet Union and the United States — which were interested only in SALT, no serious thought was given to working out either a comprehensive programme or even a new statement of principles and goals.

If progress is to be made towards genuine and substantial nuclear arms control and disarmament and the reduction of the crushing burden of military expenditure, some new thinking as well as new approaches are necessary. Perhaps a possible way out of the difficulty would be to raise our sights and to aim at a more comprehensive general plan with clear objectives for both nuclear and conventional disarmament, and within a fixed but flexible target period, rather than to continue in the present haphazard way towards limited and isolated piecemeal objectives.

Practically every measure of arms control and disarmament — whether nuclear or conventional and whether it concerns armies, navies or air forces — is interlinked with every other measure from both the national and international points of view. Each step affects the broad picture of national and international security and is also interlinked in this interdependent world with problems of development and economic security. Hence larger package agreements might be easier to achieve, because it would be easier to attain a broad balance of measures than would concentrating on narrow unconnected measures. Moreover, the problem of verification would become simpler because of the reinforcing effect of controls for several measures. A comprehensive plan for real arms control and disarmament could also attract public interest and provide the necessary incentive for top political leaders, high governmental officials and scholars to give priority to the achievement of the goals and to overcome the inertia that is one of the elements helping to keep the arms race going.

The two superpowers which possess the overwhelming military forces — conventional as well as nuclear — have the main responsibility for leading the world towards peace and disarmament. The experience of the past, however, shows that it is the smaller powers, and in particular the Third World and non-aligned powers, that have made most of the proposals for arms control and disarmament and that have pressed hardest for their adoption, often in the face of superpower reluctance or opposition. For example, each year the smaller powers push many resolutions for disarmament through the General Assembly of the United Nations. In 1975, 25 resolutions were adopted, most of them without the support of the two superpowers. For years, such UN resolutions as those for a comprehensive test ban and for progress towards real quantitative reductions and qualitative limitations of strategic nuclear arms have been ignored or remained unfulfilled.

The non-nuclear and smaller powers have thus become increasingly frustrated and disillusioned with the failure of the nuclear powers to achieve any halt to the nuclear arms race. But there are many ways whereby the nuclear powers could demonstrate their 'good faith' and the seriousness of their intentions to stop the nuclear arms race 'at an early date', to which they are in any case pledged by Article VI of the Non-Proliferation Treaty (NPT). Perhaps the most important first steps they should consider taking are more in the nature of 'political' measures, aimed at what might be called psychological denuclearisation of nations and peoples. These measures would be designed to reduce the psychological and political concentration on the possible use of nuclear weapons and to reduce their role in human and national consciousness. The two most important are:

(1) A declaration by all nuclear powers *not to use or threaten to use nuclear weapons against any non-nuclear state that does not have any nuclear weapons in its territory.* China and France have already announced their support for such a declaration, and in 1966 the Soviet Union submitted a similar proposal under the 'Kosygin Formula'. The United States and Great Britain have also given a somewhat similar pledge to the countries that are members of the Latin American Nuclear Free Zone under the Treaty of Tlatelolco. Hence it should not be beyond the ingenuity of diplomats to work out some agreed formula for such a declaration. If each of the nuclear powers also undertook to give some positive security assurances that it would, subject to the UN Charter obligations, come to the aid of any such state attacked or threatened with nuclear weapons, this would help to strengthen the feelings of confidence and security of non-nuclear states.

(2) A declaration of *non-first-use of nuclear weapons by each of the nuclear powers.* This would at a single stroke reduce nuclear weapons to a legal status similar to that of chemical and biological weapons

under the Geneva Protocol.

These two political measures would also pave the way psychologically and morally for the adoption of a concrete programme of disarmament. The programme of measures discussed below is not intended to be exhaustive; it merely indicates a number of nuclear arms control and disarmament measures, some of which are meaningful and important, that the author regards as both logical and feasible in a world of relatively stable, bi-polar mutual nuclear deterrence and of developing *détente* between the superpowers. The nuclear disarmament measures are the most important and are given priority, but conventional disarmament is also a necessary part of any programme. The nuclear and conventional measures will have a mutually reinforcing effect.

(1) The most important and probably the easiest step would be for the superpowers to agree on an *underground test ban,* to which they are already committed. It would be best if all underground nuclear explosions, whether for military or peaceful purposes, were banned, until an international régime was set up that would authorise or license the nuclear powers to conduct peaceful nuclear explosions either for themselves or for non-nuclear powers. A mutual moratorium for a fixed period of years on all underground explosions, pending the working out of a treaty for such an international régime, would have a beneficial effect and would indicate the good faith and goodwill of the superpowers. It would also make an important impression if the three nuclear powers, which are parties to the 1963 Test Ban Treaty, would announce that they were beginning immediate negotiations to draft a treaty banning all underground tests for military purposes, with a view to completing the treaty within a year.

(2) The superpowers should agree on the immediate *cessation of the production of fissionable material for weapons purposes* and the earmarking of all future production of enriched uranium and plutonium for peaceful purposes. In fact, each of the three nuclear powers that are parties to the NPT could unilaterally announce its intention to take these steps. Back in 1964, all three unilaterally cut back their production of fissionable material for weapons purposes without any talk of verification and inspection, and there were no charges nor any suspicion of evasions. All the three nuclear powers have more than sufficient nuclear weapons and fissionable material for weapons than they can use, and they have been unilaterally cutting back their production as it is; there is no reason why they could not announce a complete cut-off of such production. While it would not be a very significant limitation, it would at least have the merit of meeting one of

the long-standing demands of the non-nuclear powers, and, if made permament by treaty, would signify the intention of the nuclear powers to de-emphasise weapons and shift their interest to the peaceful, civilian uses of fissionable materials. It would also make it possible for them to accept the safeguards of the International Atomic Energy Agency (IAEA) over all their peaceful nuclear activities, including the entire fuel cycle, and remove one of the discriminating aspects of the NPT.

(3) The two superpowers should begin immediate negotiations to *reduce and phase out all land-based ICBMs* with a view to their elimination within a fixed period of time, say six to ten years. Instead of each building up to the ceiling of 2,400 strategic arms (1,320 of them MIRVs) by 1985, as permitted by the Vladivostok Agreement, they should announce instead that their objective was to eliminate the 1,618 Soviet and 1,054 American ICBMs by that date. Because of the remarkable and increasing accuracy of missiles, the fixed land-based missiles are becoming increasingly vulnerable to attack and are rapidly becoming obsolete as second-strike weapons. Early in 1974, in fact, the Federation of American Scientists issued a call to eliminate all ICBMs in three stages of five years each. Several American officials, including the Director of the Arms Control and Disarmament Agency (ACDA), saw merit in the proposal. Since missile silos are easily subject to surveillance by satellite, the complete elimination of ICBMs would obviate the problem of verification that would arise under the Vladivostok Agreement, which would require that the number of MIRVed missiles be verified. If it would help to obtain Chinese participation in an agreement, some provision might be made for them to make and retain a very limited number of ICBMs, say about 50.

(4) The two superpowers should also begin immediate negotiations to *reduce their SLBMs drastically.* If the concept of stabilising the deterrent on the basis of mutual assured destruction − that is, by each side's retaining a second-strike capability − has any validity, its effectiveness would be greatly increased by each side's agreeing to limit its strategic nuclear forces to sea-based missiles and at a much lower, balanced level. Each side now has a tremendous, useless overkill capability which it attempts to justify on the basis of matching the other side in order to deter or cope with a counter-force strike. The security of both superpowers and of the whole world would be vastly enhanced if the superpowers were to stabilise their deterrents on the basis of a small number of SLBMs, which will continue to be practically invulnerable to attack for as far ahead as anyone can see. This, of course, raises the questions of how much assured destruction capability is

enough to deter an attack. In the author's opinion, 10 per cent of the missile-firing submarines permitted by the 1972 SALT agreements (62 for the Soviet Union and 44 for the United States) would be more than sufficient for any conceivable rational purpose. If the Soviet Union were permitted to retain, say, seven missile-firing submarines (with 112 SLBMs) and the United States, say, five submarines (with 80 SLBMs), it should be more than enough to ensure mutual deterrence on a more stable basis than at present. Such an agreement might also ban the construction and deployment of the Trident submarines, which would have 24 missiles with up to 20 or 24 warheads each instead of the 16 missiles with ten warheads each on Poseidon submarines. The author believes that both Great Britain, with four nuclear-missile submarines, and France, which will have five such submarines, although without MIRVed missiles today, have very credible deterrent capabilities — even if only half of their submarines are normally at sea at any one time. When one contemplates the fact that the Poseidon missiles are MIRVed with an average of ten warheads each, it can be argued that even the limited number of SLBMs suggested here, with the United States having some 800 warheads and the Soviet Union (if it also builds ten warheads for each missile) having 1,120 warheads, is much more than would be required for mutual deterrence. Their numbers could, of course, be reduced further in subsequent negotiations. Since the submarines and their launchers can easily be photographed by 'spy satellites', which are the 'national technical means of verification' officially sanctioned by the 1972 SALT agreements, no problems of verification or of international inspection would arise.

(5) Each of the two superpowers has unilaterally reduced the number of its long-range bombers over the past decade to 432 for the United States and 135 for the Soviet Union. Many authorities are convinced that the day of the bomber is past and that these strategic arms are obsolescent. Although military establishments still argue the necessity of a 'triad' of strategic arms (ICBMs, SLBMs and bombers) for greater flexibility, many experts regard this attitude as having more to do with inter-service rivalry than with defence needs. In any case, if both superpowers were to agree to *reduce and eliminate their strategic bombers,* the balance of deterrence would be preserved and net security enhanced. In this case, too, since bombers are difficult or impossible to hide, verification would not be an obstacle.

(6) The two superpowers should also begin immediate negotiations to *ban the testing, manufacture and deployment of new strategic nuclear weapons and delivery systems.* While it is practically impossible

to ban research and development of new nuclear weapons because of the difficulties of verification, it is easy to monitor a ban on their testing and deployment. If they cannot be tested and deployed there is not much likelihood of their being manufactured, either openly or secretly. A ban of the nature proposed here should begin with a prohibition on the flight testing of missiles and other nuclear delivery vehicles, including long-range bombers, which is easy to verify. Such a ban, coupled with that on all underground nuclear testing (as proposed here above), would put a very effective limitation on the development of new nuclear weapons systems and on the technological strategic nuclear arms race. It would mean ending the programme for the Trident submarine, MARVs, cruise missiles, mobile land-based missiles, and new types of long-range bombers. It would mark a giant step toward the objective of a 'cessation of the nuclear arms race at an early date'. It would also represent a major increase in international security by removing the fears — and the possibility — of either side's achieving a breakthrough in nuclear weaponry that could threaten the stability of mutual deterrence.

(7) While it would be much more difficult to verify a *ban on new tactical nuclear weapons and 'mini-nukes',* the superpowers could begin negotiations for pulling them back from frontier and border areas separating the NATO and Warsaw Pact forces in Europe and drastically reducing their numbers. The United States, with over 20,000 tactical nuclear weapons, of which some 7,000 are in Europe, could start a unilateral cut-back immediately. A unilateral beginning followed by a bilateral agreement would give real military significance to the Vienna negotiations for force reductions in Central Europe.

(8) All the nuclear powers should declare that they will *respect all regional treaties creating nuclear-free zones or peace zones,* and accept binding legal obligations to do so. Such declarations would merely be variants of a pledge not to use or threaten to use nuclear weapons against any non-nuclear party to the NPT that has no nuclear weapons on its territory. All the nuclear-weapon states except the Soviet Union have already given such formal legal pledges by signing and ratifying Protocol II of the Treaty of Tlatelolco. If the Soviet Union also does so, and all the nuclear powers make such delcarations, it would provide real impetus and encouragement to the negotiation of other nuclear-free zones and peace zones.

(9) The two superpowers should undertake to present, within a specified period of time, say one or two years, *new draft treaties for General and Complete Disarmament* (GCD). Both of them have paid

lip-service to the idea of general and complete disarmament ever since the unanimous adoption of the United Nations resolution approving it in 1959, and both have voted in favour of many resolutions over the years calling for concrete progress toward this goal. Neither one, however, has shown much interest in revising or updating its 1962 draft treaty outlining a disarmament programme. While it would be highly unrealistic to expect that GCD would be attained at any time in the foreseeable future, the very efforts of each of the two superpowers to work out new programmes and the negotiations on such programmes might have a very salutary effect on all disarmament efforts, conventional as well as nuclear, regional as well as global. They could help to revive and give much-needed impetus to the whole range of negotiations on arms control and disarmament, which are bogged down in discussions of relatively minor measures and incremental steps of relative insignificance.

(10) The two superpowers, who, together with their NATO and Warsaw Pact allies, are responsible for more than 80 per cent of world military expenditures, should take the lead in first *freezing and then reducing their expenditures.* If they would agree to freeze their military expenditure, it would in fact amount to an actual reduction because of inflation. They could even begin the process by reducing their military expenditures unilaterally, as both powers did in 1963-4. The implementation of the nuclear arms limitations outlined above would lead to substantial reductions. Unless and until states begin to reduce their military budgets, all arms limitaton agreements, are, if not meaningless, then illusory. They merely give the illusion of progress toward disarmament, whereas the reality is that the course of the arms race is merely being shifted to new and probably more dangerous channels.

(11) The two superpowers not only possess the overwhelming proportion of conventional armaments and armed forces in the world, they are also by far the largest suppliers of conventional armaments to other countries, including those of the Third World as well as their own allies in NATO and the Warsaw Pact. The superpowers should take the lead in reducing *their armed forces and conventional armaments,* as they have done by unilateral action at various times in the past. Some unilateral actions can be undertaken on a permanent basis, but others may have to be on a temporary or trial basis pending reciprocal action by the other side.

(12) The superpowers should also agree to *reduce drastically their sales and transfers of arms to Third World countries,* in particular to the

Middle East and South-East Asia. If they were to take these steps, they would be in a much stronger moral and political position to urge the developing countries not to squander their very limited material and trained human resources on useless local or regional arms races. They would also thereby help to facilitate a better climate of security and confidence in the whole world.

The question of control and verification, which has in the past posed serious obstacles to agreement on substantial measures of disarmament, no longer constitutes an insuperable problem. The truly remarkable technological advances in satellite surveillance and electronic and telecommunications monitoring during the last decade or so, in addition to the traditional secret means of gathering intelligence, make it almost impossible for any country to undertake clandestine activities that could provide it with an important advantage or that could affect the basic balance of power.

The author is not so naïve as to think that the above programme of measures, whether as a means to implement the obligations of the nuclear powers under the NPT or as a sensible approach to avoiding a global nuclear holocaust, is likely to be achieved within the predictable or foreseeable future. Even the adoption of the foregoing list of items as an agenda for negotiation in the immediate future seems a remote possibility at this time. Nevertheless, the measures proposed are neither unreasonable nor Utopian. In a world in which great powers behaved rationally, they would appear so logical as to be obvious. Unfortunately, the military-industrial-scientific-bureaucratic complex in the United States and the military-bureaucratic-scientific complex in the Soviet Union will oppose these proposals with every political and propaganda weapon in their formidable arsenals.

While the superpowers are undoubtedly aware that only prompt and drastic action by them will prevent the deteriorating non-proliferation régime from eroding further, they seem unable or unwilling to take the steps necessary to salvage the situation. Unless the superpowers are able to generate the political will that is essential in order to undertake at least some of the proposed measures, the outlook for preventing the further spread of nuclear weapons is discouraging, and so too are the prospects of preventing a nuclear war. In a world of many nuclear weapons states, policies based on mutual nuclear deterrence, and even the concept itself, will lose much of their meaning and relevance.

A World Disarmament Conference, Preceded by a Special Session of the UN General Assembly

Of fundamental importance to any programme of general disarmament is the question of *convening a World Disarmament Conference* (WDC). The Soviet Union was responsible for reviving this idea in 1971, and it was taken up by the non-aligned countries and has received the official blessing of the UN. Great Britain and France also favour the idea. The United States and China are the only nuclear powers that are opposed. If the former were to announce its support for holding the WDC at the earliest possible date, say within one or two years, it would very probably become a reality and might well achieve universal participation, including that of China. Except for the measures of nuclear disarmament outlined in the first six items above, nothing could be more calculated to give renewed life and momentum to progress in disarmament than the holding of a WDC. It would deal with all aspects of disarmament, including nuclear, conventional, chemical, environmental and all other forms of warfare. In fact, the holding of a WCD may be the best, if not the only, way to awaken the serious interest of the public and of top government leaders in a new approach to nuclear disarmament.

In the last few years, the UN has convened world conferences on the environment, population, food, the law of the sea, women's rights and habitat. While none of these conferences has produced solutions to the problems dealt with, they did serve to awaken interest in those problems and to make the governments of the world face up to the dire need to begin to cope effectively with those problems. A WDC, which may be more immediately and directly concerned with the problem of human survival, could at the very least serve a similar purpose. If properly prepared, a WDC might be able to agree on a disarmament agenda that would include a number of items set forth in the foregoing programme and on new institutional and procedural arrangements to promote their adoption.

In view of the failure of the efforts during the past five years to reach agreement on convening a WDC, many of the smaller countries have turned to the idea of first holding a Special Session of the UN General Assembly on Disarmament. They point to the progress made at the two Special Sessions (1974 and 1975) on Resources and Raw Materials in moving towards a new international economic order. In addition, since China and the United States are members of the UN, it would be more difficult for them to avoid participation in a Special Session than in a

WDC. Finally, a Special Session held in 1977 could prepare the way for holding a WDC perhaps as early as 1978, or at least during the Disarmament Decade.

The adoption of this course of action will not provide any guarantees or assurances that the superpowers or the nations of the world will finally find the right path towards controlling and reversing the nuclear arms race. But the present writer knows of no better way out of our predicament and hopes that these new approaches will at least be found worthy of consideration.

APPENDIX 1: Growth in Comparative Strength of the United States and the Soviet Union in Strategic Nuclear Arms

		1959	1960	1961	1962	1963	1964	1965	1966	1967	1968	1969	1970	1971	1972	1972	1974	1975
United States	ICBM	None	18	63	294	424	834	854	904	1,054	1,054	1,054	1,054	1,054	1,054	1,054	1,054	1,054
	SLBM	Some	32	96	144	224	416	496	592	656	656	656	656	656	656	656	656	656
	Long-range bombers				600	630	630	630	630	600	545	560	550	505	455	442	437	432
Soviet Union	ICBM	None	35	50	75	100	200	270	300	460	800	1,050	1,300	1,510	1,527	1,575	1,575	1,618
	SLBM	None	None	Some	Some	100	120	120	125	130	130	160	280	440	560	628	720	784
	Long-range bombers				190	190	190	190	200	210	150	150	150	140	140	140	140	135

Compiled from various annual issues of *The Military Balance*, published by the International Institute of Strategic Studies, London, and reproduced from the author's *The Last Chance: Nuclear Proliferation and Arms Control* (New York, 1976).

APPENDIX 2: Chronology of the Development of Nuclear Weapons and of Arms Control Measures[1]

1945

16 July — First atomic bomb exploded at Alamogordo, New Mexico.

6 August — United States drops atomic bomb on Hiroshima and three days later drops another atomic bomb on Nagasaki.

15 November — The United States, Great Britain and Canada propose a United Nations Atomic Energy Commission to ensure the use of atomic energy for exclusively peaceful purposes and to eliminate atomic weapons.

1946

24 January — The UN Atomic Energy Commission, composed of members of the Security Council plus Canada, is established.

14 June — The United States presents the Baruch Plan for an international authority to own and manage all atomic materials.

19 June — The Soviet Union proposes a draft convention banning the use and production of atomic weapons and providing for the destruction of all stockpiles.

14 December — The UN General Assembly adopts a resolution on the principles for the general regulation and reduction of armaments.

1947

13 February — The UN Security Council sets up a Commission for Conventional Armaments, to deal with the general regulations and reduction of armaments and armed forces.

1948

17 May — The UN Atomic Energy Commission suspends work because of the Soviet-American deadlock over the Baruch Plan.

4 November — The UN General Assembly adopts a resolution approving the Baruch Plan.

1949

23 September The Soviet Union explodes its first atomic bomb.
5 December The UN General Assembly adopts a French proposal
for the submission by member states of full information
on conventional armaments and armed forces and
verification thereof.

1952

11 January The UN sets up the Disarmament Commission to deal
with both atomic and conventional weapons.
3 October Great Britain explodes its first atomic bomb.
1 November The United States explodes its first hydrogen bomb.

1953

12 August The Soviet Union explodes its first hydrogen bomb.
8 December President Dwight D. Eisenhower makes his 'Atoms for
Peace' proposal to the UN General Assembly.

1954

2 April Prime Minister Pandit Nehru of India proposes the
suspension of all nuclear tests by the nuclear powers.

1955

18-23 July The Summit Conference of France, the Soviet Union,
Great Britain and the United States is held in Geneva.

1957

15 May Great Britain explodes its first hydrogen bomb.
29 July Statute of the International Atomic Energy Agency
(IAEA) enters into force.

1958

31 March The Soviet Union announces a unilateral suspension of
nuclear tests.
21 August An East-West Conference of Experts unanimously agree
that it is feasible to establish a control system to
supervise the suspension of nuclear tests.
22 August The United States and Great Britain announce their
suspension of nuclear tests for one-year periods
depending on agreement with Moscow on a control

	system.
31 October	The Conference on the Discontinuance of Nuclear Weapons Tests begins in Geneva.
10 November to 18 December	East-West Conference of Experts on Surprise Attack meets in Geneva.

1959

| 20 November | The UN General Assembly unanimously adopts a resolution approving the idea of General and Complete Disarmament (GCD). |
| 1 December | The nuclear powers and other countries sign the Antarctic Treaty banning nuclear tests and military bases in that area. |

1960

13 February	France explodes its first atomic bomb.
15 March to 27 June	Ten-Nation Disarmament Committee meets in Geneva until Soviet walk-out on 27 June.
18 August	The UN Disarmament Commission urges the resumption of East-West negotiations.

1961

30 August	The Soviet Union announces the resumption of nuclear tests.
15 September	The United States resumes underground tests.
13 December	The UN General assembly approves the American-Soviet Agreed Principles for Disarmament Negotiations and the creation of an Eighteen-Nation Disarmament Committee consisting of five Eastern bloc countries, five Western bloc countries and eight non-aligned countries.

1962

14 March	The Eighteen-Nation Disarmament Committee holds its first session in Geneva. France is not represented. In 1969, it is enlarged to 26 members and its name is changed to Conference of the Committee on Disarmament (CCD). In 1974 it is enlarged to 31 members.
15 March	The Soviet Union proposes a draft treaty for GCD.
18 April	The United States submits an outline of a treaty on

GCD in a peaceful world.

1963

20 June	The Soviet Union and United States sign the 'Hot Line' agreement.
5 August	The United States, the Soviet Union and Great Britain sign the Partial Test Ban Treaty. Subsequently 106 countries become parties to it.

1964

16 October	China explodes its first atomic bomb.

1967

27 January	The Outer Space Treaty, governing the exploration of outer space and banning nuclear weapons there, is signed.
14 February	The Treaty of Tlatelolco, banning nuclear weapons in Latin America, is signed.
17 June	China explodes its first hydrogen bomb.

1968

12 June	The UN General Assembly 'commends' the Treaty on the Non-Proliferation of Nuclear Weapons by a vote of 95 to 4, with 21 abstentions.
19 June	The UN Security Council adopts Resolution 255 on security assurances to non-nuclear-weapon states by a vote of ten to five, with no abstentions.
1 July	The Treaty on the Non-Proliferation of Nuclear Weapons (NPT) is signed.
24 August	France explodes its first hydrogen bomb.
29 August to 28 September	The Conference of Non-Nuclear-Weapon states meets in Geneva.

1969

17 November	Strategic Arms Limitation Talks begin
16 December	The UN General Assembly declares the decade of the 1970s a Disarmament Decade

1970

5 March	The Non-Proliferation Treaty enters into force.

1971

11 February   The Seabed Arms Control Treaty, which bans the emplacement of nuclear weapons on the seabed or ocean floor, is signed.

30 September The Soviet Union and the United States sign an agreement to reduce the risk of accidental nuclear war. The Soviet Union and the United States sign an agreement to improve the 'Hot Line'.

25 October   The UN decides to give the seat of China to the People's Republic of China and to expel the Republic of China (Taiwan); a few days later the People's Republic of China takes the China seat; calls superpowers' arms control efforts and agreements a 'hoax'.

1972

10 April   The Convention for the Elimination of Biological and Toxin Weapons is signed.

26 May   The Soviet Union and the United States sign a treaty limiting ABM systems to two sites in each country with 100 ABMs at each. The Soviet Union and the United States sign a five-year agreement and protocol limiting strategic offensive arms to 710 SLBMs in 44 submarines and 1,000 ICBMs for the United States, and 950 SLBMs in 62 submarines and 1,410 ICBMs for the Soviet Union.

1973

21 June   The Soviet Union and the United States sign an Agreement on Principles for Negotiating Further Limitations of Strategic Offensive Weapons.

22 June   The Soviet Union and the United States sign an Agreement on the Prevention of Nuclear War.

3 July   The Conference on Security and Co-operation in Europe (CSCE) begins in Helsinki.

30 October   Conference on mutual force reductions in Central Europe begins in Vienna.

1974

18 May   India explodes its first nuclear device for peaceful purposes.

3 July   The Soviet Union and the United States sign a Protocol

to the 1972 ABM treaty limiting ABM systems to one site with 100 ABMs in each country.

The Soviet Union and the United States sign the Threshold Test Ban Treaty, limiting underground nuclear weapons tests to a yield of 150 kilotons each after 31 March 1976. No limitations are proposed on underground nuclear tests for peaceful purposes.

The Soviet Union and the United States sign a joint statement agreeing to discuss and advocate measures to overcome the danger of environmental warfare.

24 November The Soviet Union and the United States agree at Vladivostok to limit strategic offensive arms until 1985 to 2,400 for each, of which 1,320 ICBMs and SLBMs can be MIRVed.

1975

5-30 May   The NPT Review Conference meets in Geneva.
1 August   The Declaration on Security and Co-operation in Europe is signed in Helsinki.

1976

28 May   The Soviet Union and the United States sign the Treaty on Underground Nuclear Explosions for Peaceful Purposes prohibiting individual explosions having a yield exceeding 150 kilotons and group explosions having an aggregate yield exceeding one and one-half megatons.

Note

1. Reproduced from William Epstein, *The Last Chance: Nuclear Proliferation and Arms Control* (New York, 1976).

11 STRATEGIC ARMS LIMITATION AND MILITARY STRATEGIC CONCEPTS

M.A. Milstein

It is well known that the improvement in Soviet-American relations is of decisive importance for the entire process of improving the international situation. The general atmosphere in the world and the stabilisation of the entire international situation, of course, depends on the evolution of the relations between the two mightiest states, economically and militarily, and on their attitude to the solution of the most important problems of our time and, above all, to the problem of arms limitation.

The problem of strategic arms limitation is, as it was before, the focal problem in Soviet-American relations. First, strategic arms constitute the foundation of a country's military might. Second, these armaments are the main means for waging nuclear warfare and are, as it were, the main means of containing war. Third, any accord between the Soviet Union and the United States on the limitation of and even more so on the reduction of strategic arms increases trust between the two countries, strengthens the stability of relations between them and in so doing favourably influences the entire international situation by reducing the threat of war and strengthening international peace. Fourth, accords on strategic arms limitation will facilitate the solution to the problem of limitation of the arms race in other fields and, in particular, can help to solve the problem of limitation of armed forces and armaments in Central Europe. Conversely, the expansion of strategic arms arsenals stimulates the build up of armaments as a whole. Fifth, the development and stockpiling of new, even more destructive, systems of strategic arms calls for considerable military expenditure. Therefore the banning of the development of new, even more destructive strategic arms systems might lead to a reduction in military budgets.

On the whole we may say that it is impossible to think about the removal of the threat of nuclear war and at the same time not to take practical and effective measures on the limitation and, eventually, the reduction of strategic offensive arms. The interests not only of the peoples of the Soviet Union and the United States but also of all the world's nations demand that the Soviet Union and the United States which possess colossal might in nuclear arms spare no effort in finding a solution for this complex problem.

The strategic arms limitation problem is not simply an important, but also a very complex and diversified problem, which could not and cannot be solved all at once by any single agreement and which demands, as before, to a certain extent a stage-by-stage solution. That is why the talks on the limitation of strategic arms are conducted in definite phases which in their turn may be conditionally divided into a number of stages, the completion of which is the signing of corresponding agreements. At present the first phase of these talks has been completed and the sides are conducting the second phase.

The first phase was completed by the ratification in October 1972 of the Treaty on the Limitation of Anti-Ballistic Missile (ABM) systems and the approval of the Interim Agreement on Certain Measures with Respect to the Limitation of Strategic Offensive Arms. Later both sides made new important agreements: the Agreement on the Prevention of Nuclear War of 22 June 1973; the Treaty on the Limitation of Underground Nuclear Weapon Tests; and the Protocol to the Treaty on the Limitation of Anti-Ballistic Missile systems of 3 June 1974.

The whole history of Soviet-American relations has lasted over four decades, but the history of military *détente,* in the field of strategic arms limitation, is comparatively short — only a few years. The agreements that have been signed are unprecedented in nature. Henry Kissinger, the American Secretary of State, has written that never before have two important powers divided by ideology, historical traditions and contradictory interests, established officially agreed-upon limitations on the development of their principal armaments.

At the same time, if we speak about strategic offensive arms then the interim agreement, for all its positive significance, was of a limited nature. It was limited in time — for five years from 1972 to 1977 — and, which is the main point, it dealt only with the first two of the three important components of strategic offensive arms, namely inter-continental ballistic missiles and submarine-launched ballistic missiles, but not with strategic bombers. Moreover, the interim agreement also hardly imposed any limitations on the qualitative development of these arms. Nobody of course ever argued or could argue that the goal of the very first agreement would be to impose limitations on the entire complex of strategic arms and on all of their aspects. Both sides clearly realised that this would constitute the subject of subsequent talks.

The Vladivostok Accord, reached at the summit meeting in

November 1974, was thus of great significance for the further successful solution of the strategic arms limitation problem. First, as distinct from the interim agreement, it imposed limitations not only on inter-continental ballistic missiles and submarine-launched missiles but on strategic bombers as well. Second, it established the total number of strategic arms delivery means for both sides and in so doing imposed firm limitations upon a further build-up in their numbers. Third, an important and fundamentally new aspect of the accord was that a limit was established on the numbers of MIRVed inter-continental ballistic missiles and submarine-launched ballistic missiles. Limitations have thus been imposed upon one of the most important elements in the qualitative strategic offensive arms race — the development of MIRV missiles. Fourth, the new agreement will be long-term, from October 1977 to 31 December 1985. It will also incorporate the relevant clause from the Interim Agreement of 26 May 1972 which will remain in force until October 1977. The stabilisation imposed upon strategic offensive arms for so long a period, will have a favourable effect upon the development of Soviet-American relations and on the entire international situation. Moreover, these limitations will stop the race in the development of strategic offensive arms. For, as experience indicates, development, production and deployment require approximately ten years. Fifth, the signatories also declared their intention to make further progress not only in imposing limitations on strategic offensive weapons but in their reduction as well.

The new agreement, to be drafted on the basis of the principle of equality and equal security, will of course contribute greatly to the improvement of Soviet-American relations, to reducing the threat of war and to strengthening international peace. Naturally many details have to be agreed upon and a number of technical and not only technical problems have to be solved in order to compile the ultimate text of the treaty. And that is essentially what the Soviet and American delegations, having concrete instructions from their governments, are now doing at the talks in Geneva. Any objective analysis of the treaty shows that its realisation would impose serious limitations upon the strategic arms race and would develop good preconditions for reduction in the future.

The Soviet Union proposed not to stop only at the limitation of the already existing means, but to reach accord on the banning of the development of even more destructive systems, such as the Trident submarines and the B-1 strategic bombers in the United States and similar systems in the Soviet Union. The American side, however, rejected this proposal.

On the whole, we can say that the agreements already signed constitute the first steps along the road to strategic arms limitation and prove that the Soviet Union and the United States can reach accord on such complex questions which deal with their vital interests.

Many specialists and non-specialists — both those who are sincerely interested in ending the arms race and those who are for a build-up in armaments — continue to discuss the significance of these and future agreements, and especially their possible influence upon the strategic arms race and upon the stability of the world situation. What would have happened if the two sides had failed to make these first steps? Can the agreements reached be considered adequate in all respects? Who got more out of these agreements — the Soviet Union or the United States? The need for correct answers to these questions is obvious, the more so if we take into account that the existing agreements and treaties are being attacked now in the United States, mainly by spokesmen of the militarist circles and by those who have vested interests in the arms race, in building up of military efforts and in returning to the former 'position of strength' policy.

Certain military, political and research circles in the United States are even of the opinion that the Soviet-American agreements on strategic arms limitation, signed and ratified in 1972, had a very small influence upon the very process of the armaments build-up. Spokesmen of these circles declare that each of the sides continued, in fact, to do whatever it wanted to do in respect to the build-up of strategic arms and did not do anything it would not have been doing if there had been no agreements. We cannot subscribe to this opinion. First, the agreements stopped the race in the most costly and destabilising field of strategic arms — in the field of the ABM systems — and thus strengthened tha stability of the situation as a whole. Second, they have halted the build-up in the most modern strategic offensive arms — ICBMs and ballistic missiles mounted on submarines. Third, concrete obligations were undertaken on preventing a nuclear war. Therefore, these were the first concrete and important stops along the road of containing the arms race and reducing the greatest threat which has loomed over mankind in the last decades — the threat of a world thermo-nuclear war. They narrowed down the material base for the nuclear missile arms race. It is obvious that if this accord had not been reached the world would have seen a new escalation of the arms race — which is senseless politically and unimaginably costly economically.

It has been estimated in the United States that if a new agreement on strategic arms limitation had not been signed then the American military budget would have had to be increased by another $11,000,000,000. The Pentagon is planning a whole number of measures, if such should be the case. In such a strategic arms build-up, the following would be included: an increase in the Minuteman -3 missiles from 550 to 800; the development of a new generation of ballistic rockets; and the development of cruise missiles. All this would produce a new spurt in the arms race.

A strategic arms race, as had been already stressed, would have triggered off a chain reaction in the building up of conventional armaments. Moreover, and most important, the threat of a nuclear war would increase and the world would go back from the peaceful coexistence policy to the state of cold war between countries with different social systems and to the senseless arms race.

Are the existing agreements adequate? Of course, the complete liquidation of strategic offensive arms, the banning of production and use of nuclear weapons in general, and universal and complete disarmament would be the ideal state of affairs. Unfortunately, the time has not as yet come for this. But those who are really interested in strengthening security cordially greet any progress towards it. Therefore, the existing agreements and treaties signify definite headway made for the ending of the arms race and for strengthening peace. The Soviet Union has proposed, in order to abate the war threat even more and in order to create favourable conditions for making progress towards disarmament, a world treaty on the non-use of force in international relations and a treaty on banning the development and production of new types of mass destruction weapons and new systems of such weapons. It will be readily understood that agreements on these questions, together with accords in the field of strategic arms limitation, would be of great importance for strengthening universal peace.

As for the question as to who has got more out of these agreements, the answer to this is very easy. The fact is that when they make these agreements both sides must be strictly guided by the main principle on which they are based — the principle of equality and equal security. Therefore, neither of the sides receives, nor can receive, any advantages as compared with the other side. The agreements are made for mutual benefit, for the benefit of the peoples of both countries. Hence it is the cause of disarmament and strengthening of peace that gets the greatest benefit. And those who declare that the existing agreements provide advantages for any one side are deliberately distorting the truth in order to justify the slowing down of talks or a build-up in armaments and an increase in military spending.

It is impossible to overestimate the significance of the efforts made by the Soviet Union and the United States to limit strategic arms in the name of universal peace and universal and complete disarmament. The time will come when the question will arise whether other nuclear powers should also join the process of strategic arms limitation.

L.I. Brezhnev, General Secretary of the Central Committee of the Communist Party of the Soviet Union (CPSU) said at the 25th CPSU Congress when referring to the current Soviet-American negotiations on further strategic arms limitation:

> We are conducting them in an effort to carry out the 1974 Vladivostok Accord and to prevent the opening of a channel for the arms race, which will nullify everything achieved so far. An agreement on this issue would obviously be of very great benefit both for the further development of Soviet-US relations and for building greater mutual confidence, and for the consolidation of world peace.

Such is the Soviet Union's position.

From time to time, one hears responsible quarters in the United States urging accelerated arming, which they justify with reference to the dragging out of the talks with the Soviet Union — a protraction, to put it bluntly, that has occurred through no fault of the Soviet Union whatsoever. Meantime certain influential circles in the United States are trying their best not only to get approval from the Congress for developing new weapon programmes but at the same time to complicate the ongoing talks on limitation of strategic weapons. Their chief method is the same as they used ten and twenty years ago, namely, to frighten the public, the politicians and particularly the Congress with the imaginary 'Soviet menace'. Thus the so-called 'Soviet threat' is the main motive for the arms race given by its advocates in the United States. In fact, of course, there is no Soviet threat. But fictions concerning the 'Soviet menace' have become part and parcel of American politics. And the threats grow, in particular, when the American military representatives are on their way to the Appropriations Committee. This created obstacles even in the early stages of Soviet-American talks. And it creates obstacles to the implementation of the agreement reached at Vladivostok. If things continue in this way all efforts to stop or even to limit the arms race will be endangered. Therefore the task of peace-loving forces is to assist in every possible way the conclusion at the earliest possible date of a successful agreement on the problem of limitation, and thereafter also on the reduction of strategic arms. Those people who are slowing down, under different pretexts, the process of strategic arms limitation are, in fact, against making agreements and are thus opening new channels for the arms race. They should be opposed resolutely and with sound arguments. The struggle to end the arms race and for disarmament must be intensified. Political *détente* needs to be fortified by military *détente.*

We should bear in mind that measures, aimed at strategic arms limitation, at improving relations between states with different social systems and at strengthening the *détente* process by measures on military *détente,* will not produce durable results unless they are accompanied also by measures aimed at containment and limitation in the field of military strategic concepts and military doctrine as a whole. We know that military doctrine and military-strategic concepts are important components in the entire mechanism of military policy and among the more important factors having a substantial influence upon the arms race, both quantitatively and qualitatively. The present military-strategic concepts of the Pentagon provide particular evidence of this.

The present military policy and strategy of the United States and especially the process of its formulation and realisation reflect the complex interaction of the two main trends in the world situation – the dominating tendency towards the development and expansion of *détente* and the opposite tendency leading to material preparations for war and interference in the affairs of others. It is not by accident that the United States has been reconsidering its military strategic concepts in the last few years.

The most acute discussion is carried on around the main problem of military strategy and military doctrine – the problem of using nuclear weapons. There is much discussion as to what a nuclear war may be like, what strategic forces the United States must have to wage it and what demands should be placed on these forces, which targets should be hit first and whether theatre nuclear forces could interact with strategic nuclear forces. Essentially the idea is how to be able to utilise their tremendous nuclear weapon arsenal as a means of dealing with international problems and at the same time avoid the threat that the United States could suffer 'unacceptable' losses. In other words, the discussion centres around the far from new problem – how to make nuclear war 'acceptable'. James Schlesinger, the then American

Secretary òf Defense, declared at the beginning of 1974 that some principles of American military strategy had been changed and that a new strategic concept had been adopted. He said that at present both sides have and would have in the future indestructible means of delivering a retaliatory blow. It was inevitable, therefore, that a strike made by one side upon the cities of the other in the course of a total attack would almost immediately bring a disastrous blow at its own cities. As a result of this, the range of circumstances under which the question of a total strike against the enemy's cities might arise had been considerably narrowed down. The need arose to find 'alternative versions' for the use of strategic forces. This apparently signified a 'limited strategic nuclear war', in which 'it is impossible to make strikes against a large range of targets', but in which strategic forces should be used in such a way so as 'to limit the damage to both sides' taking part in the nuclear conflict. Schlesinger also declared that the American strategic nuclear forces were able to strike at the enemy's military targets with adequate yield and precision in order to destroy the chosen targets, but avoiding 'accompanying destruction' while so doing, and that this had supposedly provided the Pentagon with the opportunity 'to force the enemy, in case a nuclear war starts, not to attack the cities of the United States and its allies'.

This concept has officially become an inalienable component of the American military doctrine since 1974. For the changes in personnel in the Pentagon made in autumn 1975 were not accompanied by substantial changes in the military strategic concepts formulated before that. Judging from the report made to the Congress by Donald Rumsfeld, the New Secretary of Defense, on the American military budget for the 1976-7 fiscal year, all the main concepts (including 'limited strategic war') remain in force. True, more often than not 'approximate equality' is mentioned instead of 'substantial equality' but this purely semantic difference does not change either the essence or the trend of the Pentagon's approach.

The present Pentagon military concept envisages a spectrum of nuclear wars including one more type of 'limited strategic war' which is understood to be a 'limited exchange' of strategic nuclear strikes on a small number of military targets. It is assumed that neither side would be interested in expanding the nuclear conflict and would take measures to localise and even maybe to liquidate it. This kind of war is considered to be the most probable one in the conditions of strategic nuclear equality.

The effectiveness of this concept is seen in the context of the

constant ability to inflict 'unacceptable damage' on the other side in
any conditions. Therefore a guaranteed annihilation is not excluded.
At the same time it is planned to retarget a part of strategic nuclear
forces from cities and industrial projects at military projects, and above
all at launching sites and at air force and naval bases. It is thus deemed
necessary to improve further the American's strategic nuclear forces
so that they would be able to hit military targets with greater precision.
For the effectiveness of the so-called American nuclear umbrella for
NATO is being questioned.

The grave threat embodied in this concept is that its advocates regard
nuclear weapons as a means of waging warfare and consider a nuclear
war quite acceptable because a limited strategic nuclear war is not
connected with big risks and therefore may be regarded as something
like a conventional war. It is therefore appropriate to mention here
that Henry Kissinger himself wrote in 1960, in his book *The Necessity
for Choice*, [1] that even though a theoretical model could be designed
for a limited nuclear war the fact remains that no such model had yet
met with general recognition ever since the beginning of the nuclear
age. He said that it would be nerarly impossible to get any reasonable
definition of what should be understood as a 'limited nuclear war'
from the American armed forces. He arrived at the conclusion that
since arguments about targeting were usually decided by permission
being given to each branch of the armed forces to destroy whatever
they deemed necessary for performing their tasks, limited nuclear
war waged in such a manner could quite well become indistinguishable
from a total war.

The acceptance of the Pentagon's new concept may lead to a
stepping-up of the strategic arms race because the advantage gained in
improving the precision of missiles creates a potential for acquiring
the capability for delivering a first strike. And the possibility is
increased that conventional war would develop quickly into a nuclear
war. In short the so-called 'nuclear threshold' is objectively being
lowered.

Moreover, it is impossible to distinguish a ballistic missile attack
upon military targets from an attack on civilian targets by the same
means. But even if we say that such a war is possible, there is the
obvious risk that it can very easily develop into a total nuclear war.
No wonder that this approach is being subjected in the United States
to sharp criticism in the most diverse circles.

A critical view of the current military strategy is held by many
sober-minded American politicians, scientists and public personalities,

who stress its danger with a feeling of apprehension. So where is the way out? The possibility of using nuclear weapons as a 'flexible' and 'acceptable' means of foreign policy should be rejected once and for all. It is useless to make attempts at obtaining strategic advantages in the conditions of our time because such attempts fail to bring any political dividends and lead only to more resources being squandered on the arms race. Nuclear war cannot and must not serve as a means of settling international disputes.

The Pentagon leaders also regularly stress that the reliability of 'containment' depends, along with other factors, on the existence of the three-sided potential, namely strategic forces, theatre nuclear forces and conventional forces. And the importance of each of the three elements is always pointed out as well as the impossibility of replacing one of them by any other. At present certain changes are being made in this approach — a certain restressing of accents, while the essence is being preserved. These changes are being made first of all in the so-called theatre nuclear forces.

It is being stressed that NATO troops may make first use of tactical nuclear weapons in the theatre of hostilities. A Pentagon report indicated that it was possible to forecast hypothetical circumstances under which non-nuclear NATO forces would not be able to stand their ground faced by an attack by non-nuclear forces. Therefore, the report said, it was not possible to exclude the possibility of the first use of tactical nuclear weapons. The report then clarified what these circumstances were. It said that examples were the possibility of the loss of a large tract of territory or a big grouping of NATO troops, in which case the political leadership of NATO would, maybe, decide to take the risk and deliver the first strike.

Thus, the possibility of delivering a first strike with tactical nuclear weapons is now openly emphasised. There are more than 7,000 American tactical nuclear weapons in Western Europe. What would happen if only a small proportion of them were used? Here is one of the examples cited in *Defence and Retaliation* written in 1961 by Helmut Schmidt, later Defence Minister and Chancellor in Federal Germany.[2] NATO held a war-game under the code name 'Carte Blanche' in Western Europe in 1955. 335 tactical nuclear weapons were used in the three days of the game of which 265 had theoretically exploded on the territory of Federal Germany and the German Democratic Republic. As a result between 1,500,000 and 1,700,000 people were 'killed' (without taking into account deaths from radioactive fall-out) and 3,500,000 people were injured. As a comparison we may note that 305,000 people were killed and 780,000 people were wounded throughout World War Two during raids by the British and American air forces on Germany. Such are the possible results of using only a 'small' number of tactical nuclear weapons in Europe. All this sharply aggravates the danger of conventional conflict developing into a nuclear war.

Such are some of the new elements in the military strategic approach of the United States. These are not of course all the changes that are characteristic of contemporary American military-strategic thinking. The examples cited here were needed only to show that in spite of the fact that the peaceful coexistence principle is meeting with ever-greater recognition in the world and much is being done to normalise relations between countries with different social systems, there still exist in the United States influential forces which are opposing this process and strive to preserve the atmosphere of tension in order to justify every new stage in the arms race. These circles more often than not try to justify their ideas by declarations about the so-called Soviet threat. L.I. Brezhnev said at the 25th CPSU Congress:

> In fact, of course, there is no Soviet threat either to the West or the East. It is all a monstrous lie from beginning to end. The Soviet Union has not the slightest intention of attacking anyone. The Soviet Union does not need war. The Soviet Union does not increase its military budget, and, far from reducing, is steadily augmenting allocations for improving the people's well-being.

This enables the conclusion to be drawn that the Soviet military doctrine is not aimed at preparing but at the repulsing of an attack. Soviet military doctrine is not aimed at preparing war but at deterring it.

Quite a lot has been done in the field of Soviet-American relations in the last few years to facilitate headway for *détente*. At the same time there is no doubt but that the supplementing of the political *détente* with a military one presupposes the adoption of not only practical measures on curbing the arms race but also the imposing of limitations in relation to military strategic concepts which slow down the *détente* process and, on the contrary, lead to a stepping up of the arms race.

The realities of our time imperiously demand from the Western circles which elaborate military policy and strategy that they stop thinking in categories of war in general and of nuclear war in particular.

Any attempts made to widen the 'usability' of nuclear weapons or to threaten nuclear war of any type contradict the very spirit of *détente,* the international agreements that have been achieved and the constructive nature of the Soviet-American relations that have been developing in the last few years.[3]

Notes

1. Henry A. Kissinger, *The Necessity for Choice: Prospects of American Foreign Policy* (New York, 1960).
2. Helmut Schmidt, *Defence or Retaliation* (Edinburgh and London, 1962) — German edition published as *Verteidigung oder Vergeltung* (Stuttgart-Degerloch, 1961).
3. The author wishes to emphasise that this paper was prepared before the American presidential election of November 1976. Hence his comments about American policy apply only to the Republican Administration and do not necessarily relate to that of President Carter.

12 NUCLEAR TESTING – NO END IN SIGHT?

Thomas A. Halsted

Introduction

The Comprehensive Test Ban (CTB) is the Holy Grail of arms control.
It has been the longest-sought but most elusive prize that knights errant
have pursued since the dawn of the nuclear age. They have slain
dragons, rescued princesses in distress, scaled glass mountains, and
swum rivers of fire. Is it any wonder that with all the obstacles that
have beset them, these seekers of the Holy Grail might not at times
have grown weary in their quest, like many a Crusader of old, and
returned, not with the True Grail, but with some Woolworth imitation,
perhaps a little cracked and chipped at the edges? Thus it was that in
1963, after five years of test ban negotiations, focusing on a ban on
all nuclear weapons tests, a treaty was instead concluded which dealt
only with nuclear explosions in the atmosphere, under water, and in
outer space. It stopped the testing in those environments where public
anxiety about fall-out had been intense, but permitted it to continue
underground. One hundred and four states are parties to this Limited
Test Ban Treaty, including four of the six countries that have set off
nuclear explosions, the United States, the Soviet Union, Great Britain
and India, but not including China and France. In July 1974, a second
limited test ban agreement was signed, this time only between the
United States and the Soviet Union. It established that, after 31 March
1976, neither side would conduct nuclear weapons tests larger than
150 kilotons. This Threshold Test Ban (TTB) Treaty also provided
that a separate agreement would govern the conduct of peaceful
nuclear explosions (PNEs). Finally, on 28 May 1976, this latter
agreement, a separate Treaty on Underground Explosions for Peaceful
Purposes, was also signed. President Gerald Ford submitted the two
treaties to the United States Senate for its consent to ratification on
29 July 1976. They were submitted to the Supreme Soviet for
ratification on 11 August 1976.

Assembling the TTB/PNE Treaty package has been a slow process.
State Department and Arms Control and Disarmament Agency (ACDA)
spokesmen made much of the great complexity of the negotiations,
particularly of the PNE Treaty, which took place over eighteen months
in Moscow, beginning on 7 October 1974 and ending on 10 April 1976.

The agreements were subjected to criticism from both right and left, even before the Threshold Treaty was signed by President Richard Nixon and General Secretary Leonid Brezhnev in July 1974. Though Ford Administration spokesmen denied it, the 1976 American presidential campaign clearly also delayed the ratification process. Though negotiations were completed on 9 April, the PNE Treaty was not signed until 28 May and not submitted to the Senate until two months later. With the brief time then remaining for Congressional action in the current session, the Senate Foreign Relations Committee chose not to schedule hearings on the treaties before it adjourned in October, let alone act on them. Given the degree of scepticism the treaties had evoked, the Senate was happy to leave the question of final action on the treaties to the new Congress and administration that would take office in 1977. In his election campaign, President Jimmy Carter called the Threshold and PNE Treaties 'wholly inadequate'. Given this view of the unfinished business he has now inherited, what should he do about these inadequate treaties and about the comprehensive test ban itself?

To assess the value of the two test ban treaties, one must analyse not only their strengths and weaknesses, but also look again down the road not taken, namely towards a comprehensive test ban. Do the two treaties make the attainment of a CTB more or less likely? What obstacles to a CTB still loom so large that the two governments chose to stop short of the goal? What effect will the treaties have on the larger question of inhibiting nuclear proliferation? And, finally, what effect might their rejection have, if it turned out that the US Government in the end refused to complete the ratification process?

The Two Treaties

The Treaty on the Limitation of Underground Nuclear Weapon Tests (the Threshold Test Ban Treaty or TTB Treaty) is much the simpler of the two instruments. It provides that neither party shall carry out nuclear weapons tests above 150 kilotons yield at any place under its jurisdiction or control after 31 March 1976; that verification of the TTB Treaty shall be by national technical means, and that neither side shall interfere with such means — the language here is identical to verification provisions of the 1972 SALT agreements; that the TTB Treaty does not apply to underground explosions for peaceful purposes and that a separate agreement to govern the conduct of such explosions must be negotiated as quickly as possible.

A separate protocol to the TTB Treaty calls for an exchange of information on the geographical location and geological characteristics of nuclear weapons test sites, the geographic co-ordinates of individual nuclear weapons tests, after they have been conducted, and specific calibration data (yield, date, time, depth and co-ordinates) on two nuclear weapons tests in each testing area detonated at as close to the 150 kiloton threshold yield as possible. If either party decides to establish a new test site, the same descriptive information, including calibration data, must be exchanged for that site. All tests conducted at these designated sites, including PNE tests, are to be considered weapons tests.

The Treaty on Underground Explosions for Peaceful Purposes (the PNE Treaty) and its accompanying Protocol affirm the fact that it is not possible to distinguish between a nuclear explosive device used for peaceful purposes and a weapon. Accordingly, the Treaty establishes conditions for verifying that weapon-related benefits are not obtained from PNEs, that each peaceful explosion is indeed for peaceful purposes, and that the provisions of the 1963 Limited Test Ban Treaty (specifically the prohibition on venting radioactive materials into the atmosphere to the extent that radioactive debris is found outside the borders of the country where the explosion takes place) are observed. The Treaty provides that no individual explosion for peaceful purposes shall be greater than 150 kilotons, the same limit as in the TTB Treaty. 'Group explosions' consisting of simultaneous explosions of many nuclear devices are permitted, but their aggregate yield may not exceed 1.5 megatons.

The PNE Treaty provides that verification shall be both by national technical means and by a number of other provisions, depending on the yield and number of explosives involved in each PNE application. A novel, unprecedented feature is the provision in some instances for the presence at the site of peaceful explosions of 'designated personnel' or observers from the other party, whose function is to verify that the explosion is indeed for peaceful purposes, and that the yield of each explosive does not exceed 150 kilotons. The Protocol spells out in detail the amount of advance notification required, the number of observers that may be present, the equipment they may bring, and the functions they may perform. An agreed statement attached to the PNE Treaty makes clear that developmental testing of peaceful nuclear explosive devices does not constitute a peaceful application and must therefore be conducted at designated nuclear weapons test sites, in accordance with the provisions of the TTB Treaty governing nuclear weapons tests.

Both Treaties include provisions for consultation 'to promote the objectives and implementation' of the treaties. A Joint Consultative Commission for this purpose is established by the PNE Treaty. Finally, both treaties are explicitly linked to one another by Articles VIII and IX of the PNE Treaty, which stipulate that the PNE Treaty may not be terminated while the TTB Treaty is in force, and that the instruments of ratification of the two treaties shall be exchanged simultaneously.

The two treaties reflect an ingenious approach to resolving nearly all imaginable problems involved in limiting the size of nuclear weapons tests and conducting PNEs. They are extraordinarily complex – the printed text of the Treaties and their Protocols as submitted to the Senate on 29 July run for 23 pages; the accompanying letter of submittal contains an additional 26 pages. The negotiators who laboured many months in Moscow cannot be faulted for their tenacity or ingenuity.

But have they produced a positive step forward for arms control or, as many critics in the United States contend, only a rationale for continuing the arms race under new rules, in a way that may delay, rather than pave the way towards constructive new initiatives, including a Comprehensive Test Ban?

Criticism of the two treaties has concentrated on five areas:

1. The Threshold

Until the TTB Treaty was signed, discussion of a threshold on nuclear weapons testing had revolved around the issue of verification. If there is a level of seismic activity below which it is not possible to discriminate between earthquakes and nuclear explosions, it was argued agreement could be reached on a seismic threshold above which testing would be prohibited. At this point, however, many experts believe that for explosions in most geological formations the threshold for detecting a seismic event, whether an earthquake or an explosion, is virtually the same as the threshold for discriminating between the two. Small tests below the identification threshold – usually less than a kiloton – could not be detected by seismic means and would be of negligible military utility;[1] thus such a threshold test ban is no longer of value.

But the 150 kiloton threshold – more than ten times the size of the largest yield test that, under the most implausible circumstances, could escape detection by seismic means – has no relationship whatever to verification capabilities. It seems, instead, to have been set sufficiently high to allow continued testing of all but a handful of potential new weapon developments. The fact that the effective date of the treaty was 21 months after it was signed permitted both sides to complete larger-yield test programmes ahead of the deadline. Both the United States and Soviet Union did, in fact, conduct such tests, presumably to complete development of such weapons as the warheads for the American Trident and MX missiles, and the Soviet SS-17, -18, and -19 ICBMs, all of them presumably over the 150 kiloton limit.

A limit based on weapon yield introduces added complications because of the difficulty of correlating yield and seismic magnitude. Even with calibration shots at every testing site, there will still be sufficient imprecision in the determination of yield to generate uncertainties in cases when planned yields are near the 150 kiloton threshold. The negotiators recognised this potential ambiguity but chose to deal with it in a manner which is likely to undermine public confidence in the two treaties and further complicate prospects for their ratification. It was revealed by an American radio reporter in June 1976, and officially confirmed in the letter of submittal accompanying the treaties, that a 'mistakes understanding', allowing one or two 'slight, unintended breaches of the 150 kiloton threshold' each year, had been reached between the two parties, but not included in any treaty or protocol language. Coincident with the revelation of this understanding was the detonation by the Soviet Union of two underground nuclear explosions, on 4 July and 29 July, one or both of which appeared to have exceeded 150 kilotons. Since the TTB Treaty had not been ratified, tests over the limit would not have violated any treaty, but they would certainly have violated its spirit, and several newspaper editorials and columnists promptly said as much. The Soviet Embassy in Washington dismissed the allegation as groundless. The US Energy Research and Development Administration, which normally announces Soviet nuclear tests of this magnitude, curiously made no such announcement until 3 August, when it issued a brief statement reporting that both Soviet tests had taken place, but providing no details on their yields. Two more large Soviet tests, on 28 August and 29 September, raised similar questions. Further analysis may determine that none of the tests exceeded 150 kilotons, but an atmosphere has been generated which predictably has led to a number of unofficial charges of Soviet bad faith, reminiscent of earlier allegations that the Soviet Union was violating elements of the SALT I agreements.

The problem of yield determination when detonations could exceed

150 kilotons is also reflected in the Protocol to the PNE Treaty. It provides that designated personnel shall have access to any group explosion with a planned yield greater than 150 kilotons, but it also provides that they may also be present if the planned yield is lower, between 100 and 150 kilotons, if both parties agree to their presence.

Access by observers in such instances may relieve uncertainties about PNEs near the threshold, but no such access is granted to weapons or PNE tests taking place within test sites; hence doubts are bound to arise from time to time. Ironically, no such doubts would arise in the case of a Comprehensive Test Ban, since any explosion of any size would constitute a violation.

2. Legitimising Peaceful Nuclear Explosion

Peaceful nuclear explosions can be used by other countries as an excuse to justify nuclear weapons development. There was understandable scepticism when India detonated its 'peaceful' device in May 1974, and India is rightly viewed almost universally as a *de facto* member of the nuclear weapons club. Any action that gives increased respectability to PNEs can only undermine efforts to persuade other countries, such as Argentina and Brazil, that their interest in PNEs is not justifiable. Yet the PNE Treaty does just that.

The United States has essentially abandoned its PNE programme, after years of research and experimentation into the use of nuclear explosions for excavation, for underground gas stimulation, oil recovery, creation of underground storage cavities, mining of copper ore, and for electric power generation. In each instance it was ultimately concluded that conventional means of accomplishing these projects would be preferable, for economic, environmental or political reasons. By agreeing to a treaty licensing PNEs, the United States seems to have reversed its position.

Article V of the Non-Proliferation Treaty provides that nuclear weapons states shall make available the potential benefits of peaceful nuclear explosions to non-nuclear weapons states, but it has been the position of the United States, at least, that no such benefits have been proven, and that implementation of this article would therefore be premature. The PNE Treaty, which is clearly intended primarily to benefit the Soviet PNE programme (though it does provide for conducting PNEs in other countries), is likely to stimulate more complaints from Third World countries that the nuclear superpowers are discriminating against them.

3. A Freeze on Future Test Limitations

The TTB and PNE Treaties are necessarily linked, because of the impossibility of distinguishing peaceful nuclear explosive devices from nuclear weapons, but this linkage assures that, as long as the Soviet Union retains its interest in PNEs, the threshold is likely to remain at 150 kilotons.

Clearly, there is strong interest in PNEs in the Soviet Union. Soviet scientists have described the use of PNEs to excavate canals, to construct a large dam to build a lake, and to snuff out a runaway fire in a natural gas field, and have indicated interest in various underground engineering projects. An ambitious plan to link the Kama and Pechora rivers with a 65-kilometre-long canal blasted by nuclear explosives has been discussed for some time. Its purpose would be to reverse the flow of the Pechora River, which now empties into the Arctic Ocean, into the Caspian Sea, which has been experiencing a steadily dropping water level. One experimental nuclear test has been conducted on the site of the proposed canal.

The Soviet negotiators initially hoped to be allowed to conduct PNEs at yields higher than 150 kilotons, and will doubtless find some of their ambitions curtailed by the lower limit. There is, however, an escape clause (Article III, paragraph 3) in the PNE Treaty which provides that 'The question of carrying out any individual explosion having a yield exceeding 150 kilotons will be considered by the parties at an appropriate time to be agreed.' President Ford's letter of submittal to the Senate makes clear that such an agreement would require amendment of the treaty, and consent to ratification of the amendment by the Senate. It would be ironic if the threshold, far from being lowered over time, were instead raised, as this provision implies is possible. But there is no provision in the treaty for lowering either the threshold or the number of permitted tests to zero, and the link between the two treaties effectively makes any eventual comprehensive test ban treaty hostage to continuing Soviet interest in PNEs.

4. The 'On-Site Inspection Precedent'

The provision for 'designated personnel' from one party to be present and to take measurements at the site of certain large PNEs has been widely hailed as a 'breakthrough' for on-site inspection. The scheme is certainly unprecedented, but there is a danger that too much will be made of it. Undeniably, it must have been an extraordinary wrench for the Soviet government to agree to allow adversary inspectors on

Soviet soil, and to grant them at least some latitude in the activities
they may conduct at the site of an explosion. No such access or right
to conduct confirming investigations has been granted to anyone before.
But the activities of these observers is also severely circumscribed, to
the point where their role bears no relationship to the on-site inspection
sought in test ban negotiations in the 1950s and early 1960s. The
principle American and British negotiators then sought to establish
involved the despatch of Western or Soviet inspection teams, on
acquiring suspicious information suggestive of nuclear testing, to *any*
location *anywhere* in the Soviet Union or the United States, at *any* time.
That principle was never accepted, as agreement was never reached on
how many such inspections would be permitted. At one point the
Soviet negotiators had reluctantly conceded that there might be some
instances where on-site inspection could help in resolving uncertainties
about suspicious events, and suggested that they might permit a quota
of no more than three inspections per year — but at that time the
Western side would accept no less than seven.

Since then, furthermore, the science of nuclear test detection has
reached the point where almost all seismic events that can be detected
at all can also be identified, either as earthquakes or explosions, by a
combination of seismic means, involving more sophisticated analytical
techniques than were available in 1963, and intelligence, chiefly
photographic satellites. There would hardly ever be any occasion to
call for an on-site inspection.

In addition, research on on-site inspection technology has shown
that such inspections are easily made unreliable by a determined
evader. Thus on-site inspection, as it was conceived years ago, would
no longer contribute in any practical way to the verification of a
comprehensive test ban. Such specialised verification techniques
as have been devised for the PNE agreement might have some relevance
to some equally specialised verification problems, but essentially none
in the case of a comprehensive nuclear test ban.

In a memorandum to the UN Secretary-General, dated 28 September
1976, Soviet Foreign Minister Andrei Gromyko observed that the view
is 'practically unanimous' that on-site inspections are unnecessary but
added, surprisingly, that some 'voluntary framework' for on-site
verification might be attainable. This suggests some new flexibility in
the Soviet position and should be given serious consideration.

5. Commitment to the Non-Proliferation Treaty

The United States and the Soviet Union have been criticised widely for their failure to implement the obligations they accepted under the Non-Proliferation Treaty (NPT), particularly with respect to strategic arms control and nuclear testing. A Comprehensive Test Ban, adhered to by as many nations as possible, but in particular by the two states that have carried out the bulk of the more than 1,000 nuclear tests conducted over the past 31 years, has come to be viewed as a symbol of a serious commitment to ending the nuclear arms race at last. The Threshold and PNE Treaties appear to point in the opposite direction. They permit continued weapon-testing at high yields; they pay no more than lip-service to some day ending all testing; they are bilateral, rather than multilateral. To too many critics they appear to have been drawn up largely for the mutual convenience of two superpowers to keep all possible testing options open. If, instead of the TTB and PNE Treaties, the United States and the Soviet Union, together with others, were to enter into serious negotiations for a comprehensive test ban, their action would, in the words of Mrs Inga Thorsson, leader of the Swedish Delegation to the Conference of the Committee on Disarmament, 'be greeted with joy and relief all over the world'.

Three of the six countries that have conducted nuclear tests are parties to the NPT. Year after year since that treaty went into effect, and particularly at the 1975 NPT Review Conference, the non-nuclear weapons states party to the treaty have warned the nuclear weapons states that they cannot go on forever building up nuclear arsenals, threatening to use nuclear weapons, and most of all, continuing to test nuclear weapons while still expecting other nations to agree to forgo nuclear weapons of their own. A CTB would undeniably be a symbolic gesture towards these critics. It would not end the arms race, and might not dramatically affect the decision of potential nuclear weapon states to acquire the option to build nuclear weapons, but it could be a strong influence on the debate in those countries. Certainly the *lack* of a CTB, and the evidence of continued reliance on nuclear weapons by the big powers, makes it all the harder for them to dissuade these countries from the nuclear option.

Why Not a Comprehensive Test Ban?

The major obstacle to a CTB is neither technical nor military, but rather a lack of political will. Neither the United States nor the Soviet Union has adopted a public position which would make achievement of a CTB realistic. The United States contends that it would be possible for the Soviet Union to conduct militarily significant tests in secret unless the CTB included a provision for on-site inspection to resolve any ambiguities. The Soviet Union asserts that such inspections are unnecessary, but insists on the right to conduct PNEs, and further declares that all nuclear weapons states must be party to a comprehensive test ban — a condition to which China and France, neither of them a party to the 1963 Limited Test Ban or the Non-Proliferation Treaty, are unlikely to agree.

These arguments provide a convenient smokescreen for a more basic objection to the CTB: neither the United States nor the Soviet Union wants to give up the option to conduct nuclear weapons tests; the TTB and PNE Treaties will permit them to continue. As far as the capability of identifying small nuclear tests is concerned, it is highly improbable that the Soviet Union could confidently conduct clandestine, *militarily important* nuclear tests without detection by a combination of seismic and other intelligence means. Tests above one kiloton or so would almost certainly be detected, and the Soviets would be further deterred from clandestine testing of even smaller yield devices by the prospect that their tests might even then be detected. On-site inspection is no longer necessary. Furthermore, a test ban observed by only the United States and Soviet Union, without the participation of other nuclear weapons states, would not affect the security interests of either superpower for many years, regardless of the amount of testing France or China conducted. The utility of PNEs is so dubious that further efforts should be made to persuade the Soviet Union to shelve its PNE programme, as the United States already has. In no event should the unlikely prospect that they might some day prove to be useful be allowed to stand in the way of a ban on all nuclear tests.

A recent Energy Research and Development Administration (ERDA) report provides for the first time some public details of the accomplishments of thirty years of US nuclear testing:[2] 74 different types of weapons have been tested, 50 of them accepted in the stockpile at one time or another, 26 of them currently in the stockpile in 33 different weapons systems. It can be assumed that Soviet weapons development is at a comparable level of diversity. There is hardly any theoretically possible development that has not been explored by now, at least by the two superpowers, and scant reason to expect such developments in the future. To be sure, weapons designers can always come up with new concepts to explore; under a CTB, they would have to make do with extrapolation from existing designs. Under the 150 kiloton TTB Treaty, in fact, the ERDA report acknowledges that such adaptation would be necessary for any higher-yield weapons that might be required.

What about the reliability of nuclear weapons already in the stockpile? It has been suggested that, if there were no opportunity to test stockpile weapons, confidence in the weapons and thus in the deterrent would be degraded. The US Defense Department testified in 1971, however, that such confidence tests seldom take place — only five times since the mid-1950s, in fact, had a nuclear explosion been involved in validation testing of stockpiled weapons.[3] Confidence could be maintained by replacing defective warheads or testing which did not involve nuclear explosions. It is worth noting as well that the same degradation would occur for Soviet weapons.

Large and well-established bureaucracies exist in the United States and the Soviet Union which have an unavoidable vested interest in the continuation of nuclear weapons programmes, including testing. According to the ERDA report, in 1975 the 'weapons complex' — the US weapons laboratories, the Nevada Test Site, and the seven government-owned plants which produce nuclear weapons — 'employed more than 40,000 people, had an operating budget of more than a billion dollars, and represented an investment of more than $2.6 billion'. In the event of a comprehensive nuclear test ban, many of these individuals, a large number of whom may have devoted their entire professional lives to nuclear weapons, would need to acquire new skills and seek work elsewhere. They and their supporters in the Executive branch and Congress could be expected strongly to oppose a CTB. In a recent speech, Lt.-Gen. Edward B. Giller, Director of Weapons Development for ERDA, expressed his concern about this possibility:

> Above all we must not allow the nuclear weapons development and production complex to erode. In many respects this complex is unique and some of the assets are unreplaceable. The weapons laboratories represent a combination of trained manpower and physical resources that is available nowhere else in the West.

Some CTB opponents contend that ending nuclear testing, because it means foreclosing options to test in the future, is *ipso facto* a bad thing for the United States.[4] But would a CTB really hinder national security? There are scarcely any new developments 'interesting. enough to justify further weapon-testing; a CTB would inhibit Soviet as much as American developments. The security issue therefore becomes one of whether the United States is better off in a situation where neither side is testing than in one where both continue to test.

Since the present trend in American weapon development is towards more accurate delivery systems rather than higher yields, future concerns lie more in missile guidance developments than in nuclear weapon-testing. If there are possible 'breakthroughs' ahead, a CTB would inhibit their likelihood for both the United States and the Soviet Union.

A Fresh Start

The shortcomings of the TTB and PNE Treaties, together with the obvious advantages and lack of obvious obstacles to a CTB Treaty, argue that the new treaties should simply be shelved and serious efforts begun to achieve a CTB Treaty at the earliest possible time. If it could be demonstrated that a CTB Treaty would be facilitated by the TTB and PNE Treaties, there would be little wrong with hastening their ratification and getting on with the job of negotiating a CTB. But the TTB is an idea whose time is past; linking the PNE Treaty to it has ensured that no CTB will be possible as long as the Soviet Union retains an interest in peaceful nuclear explosions. Furthermore, the suspicions that are bound to arise because of the difficulty of verifying that explosions are kept below the threshold, as already evidenced by the recent experience with the two Soviet tests in July 1976, are unlikely to provide an atmosphere conducive to productive test ban negotiations.

It may be difficult to persuade the Soviet Union to give up its PNE programme, but it is conceivable that more of the scepticism that eventually led to the abandonment of the PNE programme in the United States may surface in the Soviet Union as well. By agreeing to a 150 kiloton limit on PNEs, Soviet negotiators have had to give up some of their more ambitious concepts, possibly including the Kama-Pechora Canal, for which at one time individual explosions as large as three megatons had been contemplated. In theory, the canal project might still be possible using smaller explosions, but it (and other large-scale cratering projects) essentially have already been ruled out by the Limited Test Ban Treaty, which prohibits explosions that cause radioactive debris to be present outside the territory of the state carrying out an underground explosion. The PNE Treaty reaffirms the commitment to the Limited Test Ban Treaty, and the State Department's letter of submittal explicitly states: 'this. . .provision is important because US studies indicate that it does not appear possible to carry out major excavation PNE projects without violating the

Limited Test Ban Treaty.' Thus one solution to the PNE problem would be a moratorium on their use while an acceptable way is devised to carry out both developmental tests and actual applications of PNEs under adequate international supervision.

What would be the effect of rejection of the Treaties? It has been suggested that other arms-control negotiations would be jeopardised, and that détente would suffer still further. But this means that any agreement, no matter how inadequate, must be approved for détente's sake. It would be more constructive for the super-powers to work out a test ban treaty with real significance for arms control and, ultimately, for East-West security.

The Carter Administration has stated that it supports the TTB and PNE Treaties, and sees no inconsistency between backing them and 'proceeding quickly and aggressively', as President Carter put it shortly after his inauguration, to achieve a Comprehensive Test Ban Treaty. Secretary of State Vance has called the two Treaties 'stepping stones' on the road to a CTB. Let us hope they do not turn out to be stumbling-blocks instead.

Notes

1. For a discussion of verification capabilities and prospects for their improvement, both with seismic and other means, see 'Prospects for Comprehensive Test Ban Treaty', Hearings before the Subcommittee on Arms Control, International Law Law and Organization of the Committee on Foreign Relations, United States Senate, 22 and 23 July 1971, and 'Status of Current Technology to Identify Seismic Events as Natural or Man Made', Hearings before the Joint Committee on Atomic Energy, 27 and 28 October 1971.
2. Energy Research and Development Administration, *Funding and Management*

Alternatives for ERDA Military Applications and Restricted Data Functions (Publication no.97, Washington, D.C., 1976).
3. See 'Prospects for a Comprehensive Nuclear Test Ban', p.106.
4. See, for example, Michael May, 'Do We Need a Nuclear Test Ban?', *Wall Street Journal*, 28 June 1976.

13 RECONNAISSANCE SATELLITES AND THE ARMS RACE

Herbert F. York

The United States, the Soviet Union and China have all launched satellites for the purpose of taking pictures designed to obtain intelligence which otherwise would be hard to secure or even completely inaccessible. The first important point to grasp is that these reconnaissance satellites are extremely large objects. Precise information on their size is, however, difficult to obtain. But an average-sized version might be of the order of 5 metric tons, though Chinese satellites, in particular, are probably quite a bit lighter at present. Nevertheless, most of such satellites are vast devices. Hence they are launched into space by very large rockets. Indeed, the boosters for inter-continental ballistic missiles and the rockets which launch reconnaissance satellites into space are essentially the same.

Rockets were invented in China more than ten centuries ago. They were used in China first for ceremonial purposes and later for military purposes. But probably the first suggestion for a practical application of satellites was made by Edward Everett Hale — Americans will remember him as the man who gave the other speech at Gettysburg when Abraham Lincoln gave his famous address. He wrote a story which was published in *Harpers* in 1868 in which he mentioned the fact that it was difficult to measure longitude by any simple means and he accordingly suggested that satellites be put into orbit as a means of doing so. He did not suggest that this be done with rockets. Instead he imagined a device which involved huge fly-wheels. Thus he did not suggest the rocket-launched satellites we have today. That, then, was the second historical bench-mark: the first suggestion of a practical application of satellites came just after the American Civil War.

The basis of modern rocketry — the use of liquid propellants and of multi-stage variations — was propounded at the end of the nineteenth century by a Russian physics teacher named Constance E. Tsiolkovsky. He was the first person to make various calculations of how one might achieve the velocities necessary to get and keep things in space. He actually made a series of calculations about rockets which were remarkably accurate and he considered the matter of

weightlessness and the use of multi-stage rockets as a means of getting
very high velocity. It was all rather elementary but nevertheless it was
fairly complete. Incidentally, Tsiolkovsky said that he was inspired by
reading the works of Jules Verne and, in particular, by his ideas for
using large cannons to get to the moon. Tsiolkovsky decided that it
could not be done that way but considered that rockets were the right
way to do it. His ideas were not, however, followed up and were almost
forgotten. Indeed, it is almost by chance that we recognise today that
it was he who first did these calculations.

The first people to build rockets which were anywhere near large
enough to keep satellites in orbit were the Germans in connection with
the rearmament of the 1930s and the construction of the V2 as a
bombardment device during World War Two. The V2 was in itself not
large enough to launch satellites but rather simple extensions of the
technology would have made it so. Hence the V2 was the first large
rocket that was in the general size class that is necessary for this kind
of purpose. As early as |1946, in the United States and evidently also
in the Soviet Union, the people who had been working on small rockets
on their own in both countries came into possession of these large
rockets which the Germans had developed, combined their ideas, took
the technology further and began to study the consequences. Here we
shall concentrate on the American side of the story, since the present
writer knows relatively little about what happened in the Soviet Union.
In 1945 the German group which had built the V2 surrendered to the
Americans and were 'de-briefed' about their ideas. Wernher |von Braun
gave a long description of how one might improve rockets and produced
papers explaining how they might be used for launching satellites. It is
another historical curiosity that the American who actually de-briefed
von Braun and wrote up these details was a Chinese by the name of
|H. S. Tsien who went to China in 1954 and is presumed to be the
individual who played the major role in the development of modern
rockets there. Thus it happened that both the Americans and Chinese
development owed much to the individual who de-briefed von Braun.

The first serious post-war study in the United States of what was
necessary to launch satellites and how they might be used can be traced
to the Rand Corporation: a so-called think-tank which works on
military and other problems of the United States. The very first study
produced by the Rand Corporation is entitled *An Experimental
World-Circling Space Ship* and it takes up the questions of how one
might launch satellites, what one might do with them and why.
It mentions reconnaissance but only very lightly; one of the main

reasons that it gave in support of Americans getting on with this programme is to ask readers to imagine what might happen if someone else did it first! So they predicted the political effects of Sputnik eleven years before it happened. The reason they did not think seriously about reconnaissance was that they did not believe it was possible to launch weights which were large enough to carry adequate cameras and in any case they did not think it would be practical to get the data back. But the Rand staff studied the problem continuously thereafter and they soon came to realise that if they extended the rocket technology a bit further, and developed the technology of cameras, then something of value could be produced.

Nothing much happened except for study for some years, and then a series of events caused a major re-evaluation in the United States of the role of technology in military matters. These were the Soviet atomic bomb test in 1949; the sudden onset of the Korean War in 1950; and the re-evaluation of military policy that took place when the Korean War was over. That re-evaluation of military policy had many elements to it. One of them involved the construction of large rockets and another was the forging of a much closer connection between science and technology on the one hand and military affairs on the other. All this came out of the series of events between 1949 and 1953. The result was that in 1954 the development of rockets of a size suitable for putting large satellites into space began in the United States at about the same time as in the Soviet Union. In each country there had been development of other kinds of rockets before that, but the development of really large rockets began in both countries only in 1954. At the same time that the development of the rockets began, the people studying the problem of the relationship of science and technology on the one hand and national security, and military affairs on the other, produced several very important reports. One said that there was a great need for technological intelligence and that instead of trying to get it in the classical way by relying on spies and depending on occasional defectors and others, the most efficient way to gather technological intelligence was to use technological means. These suggestions were taken seriously, and they took two forms. One of them led to the development of the U2 aeroplane as something which could be prepared quickly, and in fact U2s were flying about a year and a half after this decision was made. The other form was the building of reconnaissance satellites which would be a surer and more long-range method and one which would (they correctly presumed) be a more acceptable means for accomplishing reconnaissance. So in 1955 both the U2 and the programme to build reconnaissance satellites were authorised.

The first satellite of any kind was the Soviet Sputnik launched in 1957. But, according to the Stockholm International Peace Research Institute (SIPRI), the first satellite whose purpose was actually to conduct reconnaissance was not launched until 1960. The earlier ones were apparently intended only for preliminary scientific purposes or just to carry the development of satellites further. But since 1960 the programme has taken a serious form and there have been a great number of satellites launched. There are some estimates from SIPRI which are worth quoting: in 1975 the Soviet Union launched 33 reconnaissance satellites, the United States four and China one. SIPRI advances the view that the reason for the large number of Soviet launches may be that the United States satellites stay up longer and deliver more data per satellite. Hence, so far as the amount of reconnaissance being carried out, there is probably something like parity between the two superpowers and thus the large discrepancy in the number of launches is probably not significant.

Let us now turn to an overall discussion of the satellites themselves and give two references for those who would like to know more about the details of satellites. The best paper that I am aware of on the subject that actually describes the satellites is one by Ted Greenwood in *Scientific American* in January 1973. Greenwood is a Canadian who was a student at Massachusetts Institute of Technology and who did this work while still a graduate student. He also wrote a similar paper published by the International Institute for Strategic Studies.[1] In addition, SIPRI has been making general observations of the world's satellites and by taking data from a great number of sources concerning orbits, orbit inclinations, altitudes and all other kinds of data on the track — where satellites are at different times — has made deductions about satellites, about whether they are reconnaissance satellites or whether they are another kind of satellite. For example, in the *SIPRI Yearbook, 1976* we find the speculation that the Chinese satellite is also a reconnaissance satellite.[2] This speculation does not apparently derive from any other source, but is based on SIPRI's analysis of the orbital characteristics of the Chinese satellites.

Let us next describe briefly the characteristics of reconnaissance satellites. The principal points of interest relate to their cameras and to the apparatus necessary to get the data back to earth. First, we may usefully compare the cameras with the cameras used by the average tourist. We are talking about satellites which are extremely large, probably around five metric tons. For this reason their cameras weigh 10,000 times as much as the tourist's equivalent. Of course another difference is that they are designed to take the best possible picture of something one is not particularly sure about from about 100 kilometres, or possibly a little further away; hence they are not designed to take a picture of a friend from a few metres away. Now the dimensions of them, thinking of them as cameras, are not given by any sources which actually have all the facts, but Greenwood has made some very good guesses about these things. We know, for example, that the satellites are typically cylindrical and two or three metres in diameter and maybe 10 metres long. Hence these are the dimensions in which the camera normally has to fit.

From these dimensions, one can begin to get some idea of what the performance might be. Imagine the lens in a camera has a two-metre diameter, then from a point 100 km away, if everything is perfect (and I emphasise that nothing is ever perfect), this lens would have a resolution of around a few centimetres. That means that if there were two lines on a background more than, say, 2½ centimetres apart, one could tell that they were two lines, but if they were less than 2½ centimetres apart one could not tell they were two lines. If there is only one line and it is a white line on a black surface one could see it even if it were only a few milimetres wide because of the contrast. The resolution given does not say one cannot see anything smaller than 2½ centimetres, but says that if there are two objects that are closer together than that, one would not see them as separate objects. The human eye does not have enough resolution to see wires hung between electric poles but one can see them there because of the contrast. Now this is the resolution considering just the size of the lens. But there are many other considerations effecting resolutions. These include the quality of the film and the size of the image on the film. Moreover, there are many other factors which tend to make the resolution much poorer than might ideally be the case. The atmosphere, for example, distorts any photographs. There is in fact what one might call an absolute minimum resolution of the order of five centimetres and that the practical resolution is surely something bigger than that, perhaps substantially bigger. Instead of five centimetres it may be thirty centimetres or even bigger. The order of magnitude which we are discussing is thus resolutions which are a few inches or a few centimetres.

A second question concerns how data is to be got down to earth.

There are two hypothetical ways to do it. One is to bring down the film itself; the other is to send the picture down by television. Both of these methods are hypothetically possible and both have been debated for a long time and both are discussed in Greenwood's papers. To appreciate the problems involved it is necessary to realise another difference between the cameras in satellites and those used by tourists; namely the amount of film required. Let us suppose one wished to take a photograph of the Soviet Union or North America at a resolution of 10 centimetres. Given that both North America and the Soviet Union are about 20 million square kilometres and given that if the television system was continuously broadcasting the data down to earth, one would require more than a hundred megacycle band width to handle one picture per year. That is in turn a very broad band width, much broader than ordinary television. Another problem concerns data handling. To examine one complete picture of North America at a 10-centimetre resolution would take about 10,000 to 100,000 man years. So it is not just a matter of building rockets which are big enough, nor just the problem of bringing the data down, but also the additional problem of what to do with this enormous amount of data after one has it. Accordingly there has developed a major industry called photo interpretation, which must exist in both the Soviet Union and the United States, and probably tens of thousands of people in each country are employed to do nothing but look at satellite photographs of the other country. Now that explains something else which is commonly discussed by Greenwood and others. They say that there are two different kinds of satellites. First there are those designed to take a broad look at the whole country for the purpose of finding large objects or land configurations or finding scars left by earth movements and so forth. In this case one deliberately reduces resolution so that there is not so much data to handle. Secondly, there is the so-called 'close-look' satellite where one takes a picture with the best resolution possible. So there are basically two kinds of reconnaissance satellites, those with poor resolution and those with high resolution: the former are poor not because they could not be made better but because one simply could not cope with the information that a high resolution system would produce.

The 1972 SALT Treaty on Anti-Ballistic Missiles (ABM) and the Interim Agreement on Offensive Weapons each contain a section which specifically legitimised the use of satellite reconnaissance but only by employing euphemisms. The formula was that 'each side shall verify the compliance of the other side with the Treaty by the use of national technical means of verification'. There was the qualification, however, that parties must conform to the norms of international law. Specifically what that means is that satellites have to be non-obtrusive and non-challenging. In other words, reconnaissance satellites are acceptable, U2s are not. And surveillance by vessels which are a given distance offshore are acceptable but not otherwise. This, then, is 'national technical means of verification'. It is an interesting point that each side knows that the other side is talking about satellites and each side knows that the other side knows that they know they are talking about satellites but they never say it. The reason is an historical one. In the late 1950s the Americans at least knew that they wanted to build these devices but they did not want to make any kind of challenge with respect to them. The idea was that if one said one intended to do this and boasted that the other side could not do anything to stop it, then that would have created a challenge to which there had to be a response. Therefore, from the very beginning, each side has been very careful to avoid challenging the other side in this field.

The Treaty of 1972 also provided that neither side should interfere with these means of verification, and it is stated in such a way that makes it clear that two kinds of interference were being prohibited. First, direct interference with these devices, for example by shooting them down, is ruled out. Secondly, words are used which imply that camouflage designed to spoof these devices is also illegitimate except for that which is already being used. One of the major purposes of the Standing Consultative Committee established by the 1972 Treaty is to discuss any questions which come up between the two sides with regard to SALT, and evidently a fairly large proportion of their time has been spent in discussing purported incidents in which one side or the other is said to be trying to introduce means which confuse the other's satellites. Let us, for example, take the question of how submarines are built — whether they are built in facilities which are covered or not. The rule is that they have to be built covered and uncovered in the same proportion as before the 1972 Treaty went into effect.

So what began as a purely unilateral matter, namely the development of reconnaissance satellites for the purpose of gathering intelligence as simply a technical substitute for the thousand-year art of gathering intelligence, has become codified as an essential element of the existing SALT agreements. Presumably the same will apply to any future SALT agreements also. Hence as verification has been from the beginning one of the toughest problems involved in achieving any kind of disarmament, the development of reconnaissance satellites could constitute a major political breakthrough in the quest for international agreements to end the arms race.

Notes

1. Ted Greenwood, *Reconnaissance, Surveillance and Arms Control,* The International Institute for Strategic Studies Adelphi Paper no.88 (London, 1972).
2. Stockholm International Peace Research Institute, *World Armaments and Disarmament: SIPRI Yearbook, 1976* (Stockholm, 1976), pp.102-6.

14 THE REALITIES OF ARMS CONTROL: THE CRUISE MISSILE CASE

Robert A. Nalewajek

Introduction

The literature available on arms control and disarmament proposals is voluminous,[1] yet sorely lacking in practicable solutions usable by policy/decision makers. One can find no end of logical, moral and even intellectually exciting arguments which, regrettably, are of little value when balanced against the political realities facing national leaders. The field is replete with authors fascinated with the integrity or morality of their arguments and not with the mechanics needed to obtain viable results. Another shortcoming of many writers on arms control is that they deal mainly with the control and reduction of arms which are either already integrated into the various force structures of the superpowers or are so far along in development that they almost are. The problem of limitation before the 'final development', that is at the national stage, is left largely unconsidered.

The purpose of this paper is first to describe the cruise missile and its capabilities, and then to present and analyse five hypotheses which purport to explain the rationale for cruise development, and its integration into the United States' strategic arsenal. For only by understanding how strategic arms are developed and deployed, and by understanding the policy-makers' decision processes, is it possible to identify politically feasible courses of action to effect the limitation of arms at the developmental stage, prior to their introduction into the force structure.

What is a Cruise Missile?

The current generation of cruise missiles are air-breathing, subsonic, non-ballistic (continuously powered) missiles which may be launched from a torpedo tube, aeroplane, surface ship or land vehicle. They are approximately 14 or 21 feet long (depending on the type), approximately 21 inches in diameter and weigh about 2,000 pounds. They will travel at altitudes varying from tree-top level to 45,000 feet and be continuously guided. The missiles will vary in range from 850 nautical miles (nm) to 2,000 mm, carry a 200 KT warhead, and will have a CEP of 0.1nm. The anticipated final production cost per missile is between $500,000 and $800,0(

The cruise missile was born during World War Two, when German scientists developed the V-1 rocket used in the air war against Great Britain. After the war, the Americans developed and deployed a submarine-launched cruise missile called Regulus I. The Navy was in the late development stage of Regulus II when the successful launch of Sputnik I, coupled with a decision by the Presidential Science Advisory Committee (PSAC) to place American emphasis on the development of an ICBM, killed the project. It took technological breakthroughs in three areas (nuclear warheads, guidance and engine miniaturisation) to make a cruise missile again viable in today's nuclear arsenal.

The Engine

Research done in the 1960s by the Advanced Research Projects Agency (ARPA) to create a jet belt capable of flying soldiers around the battlefield resulted in the development of technology making a powerful miniature turbo fan jet engine possible. This technology was subsequently used by the Williams Research Company in developing the engine for the SCAD (Subsonic Cruise Armed Decoy) missile which would have been used as penetration aids for attack bombers. When this project was cancelled by Congress in 1973, the Williams Research Company went into competition with Teledyne CAE for the contract for cruise missile engines. Williams Research was subsequently awarded the contract and its F107-WR-100 turbo fan engine will be used in both air-launched and sea-launched cruise missiles. Although the F107-WR-100 weighs only 125 pounds, is approximately 33 inches in length and 12 inches in diameter, it will be capable of powering the 2,000-pound cruise missile at between mach 0.5 and mach 0.85 for distances of between 850 and 2,000nm, depending on specific configuration.

The Warhead

Advances in miniaturisation of nuclear warheads have made it possible to manufacture'. . .small warheads with [an] explosive yield of about one kiloton TNT equivalent per pound of warhead weight'.[2] It is anticipated that the cruise missile will carry a warhead in the 200 KT range.

The Guidance

Until recently, electronics technology did not provide the means for long-range continuous missile guidance, but recent advances in the micro-miniaturisation of electronic hardware and electromagnetic radiation sensors now make accurate, long-range delivery possible. (In order to self-guide itself, a cruise missile must be able to correlate information about overflown terrain, via an on-board sensing system, with information contained in an on-board memory).

The McDonnell Douglas Corporation won the guidance contract for both air- and sea-launched cruise missiles in October 1975 in run-off tests against E-Systems Inc. The McDonnell Douglas package will utilise two guidance systems, incorporating relatively accurate inertial guidance (updated and corrected periodically by terrain matching) and terminal/secondary radiometry microwave guidance.

The TERCOM (terrain matching device) works by bouncing radar waves off the terrain below the missile, at various angles, to determine altimeter readings. This information is then fed into the guidance memory where various algorithms are utilised to determine if the missile is on its predetermined flight path. Since it is usually impossible to determine position by a single elevation reading, a trajectory (a sequence of numbers, each corresponding to an elevation of the terrain) will be determined. If the guidance system discovers that the missile is off course (that is if the digital read-outs of pre-planned trajectory do not match the altimeter readings), the computer will quickly scan all possible sequences of numbers that can be formed by moving from the left to the right — or vice-versa — of the digital map stored in its memory and correlate each one with the sequences being given by the radar altimeter. The computer will then 'instruct' the missile to its correct course.

In the event that the terrain in the target area is quite featureless, the terminal radiometry guidance would be used to guide the missile. (This system could also be utilised for in-flight trajectory checks along featureless terrain.) A radiometer will measure the ground reflectively at one or more radio frequency wavelengths and the computer will convert these readings on to a digital map of the area and designate the target. Weather conditions and electronic counter-measures are not expected to interfere with the TERCOM guidance, although nuclear blasts in the vicinity of the target would affect the terminal guidance.

As advanced as this system is, with CEP of 600 feet, it is expected that when the Global Positioning Satellite system is operational in the 1980s, the continuous guidance then made possible will provide for cruise missile accuracies of up to a 30 foot CEP.[3]

Two Types of Cruise Missile

The technologies just described have been combined by both the Navy and Air Force in developing service-specific versions of the cruise missile. Each version is being developed to enhance the respective service's combat capabilities — air and sea delivery of weapons.

The Sea-Launched Cruise Missile (SLCM)

Two companies were competing for the SLCM contract, LTV Aerospace and General Dynamics.[4] Underwater launch tests of the missile took place in February and March 1976, with General Dynamics being awarded the contract. The SLCM will be approximately 21 feet long, 20.5 inches in diameter, have an aluminium alloy-based body, and an in-flight deployed fibreglass wing with a span of 10.5 feet. The Navy has nicknamed their SLCM the Tomahawk.

The key to Tomahawk design was to make the missile deployable from a submarine torpedo tube. This was accomplished by encapsulating the missile in a steel jacket and placing the entire assembly into the torpedo tube. A 32-inch solid propellant is used to eject the missile from its capsule to the surface (and is also used to eject the capsule from the torpedo tube). Upon breaking the surface, air inlet covers pop off the missile and the exhaust from starter cartridges start the turbine in the engine spinning up to 30 per cent of its maximum capacity. At this point, the fuel flow starts and is ignited via pyrotechnic charges. The missile would then fly at high altitudes — between 20,000 and 40,000 feet — at a cruise speed of approximately mach 0.5 until reaching a point within enemy radar capabilities, where it would drop to its terrain-following altitude. The SLCM range, with full fuel load and warhead, will be 2,000 nm.

The SLCM is expected to increase the combat capability of the American submarine force in three ways:

1. Since SLCMs are fired from torpedo tubes, American non-nuclear attack submarines will effectively be given a strategic nuclear capability.
2. Submarine-launched ballistic missiles (SLBMs) have a high traceable trajectory which can compromise a submarine's location and hasten its destruction, while SLCMs will allow for no retracking.
3. SLMB launch tubes are not easily reloadable, while the number of SLCMs with firing canisters that may be stored and fired is

limited only by available storage space on the submarine.

Although designed primarily for torpedo-tube launch, the SLCM will also have the capability of being fired from a variety of platforms, including surface ships and ground vehicles. The US Navy is accordingly expected to order between 1,000 and 2,000 SLCMs.[5]

The Air-Launched Cruise Missile (ALCM)

The Air Force's Boeing-designed ALCM will be approximately 14 feet long, 18 inches wide, have an aluminium body and a deployable 14-foot-long fin, elevon, and deployable wings.

The ALCM has had a more tempestuous history than the SLCM. In late 1974 the Defense Systems Acquisition Review Council (DSARC) terminated ALCM development; but this decision was reversed in February 1975 and the ALCM moved into advanced development. Then after surviving the fiscal 1976 authorisation, the House of Representatives eliminated all ALCM funding. But again the programme was saved, when first a Senate Committee and then a Joint Conference Committee voted to restore $51 million for fiscal year 1976.

Whereas the key to SLCM design was to make it launchable from a torpedo tube, Air Force design criteria were dictated by the need to make the ALCM compatible with the $5,000,000,000 investment in the Short Range Attack Missile (SRAM) on board and with ground support equipment facilities. To do this, the ALCM had to be made launchable from the on-board SRAM Rotary Rack. This allows a mixture of 8 SRAMs/ALCMs to be carried on the rotary rack and 12 on the wing pylons of a B-52.

The launch/deploy sequence of an ALCM fired from a rotary rack is critical. Air inlets must extend 0.1 seconds after launch. Elevon unfolding must begin 0.13 seconds after launch and be complete at 0.24 seconds. Fin unfolding must begin at 0.23 seconds and be complete at 0.49 seconds. This is followed by engine start at 0.5 seconds and wing deployment at 1 second, completed by 2 seconds. If this precise timing is not achieved, the missile could fly up and hit the bomber. In fact, in order to prevent this, the elevons must have control of the missile even before it clears the bomb bay.

Design criteria also limited the range of the ALCM. Although both the ALCM and SLCM have the same basic Williams Research engine (parts commonality is 80-90 per cent), the ALCM version had to be configured differently to fit the ALCM's different shape and size. The ALCM engine also uses a different fuel. This, coupled with a smaller fuél capacity, will give the rotary rack launched ALCM a range of approximately 650 nm.[6] The McDonnell Douglas guidance package for the Boeing ALCM is also repackaged to fit its smaller, flatter nose.

The ALCM launch/deploy sequence will probably take the following form: after being launched at x feet, the ALCM would lose altitude incrementally until it reaches radar detection range – by which time it would be a few hundred feet above the ground. It would then cruise at around mach 0.55 until it is approximately 50 miles from its target, when it would drop to 50 feet and speed up to between mach 0.7 and mach 0.85 for the final approach/kill. (This sequence is also applicable to the SLCM after it has dropped to its radar guidance altitude.)

A number of scenarios for ALCM deployment are possible. One is to use them from a stand-off range, prior to bomber penetration. This would effectively defeat the 2,600 Soviet interceptor aircraft, 4,000 radar and 12,000 SAM launchers.

ALCMs may also be used to compliment bombers in an advanced threat environment by:

(1) Utilising the B-52G and H series bombers with ALCMs to mask the penetration of B-1s;

(2) Launching B-52 ALCMs from a stand-off distance and timing their radar penetration and altitude to coincide with B-1 penetration;

(3) Utilising B-1/SRAMs to attack terminally, well-protected sites and B-52/ALCMs to attack less protected sites.

The Air Force has shown some reluctance in identifying a B-1/ALCM combined role. Understanding, though, that the essence of the Air Force's Strategic Air Command (SAC) is to deliver nuclear bombs on target, it may not be so surprising that no scenario offered by the Air Force foresees such a role for the new B-1, but relegates it only to the older B-52s.

Why Cruise?

The following section will present five hypotheses which attempt to explain the US Defense Department's decision to proceed with cruise development. Although treated separately for analysis, the five hypotheses are reflective of a synergistic relationship encompassing an entire spectrum of executive branch decision-making.

Keeping Up with the Joneses

The Soviets now have two types of SLCMs in their inventory. One, the

SS-N-7, can fire submerged and has a range of 30 nm. This is an undeniably tactical cruise which is carried on Charlie Class submarines. The other is the SS-N-3 Shaddock cruise missile which is carried on Soviet Echo Class submarines (Echo 1 has 6 Shaddocks; Echo 2 has 8). These missiles, which have an estimated range of over 550 nm, are one of the reasons now given for American strategic cruise development. Because the Shaddock's range can be extended to 1,200 nm and since it can carry a warhead in the high kiloton (possibly a megaton) range, ex-Secretary of Defense Donald Rumsfeld was led to say: 'If the Soviets were to divert their sea-based cruise missiles from the anti-shipping missions to which we believe they are currently assigned and extend their range, they could attack large portions of the US population and industry.'[7]

Additionally, the Soviets are developing a new SLCM (the SS-X-12) as an apparent replacement for the Shaddock. This new cruise missile will fit into the Shaddock firing canister and achieve a range of 2,000 nm with a speed of mach 2.5. (The SS-X-12 would have to fly at high altitudes and slower speeds to attain its maximum range). The AS-4 ALCM is also undergoing extensive modification to make it compatible with the Soviet Backfire bomber. The new missile can attain a range of 425 nm at supersonic speeds. By flying a higher profile, the AS-4 could greatly extend its range and attain a true stand-off capability.

Although Rumsfeld qualified the significance of these Soviet advances by pointing out the large lead in American ALCM and SLCM development, they are nevertheless cited as a rationale for continued development and deployment of American cruise missiles. This is, however, an 'after the fact' development, since as late as the SALT I agreement, Soviet cruise missiles were barely mentioned. Indeed, the recentness of reports about the upgrading of SS-N-3s and AS-4s and the development of the SS-X-12 would tend to indicate that Soviet cruise development is a reaction to the widening American lead in this field.

Kosta Tsipis has presented evidence which tends to support this 'Keeping up with the Joneses' rationale as having been used to defend cruise development. For example, in his 1972 testimony before the Senate Armed Services Committee, Secretary of Defense Melvin Laird inaccurately likened the American SLCMs to the Soviet Shaddock cruise missile, indicating a tactical role for the American cruise. He further said that American SLCM development would assure availability of American options, *if needed.* Tsipis's summary of the 'Keeping up with the Joneses' argument for cruise missiles is that there appears to be little pragmatic need to develop and deploy these weapons as a response to Soviet initiatives.[8]

The Bureaucratic Imperative

Morton Halperin identifies the essence ('the view held by the dominant group in an organisation of what the missions and capabilities should be') of the US Air Force as the flying of aeroplanes designed to deliver nuclear weapons against the Soviet Union. Armed with such a unified/unifying position, Halperin contends that an agency will do all in its power to enhance and advance that mission. The Air Force's push to develop and deploy the strategic ALCM may be placed in this context.

Although Halperin reports agreements among American Naval Officers as to the essence of the Navy, namely to maintain combat ships in order to control the seas, he also identifies a 'serious dispute' among four naval officer groups as to where naval emphasis should be placed; two such groups opting for either attack submarines or nuclear submarines. Since the SLCM would enhance the role of both these groups, the Navy's impetus for development can thus be identified.

Aside from these individual agency imperatives, bureaucratic competition between the Navy and Air Force may also account for cruise development. Halperin contends that:

1. 'An organization favors policies and strategies which its members believe will make the organization as they define it more important.' The cruise, although not in itself a policy or a strategy, would definitely enhance the Navy's and Air Force's importance by placing in their hands a new, superior weapon system.

2. 'An organization struggles hardest for the capabilities which it views as necessary to the essence of the organization. It seeks autonomy and funds to pursue the necessary capabilities and missions.' That the Navy and Air Force pursued their cruise programmes independently until forced by Congress to combine certain elements would indicate this second point is in operation. Officers in both services have identified their service's essence and the cruise as one, and have avoided 'encroachment' on their respective development of the missile.

3. 'An organization resists efforts to take away from it those functions viewed as part of its essence. It will seek to protect these functions by taking on additional functions if it believes that forgoing these added functions may ultimately jeopardize its sole control over the essence of its activities.'[9] Here it is difficult to determine which

service initiated cruise development and which reacted to protect 'part of its essence'. In any case, cruise development may be viewed as representative of the converse of this point, in that the reactive service may have perceived that not developing a cruise missile would give the other service a qualitative edge in its ability to deliver nuclear weapons to an enemy's territory. One-service control of what has been called the fourth major weapons system[10] would lessen the importance, whether internally or externally perceived, of the other service.[11]

Another thesis which may be grouped under this Bureaucratic Imperative category is that cruise development, together with the Trident programme, was the price paid to obtain Department of Defense support of the SALT I agreement.[12]

This bureaucratic interpretation of decision-making clearly provides a substantial backdrop for analysing why cruise missile development was pursued. Although the approach is relatively recent (at least in its current formulation),[13] further explanations of decisions as seen in this framework will yield fruitful results, and will suggest new practical approaches to arms control.

The Capitalistic, Technological Imperative

The rationale of this argument is basically deductive and builds on the following facts:

(1) The Williams Research Company invested a good deal of time, scientific manpower and money into the engine development for the Air Force's SCAD missile. Since this project was cancelled by Congress, the company had an available technology with no readily available buyer.

(2) This same defunct SCAD project (coupled with Skybolt) left certain air frame developers, who had also made a financial/technological commitment, without a market.

(3) These two occurrences led to the establishment of a techno-bureaucracy centred around ALCM development, without an ALCM project.

(4) Successful development of the Harpoon missile (a ship-to-ship tactical cruise) created a like techno-bureaucracy spanning private corporations and the Department of the Navy.

(5) Advances in large array microcircuits and sensing devices during the late 1960s and early 1970s created a utilisation vacuum which corporations were eager to fill.

These facts then tied together to form an economically motivated, technological imperative argument for the development of the cruise missile which runs basically:

(1) Previously, technological developments centred around defunct projects, coupled with new technologies in search of application, led to the creation of technologies without fully exploited markets.

(2) These same developments led to the establishment of a specialised techno-bureaucracy.

(3) *Ergo,* a search for profits and the existence of an under-utilised, available technology, coupled with the presence of an influential group sympathetic to its application, led to cruise missile development.

Although simply stated, this hypothesis warrants further study, not only *vis-à-vis* the cruise missile, but as a general factor in all arms development/procurement. An exposé of the private sector's ability to coerce force-structure decisions would be one way to attempt more stringent Congressional oversight in this area.

The Strategic Capability Argument

This argument is built around demonstrations of the cruise missile's unique strike capabilities and emphasis on its multiple strategic advantages. A sample of these type of arguments is:

(1) Since it is now generally accepted that missile accuracy is the more important attribute in a weapon's destructive capability,[14] it is argued that the cruise will enhance American second-strike capability by being able to knock out Soviet silos before they can be reloaded and thereby also decrease damage to the United States.[15]

(2) As the cruise missile will be launchable from almost any platform, their deployment would enhance the survivability of the American second-strike force.

(3) The cruise missile's low flying capability almost negates the use of any of the Soviet Union's 2,600 interceptor aircraft, and all but the terminally located SAMs.

(4) Since SLBMs are relatively easy to retrack to the source of fire, the employment of cruise missiles would extend the survivability of the American submarine force.

(5) The torpedo and aircraft launching capabilities of the cruise will do for our bomber and submarine forces what MIRV did for the ICBM, namely multiply cheaply and quickly the number of warheads that can be delivered on target.

This small sample should leave little doubt as to the strategic capabilities of the cruise missile. In fact, there is no controversy as to the missile's potential effectiveness. A discussion begins, though, when the group advancing this argument in favour of American cruise development correlates these strategic capabilities to the stability aspects of the American nuclear forces. The interpretation taken here by cruise supporters was best summarised by Admiral G.E. Synhorst in testimony before a Senate Sub-Committee in 1974:

> The Soviets will always have to consider that even if they could get everything else, if they could target our SSBNs, if they have an ABM system, if they can target our Minutemen, we would still have every submarine torpedo tube we have at sea that can employ this missile. That should be stabilizing.[16]

More 'complete picture' analysis of weapons systems presented by means of effective lobbying at Congressional committee and subcommittee levels is one potential vehicle for preventing this type of 'strategic capability' argument from dominating the decision-making process. To accomplish this, an effective lobby can be set up on the lines of Common Cause, which has had amazing success in pressing for both particular legislation and Congressional reform.

The Official Position

In *The Report of Secretary of Defense, Donald H. Rumsfeld, to the Congress on the Fiscal Year (FY) 1977 Defense Budget and its Implications for FY 1978 Authorization Requests and the FY 1977-1981 Defense Programs* (DODRTC), four 'basic objectives' for American strategic nuclear forces were definition, regardless of how those forces are comprised:

(1) 'To have a well protected, second-strike force to deter attacks on our cities and people, at all times'.

(2) 'To provide a capability for more controlled response, to deter less than all out attacks.'

(3) 'To ensure essential equivalence with the USSR, both now and in the future, so that there can be no misunderstandings or lack of appreciation of the strategic nuclear balance.'

(4) 'To maintain stability in the strategic nuclear competition, forsaking the option of a disarming first strike capability and seeking to achieve equitable arms control agreements when possible.'[17]

Analysing the cruise in the light of the United States' stated nuclear force objectives will demonstrate the almost *prima facie* case that can be made for cruise deployment as part of those forces:

(1) 'To have a well protected, second strike force. . .' As indicated earlier, the cruise missile's ability to be launched from almost any

platform and to penetrate Soviet air defences, both passive and active, would provide an almost undefeatable second-strike capability.

(2) 'To provide the capability for more controlled and measured response. . .' The goal here is to provide an alternative to the assured destruction policy and allow American nuclear forces to be used against *selected* economic, military and population targets. This objective, commonly called flexible response, requires an accurate missile to prevent collateral damage, coupled with good command and control. Since the cruise will be the most accurate strategic nuclear weapon in the world (CEP = 0.1 nm), its deployment would guarantee a flexible response option being available to American decision-makers. This accuracy, coupled with a lower-yield warhead, would also limit collateral damage.

(3) 'To ensure essential equivalence with the USSR. . .' Throughout the DODRTC, Rumsfeld stressed the advancing vulnerability of American nuclear forces based on a situation where major asymmetries developing between the superpowers' strategic nuclear forces are possible. He stressed the ageing character of the American bomber force and the need for the B-1 to maintain that arm of the Triad. Even assuming the B-1, he says that 'equipping the B-52Gs and Hs with cruise missiles will alleviate to a degree any loss of effectiveness and contribute to stability' and also ensure the viability of the B-52 into the late 1980s/early 1990s. With the future of the B-1 bomber being called into question more and more by the Congress, cruise deployment becomes even more critical (based on DoD arguments). Rumsfeld also pointed out that Soviet advances in MIRVing and accuracies will jeopardise the American ICBM force by the 1980s. Accepting this premise, the cruise missile would have to be viewed as a possible replacement for the loss of that capability's effectiveness, and its development/deployment would become mandatory. The increasing possibility that major asymmetries will develop due to Soviet momentum in offensive and defensive weapons is mentioned both specifically and indirectly throughout the report. Again, accepting this premise would make any American decision to cease development of a weapons system in which they possess a large lead ridiculous, for both American security and deterrence/stability capabilities would be sacrificed.

(4) 'To maintain stability in the strategic nuclear competition. . . and seeking to achieve equitable arms control agreements. . .' This is the objective which caused the present writer to preface his earlier *prima facie* case for cruise deployment statement with the qualification

'almost'. The addition of a new weapons system is rarely stabilising since it leads to accusations of aggressiveness; calls into question 'good intentions'; causes insecurity about one's security; and forces a rush to develop a like-better system to counter the original threat. In sum, introducing new systems is de-stabilising.

Apart from this fourth objective, however, it can be seen that cruise development enhances all American objectives for a strategic nuclear force; and by doing so, it enhances deterrence:

> We believe that deterrence is best achieved by maintaining a well designed, second strike-force which has the capability for assured retaliation and the flexibility to cover a wide variety of military, economic and other targets with a minimum of collateral damage and a maximum of choice and control.[18]

A weapons system which so thoroughly meets American stated objectives is not likely to be ignored, especially when it can be bought as cheaply as the cruise. Moreover, to forgo the development of a weapon system perceived as necessary for security, simply for the purpose of promoting arms limitations, would be nonsensical. Those who disagree with this view would have to develop an argument for non-implementation of cruise based on a proof that the detriment to goal number 4 ('to maintain stability in strategic nuclear competition') is greater than the sum of the enhancement of the other objectives if the cruise is deployed. Moreover, to win decisive support for such a thesis would necessitate strong, goal-orientated action, possibly centrally directed by a lobby organisation, designed to place effective pressures wherever possible in the decision-making channels.

Conclusions

This attempt to analyse weapon-systems procurement arguments and accompanying suggestions of strategies for countering such a development is by no means complete or conclusive, nor was it intended to be. The objective has been to stress the importance of the pre-development stages in arms acquisition and to demonstrate the various arguments deployed in support of arms development. Studies along these lines may help to suggest politically viable approaches towards the desired goal of arms reduction. Such a goal, though, must also encompass both superpowers and hence practical methods for inducing Soviet arms limitation must also be developed. The search for control by international negotiation should not, of course, be forsaken.

But the alternative route of individual national restraint needs to be more fully explored and exploited, with an emphasis on the most politically practical courses available.

Notes

1. Bernard Brodie, 'On the Objectives of Arms Control', *International Security,* I (1976), p.17, states that Richard Burns has compiled, in manuscript form, a 900-page, double-spaced bibliography of arms control works.
2. Kosta Tsipis, 'The Long Range Cruise Missile', *Bulletin of the Atomic Scientists,* XXI (1975).
3. This TERCOM guidance system was successfully tested in conjunction with a turbo fan engine at the White Sands, New Mexico, missile range during the late spring of 1976 *(Army Research and Development News Magazine,* July/August 1976). Tests, up to November 1976, of the TERCOM and Radiometry guidance systems have continued to be successful.
4. The SLCM and ALCM, although having different air frames, will utilise the same Williams Research F107-WR-100 engine and McDonnell Douglas guidance package.
5. Deborah Shapley, 'Cruise Missile: Air Force, Navy Weapon Poses New Arms Issues', *Science,* 7 February 1975.
6. The wing-mounted ALCM can be fitted with a belly tank which would extend its range to 1,000 nm, but this would require longer periods at high altitudes and slower speeds. The belly tank also increases the ALCM's radar cross-section size, making it easier to detect.
7. As reported by Clarence A. Robinson, Jr., 'Soviets Make a New SALT Bid', *Aviation Week and Space Technology,* 16 February 1976.
8. Tsipis, loc.cit.
9. Morton H. Halperin, *Bureaucratic Politics and Foreign Policy* (Washington, D.C., 1971), pp.28, 29.
10. The United States' current strategic nuclear arsenal consists of intercontinental ballistic missiles (ICBMs), sea-launched ballistic missiles and strategic bombers.
11. See Alexander R. Vershbow, 'The Cruise Missile: The End of Arms Control?' *Foreign Affairs,* LV (1976-7), pp.135-6.
12. Lawrence Weiler, 'Strategic Cruise Missiles and the Future of SALT', *The Arms Control Association,* V (1975), no.10. This aspect of bureaucratic politics is more fully described in Halperin, *Bureaucratic Politics,* pp.99-232.
13. In addition to ibid., see Graham T. Allison, *Essence of Decision: Explaining the Cuban Missile Crisis* (Boston, 1971) and Anatol Rapoport, *Conflict in Man-Made Environment* (Baltimore, 1974), p.133.
14. Kosta Tsipis, 'Physics and Calculus of Countercity and Counterforce Nuclear Attack', *Science,* 7 February 1975, provides mathematical evidence that 'the lethality (lethality = $Y \, 2/3 \div (CEP)^2$) of a warhead against a missile silo rises much more rapidly with improvements in accuracy of delivery than with yield.'
15. Even if a silo is able to withstand the overpressure caused by a nuclear weapon, the high level of electro-magnetic pulse (EMP) caused by a 200 KT warhead delivered within a 0.1 nm radius is expected to damage or destroy the electronic equipment of a missile and its attenuating launch facilities.
16. Shapley, loc.cit.

17. *Report of Secretary of Defense, Donald H. Rumsfeld, to the Congress: Fiscal Year 1977 Defense Budget and its Implications for the Fiscal Years 1977-1981 Defense Programs* (Washington, D.C., 1976).
18. Ibid.

15 THE DIFFUSION OF ECONOMIC AND MILITARY POWER AND ITS IMPACT ON THE MIDDLE EAST CONFLICT

Mario'n Mushkat

The transformation of oil-producing countries into important actors in present-day international life and their well-coordinated strategy has led to the creation of non-traditional centres of financial might. This in turn has opened new avenues not only for the reconstruction of the world economy but also, unfortunately, for the diffusion of military power as well. These ongoing changes have already greatly affected international politics. They are felt above all in the process of economic decolonialisation, which is now succeeding political decolonisation.

The oil-rich Arabs are not, however, investing, at least for the time being, any important part of their surplus petro-dollars in the black African and other underdeveloped countries. The Organization of Petroleum Exporting Countries (OPEC) is used less for developmental purposes and more for the military aggrandisement of their allies and of themselves. The tremendous increase of arms shipments, strengthened by the keen competition between suppliers attempting to improve their payment balances, involves the proliferation of advanced conventional and even nuclear technology.

The fundamental equations of economic and military power have thus changed decisively not only in the Middle East and Africa. This has occurred, moreover, in a situation characterised by a perceived steady decline in the practical possibilities for the use of military force by all the industrialised states, including the superpowers. This trend has been particularly evident following the withdrawal of the Soviets from Egypt, and the Americans from Vietnam.

Another contemporary feature of the international scene is the growing awareness of the dangers to peace in many different regions inherent in the arms race. This has found expression in negotiations, for arms reduction and control. True, these endeavours have so far failed to stop the growth of arsenals and military technological advance. This is not only because of the distrust between the major actors of the blocs dividing today's world; it is also the result of the failure to conceive arrangements on arms control as steps towards more comprehensive disarmament, and the difficulties in initiating negotiations, above all on the level of the superpowers, designed to halt their continuing reliance on deterrence concepts; their dialogue is marked above all with the concern to avoid a clash between themselves and with stability in Europe. The Third World concerns the superpowers only to a lesser extent.

Ironically, the region where 3,000 years ago disarmament was first conceived as a condition for human coexistence by the prophet Isaiah is now heavily armed, and is arming itself still further at an unprecedented pace. Thus for Israel and other poor nations of the Middle East the principles of disarmament evoke not only a basic premise in their moral make-up, but also practical considerations of the most direct significance in terms of the threat inherent in high levels of armaments and in terms of the crushing burden of expenditure involved in fulfilling the vast requirements of modern defence. For Middle East countries, particularly those which cannot rely on rich sources of income, the problem is becoming increasingly more difficult.

The Middle East conflict, proving that *détente* does not mean a smooth process of co-operation but rather a non-belligerent competition between the superpowers, reflects virtually all the major developments of present global interaction. The *1976 Yearbook* of the Stockholm International Peace Research Institute (SIPRI) shows, *inter alia,* that in 1975 world military expenditure reached $280,000,000,000. It is of great significance, moreover, that the share attributable to NATO and Warsaw Pact states is declining, being 78 per cent in 1975 compared with 91 per cent in 1955. Another key fact is that the value of major weapons transferred to the Third World countries increased by over 70 per cent in 1975 following a 40 per cent increase in 1974. More than half the total arms supplied in 1975 went to the Middle East. Indeed the number of jet aircraft for combat purposes and tanks deployed in the Middle East are now comparable with those of NATO forces in Europe.

The Middle East is, in fact, the most militarised region in the world. In 1974, the latest year for which data was available in SIPRI, *per capita* gross national product (GNP) for the Middle East as a whole was about $845 and *per capita* military expenditure about $135. Nearly 16 per cent of the combined GNPs of the Middle East countries was spent for military purposes. SIPRI *Arms Trade Records* show that about 4,100 jet aircraft for combat purposes, excluding trainer versions of combat types, were transferred to the Middle East between 1950 and 1975. Deliveries of heavy, medium and light tanks amounted to about 13,500. Operational jet aircraft for combat in the Middle East probably numbered about 2,300 at the end of 1975, while the number of tanks was approximately 10,500. By comparison, NATO forces in Europe have about 3,000 tactical aircraft and 12,250 main battle tanks. Moreover, Middle East arms are among the most up-to-date in the world, perhaps even more than those of NATO.

There are also clear findings as to the implications of the burden of this flow of more and more sophisticated weapons into the region. These include direct effects on the economies of all countries involved, the waste of natural resources, the social regression caused by it, the growing political dependence of Middle East states on foreign powers, and the decline of the prospects for reconciliation.

There is, then, an obvious need to halt the arms race in the Middle East both for the benefit of the peoples of the area and for peace in the world. Any agreement on this subject, as on greater stability in the region, seems to be dependent on an agreement above all between the two superpowers, since both have political and economic assets in the area, since both are seeking to increase their influence, and since both complicate, if not hinder through their rivalry, the reconciliation between the conflicting parties, a situation which is likely to continue as long as arrangements are not shaped in accordance with their vital interests. The kind of arrangement that would be highly profitable for Middle East nations would be one linked to the main principles of *détente* as agreed by the superpowers. Possibly it could be based on the outlines of the once-renowned Rapacki Proposal concerning Central Europe. It could involve freezing the arms build-up in the Middle East and a halt to the further transfer of all kinds of sophisticated weaponry.

This is the background against which Israel's Foreign Minister, addressing the General Assembly on 30 September 1975, outlined his country's position concerning arms reduction and control in the Middle East, including a proposal for making the Middle East a nuclear-free zone. According to his statement, Israel would be most willing to participate in any kind of inter-governmental consultation with its neighbours in a genuine effort to reach agreement in these matters.

Various experts and government officials have pointed out the complications that preclude any simple solutions. However, in the light of the civil war in Lebanon and various conflicts in other Middle East countries, the necessity of working towards disarmament and peace is becoming increasingly more urgent, above all because of the existing danger of new confrontations, which may be easily provoked under the conditions of an uncontrolled arms race, and because of the disastrous economic and social situation resulting from the continually growing militarisation of the region.

According to scholarly findings, military expenditure and losses in GNP following the wars between 1949 and 1969 in the Middle East reached the sum of 55,000,000,000 dollars at 1960 prices. In 1969 alone the sum was more than $8,900,000,000, which was more than the total income from oil revenues in the region that year. Egyptian losses in that year were ten times greater than its income from the Suez Canal in 1966, and Israel's losses were three times greater than all capital imports, governmental and private alike.[1]

The disastrous impact made by the rise of military expenditure on the Middle East economies had already become evident in the period between 1953 and 1970, but became especially alarming after the 1973 war. It rose in the five Arab confrontation states from $258,000,000 in 1953 to $2,066,000,000 in 1970, and in Israel from $64,000,000 to $1,075,000,000. The respective changes in the proportion of the GNP were from 5.5 per cent to 14.6 per cent and from 6.1 per cent to 19.5 per cent. By contrast, in the Arab countries military expenditure rose from $2,400,000,000 in 1973 to $8,300,000,000 in 1974 and to $16, 500,000,000 in 1975; and in Israel it rose from $1,700,000,000 in 1973 to $3,600,000,000 in 1974 and to $3,500,000,000 in 1975.[2]

Consequently the economies, above all of Egypt and Israel, were severely strained and a continual deterioration in the balance of payments became characteristic of these countries. In Egypt, the deficit grew from $516,000,000 in 1972 to $3,000,000,000 in 1975, and in Israel, from $1,100,000,000 to $3,700,000,000.[3] The sum total of Egypt's external debts in 1975 reached $1,100,000,000 and Israel's were $8,200,000,000.[4] These debts limited the prospects of achieving further credits and of promoting new investments and development. In turn this caused increasing unemployment, soaring prices and growing inflation, and the failure of plans for improvements in agriculture and industry, in education and research. This is a feature more or less in all the confrontation states but particularly in Egypt and Israel, where economic growth, which before 1973 was fluctuating between 8 and 12 per cent, became almost nil, while the rise in prices was 20 per cent in 1973 and 40 per cent in 1974 and is continuing.[5]

Yet some political factions in Israel and in Egypt have yet to abandon the nuclear option. Steven Baker has argued that, although Israel is not a nuclear weapons state in terms of the NPT, namely one that has detonated a nuclear device, there exists a growing consensus that Israel has indeed manufactured a number of nuclear weapons.[6]

Even among those who are not convinced that this is the case, there seems to be a readiness to concede that Israel is between 12 and 48 hours from doing so. According to Baker, Israel's nuclear option is based on a small plutonium production reactor, not subject to international safeguards. Plutonium has apparently been separated in a small fuel reprocessing facility and secretly manufactured into nuclear devices. There has been no demonstration of nuclear capacity — but sufficiently credible information has leaked abroad, convincing many observers that Israel does have nuclear weapons. According to Baker, Israel's route involves minimal vulnerability to nuclear-related sanctions from outside: having broken no international commitments, and having no nuclear power industry open to technological embargoes or fuel cut-offs, Israel has preserved its freedom of action in the nuclear field.

The fact remains, however, that there is no proof at all that the manufacture of nuclear devices has actually taken place in Israel, and the Israeli Government has declared many times that it will not be the first to introduce nuclear weapons into the region. Nevertheless it seems that the nuclear argument has been used by some Israeli politicians as a refined instrument of psychological warfare, and for this reason the Israelis have also been reluctant to sign the Non-Proliferation Treaty (NPT). Some Israeli hawks continue to take this line and they choose to disregard the possibility that it may lead to further political isolation. Moreover, the economic results of this approach could be catastrophic, in that a technological recession could result from the application of external sanctions.

It should also be unnecessary to stress that while nuclear deterrence may have some validity in superpower relationships, it is devoid of any meaning in a limited area such as the Middle East, where no second strike possibility exists. Moreover, even if a majority of the more than 100 million Arabs living in territories stretching from the Atlantic to the Indian Ocean could survive following a localised nuclear war, it might very well be doomsday for Israel.

The recent statement by Dr Sigward Eklund, the Director of the International Atomic Energy Agency, after his last visit to Israel, during April 1976, confirms that Israel is not a nuclear power, proving that the Israeli Government is aware that by becoming a party to the NPT, it will receive more profit than from the nuclear option. Hopes for peace will only grow and become real, however, by crushing self-delusions involving nuclear power.

A nuclear-free zone is vital, above all, for Israel and Egypt. Once achieved, possibly under United Nations supervision, it may lead to a cooling-off period, to arrangements for ending arms deliveries, and to the beginning of negotiations between the conflicting nations. Peace negotiations are more likely to succeed if based on Security Council resolutions 242 and 338, which have been formally accepted by a majority of the concerned parties. Effective steps towards the implementation of these resolutions and the establishment of conditions not only for the peaceful coexistence of all nations in the area but also for their disarmament might include: the prohibition of the introduction of foreign military forces into the area; the creation of a demilitarised zone; and the designation of neutralised zones.

Consensus between the conflicting parties in accepting a superpower agreement on stopping at least the advanced arms race in the region will occur only if it follows the first step towards reconciliation, and not, if as proposed by the Soviet Union, Israel's withdrawal from the occupied territories is a precondition. On the other hand, the Soviets claim that stopping the arms race in the Middle East is vital and even desired by all parties concerned. It will remain unattainable, however, as long as the present stalemate in the attitude of the superpowers continues concerning this question. The arms race in the Middle East, as well as in other parts of the world, is above all a reflection of the present international system, determined by new forms of the East-West antagonism and strengthening different aspects of deterrence and of the militarisation process in a growing number of developing countries.

Some experts take an extremely pessimistic view of what the future will hold. Some of them are of the opinion that this results from the belief of many decision-makers in different countries that armaments are indispensable for the continuation of their rule, for the realisation of their undertakings in the area of development, and for their struggle for expanding influence. Others are so fascinated with the perfection of military technology that they overplay its significance in international relations, equating security with power and with preparedness to knock out real and imaginary enemies, and subscribing to the dangerous belief that the arms race promotes progress in science and technology.

Those who see the arms race as a means of achieving political and security aims always have a strong argument at their disposal. Many of these people were against the first partial Nuclear Test Ban Treaty, the Non-Proliferation Treaty, the SALT commitments, the discussion of security problems and other issues of co-operation in Europe, and the least interim agreement in the Middle East. But in the end the majority has acquiesced in the aforementioned steps. Therefore, it is not at all Utopian to argue that the hawks are entirely immune from attempts to change their minds. It will, for example, become increasingly more difficult for them to argue without reservation that without the present arms race, growth and future development will become less and less certain. If the pressures of the intellectuals, of military and technological experts, of public opinion, and of different governments suffering economically and socially from the impositions made upon them by the armaments burden continues to grow, then with them will grow the awareness that unlimited and uncontrolled vertical and horizontal proliferation above all of weapons of mass destruction might one day produce by accident or by miscalculation either genocide or even a suicidal world-wide holocaust.

The increase in the dangers associated with technological improvements can lead to a catastrophe. But it can lead to disarmament as well. The latter development will be attainable only with the strengthening of *détente* and supplementing it continually with different forms of co-operation — which is the best and probably the only tool for reducing distrust between the superpowers and for enlarging their role in the peace-building process, not only in Europe but in the Middle East.

Hence, getting to the core of the problem seems dependent not on minimising the proliferation of nuclear weapons and of partial arms control arrangements, which are often seen as an end in themselves, actually favouring deterrence theories and other stop-gap measures, but on building a new international peace structure. Such a structure cannot, of course, be built overnight, but the incremental approach, and all other step-by-step control arrangements, if conceived as links in a comprehensive disarmament scheme, may be very helpful. They favour the evolution of a new form of enlightened *Realpolitik* rooted in the progress of *détente*. This does not seem in fact to be a temporary trend in world politics. Rather, it is determined by a historical process, the imperatives of the nuclear age, the decolonisation process and a long East-West dialogue, which has facilitated also a gradual North-South dialogue, and the realisation of a new economic world order.

Recent political developments in the Middle East, above all in Israel and Egypt, where pressures for giving priority to economic development and to diplomatic solutions which do not rely upon military strength, are growing. Although the situation does not yet permit over-optimism, there is proof that efforts to bring about an end to irrational politics in the relationships of the bitterly divided Semitic family and other regions of the world are inherent in the condition of growing interdependence between all nations, and not just an exercise in semantics.

War and peace are man-made phenomena, and dreams of achieving true Shalom and more of it in the world may become less and less Utopian. This will be all the more the case if researchers provide information and guidance to governments, parties and mass movements concerning the necessity of breaking away from the constraints of power politics.

Notes

1. H. Askari and V. Corbo, 'Economic Implications of Military Expenditures in the Middle East', *Journal of Peace Research,* IV (1974), p.341.
2. Institute for Strategic Studies, *The Military Balance, 1970-71* (London, 1970) and International Institute for Strategic Studies, *The Military Balance, 1975-76* (London, 1975).
3. *The Economist,* 28 June 1975; *Newsweek,* 13 October 1975; and *The Israeli Statistical Yearbook, 1975,* p.177.
4. *Newsweek,* 13 October 1975; and *The Israeli Statistical Monthly,* September 1975.
5. *The Israeli Statistical Yearbook, 1975,* pp.151, 237.
6. Steven J. Baker, 'The International Political Economy of Proliferation', above, pp.70-101.

16 THE FALLACY OF THINKING CONVENTIONALLY ABOUT NUCLEAR WEAPONS

Hans J. Morgenthau

It is unsound to think in conventional terms about nuclear problems and, more particularly, about nuclear disarmament. But what is obvious to people reflecting theoretically about certain issues of the contemporary world is not necessarily obvious to the policy-makers. In other words, there exists a profound and wide gap between, on the one hand, our traditional modes of thought and action, and, on the other hand, the objective conditions under which we live.

The availability of nuclear power, more particularly in the form of nuclear weapons, has ushered in a new period of history which is at least as different from all of recorded history until 1945 than are, say, the Middle Ages from the ancient world or modern times from the Middle Ages. The very conceptions of nuclear 'weapon' and of nuclear 'war' are misnomers. For when we speak of weapons, we have in mind a rational relationship between a means, an instrument and an end. That is to say, we can use a gun to kill a man, we can use a cannon to breach a wall, and if we have set our mind upon killing a man or breaching a wall, then the use of a gun or of a cannon is a perfectly rational means to a rational end. The same is true of conventional violence in the collective sense, that is war. War, in the conventional sense, is a perfectly legitimate instrument of national policy in a society which is composed of sovereign nations, that is to say, of nations which have no secular superior above them, which cannot be forced to do something, which cannot be compelled to engage in certain behaviour, by legitimate superior authority. Violence, for better or for worse, its threats or actual application, is the inevitable result of the anarchic character of a society composed of sovereign nations. Thus it was from the beginning of history to 1945 perfectly legitimate, perfectly rational to use the threat or the actuality of war for the purpose of defending or promoting the interests of individual nations. All this has been radically changed through the impact of the availability of nuclear weapons. For a nuclear weapon is not a weapon in the conventional semantic sense. It is not a rational means to a rational end. It is an instrument of unlimited, universal destruction, hence the threat or the actuality of a nuclear war is not a rational instrument of national policy because it is an instrument of suicide and genocide. It is exactly for this reason that for more than a quarter of a century the two major nuclear powers have been extremely careful not to come too close to the brink of nuclear war, both being fully aware, at least in a general philosophic sense, that nuclear war is a self-defeating absurdity.

However, from the beginning of history to 1945, when mankind thought naturally in pre-nuclear terms, it developed certain conceptions about weapons and war, which have not yielded in the minds of certain theoreticians, or even in the minds of practitioners, when they have time to think in theoretical terms, to the impact of an entirely novel phenomenon, the availability of nuclear weapons and of what we call euphemistically a nuclear war. So we have a disjunction between the conventional ways we think and act about nuclear weapons and the objective conditions, under which the availability of nuclear weapons forces us to live. Let me give a simple example of this disjunction from recent history. One of my former students, who has reached a kind of eminence, was for a considerable period of time one of the leading members of the Central Intelligence Agency (CIA). One of his tasks was to brief the Joint Chiefs of Staff about the basic issues which arose in the foreign and military policy of the United States. This official said to me that when he talked to General X about the difference between conventional and nuclear weapons, the latter said, of course, obviously, but when the former read this general's position papers, there was no trace of that recognition in them. There is a psychological and sociological problem here, which is of the most crucial importance for the future of humanity, that is our seeming inability thus far to adjust our conventional modes of thought and action to the objective conditions which the nuclear age imposes upon us. This is particularly true when consideration is given to the approaches to a nuclear strategy which have followed each other in the last 25 years in the United States. From the clean H-bomb through graduated deterrence, to the counter-force strategy of ex-Secretary of Defense, James Schlesinger, there is one impulse tying those different strategies together: to find a way by which a nuclear war can be fought in a conventional way, that is, to conventionalise nuclear war in order to be able to come out of it alive. In other words, there is what I would regard as an absurd attempt, not to adapt our modes of thought and action to the new objective conditions of the nuclear age but to transform those objective conditions in the light of the pre-nuclear modes of thought and action.

We have tried, then, instead of adapting our modes of thought and action to the objective conditions of the nuclear age, to conventionalise nuclear war in order to be able to fight and win it and to come out of it alive. And this is true not only with regard to military strategy but also with regard to disarmament and the attempts to develop a defence against nuclear war. For it is one of the characteristics of the nature of nuclear weapons that their destructiveness is so enormous that it has simply destroyed, disintegrated like an atomic bomb, the very conceptions from the beginning of history to the beginning of the nuclear age.

Let us very briefly consider the different attempts at a new strategy, which would allow us to use nuclear weapons without the universal, uncontrolled destructive effects, which, in theory, we correctly associate with nuclear weapons. Take the so-called clean H-bomb, which made its appearance at the beginning of the 1950s, that is an H-bomb that would not have the devastating indiscriminate effects which even the kiloton bombs dropped on Hiroshima and Nagasaki had. It was a bomb which would have very little if any fall-out and whose effects would be those of a gigantic conventional bomb. In the immortal words of a former Chief of Staff of the American Air Force, General Curtis Lemay, the nuclear bomb is just another bomb. The US Atomic Energy Commission in a book entitled *The Effects of Nuclear Weapons*, published in 1962, made short shrift of this idea when it said that there is no such things as a clean H-bomb, and that all H-bombs are more or less unclean even though the distribution of blast, fire and radiation effects may be different in different designs of the bomb. But the idea that it is possible to devise an H-bomb which is not essentially different from a conventional bomb is utterly mistaken. Take the conception of graduated deterrence, that is a method of waging nuclear war, which does not escalate almost immediately into all-out war, but in which in a rational, almost predetermined way, similar to a chess game, one side makes a move by, say, taking out one city, and the other side makes another move taking out a city of its opponent. Thus each side in a perfectly detached, rational way inflicts a certain degree of damage upon the other. It is this idea, which has gained wide acceptance in certain think-tanks where this kind of playing games with survival issues is highly developed. There is something to be said in favour of them in terms of the hypothetical possibilities that exist. However, in practical terms, it is inconceivable that living human beings, with the ideological conceptions and values which the policy-makers in the Soviet Union, the United States and China possess, would look at, say, the destruction of Chicago by the

Soviet Union or at the destruction of Minsk by the United States with the same detachment with which chess-players would look at the exchange of pawns. They are bound to arrive very quickly at a point at which, aside from the aroused emotions, one side or the other or both sides will feel that in this rational simulation of a chess game, one or the other side will take advantage of the other, that is the equivalence, which is theoretically assumed between Minsk and Chicago, will not be self-evident to the players of the game. The Soviet Union will inevitably find that Minsk is more important than Chicago and the United States will find that Chicago is more important than Minsk. Thus they will find that this type of graduated deterrence is really not deterrence at all, because it leads inevitably by its own dynamism to escalation and to an all-out strategic war, which it was the first purpose of the enterprise to avoid. For once the United States has arrived at the conclusion that Chicago is more important than Minsk, it will take out two Soviet cities, which are regarded as the equivalent of another American city, whereupon the Soviet Union will take out two American cities, which are regarded as the equivalent of one Soviet city and before we know it, we shall be in the middle of the all-out nuclear war which we wanted to avoid in the first place. Furthermore, we have to reckon with the emotions, the passions of the people at large and of the policy-makers, for in such an undertaking started in the rational way I have indicated, enormous powers of passion are of course involved on both sides. The population of the United States will not look with equanimity at the successive, however rational, elimination or partial destruction of American cities and their inhabitants, nor will the people and the government of the Soviet Union, and hence again we have a force which almost inevitably will lead to escalation and to the various effects which the graduated deterrence was intended to avoid. Incidentally, those conceptions of limiting nuclear war, of making it possible to wage it withoug destroying oneself and one's enemy are peculiarly American and are the result of a humanitarian impulse within the framework of an utterly inhuman enterprise. Since we are confronted with the possibility of nuclear war, we want to make nuclear war as painless as possible, as limited as possible, one might even say, if so grotesque a juxtaposition is allowed, as humane as possible. On the other hand, the official military doctrine of the Soviet Union has never accepted those distinctions. That doctrine assumes that a war, especially a European war, which starts as a conventional or limited nuclear war and whose stakes the belligerents regard as being of prime importance, is bound to escalate into all-out nuclear war. Thus the idea of the fire-break or the pause between either conventional war or limited nuclear war, on the one hand, and all-out nuclear war, on the other, is alien to the military doctrine of the Soviet Union.

We shall next examine the counter-force strategy, whose philosophy the then Secretary of Defense, Robert S. McNamara, explained to an audience at the University of Michigan in 1962. It was an attempt to limit nuclear war, to make it acceptable as an instrument of national policy. The counter-force strategy is very simple; in fact, it assumes that a nuclear war can be waged and ought to be waged not against population and industrial centres, but against strictly military objectives. The revival of this doctrine in very recent times starts with the same assumption, fortified by the increase in the sophistication of nuclear weapons during the last twelve years. For in 1962 one could well make the case that it was impossible, in view of the character of nuclear weapons, to distinguish in practice strictly between military and civilian objectives, that the indiscriminate and widespread destructiveness of nuclear weapons was so enormous that a nuclear weapon aimed at a military objective was bound to destroy, by virtue of the mere proximity of civilian objectives, the latter as well. That argument is still valid, in my opinion. If the Soviet Union tries to take out the missile sites near Phoenix and Cheyenne, to give only two examples, the Soviet missiles are not likely to be so accurate as to be capable of destroying the missile sites without having any negative effect upon the adjacent population and industrial centres. But recent increases in accuracy may have improved the situation somewhat in this respect, and therefore there is a grain more merit in the recent revival of the counter-force strategy than in its original formulation. There is, however, a more profound argument against the counter-force strategy, namely its ultimate military purpose. In the case of the American version, which is the main version of the counter-force strategy, the United States will not initiate a nuclear war by a first strike. It will wait, in other words, until the other side has initiated a nuclear war by a first strike and then will attack the military targets, which the other side presents not merely in the form of missile sites, but of the missile themselves. But the first strike has already emptied most or many of the missile sites. So it is necessary, then, to make a distinction — I have been assured that it is possible, even though I cannot see how it can be made — between missile sites which still contain their missiles and the other missile sites from which the missiles have already departed. Now let us suppose that this distinction can be made, and that this exchange operates as intended. This of course depends on the enemy who started the war with the first strike not having destroyed all one's missile sites, and on one having a sufficient number of missiles left with which one can destroy the enemy missile sites which still contain missiles. Accept all of this and assume that the two belligerents knock out their land-based missiles reciprocally, what have they gained? They are in the same position that they were originally, except that now they have to rely exclusively upon the sea-borne deterrent and perhaps upon the airborne deterrent. So one would have the same distribution of destructive power with the same deterrent effect one had at the beginning of the war with only the difference that the mechanics of deterrent would have changed from land-based to sea-based missiles. Now there are people who say that land-based missiles are obsolete anyhow, and that they should be phased out through the arms control negotiations between the United States and the Soviet Union. If this position is correct, then in the projected counter-force encounter we would simply have engaged in a mutual disarmament enterprise by knocking each other's land-based missiles out and be in the same position as we were before, that is to say, there would be no victor and no vanquished.

This brings us to another point, that is the basic distinction between victory and defeat in war, which is again a distinction that is deeply ingrained in our consciousness, because it has been imposed upon us through millenia of historical experience. Thus the military, in particular, have found it unacceptable both in Korea and Vietnam that a conventional war should not end in the clear-cut victory of that side whose cause is regarded to be just, which is of course one's own side. The same reluctance to give up the distinction between victory and defeat can be noticed in our thinking on nuclear war. The idea that a nuclear war should necessarily end in a stalemate or in the mutual destruction of the belligerents is simply unacceptable to people who have made it their business to prepare for victorious wars. They are in the position of a banker or a business in general, whose purpose in life is to make a profit for his company, and all of a sudden he is faced with the contingency that the best he can hope for is to break even. He will never make a profit and pay a dividend on the stock of his company, which goes against his grain, against his nature. As far as nuclear war is concerned, this is the objective situation we face, a situation which again is utterly different from any situation which any nation has faced in the past: war itself becomes a completely senseless, irrational enterprise in that if it can be limited in terms of counter-force strategy, it will simply end in the same kind of equilibrium with which it started, only that the composition of the forces through which the equilibrium is presented will be different.

Take the concept of defence. It has been axiomatic throughout history that any new weapon will call forth sooner or later a counter-weapon, a defence against it. Let us assume that this axiom is borne out by historical experience. But it is still true that the destructiveness of nuclear weapons is so enormous, is so staggering to the imagination, that it is inconceivable in view of present technology to devise a defence against nuclear weapons. Thus, the abolition, for all practical purposes, of Anti-Ballistic Missiles (ABMs) by the two SALT negotiations, simply recognises an objective fact of nuclear life. But it should again be kept in mind how insistent the attempts were on both sides to find a defence against nuclear weapons, for once we have a defence against nuclear weapons, we have removed the main deterrent against nuclear war. If we can expect to come out of a nuclear war alive, then to wage or not to wage nuclear war becomes simply like the approach to conventional war, a matter of pragmatic, expedential calculation.

Let us now consider tactical nuclear war, which is another attempt to wage a nuclear war, which will not lead to the destruction of both sides, and which can lead to the victory or defeat of one or the other side. The conception of tactical nuclear war, that is to say, of the battlefield use of nuclear weapons, first of all is up against the impossibility of drawing an objective, generally recognised and recognisable line between tactics and strategy in general. The military schools in all countries have debated this question without ever arriving at a conclusion. For the distinction is not so much in the objective situation on the battlefield as in the minds of the military planner or director of military operations. Incidentally, the fact that the Hiroshima and Nagasaki bombs today are classified as tactical nuclear weapons, shows how far tactics can be stretched to cover what generally would be regarded as strategy. What might be intended by one side as a tactical manoeuvre may thus be interpreted by the other side as a strategic move, and the reply of the other side may either be interpreted in tactical or strategic terms by the first side. Since in such situations both sides are inclined to use a worst-case approach to the problems, that is to assume the worst in terms of the intentions of the enemy, the distinction is bound to break down very quickly. This is true not only of nuclear but of conventional war as well. But the problem is aggravated by the nature of nuclear war.

Assume for a moment as a hypothetical case that a conventional war breaks out in Central Europe, in which the United States and the Soviet Union are involved. The United States, which has about 7,000 so-called tactical nuclear warheads in Europe uses some of them against the military objectives presented by the Soviet Union, such as bridges, military concentrations, ammunition dumps and logistic installations. But that may lead to the destruction of, say, certain cities in White Russia. The Soviet Union replies in the same tactical spirit by attacking the Channel ports, Brest, Cherbourg, Le Havre and so forth, in order to inflict upon the Western armies the same tactical disadvantages the Americans have tried to inflict upon the Soviet Union. But since the tactical targets are different in nature, asymmetric in the extreme on both sides, the Americans will ask themselves when they see Le Havre, Brest and Cherbourg going up in flames, what are the Soviets after? Is this tactical or is it strategic? Applying the worst-case interpretation, the Americans take out some of their cities as a reply to their move. The Soviets then reply in kind: if the Americans take out some of our cities, we take out some of theirs. And one morning we wake up, if we wake up at all, and we find that both sides are engaged in an all-out strategic war, not because either side wanted it, but because the objective dynamism of the initial act leaves neither side a choice.

Another rationalistic fallacy is causally connected with the attempt to make a distinction between all-out nuclear war and a civilised nice little nuclear war out of which both sides will come alive, namely the idea that the nature of war, as it appears to the historian in retrospect, is a result of conscious designs of the war-makers. This may sometimes have been the case, but it is by no means typically the case. It is much more likely that you take one step, to quote Goethe's Faust, which you are free to take, yet from the second on you are a slave of the first. That is to say, the consequent action is predetermined by the first step one has taken and one is not able to escape the inner logic, the inner dynamism of the first step. So it is a naïve, rationalistic illusion to think that the war-makers remain in control of the war. They are in control before they take the first step. Once they have taken the first step, the dynamism of that first step pushes them in the direction which that first step indicates. Abraham Lincoln said at the end of the American Civil War: 'It is sure that I have not controlled events, events have controlled me.' So here is a philosophic fallacy which attaches to the conception of the nature of man as a war-making animal, and that is another factor in the confusion and delusions to which the attempts at developing a rational strategy of nuclear war and nuclear disarmament are exposed.

Take, finally, the problem of nuclear disarmament which is, because of the nature of nuclear weapons and of nuclear war, fundamentally different from the problem of conventional disarmament. The conventional arms race is indeed an inescapable function of the balance of power. To simplify the situation by only speaking of two nations, we may say that both nations want to maintain an equilibrium between them. But they can never be sure whether they have calculated correctly their own military strength or that of the other side. So they need a certain insurance against miscalculation in their disfavour. In consequence, if the quantity of x would establish and maintain a balance between themselves and the prospective enemy, they must add to x a y, say 10 per cent more, in order to be sure that even if they have made a mistake in their disfavour, the balance is still maintained. The other side, seeing this addition of 10 per cent or y, must add z to its military power in order to make sure that it is not disadvantaged by the increase in the military power of the other side. The other side notes again that the enemy has added z to its power, so they add more and vice versa. So there is a cumulative inevitable increase in military power, which is another term for the conventional arms race.

To stop this arms race by disarmament agreements has proved to be possible only if the underlying political conflicts, which have given rise to the arms race in the first place, have been mitigated or eliminated. When one reviews the history of attempts to secure conventional disarmament from the end of the Napoleonic Wars to the present — there have been scores of them — one realises that there have been only two successes, one temporary, the other permanent: the Washington Treaty for the limitation of naval armaments of 1922 and the disarmament of the American-Canadian frontier, both having been the result of the permanent or temporary elimination of political conflicts. So there is an element of hopelessness in the numerous attempts at conventional disarmament by means of an isolated technical approach.

The situation with regard to nuclear disarmament is, however, utterly different. For the dynamism which characterises the conventional military balance of power policies of nations does not apply to nuclear weapons. When it comes to machine-guns, one can never have enough of them, because there are always many more possible targets available than there are weapons to eliminate the targets. When it comes to nuclear weapons, there exists an optimum, which does not exist with regard to conventional weapons, beyond which to go is utterly irrational. If we are capable of destroying our enemy 10 times over, under the worst of conditions, it becomes utterly irrational to compete with him for the sake of being able to destroy him 15 times over, and our enemy, who is only capable of destroying us 6 times over, is by the same token not inferior at all. This simple and obvious syllogism has not escaped policy-makers in theory but it has escaped them in practice, because the impulse to get more and better nuclear weapons has proved to be irresistible. So the modes of thought and action which are perfectly appropriate for conventional weapons and for the conventional arms race have been transferred to the nuclear field, where they are bound to prove, and have already proved to be, to a certain extent, catastrophic. They have proved to be catastrophic in the economic sense, and they are bound to prove to be catastrophic in the very vital sense of the survival of Western civilisation, if not humanity, if the nuclear arms race is not stopped. In theory the Americans have recognised this, as have the Soviets. For this reason we have had the SALT talks. But when politicians get down to business and when they need the approval of their military establishments, they find themselves handicapped in transforming their theoretical insight into practical measures of nuclear arms control and later on disarmament.

We may thus conclude as we began: the issue of nuclear disarmament or at least of arms control is a literally vital issue, not only for the superpowers, not only for their allies, but for humanity. For with proliferation now having started in earnest, there is no doubt in my mind, and I think in the minds of most experts, that a nuclear arms race, not limited to two superpowers having responsible governments mortally afraid of each other, but spreading over the whole globe is bound, sooner or later, to lead to an unspeakable catastrophe. For history shows, if history shows anything, that all nations have been governed at times by fools and knaves, and even a combination of both. That was bad enough before nuclear weapons existed. But imagine a fool or knave or a combination of both in the possession of nuclear weapons, and nuclear war will be unavoidable. So it is the almost inevitable danger of actual nuclear war, inherent in the dynamism of a generalised unlimited nuclear arms race, which makes nuclear arms control and in the end nuclear disarmament a question of life or death for all of us.

17 ALL AT SEA? A CRITIQUE OF THE AMERICAN STRATEGIC FORCE STRUCTURE

Peter King

James Schlesinger, former doctoral student of Harvard, former professor of the University of Virginia, former systems analyst at the RAND Corporation (1963-9), and former bureaucrat — Bureau of the Budget (1969-71), Chairman of the Atomic Energy Commission (1971-3), Director of the Central Intelligence Agency (1973), and Secretary of Defense (July 1973—November 1975) — is the first civilian strategist to reach the top of the American defence hierarchy, although the influence of such professionals was strong in the McNamara period, and subsequently.[1] Schlesinger's chief doctrinal contribution whilst in office resembles Robert McNamara's — the doctrine of 'counter-force', city-sparing warfare, 1962-3, although later repudiated publicly by McNamara, has remained important in the Defense Department's operational plans.[2] Schlesinger has revived it, with original variations, as declaratory policy. Schlesinger's 'selective, flexible response' means readiness to mount a wide range of nuclear responses (including extremely 'restrained' ones) to less than all-out strategic attack. While it is new as official American declaratory policy, war-fighting plans in the Single Integrated Operational Plan (SIOP) since 1962[3] have embodied progressively more and more selective, targeting options, especially city-avoiding options, as Schlesinger himself has acknowledged under Congressional questioning.[4]

Schlesinger apparently 'went public' with selective, flexible response partly in order to acquire the means necessary (in his view) to implement it. He had more success than his immediate predecessors in securing funds specifically to upgrade the hard target kill capability (yield and accuracy) of the United States' strategic missiles.[5] Like this predecessors, however, he disclaimed the intention to develop a disarming or even 'major' counter-force capability, although he has made a more vigorous case for deploying limited counter-force capabilities,[6] and on what may be regarded as a central question for strategic arms control in the long run — the preservation of the American strategic TRIAD of bombers, submarine-launched ballistic missiles and inter-continental ballistic missiles — Schlesinger was indistinguishable from his predecessors.[7] Thus he pushed funding for the new Trident submarine-launched ballistic missile (SLBM) system, due to begin operational deployment in 1978; for the B-1 bomber whose prototypes are flying in readiness for a 'production decision' late in 1976, and which is designed to replace the B-52 force in the course of the 1980s;[8] and finally for the MX missile, an entirely new inter-continental ballistic missile (ICBM) with an advanced inertially guided warhead, for the long term ('mid-1980s and beyond').[9]

This paper is principally a critique of ex-Secretary Schlesinger's policies in office; but it draws on his writings while at the RAND Corporation to throw light on those policies and to define the distinctive qualities of his strategic outlook. It also, on the other hand, treats Schlesinger as a representative figure (a whipping boy, at times), especially in arguing against a large strategic force and, in particular, against the land-based elements of the strategic TRIAD.

Much of the paper is written as if Schlesinger were still in office. For he may very well be back in the office within a year or two, and the influence of his initiatives on his successor is already apparent. According to the 1977 Defense Report:

> a continuation of current strategic programs — even within the constraint of SALT — by the Soviet might give them the ability to knock out the highly accurate Minuteman force which the American President might want to use for surgical strikes before resorting to all out war.[10]

This is pure, if slightly clumsy (in its last clause) Schlesinger, as will be shown. Indeed the FY 1977 Report seems to be largely Schlesinger's doing, and there is little likelihood of major new departures in American strategic policy before 1977.

The United States quietly abandoned the goal of 'strategic superiority' over the Soviet Union in favour of 'sufficiency' during the early months of the Nixon presidency. Under the terms of the SALT I accords of 1972, the United States accepted plain inferiority in two measures of strategic strength — deployed numbers of long-range nuclear missiles (ICBMs and SLBMs) and ICBM throw weights.[11] However, the Americans retained (and still do) a substantial overall edge in the strategic balance as conventionally measured. They remain ahead in strategic bomber strength and overall re-entry vehicle (RV) numbers, in missile RV accuracy, and also in strategic command, control and communication (C3), and strategic surveillance and warning systems.

Table 17.1: Capabilities of American and Soviet Strategic Missiles, 1975

Missiles	Y (Megatons)	CEP (Nautical miles)	n	m
		United States		
Minuteman III	0.160	0.2	3	550
Minuteman II	1	0.3	1	450
Titan	5	0.5	1	54
Poseidon	0.05	0.5	10	496
Polaris	1.200	0.5	3	160
Totals				1,710
		Soviet Union		
SS-9	20	*1	1	288
SS-11, 13	1	*1	1	1,030
SS-N-6 (SLBM)	1	*1-2	1	544
SS-N-8 (SLBM)	1	*1-2	1	156
SS-7, 8	5	*1.5	1	209
Totals				2,227

Abbreviations: Y = yield; CEP = circular error probable; n = re-entry vehicles per missile; m = number of missiles.

*Estimates

Source: Kosta Tsipis, 'Physics and Calculus of Countercity and Counterforce Nuclear Attacks, *Science CLXXXVII* (1975); and IISS, *The Military Balance 1975-1976* (London, 1975).

Tables 17.1 and 17.2 indicate the American qualitative lead, and show the dramatic effect of MIRVing on the quantitative balance. (For the strategic bomber balance, see also Table 17.3.)

For some administration spokesmen 'sufficiency' remained superiority writ small, and they occasionally almost said so.[12] Under Schlesinger sufficiency was in turn quietly dropped in favour of 'essential equivalence' — put forward as one of 'four major requirements' for credible strategic nuclear deterrence.

First, we must maintain an essential equivalence with the Soviet Union in the basic factors that determine force effectiveness. Because of uncertainty about the future and the shape that the strategic competition could take, we cannot allow major asymmetries to develop in throw-weight, accuracy, yield-to weight ratios, reliability and other such factors that contribute to the

Table 17.2: Numbers of American and Soviet Strategic Missiles and Re-entry Vehicles, 1966-75

Missiles and Re-entry Vehicles	1966	1967	1968	1969	1970	1971	1972	1973	1974	1975
				United States						
Minuteman I	800	800	750	650	550	490	400	300	140	0
Minuteman II	50	200	250	350	450	500	500	500	500	450
Minuteman III	0	0	0	0	0	10	100	200	360	550
A2 (Polaris)	208	208	208	208	208	160	128	64	0	0
A3 (Polaris)	448	448	448	448	448	432	368	272	240	160
B3 (Poseidon)	0	0	0	0	0	64	160	320	416	496
Titan	54	54	54	54	54	54	54	54	54	54
Total Missiles	1,560	1,710	1,710	1,710	1,710	1,710	1,710	1,710	1,710	1,710
RVs	1,554	1,710	1,710	1,710	1,710	2,300	3,250	4,990	6,154	7,594
				Soviet Union						
SS-7, 8	220	220	220	220	220	220	210	209	209	209
SS-9	108	162	192	228	288	288	288	288	288	288
SS-11	31	340	500	730	960	960	970	970	970	970
SS-13	0	0	0	30	40	60	60	60	60	60
SS-N-6 (SLBM)	0	0	32	96	224	336	432	528	528	544
SS-N-8 (SLBM)	0	0	0	0	0	0	12	36	80	156
Total Missiles	359	722	944	1,304	1,732	1,864	1,972	2,091	2,075	2,227
RVs	359	722	942	1,304	1,732	1,864	1,972	2,091	2,075	2,227

Source: Adapted from Kosta Tsipis, 'Physics and Calculus of Countercity and Counterforce Nuclear Attacks', *Science,* CLXXXVII (1975), p.394. But see also Thomas A. Brown, 'Missile Accuracy and Strategic Lethality', *Survival,* XVIII (1976), pp.52-9. He maintains that Tsipis has underestimated Soviet ICBM and SLBM accuracies.

effectiveness of strategic weapons and to the perceptions of the non-superpower nations. At the same time, our own forces should promote nuclear stability both by reducing incentives for a first use of nuclear weapons and by deterring and avoiding increased nuclear deployments by other powers.

The second requirement is for a highly survivable force that can be withheld at all times and targeted against the economic base of an opponent so as to deter coercive or desperation attacks on the economic and population targets of the United States and its allies.

The third requirement is for a force that, in response to Soviet actions, could implement a variety of limited preplanned options and react rapidly to retargeting orders so as to deter any range of further attacks that a potential enemy might contemplate. This force should have some ability to destroy hard targets, even though we would prefer to see both sides avoid major counterforce capabilities. We do not propose, however, to concede to the Soviets a unilateral advantage in this realm. Accordingly, our programs will depend on how far the Soviets go in developing a counterforce capability of their own. It should also have the accuracy to attack — with low-yield weapons — soft point targets without causing large scale collateral damage. And it should be supported by a program of fall-out shelters and population relocation to offer protection to our population primarily in the event that military targets become the object of attack.

The fourth requirement is for a range and magnitude of capabilities such that everyone — friend, foe, and domestic audiences alike — will perceive that we are the equal of our strongest competitors. We should not take the chance that in this most hazardous of areas, misperceptions could lead to miscalculation, confrontation, and crisis.[13]

For Schlesinger, then, there are two very different reasons for maintaining essential equivalence with the Soviet Union. One is favourably to affect *perceptions* of the strategic balance by 'non-superpower nations' and by 'friend, foe and, domestic audience', and thus maintain the political effectiveness of the United States in alliance diplomacy, adversary crises, Third World politics and domestic politics as well. The other is favourably to affect the capabilities of the United States for fighting nuclear war. The two are related, of course, but Schlesinger's case for a large strategic force rests heavily on concern about the perceptions of non-Americans (and non-responsible Americans), even though it is clear that non-American perceptions of the strategic balance, even Soviet ones, are greatly conditioned by what official Americans say about it.[14] It is curiously fortunate for the Schlesinger policy that the imperatives engendered by outside (and domestic) perceptions always point one way — to a large or larger force.

Of course it is primarily Soviet perceptions which concern Schlesinger:

> Until the late 1960s, US superiority in launchers, warheads, and equivalent megotonnage was so great that we could ignore or disparage the importance of such 'static' measures in comparing our forces with those of the USSR. Now, however, our numerical superiority has disappeared in almost every category except that of warheads, and it could dwindle very rapidly there as well. . .
>
> Their words, at least, have suggested that they see these asymmetries as giving them diplomatic if not military leverage.
>
> As far as we can judge, moreover, the Soviets now seem determined to exploit the asymmetries in ICBMs, SLBMs and payload we conceded to them at Moscow [in the SALT accords of 1972]. Apparently, they are considering the deployment of large numbers of heavy and possibly very accurate MIRVs. As I have already indicated, this kind of deployment could in time come to threaten both our bombers and our ICBMs. Admittedly, we would still retain immense residual power in our deployed SLBM force, and the Soviets would surely know it. But to many interested observers, the actual and potential asymmetries (as measured by those 'static' criteria) would look even more pronounced in favour of the USSR. . .The United States is willing to tolerate the existence of asymmetries provided that, in an era of alleged parity, they do not all favour one party. But we are not prepared to accept a situation in which all the visible asymmetries point in one direction. . .
>
> A more equitable and stable arrangement would be one in which both sides maintain survivable second-strike reserves, in which there is symmetry in the ability of each side to threaten the other and in which there is a perceived equality between the offensive forces of both sides.[15]

More specifically (and Schlesinger echoes ex-Secretary Melvin Laird in this), the Soviet Union must not be permitted to acquire 'a capability for damage and disruption that we ourselves would lack'.[16]

Now it is easy to criticise or even ridicule the very special *official American* perception of the strategic balance manifested here. American superiority has dwindled in 'almost' every category except one — but in fact there are only a few major quantitative categories, however the measuring is done, and the United States is overwhelmingly ahead in two ot them — numbers of long-range bombers, and, of course, warheads, the most important quantitative measure of all. While , 'warhead consciousness' is undoubtedly quite high, 'bomber consciousness' has almost disappeared from the public mind; yet Schlesinger himself is confident that the bulk of the ground-alert B-52 force can survive a Soviet surprise attack and penetrate Soviet air defences.[17]

Now the Soviet Union, which accepted 'strategic inferiority' for most of the Krushchev years, was apparently moved to seek missile parity (and more) with the United States after experiencing diplomatic collapse in the Cuban missile crisis. By the time the catch-up began the United States had deployed over 1,000 ICBMs, and the Soviets were eventually to deploy many more. But it remains a question whether the Soviet leaders misperceived the cause of their failure.[18] Would a Cuban missile crisis in 1976 or 1986 unfold differently, given the overwhelming local conventional military superiority of the United States? And it remains a question — actually raised by Henry Kissinger — whether there is any diplomatic leverage in the persisting 'strategic superiority' of the United States.

Now any American Secretary of Defense urging budget increases in the present economic climate may face a dilemma. To defend himself and the national interest he can say that defences are sound; to get extra funds he may feel compelled to say they are not. In fact Schlesinger's alarmism can often be refuted out of his own mouth, even on the key question of the balance of counter-force capabilities:

> If you believe the results from our own test ranges would be applicable in operational conditions and if you infer what you must infer about present-Soviet accuracies, I think one would conclude that we now have greater operational counterforce capabilities than they have.[19]

As for assured destruction:

> I can say with confidence that in 1974, even after a more brilliantly executed and devastating attack than we believe our potential adversaries could deliver, the United States would retain the capability to kill more than 30 per cent of the Soviet population and destroy more than 75 per cent of Soviet industry. At the same time we could hold in reserve a major capability against . . . China.[20]

So far as *capabilities* are concerned, Schlesinger is anxious only about the future — in particular about future threats to the United States' capacity to exercise 'selective flexible response':

> Since both we and the Soviet Union are investing so much of our capability for flexible and controlled responses in our ICBM forces, these forces could become much more substantial hard-target kill capabilities than they currently possess. If one side could remove the other's capability for flexible and controlled responses, he might find ways of exercising coercion and extracting concessions without triggering the final holocaust. . .No opponent should think that he could fire at some of our Minuteman or SAC bases without being subjected to, at the very least, a response in kind. No opponent should believe that he could attack other US targets of military or economic value without finding similar or other appropriate targets in his own homeland under attack. No opponent should believe that he could blackmail our allies without risking his very capability for blackmail. Above all, no opponent should entertain the thought that we will permit him to remove our capability for flexible strategic response. . .In some circumstances, we might wish to retaliate against non-collocated, small soft targets, or facilities near large population centres; high accuracy and a low-yield, air-burst weapon would be the most appropriate combination for those targets. In other cases, we might wish to respond with attacks of a limited number of hard targets such as ICBMs, IRBMs, and MRBMs. The desired combination for these latter targets, especially as long as we have to depend on all-inertial guidance systems, is high accuracy and a higher-yield warhead than we now deploy.[21]

To meet this supposed danger Schlesinger, as already quoted, has disclaimed and discounted the option of developing a 'major' counter-force capability against Soviet strategic forces — a disarming strike capability or even a significant damage-limiting capability.[22] What interests him is strategic flexibility. At one point he even temporarily re-defined 'counter-force' to include conventional military as well as nuclear targets:

> Counterforce can go [sic] against any military target. . .It could go against airfields or Army camps. . .It has a range and one can go counterforce rather than countervalue without necessarily putting himself [sic] into a position of having a disarming first strike

capability.[23]

'Counterforce' strategies (in the wide sense here favoured by
Schlesinger) and countervalue strategies become indeed a continuum
in which Schlesinger seems to see the role of limited strikes of whatever
kind as principally to warn, punish, or dissuade an adventurous
opponent, rather than militarily to defeat him. Schlesinger may have
in mind that if counterforce strikes in the classical sense (strikes against
strategic forces) are militarily insignificant or at least indecisive, what
may matter most is the 'value' losses (lives, property, dollars or roubles
and perhaps 'honour') associated with them. In Robert Sherman's
words: 'a counter-force attack in reality functions as a *countervalue*
attack.'[24]

Do emerging Soviet missile capabilities threaten the United States'
ability to conduct this kind of limited counter-force or countervalue
strategy? What is the significance of the three to one disparity in
ICBM throw weights (six to two million pounds) which some critics of
SALT have said may become six to one? Not only the land-based
ICBMs but the other two legs of the strategic TRIAD have virtues as
well as drawbacks for Schlesinger-style selective, flexible response.
Submarines are relatively invulnerable and therefore ideal for riding
out an attack and for 'slow motion' war, while SLBM accuracies are
now similar to ICBM accuracies; but one strike may 'give away the
boat', and two-way communication is difficult to sustain in war
conditions. Bombers, once airborne, are much less vulnerable than
ICBMs in silos, and could be withheld or maintain 'loiter capability' in
some strategic scenarios (if their bases — and their tankers' bases —
were not destroyed),[25] while bomber weapons are extremely varied
and accurate; but without long-range stand-off weapons the bomber's
ability to make limited strikes in the deep interior of the Soviet Union
without a sort of 'limited saturation attack' would be limited. As for
the fixed land-based ICBMs they must eventually be highly vulnerable
to saturation attack by MIRVs, and they have no loiter capability
(although it may be possible to abort them), except in so far as they
stay in their silos and ride out any attack. However the Circular Error
Probable (CEP) of ICBMs is still superior to that of SLBMs, and the
Minuteman force can be quite rapidly retargeted and selectively
launched, while maintaining central control is relatively easy.
Nevertheless, long-run technical developments (especially accurate
MARVs and airborne and satellite-borne Very Low Frequency
communications) promise to make SLBM systems clearly superior on

balance to all land-based systems for flexible response, although this potential finds little place in Schlesinger's thought. He is almost obsessed with threats to the land-based missile system.

When he briefed a subcommittee of the Senate Foreign Relations Committee on 'nuclear counterforce' attacks against the United States in September 1974,[26] he set out to show in detail that such attacks could be designed to minimise civilian casualties; could — at least in the long run — destroy a large fraction of the Minuteman force; and could thus jeopardise American capacity for flexible, selective response. He argued strongly against an assured destruction type response to such a discriminating, or at least restrained, Soviet attack.

The content of the briefing was remarkable. On Schlesinger's own estimates, up to about eight million Americans could die in such attacks — confined to 1,054 ICBM silos, 46 SAC bomber bases, and two SLBM bases — largely as a result of fall-out;[27] and it transpired that Arms Control and Disarmament Agency (ACDA) casualty estimates ranged much higher.[28] A large fraction of the Soviet ICBM force would obviously have to be committed to produce this result — and Schlesinger notably failed on this occasion to supply a careful accounting of the post-attack strategic balance which would pose America's surviving ICBMs, most of its strategic bombers (which would be free to land at 100-plus dispersal bases in the continental United States after the assumed Soviet attack) and all of its SLBMs at sea against a substantially used-up Soviet ICBM force, an inferior SLBM fleet, and a vastly inferior bomber force.

Clearly there would be a strong case for diplomatic management and even exploitation of the situation *without retaliation* if the strategic balance had shifted in favour of the United States. When Schlesinger says that 'we do not propose to let an enemy put us in a position where we are left with no more than a capability to hold his cities hostage after the first phase of a nuclear conflict',[29] he is apparently forgetting the counter-force potency of the Polaris-Poseidon fleet, which is quite well documented by now,[30] and also that the opponent would have substantially depleted the main element of his strategic arsenal.[31] Even if the force exchange ratio favoured the Soviet Union in an ICBM duel, the ratio of total unused strategic forces might favour the United States at the end. In any case, even if the United States lost all its ICBMs and the Soviets retained a substantial number after such an exchange, nothing essential would have changed in the strategic balance if SLBM forces remained untouched.

Robert Sherman's conclusion that the significance of a Soviet counter-force attack would lie solely in destroying American values (especially lives) follows from this analysis. Sherman therefore recommends discriminating counter-value instead of all-out counter-force relation for such an attack.[32] But this course of action would risk counter-counter-retaliation, and would preclude one major diplomatic possibility, which is also neglected by Schlesinger — Soviet disavowal of the attack and compensation for lost American lives and property.[33] In any case Schlesinger has to assume an extraordinary mode of attack by the Soviet Union to produce his low casualty forecast, for while air-bursting does minimise fall-out, counter-force effectiveness against hardened silos demands ground bursts; air-bursting would virtually ensure Soviet ICBM inferiority at the end of the exchange.[34] It is absurd to assume that the Soviet Union will try to eliminate the Minuteman force by adopting an attack mode which guarantees failure, particularly as Soviet strategic writers and spokesmen have in any case shown no interest in an isolated attack on American land-based strategic forces or in minimising civilian casualties during such an attack.

Despite the dialectical difficulties which Schlesinger encountered in defending his new policy, he remained adamant that the United States does need a counter-force capability at least 'comparable' to that of the Soviet Union,[35] which would nevertheless, he maintained, not be viewed as threatening by Soviet leaders.[36]

For Schlesinger, 'essential equivalence' means not only enhancing the flexibility and second-strike counter-force capability of the Minuteman force, but also preserving the two other elements of the TRIAD indefinitely, with a powerful presumption that the systems currently constituting the TRIAD will all need to be replaced by the end of the 1980s. The relevant weapon programmes — the MX missile (more accurate and powerful and probably land-mobile),[37] the Trident SLBM (MARVed, longer-range and in a deeper-diving, quieter parent boat), and the B-1 bomber (larger payload, supersonic and with terrain-following capability) — are already being substantially funded. Moreover, the cruise missile, which may be coupled with bombers, hunter-killer submarines or the surface fleet, promises a vast, possibly cheap increase in accurate inter-continental striking power, although a SALT II agreement may put limits on its range and numbers.[38] Are those replacements, innovations and new deployments necessary? Is the continuation of the TRIAD justified? Schlesinger has added little to the conventional wisdom on behalf of the TRIAD except in making his somewhat idiosyncratic case for Minuteman. It has often been acknowledged in American strategy circles that the TRIAD 'just happened' − a product of service-lobbying energies more than a grand, rational strategic design.[39] However, Schlesinger has endorsed all the main conventional arguments: that the TRIAD is a 'hedge' against technological breakthroughs threatening any single element of the system;[40] that each of the three legs has special virtues for nuclear war-fighting;[41] that 'each element of the TRIAD would enhance the potential of the other in a retaliatory blow'; that the mere existence of the TRIAD greatly complicates the attacker's porblems;[42] that the enemy has an (albeit inferior) TRIAD of his own, which must be matched; and so on. In February 1975 Schlesinger issued a table to summarise the strategic force balance as it would be in 'mid-1975'[43] (Table 17.3). The figures in this table take no account of the 7,000 tactical nuclear warheads available to the NATO command in the European theatre, or of the American tactical nuclear weapons deployed in the Far East, or of the (much smaller) numbers of Soviet MRBMs and other short-range nuclear weapons deployed against NATO and also in the Far East − but even with the tactical nuclear balance excluded, the American warhead lead remains striking. Yet, despite the overwhelming American bomber superiority, for instance, Schlesinger has spoken out for active development of the B-1 follow-on option 'for the 1980s and beyond',[44] which would bring about a great increase in the striking power already available with the fabulously destructive B-52. Schlesinger has argued that, despite the lack of a significant present-day threat to the ground-alert B-52s, which would require 'SLBMs. . .launched on depressed trajectories from Soviet SS-BNs [ballistic missile-firing nuclear submarines] operating close to

Table 17.3: The American-Soviet Strategic Force Balance According to Secretary Schlesinger, 1975

	United States	Soviet Union
ICBM launchers	1,054	1,590
SLBM launchers	656	700
Inter-continental bombers	498	160*
Force loadings weapons	8,500	2,800

*This figure apparently includes an initial deployment of the new Backfire Bomber whose inter-continental capability has been in doubt.

our shores', or 'major new [Soviet] air defense programs at home', nevertheless 'all of these capabilities will clearly be within its [Soviet] technical competency and economic capacity' — eventually. To counter this threat,

> It [the B-1] will have a distinctly shorter escape time and much better resistance to nuclear effects, than the B-52, and by virtue of its lower flight altitude, greater speed and smaller radar cross-section, it should have much better capability to penetrate improved Soviet air defenses. Moreover, because of its wider range of altitude and airspeed options, the B-1 will provide greater flexibility in employment than the B-52, thereby enhancing our ability to execute a wide range of attack options in response to potential enemy action.[45]

A case along the same lines is made for the MX ICBM replacement and for the Trident submarine, both of which also in effect seek to pre-empt advanced technology threats which are many years if not decades away.

Schlesinger in office was fully committed to the deployment of only one of the follow-on strategic systems then in the pipeline, the Trident: and, if the strategic philosophy of his RAND papers is a guide, he still places extraordinary value on creating options to deploy (and also options to push promising lines of research and development), not just on deployments themselves.[46] But there seems little doubt that Schlesinger will favour deployment of the B-1, at least, and probably the MX also, given his special anxieties about the Minuteman force. It is also fairly clear that this force of the future is designed to furnish new or to upgrade old counter-force capabilities against the Soviet Union rather than simply to make assured destruction trebly sure. Even the old argument that the United States needed a special counter-force capability to 'look after' China seems to have lost some of its force for Schlesinger, given his estimate that China will only have 'regional' nuclear capability until a Chinese ICBM is 'possibly. . .ready for deployment in silos by mid-1980'.[47] There are no other nuclear powers which would require American deployment of a counter-force arsenal in the foreseeable future, certainly not in the immediate future. (The situation if, of course, very different for the Soviet Union, which is significantly tied down in nuclear terms by France, Britain and China.) Why, then, upgrade or even keep these vast forces which cannot plausibly be fitted into limited nuclear war scenarios, and yet cannot significantly limit damage to the United States in any but the most far-fetched general nuclear war scenarios, namely ones in which both sides have traded blow for blow down to a low level of withheld, vulnerable forces?

The superpower nuclear balance of the future could be very different. There are glimpses of new and different 'force-sizing' criteria in Schlesinger's own formulations, and even stronger intimations in the writings of one of the most interesting officials of the Nixon and Ford administrations, Fred Iklé, Director of the Arms Control and Disarmament Agency since early 1973. Iklé, in office as well as out, has stressed the disastrous all-round effects of actually firing off thousands of megatons, even for the nuclear attacker himself.[48]

My own view is that, whether bilaterally or unilaterally, superpower nuclear forces should be reduced drastically in megatonnage; deployed exclusively at sea; and targeted for executing not 'counter-force' (in the usual sense) and not 'assured destruction', but what might be called 'assured paralysis' (of conventional military forces). Finally, superpower nuclear forces should be capable of and oriented towards 'protracted unconditional withholding'.[49] In particular, weapons above a few kilotons at most in yield would be excluded from inventories (there would be no capability to 'bust up' large cities with individual weapons); fission yields would be minimised;[50] delivery would be extremely accurate; and there would be greatly reduced numbers of re-entry vehicles available for laying waste the planet, but increased efforts to reduce their vulnerability and ensure control of them.

Could such a strategic deployment by the United States (counter-force and damage limitation being ruled out) perform the deterrence function more safely, cheaply and humanely than the TRIAD? Schlesinger himself has raised the spectre of a strategic nuclear war fought exclusively between presently deployed forces, which would be at once militarily futile, and also — because of collateral radiation, blast and fire damage — catastrophic for the belligerents and for the world at large. In general, taking due account of the size of the enemy force, a small strategic force (especially one which eschews the counter-force role) is preferable to a large force, for several reasons. A large force increases the statistical likelihood of accident and accidental war. In war it makes for high levels of collateral, 'unintended' damage for the opponent's civilian population and ecology, and it increases expected radiation 'backlash' for one's allies and oneself (self-inflicted collateral damage). In so far as targets are multiplied on one's home territory, the opponent is given an incentive both to deploy counter-weapons and thereafter to use them in war — thus, again, increasing expected collateral damage to oneself if war comes. Finally, the deployment of large forces plainly designed for 'taking out' enemy missiles must always give rise to the possibility of pre-emptive or preventive attack in a crisis or in an accident-clouded situation — either by the enemy or, equally important, by oneself. Designing forces which will tend to restrain oneself or one's successors is a neglected skill. Trust in 'oneself' — in reality a complex of persons and organisations often at cross-purposes — is grossly misplaced.

Now the pre-emption danger is usually over-stated by opponents of counter-force. After all, a resolutely 'rational' adversary will be reluctant to pre-empt if he believes that one has an impregnable second-strike capacity, even if he believes that he himself is about to be substantially or even totally disarmed. (Any strike of his may bring down counter-strikes on his own cities.) The situation changes radically only if he believes that one's own strike will be *self-disarming*. But even then he should prefer diplomacy to launching a strike without further ado (if he can). However, clearly, the incentive for a power to withhold nuclear retaliation will be strongest when there is no possibility of its being significantly disarmed by a first strike. Despite their vulnerable weapons the superpowers are both essentially in this situation at present. Both have a few huge, very valuable and very vulnerable targets (Moscow, Leningrad, New York, Washington), which a handful of surviving 'enemy' thermonuclear weapons would suffice to eliminate. However, both sides do have capabilities to deplete the other's missile force substantially (even if the 'trade' might not favour the aggressor), and the military on both sides have certainly spoken out for pre-emptive and other variants of a launch-on warning strategy. Even Schlesinger has said that if the Soviets should launch a preventive strike,[51] withholding ICBMs initially in order to attack unalerted Strategic Air Command (SAC) bomber bases with SLBMs,

> this would mean that the first SLBM warheads would detonate over our bomber bases 15-20 minutes before the first ICBM warheads reached our Minuteman silos. Whether our National Command Authorities would, under these circumstances, choose to launch some or all of our Minuteman missiles before they were struck, no-one, including the Soviet planners, can foretell in advance of the actual decision.[52]

If the Soviet ICBM attack follows at the 'rational' interval of '15-20 minutes' mentioned by Schlesinger, then the result might be true strategic theatre of the absurd – Soviet ICBMs impacting on empty American silos and American ICBMs impacting on empty Soviet silos!

The heart of the self-interested case against large land-based forces – bombers and missiles – is the heavy weight of attack that they tend to attract on the deploying power in war, whether the attacking power is seeking to avoid damage to the civilian economy and population or not. There is irony in hardening missile silos to ride out all but the most accurate attacks. While hardening may persuade an aggressor to stay his hand, it also means that an effective and therefore ground-burst attack will cause higher levels of long-term radiation damage than an air-burst attack on a 'soft' or unprotected system. Hardening, also rules out the possibility of drawing a sharp distinction between the strategic nuclear and the civilian economic target system in practice. Schlesinger seems to believe that bomber bases and ICBM silos should continue to lie scattered about the continental United States indefinitely; but this virtually guarantees escalation in his favourite limited counter-force war scenario.[53]

Schlesinger, it seems, ought to be a proponent of Deterrence All At Sea. If American strategic forces were concentrated exclusively in submarines there would be few, if any, 'time-urgent' strategic targets for the Soviet Union to hit in the continental United States, at least for the time being.[54] The only high-priority targets directly connected with the strategic force would be two Polaris-Poseidon submarine bases.[55] While strategic weapon storage sites and a few other locations might be seen as important counter-force targets for a Soviet attack, such a target system would be vastly less damage-inviting than one containing 1,300-plus time-urgent and mostly hardened targets. And certainly a war of forces would be much less likely to escalate to general war if civilian and nuclear strategic target systems were systematically separated. (The American bomber force is actually superior to Schlesinger's cherished Minuteman force from this point of view. Discriminating but effective air-burst attacks on bomber bases are at least possible, not that the Soviets yet have the low-yield warheads in their strategic missile arsenal for executing them.)

The objection that Deterrence All At Sea would remove two large 'hedges' against sudden technical changes making the strategic force vulnerable to surprise attack – namely bombers and land-based missiles – has much less force than is commonly supposed. Admittedly, existing Polaris and Poseidon boats represent a great prize for anti-submarine warfare (ASW) forces in a surprise attack. Poseidon-equipped submarines have 16 missiles with about 10 warheads apiece – a total of up to about 200 fifty-kiloton warheads capable of being taken out in one torpedo attack. One Trident boat will concentrate about 24 x 24 = 576 warheads into one corner of the ocean. However, the pattern of American SLBM design and deployment could be radically changed not only to avoid this warhead concentration, but to emphasise a 'considered' second-strike capability. At 16,000 tons the Trident submarine has twice the displacement of its predecessor. The ranges of the Trident 1 and Trident II missiles are 4,000 and 5,000 nautical miles respectively, compared with the Poseidon C3's 2,500 natical miles. The Trident II missile will permit the boats to cruise almost anywhere while remaining on station — but, of course, any nuclear submarine can cruise where it will and rely quite confidently on getting to station after an attack. Being continuously on station is only important for urgent counter-force strikes. Trident seems likely to be the most expensive strategic weapon programme in history, and the present need for it is very doubtful.[56] In any case, it can be stated flatly that submarines simply are not and never will be as vulnerable as fixed ICBMs, which eventually must bow out to the threat of accurate MIRV attack. They are also a more secure — and even more flexible —war-fighting instrument than bombers (which eventually must return to vulnerable bases) for the type of protracted strategic conflict which Schlesinger, for one, has been disposed to expect.[57] Finally, technical innovations do seem capable of mitigating the command and control problems of the submarine fleet.

A possible objection to Deterrence All At Sea is that many Soviet ICBMs are presently targeted against American ICBM silos and Strategic Air Command (SAC) bases, and might therefore be re-targeted to threaten a large number of otherwise untargeted American cities if the American land-based forces were scrapped. In reply, it is worth noting that official Americans expect over 100 million American deaths under existing Soviet targeting practices.[58] There cannot be many untargeted American cities of size at present if this forecast is correct. In any case a forces-to-cities targeting change would to some extent run counter to Soviet strategic doctrine, which calls for the elimination of targets of major military, military-industrial and administrative importance rather than 'city-busting' as such. The Soviets might choose to reorient a larger part of their ICBM force to Chinese or European targets, or move towards a protracted withholding doctrine, or even phase out part of their strategic force altogether. In any event, the nightmare of a destructive and futile pre-emptive war of land-based nuclear forces would have been scotched by unilateral American action.[59]

Action need not be entirely unilateral. An American administration could surely secure a substantial reduction of the Soviet ICBM force in return for a move to rely exclusively on sea-borne forces for its own strategic deterrent. But even if the Soviets were not influenced by American negotiating offers or the new 'fashion' launched by an American switch to the sea, the essentials of the strategic situation would nevertheless not be disturbed. Both sides would retain a capability to wreak appalling damage on the other.

If, in addition, the American force was re-tooled to eliminate individual city-razing weapons, it would still of course be able to destroy whole cities quite rapidly by cumulative strikes. Despite this, I believe that it is worth moving in the direction of a small (say a few hundred cruise and ballistic missiles overall), exclusively sea-based strategic force of highly accurate low-kiloton weapons, as fission-free as possible. All of this is technically quite possible in the short to medium term (five to ten years), and would become politically feasible if strategic doctrine underwent the necessary (pardon the pun) sea-change; and if the service politics of the shift were carefully attended to.[60] The United States has been the world fashion leader in strategic force structuring and strategic doctrine for over a generation; the change recommended here would potently influence nuclear friends and enemies, and threshold powers also.[61]

Notes

1. See William W. Kaufmann, *The McNamara Strategy* (New York, 1964), for an unselfconscious presentation of McNamara's views by their chief inspirer, who was still drafting major policy pronouncements under Schlesinger. Kaufmann, formerly of the Rand Corporation, is now at the Massachussets Institute of Technology. On the Washington influence of Rand alumni generally, in the Schlesinger period, and before, see Desmond J. Ball, *Déjà Vu: the Return to Counterforce in the Nixon Administration,* Foreign Scholar Series, California Arms Control and Foreign Policy Seminar, Santa Monica, California, December 1974, pp.33-6.
2. Ball, *Déjà Vu,* p.17.
3. See H.D. Mariska, 'The Single Integrated Operational Plan', *Military Review,* March 1972.
4. 'US-USSR Strategic Policies', Hearings before the Subcommittee on Arms Control, International Law and Organisation of the Senate Committee on Foreign Relations, 93rd Congress, Second Session, 4 March 1974, p.38. ('Top Secret Hearing sanitized and made public, 4 April 1974') (hereafter abbreviated to 'US-USSR Strategic Policies', loc.cit.).
5. J. Newhouse, *Cold Dawn: The Story of SALT* (New York, 1973), p.158. According to Newhouse, Secretary Laird withdrew funding requests for a

more accurate Poseidon missile 'precisely to head off accusations that the United States might be headed for a first-strike MIRV'. For details of Schlesinger's budgetary proposals to upgrade Minuteman and Poseidon, see Ball, *Déjà Vu,* pp.21-3.

6. 'US-USSR Strategic Policies', loc.cit., p.18 and *passim.*
7. Annual US Defense Department Report, Fiscal Year 1976, Washington, D.C., 5 February 1975, p.49 (hereafter abbreviated to *FY 1976 Defense Report).*
8. Annual US Defense Department Report, Fiscal Year 1975, Washington, D.C., 4 March 1974, Part Two, p.38 (hereafter abbreviated to *FY 1975 Defense Report).* Schlesinger was an ardent opponent of the B-1 whilst in charge of the National Security Division of the Bureau of the Budget.
9. *FY 1976 Defense Report,* Part II, p.20.
10. *International Herald Tribune,* 28 January 1976.
11. There is also now a 'megatonnage gap'. According to the Chairman of the Joint Chiefs of Staff, Admiral Thomas H. Moorer: 'Ten years ago the US had five times the available megatonnage as the USSR. The USSR has taken over the lead in strategic offensive megatons and now far surpasses us in this measure of the strategic balance. The sharp drop in US megatons from 1966 to 1970 reflects the reduction in heavy bombers and the substitution of smaller-yield for higher-yield weapons during that period. The decline, thereafter, reflects the substitution of lower-yield MIRVs for higher-yield single RVs in our strategic missiles.' Statement before the Senate Appropriations Committee on the FY 1975 Defense Budget, 93rd Congress, Second Session, p.260.
12. For an amusing account of the debate about criteria for 'sufficiency' see Ball, *Déjà Vu,* pp.5-8.
13. *FY 1976 Defense Report,* Part One, pp.13, 14.
14. This paper assumes that a strategic force capable of exterminating the urban population of the earth after absorbing a first strike is 'large'. For a discussion of the potential diplomatic disadvantages of American official statements which exaggerate Soviet capabilities, see Robert Sherman, 'The Fallacies of Counterforce', *Strategic Review,* III (1975), no.2, p.5.
15. *FY 1975 Defense Report,* pp.43-4.
16. *FY 1976 Defense Report,* Part Two, p.10.
17. *FY 1976 Defense Report,* Part Two, pp.34ff. The United States is probably several years ahead of the Soviet Union by every major qualitative measure of the strategic balance. On the superiority of the American SLBM fleet in warhead numbers, accuracies, security and scope of operations, see J.P. Ruina, 'The TRIAD and US Strategic Policy' in Kosta Tsipis, Anne H. Cahn and Bernard T. Feld (eds.), *The Future of the Sea-Based Deterrent* (Cambridge, Massachusetts, 1973).
18. Schlesinger himself has remarked of the McNamara period: 'In retrospect it seems clear that the buildup of strategic missiles was more rapid than necessary.' See 'Organizational Structures and Planning', Rand, P-3316, February 1966, in James R. Schlesinger, *Selected Papers on National Security 1964-1968,* Rand Corporation, P-5284, September 1974, p.65. But he has never conceded that it was far *larger* than necessary – indeed he has often criticised the foreclosure of the heavy missile option ('the large payload hedge') by the 1961 decision to deploy the Minuteman ICBM, with its 'small' one-megaton warhead, almost exclusively. See 'The Changing Environment for Systems Analysis', Rand P-3287, December 1965, in ibid., p.49. This criticism interestingly foreshadows his future concern with Soviet superiority in missile throw-weight.
19. 'US-USSR Strategic Policies', loc.cit., p.50.

20. *FY 1975 Defense Report,* p.35.
21. *FY 1976 Defense Report,* Part II, pp.4, 5.
22. Also 'neither side has a high confidence capability of destroying a large fraction of the other's fixed, hard ICBM silos.' *FY 1976 Defense Report,* Part II, p.3.
23. 'US-USSR Strategic Policies', loc.cit., pp.18-19.
24. See Sherman, 'The Fallacies of Counterforce', loc.cit., p.52.
25. The Soviet attack discussed in Schlesinger's 'counterforce briefing' of the Senate Foreign Relations Committee deliberately avoided the secondary or dispersal bases of the Strategic Air Command.
26. The briefing was requested by Senator Clifford Case in a letter which questioned Schlesinger's weapon budget proposals: 'Should it turn out that the destruction to our society from counterforce attacks would be so substantial as to make this cost as unacceptable as all-out attacks specifically targeted against our population centers, then the rationale for the multi-billion dollar family of weapons designed to destroy military targets that has begun to be funded this year. . .could be called into serious question.' (This highly apposite question nevertheless contains misleading assumptions. Most American strategic weapons have been designed to destroy military targets since the mid-1950s; and funding of the coming multi-billion dollar strategic systems – the Trident SLBM, the B-1 bomber and the MX ICBM began years ago.) For the full text of the letter see Briefing by Secretary of Defense James R. Schlesinger on Casualties and Destruction Expected to Result from So-Called Nuclear Counterforce Attacks against Military Installations in the United States: Subcommittee on Arms Control, International Law and Organisation of the Senate Foreign Relations Committee, pp.1-2. ('Secret Hearing held on September 11, 1974; Sanitized and made Public on January 10, 1975') (hereafter abbreviated to 'Counterforce Briefing', loc.cit.). For Senator Case's final word in committee on what he called 'this whole razzle dazzle', see ibid., pp.35-41.
27. Ibid., pp.12, 14. The heaviest attack considered by Schlesinger involved two one-megaton warheads (MT) Soviet warheads per American ICBM silo, plus a single one-MT warhead each for SAC and SLBM bases. Deaths associated with hitting Minuteman silos would range from one million to three million, depending on whether weapons were air-burst or ground-burst, according to Schlesinger.
28. The chairman of the sub-committee, Senator Edmund Muskie, quoted the following excerpts from an ACDA memorandum at p.25 of the hearings transcript: 'Consider the following bounds on the uncertainty relative to casualties resulting from an attack against Minuteman silos if the population protection factor [i.e. the effectiveness of civil defense measures] is unknown, and the weather is not selected to minimize covering populated areas with fallout, [i.e. the winds are blowing away from cities.] The urban casualties can range from 145,000 to 50 million for two one-megaton warheads arriving at each Minuteman silo. Note this does not include casualties among the rural population.' Muskie then asked: 'if the President of the United States knows the possibility is not that the damage to our population will be only 800,000, but that it could be 50 million, why should he limit his response?', ibid., p.26. For a partial text of the ACDA memorandum see ibid., pp.30-2, where we learn that, for the ACDA estimates: 'The weather is fixed as "Winter Mean" [April, it appears, is among the cruellest months for nuclear attack] ; the fission-fusion factor [the overall ratio of the fission to the fusion yield in the warheads] is 1 and ground burst is used. . .The extreme range of population kill (P95 only) [i.e. urban only, apparently] is 145,000 to 13,000,000 for a two-1MT attack against Minuteman silos. A mean or expected kill is

4,500,000 for the above case.'
29. *FY 1975 Defense Report*, p.42.
30. See Herbert Scoville, Jr., and David G. Hoag, 'Ballistic Missile Submarines as Counterforce Weapons', in Tsipis, Cahn and Feld, *The Future of the Sea-Based Deterrent*.
31. ICBMs account for nearly 50 per cent of Soviet re-entry vehicles and megatonnage, while Schlesinger has said that 'less than 25 per cent of the US strategic deterrent capability measured in terms of missile and bomber warheads resides in fixed ICBMs'. See *FY 1976 Defense Report*, Part One, p.16.
32. Sherman, 'The Fallacies of Counterforce', p.52.
33. Imaginative and far-reaching 'positive' diplomacy may become possible beyond the nuclear brink as Thomas Schelling, for one, has pointed out. There ought to be a 'diplomatic SIOP' with a sliding scale of offers and demands for compensation in case of nuclear accidents, inadvertence, or indiscipline. Offers might range from unilateral crash disarmament to long-term loans and include various kinds of immediate direct aid. The necessary communication arrangements and agreed procedures already exist as a result of superpower agreements.
34. See S. Glasstone (ed.), *The Effects of Nuclear Weapons*, Department of Defense, Washington, 1964, pp.114, 164. Kosta Tsipis and Herbert Scoville inform the present writer that some early (and erroneous) Pentagon studies forecast advantages for low air-bursting over ground-bursting in a counter silo-attack. Schlesinger's 'Scenario assumptions' were replaced by more realistic ones in later presentations. See Sub-Committee on Arms Control, International Law and Organisation of the Senate Foreign Relations Committee, *Analysis of Effects of Limited Nuclear War*, Washington D.C., September 1975.
35. 'Counterforce Briefing', loc.cit., p.3.
36. 'We do not have and cannot acquire a disarming first-strike capability against the Soviet Union.' *FY 1976 Defense Report*, Part One, p.16.
37. 'For the long-term [mid-1980s and beyond], we can provide an option to develop an entirely new ICBM.' *FY 1976 Defense Report*, Part II, p.20.
38. Cruise missiles, whether ship-launched (SLCM) or air-launched (ALCM), will be subsonic, air-breathing, terrain-following, 'smart' flying bombs, able to fly under defensive radars and 'home' on point targets by means of sophisticated sensors. See Kosta Tsipis, 'The Accuracy of Strategic Missiles', *Scientific American*, no.233, July 1975, p.22.
39. See Ruina, 'The TRIAD and US Strategic Policy' in Tsipis, Cahn and Feld, *The Future of the Sea-Based Deterrent*.
40. *FY 1975 Defense Report*, p.49. 'You don't want to have all your eggs in one basket because if you have a breakthrough in ASW [anti-submarine warfare] capabilities your deterrence goes rapidly downhill.' 'US-USSR Strategic Policies', loc.cit., p.55.
41. *FY 1975 Defense Report*, p.49.
42. Ibid., p.51.
43. *FY 1976 Defense Report*, Part II, p.19.
44. *FY 1976 Defense Report*, p.62.
45. Ibid.
46. Note especially his repeated criticisms of what he considers the premature foreclosing of ICBM options by ex-Secretary McNamara. Schlesinger manages to criticise — consistently, I think — (a) the decision to deploy preponderantly Minuteman missiles rather than Titan, or a follow-on 'heavy' ICBM; (b) the decision to deploy Minuteman so rapidly (1,000 by 1967) in the absence of a Soviet build-up; and (c) the decision to foreclose a larger (than 1,000) Minuteman build-up in 1963-4. See Schlesinger, *Selected Papers*, pp.48, 65 and

71 respectively on these points.

47. *FY 1976 Defense Report,* Part II, p.17.

48. F.C. Iklé, *Can Nuclear Deterrence Last Out the Century* (California Arms Control and Foreign Policy Seminar, Santa Monica, California, 1973). Iklé's foreword to an ACDA report released in October 1975 stated: 'it now appears that a massive attack with many large-scale detonations would cause such widespread and long-lasting environmental damage that the aggressor country might suffer serious physiological, economic and environmental effects even without a response by the country attacked.' *Worldwide Effects of Nuclear War. . .Some Perspectives,* Report of the US ACDA, Washington, D.C., no date, p.2. This report summarises the findings of an ACDA-sponsored study by the National Research Council, which Iklé initiated. See *Long-Term Worldwide Effects of Multiple Nuclear Weapons Detonations,* National Academy of Sciences, Washington, D.C., 1975. Iklé has been even reported as being in favour of abandoning land-based missiles altogether. See *Time,* 11 February 1974, p.30. But in fact he does not — at least publicly — favour unilateral American force reductions. See *The Washington Post,* 2 February 1974.

49. It should be noted that I am recommending a targeting doctrine whose actual execution in war I do not in general favour. For the important distinction between targeting and execution doctrine see Donald R. Westervelt, 'The Essence of Armed Futility', *Orbis,* XVIII (1974), p.693. On 'unconditional withholding' see Peter King, *The Strategy of Total Withholding,* Canberra Papers on Strategy and Defence, Canberra, 1971.

50. But as Schlesinger has pointed out, even a pure (laser-triggered) fusion weapon would not be 'clean', only 'less dirty' than a fission-triggered one. See 'US-USSR Strategic Policies', loc.cit., p.28. Fission-free fusion weapons are under active development. See Ball, *Déjà Vu,* p.25, and J. Carson Mark, 'Nuclear Weapons Technology' in B.T. Feld, T. Greenwood, G.W. Rathjens and S. Weinberg, *Impact of New Technologies on the Arms Race* (Cambridge, Massachusetts, 1971).

51. For some reason the traditional and useful distinction between a preventive strike ('out of the blue') and a pre-emptive strike ('I won't strike first unless you do') has been blurred or abandoned in the American strategic literature, perhaps because preventive attack has become 'unthinkable' for Americans. But of course Soviet planners often think of it when facing East.

52. *FY 1976 Defense Report,* Part II, p.18.

53. Whiteman Air Force Base, Missouri, is particularly damage-inviting. It is a Minuteman complex located between Kansas City and St Louis, within easy fall-out range of both. Department of Defense figures in 'Counterforce Briefing', loc.cit., suggest that, according to prevailing winds and other factors, there could be up to one million casualties in St Louis and even more in Kansas City, although not in any one attack. (See ibid., pp.17-18.) According to Schlesinger, up to more than half of total expected American fatalities (urban and rural) in a counter-force attack on all six of the American ICBM fields would be due to attacks on this one field alone. The 'Whiteman' dead could number 500,000 (ibid., p.13). Schlesinger has apparently neglected an American option which would permit the Soviets greatly to reduce expected collateral damage in case they do launch a counter-force attack on the United States — namely to wind up the Whiteman base.

54. Trident SLBM missiles have true inter-continental range, and submarines carrying them would be time-urgent targets in American ports.

55. Officially epxected collateral damage for attack on these two soft targets is worth noting. According to Schlesinger: 'If the Soviets were to attack the two CONUS — Continental United States — SS-BN support bases, Charleston and

Bremerton, possible fatalities could number on the order of 100,000.'
'Counterforce Briefing', loc.cit., p.17.

56. See George W. Rathjens and Jack P. Ruina, 'Trident', in Tsipis, Cahn and Feld, *The Future of the Sea-Based Deterrent*.

57. See 'The Changing Environment for Systems Analysis', Rand, P-3287, December 1965, in Schlesinger, *Selected Papers*. This paper yields a clue to Schlesinger's urgent desire to improve the counter-force war-fighting capability of the Minuteman missile. It analyses the contrasting force requirements of 'spasm' and protracted nuclear fighting, and concludes that in 'city-avoidance' war, 'the returns for additional outlays on strategic offensive forces may be moderately high' (ibid., p.44). Also: 'If city-avoidance is to take place and a long-endurance counterforce war is the prospect, then the best allocation of the strategic budget shifts from defense towards offense.' See 'On Relating Non-Technical Elements to System Studies', Rand P-3545, February 1967, in ibid., pp.82-3.

58. 'Counterforce Briefing', loc.cit., *passim*, and *FY 1976 Defense Report*, Part II, p.7.

59. In one perhaps unwary passage Schlesinger himself has almost fully conceded the case for abandoning the counter-force mission: 'In the event of war the most desirable thing that can happen to weapons of mass destruction is that they be destroyed before they can inflict damage.' (See 'Arms Interaction and Arms Control', P-3881, September 1968, Schlesinger, *Selected Papers*, p.30.) Of course Schlesinger meant *Soviet* weapons, but the argument cuts two ways. A more 'desirable thing' of course is that weapons to destroy weapons are not deployed in the first place.

60. The army and the Navy could perhaps be interested in depriving the air force of at least one of its two strategic striking forces.

61. Thanks are due, first, to my research assistant in 1975, Rebecca Albury, not only for conventional scholarly exertions but also for her creative hostility to the subject matter of the study; to Desmond J. Ball, Strategic and Defence Studies Centre, Australian National University, whose pioneering work in the field of Schlesinger studies are, I hope, adequately celebrated in the footnotes; and to my wife, Inese Veidelis, for surgical work on the prose and other contributions and, finally, to Kosta Tsipis for permission to reproduce his tables.

18 THE FUNCTION OF MILITARY POWER

B.V.A. Röling

Introduction

Few would disagree that the present state of the arms race is very dangerous indeed. And when we look into the future matters appear likely to go from bad to worse. Here is not the place to go into details. But awareness of the character of the present danger is necessary. For every alternative solution has risks. The question is whether the present risks are greater or smaller than the new risks of any alternative we would like to see adopted. But is there any realistic alternative, that is an alternative which would have a reasonable chance of being accepted? Do we in fact really have an alternative?

Certainly it is no alternative to demand that humanity should be wiser, more kind in its relations, more restrained in its aggressiveness. We have to take as our starting point humanity as it is: self-centred, distrusting of foreigners, short-sighted, unwilling to pay attention, indifferent to far-away things and, above all, socialised in the group in which the individual is living and not inclined to change traditional opinions and habits. Nor is general and complete disarmament an alternative, but only a far-away ideal for a world system that is different from ours.

Again, unilateral disarmament is no alternative. Pacifism is good, but too good to be true, too good for this world. Our dilemma is that technology has brought into being nuclear weapons that, at least between nuclear powers, cannot be used, because their use would mean mutual destruction. But in our world we cannot do without the possession of these weapons. If we abolish our nuclear weapons, the other weapons of our adversary would become decisive. He would have the power to behave as he liked. And the arrogance of power would make him misbehave.

In our world military might is thus indispensable as a means of balancing the military might of the other party, and hence of preventing his hegemony. The balance of power signifies that no one has sufficient power to allow his will prevail. But reliance on armed force to maintain peace and security inevitably leads to an arms race such as we have experienced since World War Two. Moreover, modern arms compel us to have weapons on constant alert in peacetime because a first blow might be decisive. The necessity to possess armed force has also led to an irrational degree of over-armament and to 'overkill'. This in turn means that armed forces themselves become causes of tension and danger.

Arms are needed for the maintenance of peace and security, but they have actually become one of the greatest dangers of our time. And hitherto no one has succeeded in curbing the arms race, in stopping the increasingly sinister development of arms technology. Multilateral disarmament has been discussed for almost a century. Endless disarmament conferences have been held. They have all failed with the exception of the undertaking to abolish biological weapons.

It would seem that our approach has been wrong. If we still believe that something can be done, something else should be tried, something new. William Epstein has called for 'radical new approaches'.[1] But are his proposals radically new? Or do they only suggest trying again what failed in the recent past, in what were far more favourable circumstances? The conditions for his suggestions are in fact less favourable than in the post-war years. Mankind has got accustomed to atomic power. In the minds of people war has been replaced as the 'primary danger' by the danger of pollution and scarcity. The younger generation has forgotten about the war. And many uninformed people have started to trust in the situation of mutual 'overkill', because there has been no war of significance in Europe since 1945.

Is it possible to offer something new? The concept of newness might be further analysed. One could consider several aspects of change.

1. Change in the Groups We Want to Influence

The decision-makers, the élite, scholars, the military, the labour movements, women, the young, the small powers and the Third World are examples of such groups.

2. Change in the Method of Approach

Hitherto we have stressed the dangers of the situation. Have we given sufficient attention to why we failed to reach the groups we wanted to communicate with? Is it research on communication that we need? Or should it be something different that we ought to communicate?

3. Change in the Field Where Change Should Take Place

What are the forces behind the sinister developments we witness? Can we discover them? And when discovered, would it be possible to eliminate them?

4. Change in the Means of Change

Did we not put too much emphasis on multilateral action? Did we try enough to find out what we might do alone? Perhaps unilaterally something might be achieved that appeared to be impossible to achieve multilaterally. Such unilateral action might be considered not only with respect to the adversary in the Cold War, but also with respect to the superpower *within* each of the military alliances. Small powers may hold different opinions to those of the superpowers. Would it be desirable to start action on the principle of 'Small powers of the World, Unite!'?

5. Change in the Goal with Respect to Arms

Hitherto primary attention has been given to disarmament and rather less to weapons. Have we given enough attention to the feasibility of using other weapons? Would it be worthwhile to consider anew the function of military power, now that modern weapons cannot be used but equally cannot be abandoned? This point deserves further elaboration. The question is which military functions are indispensable and which functions might be eliminated without any danger to peace and security? It may be that some functions of weapons are dispensable, and that a restriction in the function of military power might appeal to statesmen eager to diminish arms spending. Such reduction of the accepted function of weapons might eliminate the very reason for the failure to control the arms race and promote real arms reduction.

In this discussion of the function of military power, the internal and the transnational aspects are for the moment disregarded. The internal function may be defined as that of preventing internal uprisings and of suppressing revolts. The transnational function involves participation in the carrying out of measures of collective security such as the use of national armed power in the service of the United Nations. (The role national armies play in military alliances is not transnational on this definition, for the military power of regional alliances such as NATO and the Warsaw Pact plainly takes the place, more or less, of national military power.) Both the internal and transnational functions are important, but have almost no bearing on the arms race or the arms dilemma. A fraction of the presently available national military power would suffice for these two functions. It is the other functions which stimulate the arms race, arms research and the existing overkill.

Considering the functions of military power, a distinction should be made between those functions which aim at the promotion and extension of power and interest — one might call them the *acquisitive functions* — and those functions which aim at the preservation of existing power and interests — one might call them the *defensive, negating functions.* (Some analysts prefer to designate the former category 'positive functions' but this is possibly undesirable because it might appear to indicate a positive evaluation.)

Acquisitive Functions

1. The Function of Conquest by the Use of Armed Force to Gain Territory or to Obtain Concessions in the Economic, Political or Ideological Field

This function is not on the face of it always indefensible. For example, the use of armed force for the purpose of liberation from colonial domination or apartheid falls into this category. But this armed force would be the primitive and rather unorganised military power of 'a people', not of a state. Armed state action for the purpose of liberation might come into the picture in the case of spheres of influence of superpowers becoming so marked by oppression that armed action might be used in the quest for national independence and liberty. But such armed action is rather hypothetical, taking into account the might of the superpowers. The extent of the oppressive impact of the superpower might better be reduced by non-violent action and by the impact of world public opinion.

2. The Function of Conquest by the Threat of the Use of Armed Force

Thomas Schelling has defined this as 'coercive diplomacy'. In Schelling's theory, power is the central concept in the relations between states, especially 'the power to hurt'. Threatening to use this power is part of diplomacy: 'The power to hurt is bargaining power. To exploit it is diplomacy, vicious diplomacy, but diplomacy.' According to Schelling, in former times this coercive diplomacy was used in exceptional circumstances, it was

> abnormal and episodic, not actual and continuous. . .For the last two decades, though, this part of diplomacy has been central and continuous; in the US there has been a revolution in the relation of military to foreign policy at the same time as the revolution of explosive power.

In his chapter 'The Strategic Role of Pain and Damage', Schelling observes that 'it may be possible to bypass the military stage altogether and to proceed at once to coercive bargaining.' He refers in this connection to Hitler's policy with respect to Denmark and Austria, noting that 'proud military establishments do not like to think of themselves as extortionists'. But more can be achieved with threats than with military action, especially at the present period 'in which the power to hurt is more impressive than the power to oppose'. Coercive diplomacy aims at 'compellence'. 'Compellence' differs, according to Schelling, from 'deterrence'. It is the difference between 'inducing inaction and making somebody perform'. In his opinion deterrence has the function not only of deterring armed action, but also of deterring non-violent action which would harm our interests.[2]

3. The Function of Armed Force in a Strategy of Indirect Aggression

This third acquisitive function may be mentioned, though military power appears here to be strictly defensive. This is the function of military power in a strategy which André Beaufre called 'une stratégie d'ensemble', or 'une stratégie totale'.

According to Beaufre, extension of power and interests can be achieved in the direct way, by military conquest, or in the indirect way, by economic or ideological means. But at the present time freedom of military action no longer exists because modern weapons are too destructive. Their direct use has become too dangerous. The only way to achieve advantages is the indirect way. Freedom of action still exists in the economic and ideological field.[3] But if a state is successful in this indirect way, and, for example, succeeds in luring another state into its own alliance, the possibility will exist that military action will be taken by the opposing superpower to regain with military means what it has lost in the indirect way. Here, then, appears the military function in the totality of the 'stratégie d'ensemble': the use of military power to deter such military reaction, and by doing so to prevent the military retaking of that which was lost in non-violent aggressive action.

Beaufre's theory has gained political significance, since his doctrine was taken up by the German statesman Franz Joseph Strausss. Strauss aims at a United Europe extending to the borders of the Soviet Union. The 'satellite states' should be seduced into coming over to the West, by the latter's wealth and liberty. The military might of a united Western Europe — 'die Kraft eines integrierten Grossraumes' — should be great enough to deter the Soviet Union from militarily retaking what it lost. A European nuclear force would be indispensable to the performance of this function.[4]

Defensive, or Negating Military Functions

Here we are concerned with the functions of military power which aim at the prevention of damage to our own interests or, otherwise defined, at the prevention of gains by another state.

1. The Function of Deterring Armed Conquest

Deterrence is a well-known concept in Western military philosophy. Usually it means that a country is willing and able to defend itself if it is attacked. If a country did not have this willingness and this capacity, it would be at the mercy of every mighty, well-armed neighbour. Lack of power would work out almost as a kind of 'negative provocation'. The neighbour could use military power effectively, and it would be almost impossible for him to resist the temptation. Therefore such a deterrent military function is indispensable, and the Charter of the United Nations in Article 51 recognises this inherent right of using arms in self-defence against armed attack (until the Security Council has taken steps to maintain international peace and security).

This deterrent function can operate at all levels of military strength, and consequently at all levels of intensity of the deterrent function. A small country, like Switzerland or Sweden, cannot build up an army really able to repel a mighty neighbour in case of attack. But its army has still a powerful deterrent effect. The costs would be high for an attacker, and they probably would not outweigh the gains. In short: the deterrence function of a small country such as Switzerland has the effect of raising the entry-price in such a way that armed aggression will not be probable, the more so because its foreign policy, based on permanent neutrality, avoids as much as possible providing any reason for attack.[5]

More powerful nations than Switzerland and especially military alliances such as NATO or the Warsaw Pact have so much military might that a premeditated aggression by one of them on another is almost unthinkable. In such a relationship the deterrence of war in the sense which von Clausewitz used it — war as a means of national policy — is almost complete. Only fear that one of the parties might be considering an attack, might induce the other to start hostilities, a pre-emptive war, especially if the weapon-posture puts a premium on delivering the first blow.

2. The function of Deterring Coercive Diplomacy

This belongs to the same category. Armed power is indispensable to prevent the use of the 'power to hurt' in diplomacy. The function of this power is to make threats and blackmail 'incredible', and therefore to reduce the military power of the opponent to that of a 'paper tiger'.

3. The Function of Deterring, with Military Means, Unfavourable Acts in the Political, Economic or Ideological Field

In this respect the function of armed force is to forestall 'indirect aggression'. A typical example of this kind of use of military threat was Henry Kissinger's warning the United States could use force in case oil supplies were again cut off.

The question is, whether such a function is indispensable. Mostly the argument goes: one has to threaten the use of force if vital interests are at stake. But in which cases are they? There may be violations of great interests. But would this justify the use of armed force in the nuclear age? Is it not a very traditional way of thinking, to consider the use of armed force in the case of non-violent hostile action? It is difficult to imagine that other means of defence would be lacking. Yet exclusion of the use of force in such circumstances – in accordance with the provisions of the Charter of the United Nations – might encourage state behaviour that would interfere with the interests of developed countries. The nationalisation of the Suez Canal Company was a case in point. But some relations should be altered. We are approaching a period in which gradually the privileged position of Europe, of the old rich nations, will be eliminated. To defend with arms those privileges would be not only illegal, but unwise. Concessions in this field are not only required by justice, but might also be called the price of survival in the atomic age.

The dilemma is, as already stated, that in our world of nuclear power armed force can no longer be used between nuclear weapons states, because the risks would be too great that a total nuclear war would be the consequence. And such a war might be the end of our civilisation. Survival of the technically highly developed world, which might, through war, perish through its technology, is a new factor playing a role in any evaluation of armed action. Regarding this intolerable risk, in general the function and use of armed force should be reduced to the cases in which that use is strictly indispensable. We cannot do without weapons, because if we unilaterally abolish them, we would be at the mercy of the states which still retained military power. But in the present situation in which we need weapons which cannot be used, their function should be reduced simply to deterring the use of such weapons. The only reasonable function of weapons is the neutralisation of the weapons of the other. Consequently the acquisitive functions of weapons should be regarded as belonging to the past, unless armed force is used on the order or the recommendation of the world organisation. The function of deterring, through the threat of the use of force, interest-damaging non-violent action, such as the cutting off of oil supplies, should also no longer be regarded as a reasonable weapon function in the hands of the national state. Such forceful action should, however, still be open to the United Nations, since the Security Council recognised correctly that the continuation of unbearable social injustice, such as 'apartheid', can be considered to be 'a threat to the peace' in the sense of Article 39 of the Charter. This revolutionary change in the interpretation of Article 39 occurred in 1966 in the decisions of the Security Council with respect to Rhodesia. The General Assembly, however, had already taken this point of view many year earlier, not only with respect to 'apartheid' but also with respect to 'colonial domination and exploitation'.[6]

At this point some consideration must be given to strategic and tactical nuclear weapons. There was a time when, according to deterrence theory, effective deterrence could only be achieved by threatening the destruction of cities. This threat of massive retaliation, if aggression occurred, was rational, be it illegal and immoral, in the period of American monopoly. As soon as the Americans became vulnerable to Soviet strategic weapons — the Sputnik announced the coming vulnerability in 1957 — this threat of massive retaliation became incredible. For years thereafter, however, it was still assumed that strategic weapons deterred war in general.

Matters have been made more complicated by the invention of new weapons — precision weapons, anti-submarine warfare (ASW), MIRVs and ABMs have opened up the possibility of a disarming first strike capability. SALT started with the principal aim of preventing that possibility, or the possibility that the parties might think that this capability had been realised. Hence the SALT I agreement practically to eliminate effective ABM systems had the main aim of keeping cities open to mutual destruction, that is to maintain, by formal treaty, the mutual capacity for genocide — for the sake of peace. It is a kind of mass hostage system. In former times the children of kings were given as hostages for the good behaviour of governments. Now it is the children of the big cities: a kind of democratisation of the hostage system.

But with the formal exclusion of effective ABM systems a greater awareness has grown concerning the disastrous results which the use of strategic nuclear counter-city weapons might have. President Gerald Ford mentioned on one occasion the possibility of 100 million dead on either side. Who would be prepared, in cold blood, and deliberately, to use these weapons in case a conventional war started? It would be either stupidity or madness. Stupidity plays a considerable role in international relations, and so does madness, or anger. But the conviction has grown that, rationally, these strategic weapons no longer deter war. Their use has become incredible, and with that their deterrent function has been reduced to the deterrence of the use of strategic nuclear weapons. One may thus take it that strategic weapons will not be used if a conventional war breaks out in Europe.

It should be noted here that the same reasoning might and should be applied to tactical weapons in the European theatre. The use of these weapons could easily lead to the total destruction of Europe.[7] The assumption that the adversaries would come to a diplomatic understanding after the exchange of some rounds of tactical nuclear warfare is highly implausible. Reference may be made here to Marshal V.D. Sokolovsky's description of what the Soviet answer would be to the use of nuclear weapons.[8]

The use of tactical nuclear weapons for defence — in accordance with NATO's military philosophy in which all options are kept open — is incredible, if rational behaviour takes place. In Europe no defence is possible in nuclear warfare: if we take defence in the sense of 'preserve, protect, keep safe by resisting attack'. As long ago as 1960 Basil Liddell Hart, asked whether Europe or the United States could be defended, said: 'The answer, if we are honest and brave enough to face hard facts, can only be that, in the present conditions, effective defence is not possible.'[9] We may, therefore, conclude that the threat to use tactical nuclear weapons has become incredible. Their primary function is no longer to deter war but to deter the use of tactical nuclear weapons. Consequently, the moment has come to have an agreement outlawing the use of nuclear weapons except as a reprisal against the use of nuclear weapons; and if such an agreement is not feasible it is desirable that states should declare unilaterally that they will never be the first to use those weapons. Such a unilateral declaration of no-first-use would enhance security in Europe, especially as deliberate attack by the Soviet bloc is highly improbable whereas local misconceptions and miscalculations may lead to inadvertent war, in which 'crisis management' would be the sole purpose of military power. In such a case the presence of nuclear weapons and the open option to use them would be an escalating factor.

If nuclear weapons have as their primary function to deter the use of nuclear weapons, the emphasis should be put on conventional weapons as a deterrent. The certainty that armed action will be met by armed action will deter armed aggression between the blocs. Who could be expected to unleash a war against a military alliance of almost half a billion people, armed, and prepared to resist any attack? Whatever might have happened beforehand, even nuclear disarmament or the outlawing of nuclear arms, every war would entail the possibility of escalating into a nuclear war. No gains, in case of victory by the aggressor, would outweigh the loss of life and the destruction any war would bring about. Only one reason might induce the adversary to launch an attack: the fear that the other party was considering one. In that case the first blow might give considerable advantage, albeit in damage limitation.

Consequently, the conventional force which has the function of deterring conventional attack by the prospect of defence *should clearly show that defence is its only function.* A state whose military philosophy restricts the function of military power to the neutralisation of the military power of the adversary should show this restricted function by the choice of its arms, by its weapon posture, by its logistics. If its purpose is only what might be called *defensive deterrence,* the force should be formidable if attacked, but utterly incapable of aggressive action outside its territory. Hence the term 'inoffensive deterrence', or 'territorial defence'. In this paper, however, the term 'defensive deterrence' is preferred in order clearly to indicate the only, and in the present world, indispensable function military power rationally can have.

The question is in what way the weapon posture could indicate the defensive function. Can the weapon posture show clearly an incapacity for attack? To what extent would this mean the adoption of 'a calculated inferiority' as suggested by General von Baudissin? What would it mean with respect to the preference for defensive weapons? On all these points further research is needed, in which military expertise is indispensable. The question would be not, as at present, 'What military power do I need to win if war breaks out?' but 'What military power do I need to prevent war breaking out?' It is here contended that what is needed for deterrence and defence is less than what is needed for victory.

The advantages of the grand strategy of defensive deterrence are many. First, there would be the elimination of fear on the other side, since attack would have become physically impossible. Secondly, if on both sides such a strategy should be applied, it would enhance the chances of arms control and disarmament. Both failed utterly hitherto, because the traditional *Siegdenken* induced both parties to strive for superiority and for enhancing their military position through arms control and disarmament. The strategy of defensive deterrence might, for the first time in history, open the road to arms diminution, to getting rid of the 'overkill' at present existing, to reversing the arms spiral and to real disarmament. But, as mentioned, further research is needed. The military philosophies of countries like Switzerland, Sweden, Yugoslavia, Finland and Romania should be analysed. The quality of a defensive armed force is not only determined by the damage and losses it will inflict upon an aggressor, though those costs should, as a matter of course, be higher than any foreseeable gains. Nevertheless defensive strength should be sufficient to offer a fair chance of repelling the intruder, since that is necessary for the morale of the defending armed forces. A third aspect of weapon posture should be the ability to contribute to 'crisis management' in case of local fighting as a consequence of internal unrest. In such a situation both blocs have as an undisputed priority of their international policy the avoidance of general war. On that basis a diplomatic solution of a conflict would be feasible, if the armed forces were able to keep matters under control, and especially, to prevent military escalation.

A strategy of defensive deterrence would have considerable political consequences, which might make the superpowers and also medium powers unwilling to adopt it. Some are listed here, although an elaborate treatment would be beyond the scope of this paper.

(1) The possibility of coercive diplomacy would be reduced, if not disappear.

(2) The possibility of intervention in foreign countries would likewise be reduced or disappear.

(3) The elimination of military action, or the threat of military action, against illegal non-violent action, as in the case of illegal expropriation of foreign possessions. This might have considerable influence on North-South relationships.

(4) National military action for humanitarian reasons would be made impossible. In case of genocide the United Nations might be able to act, but there is no certainty that it would be able to do so.

(5) There would be no possibility of a military reaction in case one of the Cold War adversaries took military action against a third party as in the Dominican Republic or Angola.

It is an open question whether the superpowers would be prepared to accept this reduction of their global roles. Probably they would not. Hitherto the strategy of defensive deterrence has been in fact the strategy of small powers. But the concept of defensive deterrence might be applied in specific theatres, for example in Europe. Since parity between the superpowers was achieved and confirmed in SALT I, Europe has had a special security problem — as recognised in the 1974 NATO communiqué. It seems feasible that this part of the world, more than any other threatened by mutual destruction, might become the first local region in which the concept of defensive deterrence could be realised. It would be in the interest of both superpowers, because both have vital interests in peace and security in this area. In general, it is one of the great advantages of this strategy that it can be realised locally, and unilaterally, even within a military alliance as, for example, with the Romanian Law on People's Defence of 1972.

The strategy of defensive deterrence presupposes a constructive foreign policy, aiming at friendly relations and co-operation. As we saw, one aspect of defensive deterrence consists in the fact that the costs, 'the entry-price' (as it is called in official Swiss statements about Swiss military philosophy), might be out of proportion to any foreseeable gains. But if the foreign policy of a state offends the vital interests of another party, it might become attractive to that party to pay the price of military action. Mention might be made here of Strauss's application of Beaufre's 'stratégie d'ensemble'.

A constructive foreign policy would entail:

(1) that, in general, account would be taken of the interests of foreign states;

(2) that a government would refrain from doing things which would touch upon vital interests of other states;

(3) that governments would be prepared to make reasonable sacrifices in favour of third parties, an aspect that might, for example, have considerable significance in relations between North and South;

(4) that government would stimulate co-operation in the economic and cultural fields;

(5) that governments would promote the strengthening of international functional organisations, and specifically of the United

Nations.

Conclusion

The thesis of this paper — with many reservations and many unclear aspects — is that the concept of defensive deterrence might be an alternative to the present disastrous situation and an alternative that may be tried out regionally in the first instance. If the thesis is valid, then the question arises what can be done to get this concept accepted by governments, by statesmen and by the military.

Hitherto peace research has had almost no influence at all, because it did not present an acceptable alternative. It has demonstrated the danger of the world situation. It has foretold the development of relations from bad to worse. It has illuminated the prevailing irrationality, even the stupidity and madness of decision-makers. It has discovered the predominance of partial rationality between the superpowers, which aim at 'security through strength' in their relationship, but neglect the disastrous results of their policy for the world at large. One of these disastrous consequences is the proliferation of nuclear weapons. If the leading nations propagate, by their statements and their actions, the view that nuclear arms are indispensable for their safety, proliferation cannot be stopped. The time is past when the world could be indoctrinated with the dictum: *Quod licet Jovi non licet bovi.* On the other hand, the doctrine of defensive deterrence would favour denuclearised zones; and the 'no-first-use principle' might, by procedural provisions, be strengthened with respect to states which adhere to the Non-Proliferation Treaty or belong to a denuclearised zone as evidenced by Protocol II of the Treaty of Tlatelolco.

Peace research, then, has given a diagnosis of the illness of the world, but has not offered a cure. General and complete disarmament was not a cure because the indispensability of military power is a consequence of the present world structure. Nor is the time yet ripe radically to change this structure into a kind of world unity. The difference in interests is still too great, as evidenced in the North-South relationship; the difference of values is still too predominant, as witness the East-West relationship; too much mistrust still prevails, and too little solidarity is apparent. The facts, influenced by technology, dictate that the world moves towards a structure of federal unity, but ethical evolution has apparently not been able to match technological developments. We live in a time of transition towards some kind of organised world unity. But it is a slow, perhaps too slow process.

Within that period of transition, we have to prevent a violent clash between the superpowers, and we have gradually to change existing relations.

In what direction should the development go? Concerning military power, it should go in the direction of a reduction of military functions. Hitherto most proposals have been aimed at diminishing armed forces without any change in their functions. This might have been one of the reasons for the failure to achieve results. Recognition of the inevitability of the reduction of military functions − due to the fact that the danger of actually using modern weapons has become too great − might be a new starting point. Reduction of the function of military power, that is reduction to the prevention of the use of armed force, might facilitate the elimination of present 'overkill', and might be a precondition for the achievement of substantial disarmament.

It is an advantage of the concept of defensive deterrence that it can be applied multilaterally, bilaterally and unilaterally. It can be applied locally within the overall relationship of the superpowers, for example in the European theatre, and it is even applicable within an alliance. Recognition of the strategy of defensive deterrence, moreover, might restore the image of the military, which in many countries, since the wars in Indochina and elsewhere, are regarded with suspicion and even contempt. But when an army is despised, it becomes dangerous, because it is powerful. As long as the world needs military forces it is desirable that the opinion of the 'honourable profession of arms' should prevail. That might again be the case if there were general recognition and acceptance that the only function of military power is the neutralisation of military power.

Perhaps the most important aspect of defensive deterrence − important with respect to the question whether it has a reasonable chance of being accepted − is the economic side of it. In the long run it would be cheaper. The costs of defensive weapons are small in comparison with the costs of offensive weapons. Armed forces dedicated to the sole purpose of providing security with respect to foreign military power might cost a fraction of the money spent at present. This economic aspect might be of decisive importance. Research about the dynamics of arms races shows that forces are at work which are stronger than the forces of reason: forces of fear, of greed, of small-group mentality, of ignorance and of indifference. We have to bring new concepts to a short-sighted and unwilling world. The general tendency, and even necessity, of cutting budgets has brought military spending into the limelight. In many countries the choice has to be made between military spending and spending for social provisions or development aid.[10] The tendency to economise in the military field is apparent. This may enhance the interest in the concept of defensive deterrence which claims to produce security for less costs. No amount of money is too much, of course, if it provides peace, security and independence. But the existing huge military spending does not contribute to peace. Weapons have become a source of anxiety and tension. Prevailing public opinion, however, does not share this view. But the reduction of military budgets might be expected to be based more on the longing for material well-being rather than on rational argument about the maintenance of peace and security. Why, one may ask, should we not try to achieve our rational aims partly on the basis of other, even irrational considerations?

Notes

1. William Epstein, 'A New Approach to Strategic Arms Limitaton and Reduction', above, pp.176-97.
2. Thomas C. Schelling, *Arms and Influence* (New Haven, Connecticut, 1966).
3. André Beaufré, *Dissuasion et Stratégie* (Paris, 1964) and *Stratégie de l'Action* (Paris, 1966).
4. Franz Joseph Strauss, *Herausforderung und Antwort* (Stuttgart, 1968).
5. For an extensive treatment of the Swiss defence philosophy see Alfred Ernst, *Die Konzeption der Schweizerischen Landesverteidigung, 1815-1966* (Frauenfeld and Stuttgart, 1971).
6. See B.V.A. Röling, 'International Law and the Maintenance of Peace', *Netherlands Yearbook of International Law, 1973*.
7. C.F. von Weizsäcker, *Kriegsfolgen und Kriegsverhütung* (Munich, 1971).
8. V.D. Sokolovsky, *Soviet Military Strategy,* edited with an analysis and commentary by Harriet Fast Scott (London, 1975), pp.291 et seq.
9. B.H. Liddell Hart, *Deterrent or Defence: A Fresh Look at the West's Military Position* (London and New York, 1960), p.47.
10. For a comparison see Ruth Leger Sivard, *World Military and Social Expenditure,* 1976 (Leesburg, Virginia, 1976).

19 116 WARS IN 30 YEARS

Istvàn Kende

The purpose of this paper is to analyse one type of social conflict — the sharpest of them: the armed conflicts *en masse,* namely the wars of the first thirty years after World War Two (1945-74). This is not the place to go into details about the definitions of war, nor to examine the philosophic and legal aspects of the extremely complex phenomenon called war. The approach is from the point of view of a contemporary historian and of a political scientist: the aim is to deal with the wars in question and also with important elements of national and international politics, and to consider the correlation of the relevant wars fought within the given period with other phenomena of international politics and with the changes in the structure of our world and of the balance of power.

I deal with 116 wars here, which are listed in the Appendix. My definition of war is one that is also acceptable to the Stockholm International Peace Research Institute:

> War is any armed conflict in which all the following criteria occur:
> (1) Activities of regular armed forces (military, police forces, and so on) at least on one side — that is, the presence and engagement of the armed forces of the government in power.
> (2) A certain degree of organization and organized fighting on both opposing sides, even if this organization extends to organized defence only.
> (3) A certain continuity between the armed clashes, however sporadic. Centrally organized guerilla forces are also regarded as making war, insofar as their activities extend over a considerable part of the country concerned.[1]

Thus the following are not considered to be wars: riots; border incidents or even a series of them; massacres where one side did not even organise its defence (for example, Indonesia, 1965); and international crises with serious military forces involved when virtually no shooting occurred (for example, the Cuban missile crisis of 1962 or Czechoslovakia, 1968).

On this definition 116 wars occurred in the thirty years between

1945 and 1974, on the territory of 69 countries, with the participation of the regular armed forces of 81 countries. Hence more countries were involved in these wars than in World War Two. The estimated total number of fatalities was around 25 million, which, although less than the casualties of World War Two, is still extremely high. During the thirty years no more than 26 days passed without any war — all in September 1945. The total duration of all the wars, that is the simple addition of the duration of each of the 116 wars, was some weeks less than 350 years. This means that on the average almost 12 (11.66) wars were being fought every day since the end of World War Two and that during the last thirty years wars were being fought — on average — in 11.66 different places every day. Nevertheless no declaration of war has been made since the end of World War Two and hence those experts who consider a declaration of war as the main criterion of war — and there are those who hold such theories — can sit back and relax, stating that no war has been waged during the last three decades.

However frightening or surprising these figures may be, they do not in themselves permit us to draw any general conclusion. To go further, it is necessary to subdivide wars by time, by space and by their differences of types. That is necessary if we are to indicate the trend in different periods, the propensity to go to war in different regions, and the causes and aims of war.

To that end some appropriate methods of quantification have been sought. Two different methods have been used. One is quite simple: merely to deal with the duration of every war, basing our calculations only on the time factor. That of course means a complete elimination of some very important differences of the kind or intensity of wars — for example, the extreme differences between a war like that in Vietnam and the guerrilla war in Zimbabwe/Rhodesia. Nevertheless the picture solely based on duration gives us a general mean for wars and this itself is extremely interesting. The other way is much more complicated. It relies to some extent on the approach of Pitirim A. Sorokin.[2] It is essentially a kind of quantification based on the intensity of each war. This calculation is based mostly on the number of fatalities and on the number of men in arms relative to the size of the population of a given country. But other parameters were also considered, such as the use of air forces or the extension of the theatre of war to the territory of more than one country. This kind of quantification is, obviously, completely arbitrary; its use is limited to making a certain comparison of the different wars and discovering such things as the general trend, the increase or decrease and the geographical location of degrees of intensity.

We found that both the curve of wars based on the simple time factor and the curve of intensity were more or less similar. That they did not strongly differ, in my view, showed that the calculation of the duration of wars gives a highly revealing picture of their development and the general trend. For this reason this factor is given primary attention, for it is easier to use and to follow.

A breakdown of our data gives on this basis the picture shown in Table 19.1 and Figure 19.1.

The general curve of wars shows a slow rise in the first twelve years, a rapid increase in the 1960s with a peak in 1967 followed by a sharp decrease.

The distribution of wars by regions proves that wars are mostly phenomena of the Third World, or rather of the extra-European and extra-North-American world (see also Figure 19.2). Europe, once the very epicentre of the most important and sophisticated wars, has become a relatively calm continent, at least from this point of view. Asia, on the other hand, has become the main centre of wars, with 34 wars, in which the region accounted for 41 per cent of all the time spent in wars during the thirty years under review. The broad tendency is, moreover, slightly upwards. The Near East, also with 34 wars, but with only 19 per cent of time spent in wars, shows a very erratic and

Table 19.1: Time Spent in Wars by 5-Year Periods and by Regions (in years)

Period	Total	Europe	Asia	North-East	Black Africa	Latin America
1945/9	32.40	6.74	21.48	0.95	0.88	2.35
1950/4	33.72	–	22.07	5.44	2.20	4.01
1955/9	48.77	0.04	20.51	17.38	6.06	4.76
1960/4	61.14	–	21.98	12.28	19.45	7.43
1965/9	99.18	0.24	26.69	21.81	33.77	16.66
1970/4	74.46	5.00	29.51	8.71	27.12	4.12
1945-74	349.67	12.02	142.24	66.57	89.48	39.33

Note: Near East comprises all the Arab countries plus Cyprus, Iran and Israel. Thus Asia and Black Africa do not include these countries, only the rest of the continents.

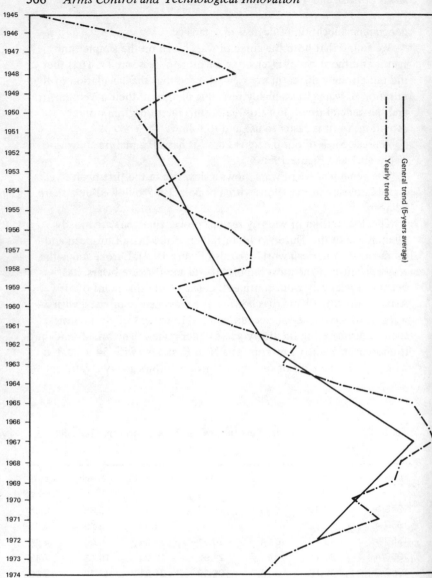

Figure 19.1: Trend of Wars (time spent yearly in wars)

changing curve. Black Africa had 'only' 20 wars but accounts for more than a quarter (26 per cent) of all the time spent in wars; this curve reveals a constant and rapidly increasing tendency until the last five-year period. Compared with Black Africa, Latin America had more wars — 23 — but a much lower percentage (11 per cent) of the time spent in wars. It also had a growing curve until the late 1960s followed by a much sharper decrease at the end of the period. Europe, with five wars, accounts for only 3 per cent of all time spent in war.

We must now consider more deeply the characteristics of these wars in order to see the interdependence of the general international political development and the evolution of armed conflicts. The vast literature about the problem of war contains quite a number of different classifications and typologies. There are classifications based on the extent of the wars, on the type of arms used, on the main features of forces involved, and so on. This is not, however, the place to discuss these typologies or even to enumerate them. Instead, a particular classification is offered for consideration. First, we may speak of 'anti-régime' wars in which the aim of one of the parties is to overthrow the given power in a country. In a more detailed version of this study a distinction was made between those wars where the government in power was a progressive one and where it was a colonial or reactionary one. But here we do not go into such details for reasons of space. Hereinafter we label wars of an 'anti-régime' type as *A*.

Second, there are internal wars, which while similar to the previous ones, are not motivated by the desire to overthrow a government or to change a régime, but by the demand for separation or some kind of autonomy for one part of the territory or of the population. These are wars of tribes, of religious groups, of national minorities, of certain regions within a country, such as the Biafra conflict. We label these wars as *B*.

Finally, a third type of war comprises those in which two (or more) countries on either side of one (or more) border(s) are involved against each other. That is the classic type of border war such as the Indo-Pakistani wars, or the Arab-Israeli conflicts. These we label as *C*.

In addition we must recognise that in many wars, third-party forces become militarily involved. Defining military involvement as active participation in military operations (that is, we did not consider arms transfers, or the presence of advisers, or military aid as foreign participation), we found that there were examples of wars of all the three main types (*A, B* and *C*) in which foreign troops participated and in which they did not. We indicated those wars where foreign forces

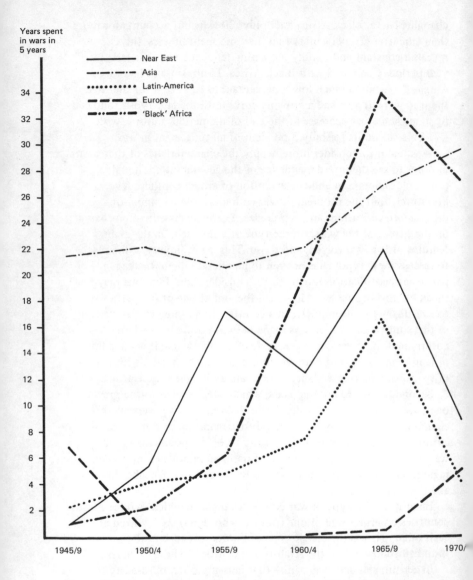

Figure 19.2: Trend of Wars by Regions (time spent in wars, in 5-year-periods)

were involved with the sign /1, while those without foreign participants were labelled with /2. Thus we have A/1 and A/2, B/1 and B/2, and C/1 and C/2 wars as the main types.

What does analysis based on this classification show? Only a few conclusions may be outlined here. But emphasis must first be placed on the fact that the type C (border wars) represents only a very tiny part of all the wars: 18 wars with only 3 per cent of all the time involved in war. Of course this kind of war was considered once − and with good reason − as the main, the classic type of war. Now this has become in our times the least frequent type of war. The main type in our days is type A, namely wars in which the force in power defends itself against a force trying to overthrow it. They are mainly wars where revolutionary or anti-colonial forces fighting to obtain or maintain independence are opposing anti-revolutionary and/or colonial/neo-colonial forces. Wars of type A are in an overwhelming majority: 70 wars with 81 per cent of all the time spent in war. The wars of type B, namely tribal, national, religious conflicts, are also more frequent than the classical C wars, but much less frequent than the 'anti-régime' wars: 28 wars of type B account for 16 per cent of all the time spent in wars since 1945.

Enquiry into foreign participation reveals another aspect. Those wars in which foreign military forces were involved form the majority: 69 wars, consuming 69 per cent of time. Incidentally, we have also calculated that this kind of war is by far the most intensive: 82 per cent of the whole 'volume' of intensity of all the 116 wars involve foreign participation. Especially grave is the participation in wars of type A: in 53 wars out of the 70 of type A there was foreign participation, while out of the 28 wars of type B only 11, and out of the 18 wars of type C only 5 were wars with foreign participation. But considering the time spent in these wars we find that 80 per cent of all the time spent in A ('anti-régime') wars involved foreign presence, while only 19 per cent of the duration of all wars of type B and half the time of wars of type C were fought with (or against) foreign troops (see Table 19.2).

The tendency is clear: foreign participation is mainly required or inflicted where the future of the government is at stake: in A wars. But foreign interventionist forces are not involved in most of the wars where minor local interests seem to be at stake. Nevertheless, even then hidden foreign interests quite often have their role, too.

As to border wars, the curve of foreign participation shows a curious trend: until 1959 all the wars of type C have been fought with

Table 19.2: Repartition of Wars by Types

Type	Number of Wars		Time spent in wars, percentage	Time spent in wars of a given category
A	70		81	100
/1		53		80
/2		17		20
B	28		16	100
/1		11		19
/2		17		81
C	18		3	100
/1		5		50
/2		13		50
Total	116	116	100	
Total				
/1	69		69	
/2	47		31	
	116		100	

foreign participation while since 1962 none of them have been.

The foreign participants do not cover a very broad spectrum. Although there were numerous cases of participation of the armies of Third World countries as foreign troops — for very different reasons and with very different aims — and some cases of participation also by troops of the socialist countries, there is no doubt that there were four major powers which can be described as the main interventionists: the United States, Great Britain, France and Portugal. Of these the United States has the leading role: it spent 94 years in 27 wars, that is 27 per cent of all the 350 years spent in wars. Great Britain follows with 20 wars over 65 years. France had 12 wars over 39 years, while Portugal had 5 wars over 35 years. But there is an important distinction to be made. While the United States spent 62 per cent of all the time spent by it in wars in the last ten years, Great Britain spent in this same period only 30 per cent and France only 11 per cent of their time of involvement (see Figure 19.3). Thus, while the interventionist activities of Great Britain and France decreased, the United States became the foremost active foreign participant (see Table 19.3). The participation of these powers also varies greatly with respect to the

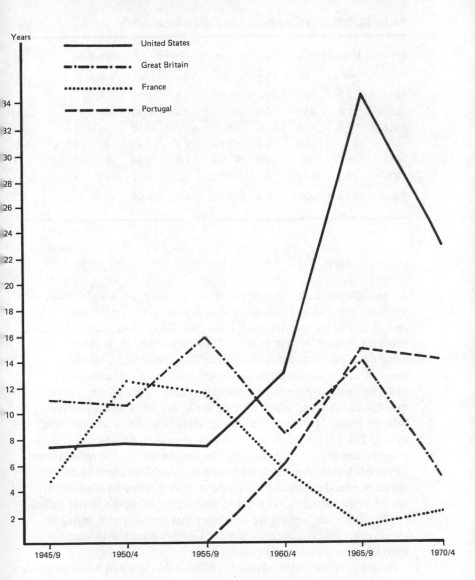

Figure 19.3: Time Spent in Wars by Main Interventionists (in 5-year periods)

Table 19.3: The Trend of Interventions (by periods)

Period	United States		Great Britain		France		Portugal	
	Years	%	Years	%	Years	%	Years	%
1945/9	7.5	8.02	11.1	17.01	4.8	12.23	–	–
1950/4	7.8	8.25	10.6	16.21	12.6	32.33	–	–
1955/9	7.5	7.96	15.9	24.35	11.7	30.10	–	–
1960/4	13.1	13.98	8.4	12.85	5.7	14.73	6.1	17.38
1965/9	34.7	36.91	14.1	21.57	1.3	3.44	15.0	42.52
1970/4	23.4	24.87	5.2	8.01	2.8	7.17	14.2	40.11
Total	94.0	100.00	65.3	100.00	38.9	100.00	35.3	100.00

various regions.

As demonstrated, the wars of our epoch are mostly fought between different social forces within one country, that is 'internal' wars, but mostly having an 'international' character due to the presence of forces foreign to the country or theatre of war. And as in the majority of cases the régime which is to be overthrown is one with colonial, neo-colonial or some other oppressive characteristics (backed very often by the above-mentioned interventionist forces), we may state that the main forces which directly shape the war trend are on one side the forces fighting for their national independence and freedom – mostly Third World countries – and on the other side the main interventionist powers, principally the United States. The international forces of the socialist countries have been much less involved in the concrete armed conflicts since World War Two. They have seldom been foreign participants (as with China in Korea, or the Soviet Union in Hungary, both backing legal governments against forces trying to overthrow a socialist régime). More often they have been victims of aggression (as with Vietnam and Cuba).

Space does not permit us here to consider the details of the strategies and aims of such different national forces as those fighting for their own independence and liberation. Nevertheless, their judged armed mass violence to be the only way of obtaining their common characteristic is that in the cases in question they judged armed mass violence to be the only way of obtaining their national aims and of overthrowing a régime in power. But we may conclude from our research that on the whole the role of American strategy seems to be the most general and most important factor in the formation of the general war curve, and obviously of the curve of American interventions.

In this connection it is interesting to note that in the first phases of our period — during the Cold War — we see a moderation in the curve of both wars in general and of American interventions in particular. That was the era when the Americans concentrated much more on Strategic Offensive Forces and were much more preoccupied by so-called massive retaliation. They counted on a general conflict, and all-out war, and hence did not concentrate on local encounters. Hence the period of Cold War was not a period of local wars. As Maxwell Taylor said, arguing against the strategy of John Foster Dulles, this strategy 'could offer. . .only two choices, the initiation of general nuclear war or compromise and retreat'.[3]

As is well known, the criticisms of the Dulles strategy — such as those made by Taylor, by Henry Kissinger, and by R.E. Osgood — led to the adoption of the strategy of flexible response, one element of which was the necessity to build up American military forces able to initiate or fight local wars all over the globe. President John F. Kennedy, who agreed to this approach, said in his special message to the Congress on 25 May 1961:

> I am directing the Secretary of Defense to extend rapidly and substantially, in cooperation with our Allies, the orientation of existing forces for the conduct of non-nuclear war, para-military operations and sub-limited or unconventional wars. . .Our special forces and unconventional warfare units will be increased and reorientated. . .New emphasis must be placed on the special skills and languages which are required to work with local populations.[4]

As a consequence of this new strategic doctrine the character of the American military budget was the subject of important changes and the proportion of expenditure for developing the General Purposes Forces drew closer to the cost of the Strategic Offensive Forces. But this change also shows up on our war-curves. As has already been shown, the increase in wars was especially strong in the 1960s, in the years of flexible response and of the strategy of local wars, in the years of the presidencies of Kennedy and Lyndon B. Johnson (see Figure 19.4). But we may also note from the figure that while the early Nixon years show a strong decrease in the time spent in different wars, the period begins with an increase in intensity. And a fact that is no less important is that more or less the same trend can be seen on the general war

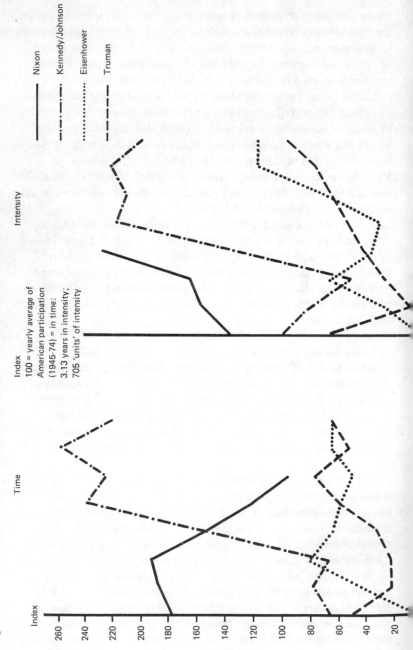

Figure 19.4: Trend of Military Involvement of the United States in Presidential Terms

Intensity

Index
100 = yearly average of
American participation
(1945-74) = in time:
3.13 years in intensity;
705 'units' of intensity

Nixon

Kennedy/Johnson

Eisenhower

Truman

Time

curve, proving that the American participation is a factor of primary importance in the evolution of wars throughout the world.

The last years – both in the evolution of the general trend and of American interventions – were years of decrease. The new balance of power which led the progressive forces to the conclusion that a new world war not only must but also can be avoided, led also to the falling back of both the war curves and intervention curves. The period of decrease in wars corresponds to the period of the beginning of *détente*. It does not follow, however, that *détente* itself was the reason. Rather it is our contention that the same reasons which caused the beginning of *détente,* which obliged some forces to accept a policy which they denied and rejected before, led to this development, as also to the victory of the revolutionary forces of Vietnam, Laos, Cambodia, Mozambique, Guinea-Bissau and, finally, Angola. Hence the decrease in war is strictly related to the emergence of new relationships of forces in the theatre of world politics. The same reasons which caused the leading Western forces to more or less accept the policy of *détente* and of peaceful coexistence led to their withdrawal from Indochina and from former Portuguese Africa.

Finally, attention must be drawn to another correlation. Figure 19.5 shows the curve of wars in duration and in intensity and the trend of military expenditure and of the arms trade in Asia, Africa and Latin America. It is clear that for most of our period the duration and intensity of wars and of military expenditure run in parallel with the war curves and with the arms trade in these parts of the world. Nevertheless – and this is an extremely important new factor – since the late 1960s this parallelism ceases. While the curve of wars falls, military expenditure does not stop growing and the arms trade curve continues its increase.

For reasons of space we did not even touch here on such important items as conflict resolution, mediation, questions of victory and defeat and the role of the United Nations and other international bodies. Nor do we seek either to draw far-reaching conclusions as to the future. We do not presume that the decrease of wars suggests something like a complete future absence of wars. While contending that there is a strict relationship between the reasons for *détente* and reasons for the decrease in wars, we have no illusions and we know that there are still many obstacles to be overcome. But is does seem that at least in the near future the main types of wars are not likely to be so-called border wars; and that for the time being there is less probability of open military interventions by foreign powers in the internal affairs and in

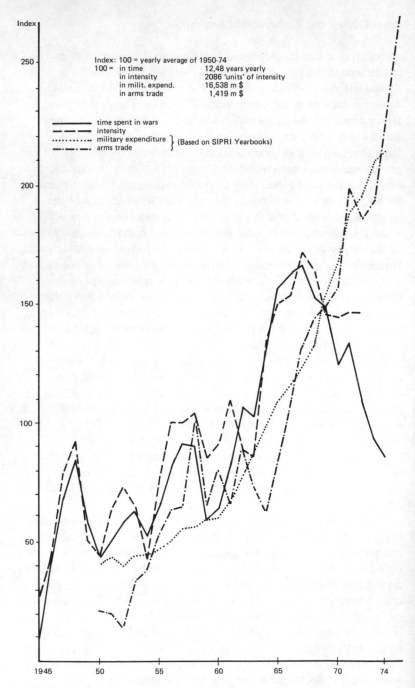

Index: 100 = yearly average of 1950-74
100 =   in time   12,48 years yearly
        in intensity   2086 'units' of intensity
        in milit. expend.   16,538 m $
        in arms trade   1,419 m $

——— time spent in wars
––– intensity
······· military expenditure ⎫ (Based on SIPRI Yearbooks)
–·–·– arms trade   ⎭

Figure 19.5: Correlations of Time Spent in Wars, Intensity of Wars, Military
Expenditure and Arms Trade

the internal struggles of other countries. The process by which several countries became independent states is near to its end; there are almost no more legally non-independent territories in the globe. Because of that new struggles for independence like those by which newly emerging nation-states came into being, as in Vietnam or Algeria, are hardly to be expected. The internal struggles against existing authorities may well have another character: they may have a greater social content and have a reduced national emphasis. Nevertheless it is not intended to offer here any clear-cut predictions. The primary aim has been to analyse the near past, dealing with only one sector of human political activities, armed mass struggles. At the same time attention has been drawn to something that Europeans are sometimes inclined to forget, namely that even in our own epoch millions have been and are subject to suffering and death because of the phenomenon called war.

Appendix: List of 116 Wars

1.	Greece	1944-5
2.	Algeria	1945
3.	Indonesia	1945-9
4.	Spain	1945-8
5.	Indochina	1946-54
6.	Greece	1946-9
7.	India (religious war)	1946-7
8.	Philippines	1946-54
9.	China	1946-9
10.	Iran	1946
11.	Paraguay	1947
12.	Madagascar	1947-8
13	India (Hyderabad, Telangana)	1947-9
14.	India-Pakistan (Kashmir)	1947-9
15.	Yemen	1948
16.	Costa Rica	1948
17.	Burma	1948
18.	Colombia	1948-53
19.	Israel-Arab countries	1948-9
20.	Malaya	1948-59
21.	Bolivia	1949
22.	Korea	1950-3
23.	Puerto Rico	1950
24.	Egypt	1951-2
25.	Tunisia	1952-4
26.	Bolivia	1952
27.	Kenya	1952-6
28.	Morocco	1952-6
29.	Guatemala	1954
30.	Colombia	1954-7
31.	Algeria	1954-62
32.	China (islands)	1955
33.	Costa Rica — Nicaragua	1955
34.	Cyprus	1955-9
35.	Cameroon	1955-63
36.	South Vietnam	1955-75
37.	Oman	1955-63

38.	India (Nagas)	1956-64
39.	Israel	1956
40.	Hungary	1956
41.	Cuba	1956-9
42.	Aden, Yemen	1956-8
43.	Indonesia	1957-8
44.	Honduras − Nicaragua	1957
45.	Spanish Morocco	1957-8
46.	Lebanon	1958
47.	Jordan	1958
48.	China (Quemoy, Matsu)	1958
49.	Nyasaland	1959
50.	China (Tibet)	1959
51.	Laos	1959-62
52.	Dominican Republic	1959
53.	Paraguay	1959-60
54.	Congo (Zaire)	1960-4
55.	Angola	1961-74
56.	Nepal	1961-2
57.	Cuba	1961
58.	Tunisia	1961
59.	Ethiopia (Eritrea)	1961...
60.	Iraq (Kurds)	1961-4
61.	Venezuela	1961-70
62.	India (Goa)	1961
63.	Indonesia (West Irian)	1962
64.	Guatemala	1962-72
65.	Colombia	1962
66.	Yemen	1962-70
67.	India − China	1962
68.	Brunei (North Borneo)	1962
69.	Guinea (Bissau)	1963-74
70.	Malaysia (North Borneo)	1963-6
71.	Algeria − Morocco	1963
72.	South Yemen	1963-7
73.	Dominican Republic	1963
74.	Somalia − Ethiopia	1963-4
75.	Congo (Zaire)	1963-9
76.	Cyprus	1963-4
77.	Rwanda	1963-4
78.	Kenya − Somalia	1963-7

79.	Laos	1964-73
80.	Colombia	1964-72
81.	North Vietnam	1964-8
82.	Mozambique	1964-74
83.	Iraq (Kurds)	1965-70
84.	India-Pakistan	1965
85.	Dominican Republic	1965
86.	Peru	1965
87.	Oman (Dhofar)	1965...
88.	Sudan (South)	1965-72
89.	India – Pakistan	1965
90.	Thailand	1965...
91.	India (Mizos)	1966-7
92.	Bolivia	1967
93.	Israel – Arab countries	1967
94.	Congo (Zaire)	1967
95.	Nigeria (Biafra)	1967-70
96.	Zimbabwe (Rhodesia)	1967...
97.	South Yemen	1968
98.	Chad	1968-72
99.	El Salvador – Honduras	1969
100.	South Yemen – Saudi Arabia	1969
101.	Great Britain (Northern Ireland)	1969...
102.	Cambodia	1970...(1975)
103.	Sudan	1970
104.	Philippines	1970...
105.	Jordan	1970
106.	Guinea	1970
107.	Pakistan (Bangladesh)	1971
108.	Sri Lanka (Ceylon)	1971
109.	Jordan	1971
110.	North Vietnam	1972-3
111.	Burundi	1972
112.	Uganda – Tanzania	1972
113.	Yemen – South Yemen	1972
114.	Israel – Arab countries	1973
115.	Iraq (Kurds)	1974...
116.	Cyprus	1974

Notes

1. Stockholm International Peace Research Institute (SIPRI), *World Armaments and Disarmament: SIPRI Yearbook, 1975* (Stockholm, 1975), p.6; and *World Armaments and Disarmament: SIPRI Yearbook, 1976* (Stockholm, 1976), p.48.
2. Pitirim A. Sorokin, *Social and Cultural Dynamics: Vol.III. Fluctuations of Social Relationships, War and Revolution* (New York, 1937).
3. Maxwell Taylor, *The Uncertain Trumpet* (New York, 1959), p.5.
4. *Public Papers of the President: J.F. Kennedy, 1961* (Washington, D.C., 1962), p.24.

20 THE ROLE OF ARMS IN CAPITALIST ECONOMIES: THE PROCESS OF OVERDEVELOPMENT AND UNDERDEVELOPMENT

Mary Kaldor

Introduction

There is a debate among students of arms control and disarmament about whether the arms race is caused by the instability of international relations, by the need to use force to settle conflicts, or whether it is caused by pressure from the military and the arms manufacturers or by the need to produce arms to maintain full employment and steady technical progress. Proposals of the first line of thought would include the more orthodox scholars, generally preoccupied with problems of strategy and military balances, as well as the followers of Lewis Richardson, the original peace researcher, who developed the 'action-reaction' model of the arms race. Proponents of the second line of thought are generally known as military-industrial-complex (MIC) or arms economy theorists.

Yet, it can be argued that the debate is a false one. It may be the case that every society has some requirement for organised force to meet external threats or to cope with domestic unrest, but every society has different answers to the question, 'How much is enough?' Every society must make decisions about how to allocate resources to meet military requirements and these decisions reflect available technology and dominant forms of social organisation. What is efficient for an Amazon tribe is clearly not efficient for the United States af America, and the people who decide what is efficient for the United States, among them the military and the arms manufacturers, have quite a different conception of efficiency from critics of military spending, perhaps those involved in underfinanced social services, for instance. In other words, the debate about the causes of the arms race is a confusion between 'Why' and 'How'. The 'Why' may originate in strategic perceptions but the 'How' necessarily has to do with the military-industrial complex and the economy.

This chapter is about the 'How' of armament decisions. The first part deals with industrialised countries, particularly the United States and Great Britain. The second part deals with the Third World, the impact of arms on development, and the role of arms in the relations between rich and poor countries, in imperialism. As a preliminary to both parts, some general remarks about the social nature of armaments and the identifying characteristics of capitalism are in order.

The specific allocation and organisation of resources for military purposes in any given society could be defined as the form of force. This comprises two elements. The first element, the relations of force — sometimes known as force structure — comprises such things as the organisation and hierarchy of the armed forces, or the methods of recruitment, for example. This tends to reproduce the dominant relationships within society as a whole; it could be described as a microcosm or epitome of society. Hence the feudal army was based on feudal levies in which serfs owed military service to their lords in much the same way as they owed agricultural service. The army was organised around a hierarchy of knights, each with their complement of serfs. The slave army was the retinue army and the liberal capitalist army was the so-called professional army in which soldiering was part of the overall division of labour and volunteer soldiers were paid for their work, like any other form of labour. The central contradiction of liberal capitalism, the need for an increasingly powerful state, was epitomised in the adoption of conscription in World War One.

The second element in the form of force, with which this chapter is properly concerned, is the technique of force, that is arms. This reflects both the available technology and the relations of force, since there may be some techniques which are inappropriate for a particular military organisation. Hence, it took the introduction of mercenaries, associated with the rise of the absolute monarchy, before gunpowder, the product of urban craftsmen, could be introduced into the feudal army.[1]

The form of force is thus the product of a particular society, but it can also influence society. Historically, this occurs through war between different types of armed forces. For example, the victory of Cromwell's New Model Army in the English Revolution represented a victory for a new form of social organisation, reflecting the rise of a new class. Today, it also occurs through the import of arms and appropriate force structure, through the adoption of a foreign form of force that is alien to local society. The implications of exporting modern industrial armies to the Third World are a major theme of this chapter.

The Western form of force is the product of capitalism, a system of competitive private ownership of the means of production, that is 'free enterprise', which involves numerous and disparate economic decision-makers. The system has given rise to a very rapid accumulation of wealth which, because of the anarchy of private neterprise, has been an uneven process. It has proceeded through the rise and fall of particular technologies, reflecting the rise and fall of institutions and even societies, such as corporations, social classes, industrial sectors, regions, communities and nations. Thus the age of shipbuilding, railways and heavy industry, which was also the British era, was replaced by the modern automobile and consumer durable age, the American era. Perhaps the age of electronics, telecommunications and chemicals will be the German and Japanese era. These features of capitalism, the decentralisation of decision-making, the rapid but anarchic expansion and the rapid but uneven technical progress are also central features of the armament process, as we shall try to show.

Western Industrialised Nations

The dominant form of force in the capitalist world, in the sense that it characterises most armed forces in capitalist countries, originates in the United States. An important starting-point, therefore, is the 'How' of the armament process in the United States. How does American society allocate resources to defence and how does this affect the economy? The present writer supports the thesis that the armament process must be understood in terms of a decline in the American economy and that the relatively high level of military spending (both in historical terms and in relation to other Western advanced industrial nations) reflects and reinforces this decline. A parallel can be drawn with Great Britain before 1914. A corollary to this argument is that the form of force could be regarded as, in some sense, decadent, the techniques and associated relations reflecting a decaying industrial structure, which is being overtaken by more 'advanced' technologies and more dynamic economies. This thesis rests on three propositions, which might be better termed as hypotheses, since only perhaps the second can claim substantiation.

The first proposition is that a secular peacetime increase in the procurement of arms, both absolutely and in relation to national income, marks the beginning of a period of economic decline. This occurred in the United States after World War Two and Great Britain in the 1880s. It was based on the decline of the dominant industries in those countries; that is to say, the industries which accounted for the largest share of manufacturing output and exports began to grow more slowly and their share in total world output began to fall. This decline was associated with the challenge of new industries (both technically and economically, as for example the challenge to railways and passenger ships from automobiles and aircraft or the modern challenge from telecommunications), the rise of industrial competitors (the challenge to Britain from the United States and Germany and to the United States from Germany to Japan), the increase in foreign investment (as funds for investment went in search of new markets and more profitable regions of production) and a deteriorating balance of trade. It was also associated with a more aggressive foreign policy — the British 'scramble for colonies' and the post-war American alliance system — and it might be argued that the association was more than coincidental as these nations struggled to preserve a dominant economic position through political and military means, or even less consciously, perceived their economic decline in political terms and reaffirmed their past dynamism in the same terms.

The most important military techniques (in terms of the quantity of resources absorbed by them) are generally based on the dominant industries; hence, the fighter bomber and the tank are the techniques of the American era, while the battleship and heavy artillery were the techniques of the British era. As the dominant industries begin to decline, certain companies face severe economic difficulties; one way of saving them is through the increased procurement of arms. Indeed, both in the 1880s and the 1940s, it was explicitly argued that British shipyards and later American aerospace companies threatened with bankruptcy should be preserved through the extension of military orders in order that their productive capacity should be available for mobilisation in time of war. It may also have been the case that the military importance of these companies increased with the advent of a more militaristic foreign policy. But the timing of the orders and previous discussion in government and company reports on the subject suggest that it was a response to industrial problems rather than any external political event which caused the initial increase in arms procurement.[2] In the American case, for example, new orders for the air force were placed *before* the formation of NATO in 1949 and before the outbreak of the Korean War.

The second proposition is that the procurement of arms gathers a momentum of its own, stemming from the momentum of the arms industry. In the traditional arms industries, technical 'progress' takes the form of product improvement, additions to the product to improve technical performance, rather than process improvement, more efficient methods of production. This results in new generations of weapons which are successively more expensive and elaborate rather than cheaper and more simple. The form of technical 'progress' is the consequence of the structure of the market which is oligopolistic, that is has only a few producers, and monopsonistic, that is dominated by one customer — the government. Because the market is monopsonistic, there is very little opportunity of reaching new customers and achieving a quantitative increase in the market which would make the development of cheap and simple arms worthwhile. By the same token, because of the oligopolistic nature of the market, any attempt to undercut rivals through the development of cheap and simple products would simultaenously undercut markets for the existing products of a company. An additional factor is the special character of the government as consumer; the fact that it is not subject to the same budgetary constraints as a civilian consumer. Indeed, there is evidence to suggest that the system of contracting whereby profits are awarded as a fixed percentage of costs has caused arms companies to be cost-maximisers rather than cost-minimisers.[3]

As the products of arms manufacturers become more expensive and elaborate, the capacity to manufacture arms becomes more specialised and more complex. As it becomes more specialised, arms manufacturers become more dependent on military orders from the government and foreign governments. As capacity becomes more complex, it expands and more orders are required to maintain employment and profits. The consequence is that military orders or arms exports must rise. Thus, in the early 1900s, Charles Beard, the American historian, wrote of the British arms manufacturers:

> after the buildings has begun and plants had been extended to meet additional requirements, gentlemen of this order [the arms manufacturers] thought the navy should be still bigger. Otherwise their enlarged establishments would be partly idle and, as they pitifully urged, their working men would be unemployed.[4]

The alternative is the rationalisation of capacity through mergers and take-overs in the arms industry or through international collaboration with foreign arms companies. This course is only adopted unwillingly where budgetary constraints are severe; it has implications for the relations of force as well as wider foreign policy which are not always easy to accept (discussion of these implications, however, would be too large a digression in the subject matter of this chapter). In practice, even those nations that have pursued rationalisation policies have found it necessary to increase procurement budgets, if not total defence budgets.

The third and last proposition concerns the consequences of an increase in the procurement of arms and/or the level of military spending. The argument is that such an increase actually accelerates the process of economic decline. This is because resources are diverted into declining industries and away from dynamic industries, into military purposes and away from productive civilian purposes. First there is a clear inverse correlation between the share of GNP devoted to military spending and the share of GNP spent on capital investment (see Table 20.1). This relationship has been shown to hold both for a cross-country NATO comparison and in the historical British context.[5] Second, a similar but less clear inverse relationship can be shown for military and civilian research and development (R and D). Those countries which devote a relatively high share of gross national product (GNP) to military R and D devote a relatively low share of GNP to civil R and D and vice versa. Also, in those countries where government spending on military R and D is low, spending by business enterprises, presumably on directly productive civil R and D is high (see Table 20.2). Moreover, military R and D, like military spending, is concentrated in certain sectors. Great Britain and the United States spend a relatively high proportion of total R and D on aerospace, while Federal Germany and Japan spend a relatively high proportion of total R and D on the chemical industry. All four countries devote a good deal of R and D resources to electronics, but in Great Britain and the United States resources are largely spent by the government for military purposes, while in Federal Germany and Japan they are largely spent by business enterprises for civilian purposes.[6]

The significance of the sectoral concentration of military resources lies in the fact that the declining sectors in which military resources are concentrated seem to be subject to diminishing returns in technical progress. That is to say, a dollar invested in a declining industry yields a smaller technical advance than a dollar invested in a more rapidly growing industry. Janstch has observed that any technology over its life-span proceeds along a sigmoidal curve; increasing performance for costs in its early growth phase and falling returns during its maturation.[7] This presumably applies as much to the technology of a whole industry as to a particular product. Certainly, there is evidence to suggest that the phase of diminishing returns has been reached by the dominant military technologies. A study undertaken by the Rand Corporation showed that, on the basis of certain subjective criteria for technical advance, the size of cost overruns was directly related to the

Table 20.1: Military Expenditure and Gross Fixed Capital Formation as a Percentage of Gross Domestic Product

		United States	Great Britain	France	Federal Germany	Netherlands	Sweden	Japan
1963	Military Burden	8.8	6.2	5.6	5.2	4.4	4.2	1.0
	Rate of Investment	16.8	15.2	20.0	25.7	22.1	22.0	27.9
1973	Military Burden	6.0	5.0	3.8	3.4	3.4	3.4	0.8
	Rate of Investment	18.0	18.0	25.0	25.5	24.0	22.0	37.0

Source: Stockholm International Peace Research Institute, *SIPRI Yearbook 1976: World Armaments and Disarmament* (Stockholm, 1976); Organization for Economic Cooperation and Development, *National Accounts of OECD Countries 1974,* vol.1, (Paris, 1976).

Table 20.2: Patterns of Resources Devoted to Research and Experimental Development in the OECD Area, 1963-71

	United States	Great Britain	France	Federal Germany	Sweden	Netherlands	Japan
Government	1.4	1.2	1.1	0.9	0.6	0.8	0.5
Defence, Space, Nuclear	(1.1)	(0.6)	(0.7)	(0.3)	(0.3)	(0.1)	(0.1)
Other	(0.3)	(0.6)	(0.5)	(0.6)	(0.3)	(0.7)	(0.4)
Business Enterprise	1.0	0.9	0.6	1.1	0.9	1.1	1.2
Other	0.1	0.1	—	0.1	0.1	—	—
Total	2.5	2.3	1.8	2.1	1.6	2.0	1.6

These figures are R and D as a percentage of GNP

Source: Organization for Economic Cooperation and Development, Paris.

degree of technical advance sought.[8]

It is evidently the case that resources devoted to military purposes are, *a priori,* likely to make less contribution to civilian technical progress than resources devoted to civilian purposes directly and also that resources devoted to declining industries are likely to yield less technical progress, however measured, than resources devoted to dynamic industries. But it could still be argued that because some military resources are devoted to dynamic industries and because the government can afford to take greater risks and to spend in larger quantities than individual business enterprises, new discoveries might be made in the military sector which could compensate for any loss of resources in the civilian sector — this is a sort of sophisticated version of the 'spin-off' argument. It is true that such discoveries are made — a favourite example is the development of integrated circuits in the United States. It is also true that because such discoveries are made by the military, there is little incentive and even perhaps disincentive to apply the discovery to civilian purposes. Thus it was the Japanese who developed standardised integrated circuits; American electronics companies tended to be preoccupied with custom-built devices for the military.[9] Similarly in Great Britain in the early 1900s, where automobiles were developed by several arms manufacturers, a plan by Armstrong to mass-produce 6,000 cars a year was rejected by the directors on the grounds that the 'profit on 6,000 cars was inferior to that on a single river gunboat'.[10]

Taken together, the three propositions — that an increase in the procurement of arms is a response to economic decline, that the procurement of arms attains an independent momentum, and that an increase in the procurement of arms accelerates economic decline — amount to a feedback mechanism in which the armament process becomes part of a more general process of economic decline. This is not to suggest that arms are the only factor accounting for this decline. On the contrary, we have suggested that the decline of the dominant industries tends to precede a secular peacetime increase in the procurement of arms and is attributable to more general mechanisms at work in a capitalist economy accounting for the rise and fall of technologies and industrial sectors. The armament process plays a critical role in reinforcing such mechanisms, as also do other processes in other spheres.

The industrial logic which necessitates the procurement of arms which might be considered superfluous in other situations also imposes a certain logic in the relations of force. Associated with the first great peacetime increase in military spending — the Anglo-German naval arms race before 1914 — was the rise of the weapons system concept which apparently imposed a rather rigid division of labour on the armed forces. The weapons system combines the weapon (for example, gun, missile or torpedo) the weapon platform (for example, ship, aircraft or tank) and the means of command and communication. Formerly the weapon was the instrument of the soldier. Today, the soldier appears to be the instrument of the weapon system. The organisation of men needed to operate a weapon system is somewhat similar to the organisation of batch production, in which each man has his allotted task, under the supervision of an officer, and none can act without the co-operation of others. A modern combat aircraft, for example, requires 50 men to keep it in operation. Furthermore, the weapons systems are themselves ranked and subdivided into a hierarchical military organisation. At the apex of the US Navy is the aircraft carrier, justifying aircraft to fly from its decks, destroyers, frigates and submarines to defend it, and supply ships to replenish it. The bomber and the battle tank have similar functions in the air force and army.

The weapons-system-based force structure directly reflects industrial structure. The weapon system is the link between a particular defence company and a particular organisational unit of the armed forces. The manufacturing capabilities of the company are at one and the same time the performance characteristics of the weapon system and the specifications needed to meet the strategic requirements of a particular military unit. Any rationalisation of the industrial structure, such as occurred in Britain in the late 1950s and early 1960s, imposes organisational and doctrinal changes on the armed forces. Naturally, such changes tend to be resisted both in military and industrial circles.

The very fact that the main contractors for weapons systems tend to be found in the declining industrial sectors implies that the relations of force are also, in some sense, decaying. We have noted that technical improvements to weapons systems appear to be subject to diminishing returns. It is also the case that these increasingly expensive and elaborate technologies have come under challenge from new technologies, themselves the product of newer and more rapidly growing industrial sectors. Thus technical advance in the electronics field has made possible a revolution in the guidance systems of munitions, which renders all weapon platforms extremely vulnerable and calls into question the utility of weapon systems which are difficult to hide and expensive to replace.[11] Since the new technologies are relatively cheap (a modern combat aircraft costs 1,000 times more than an anti-aircraft missile;

a battle tank costs around 200 times more than an anti-tank missile) they introduce the option of a much more cost-effective solution to most modern military problems. Naturally, there is disagreement about their potential and since the criteria for military efficiency are, as noted at the beginning of this chapter, subjective in peacetime, only the test of war can demonstrate their superiority and, hence, the decaying nature of most existing techniques of force. To some extent, wars in South-East Asia and the Middle East have provided such a test.[12]

This association between decaying or baroque techniques of force and a declining economy is by no means permanent. Indeed, it contains within it the necessity for change. It is not simply that the techniques will, sooner or later, be subjected to the test of war, in which the 'Why' of the armament process is more rigorously defined. It is also that the industrial structure has resulted in two irreconcilable trends, that the traditional answer to the 'How' of the armament process will no longer suffice. On the one hand, the momentum of the arms industry has resulted in more expensive and elaborate weapon systems. On the other hand, the decline of the economy has meant that governments are becoming less able to afford the weapon systems and will be forced to seek alternative solutions to military problems. This stage was reached by Britain after World War Two and has recently been reached by the United States, as evidenced in the attempts to narrow the range of weapon systems and to promote arms exports.

An obvious solution is adaptation to the PGM revolution, but like all solutions which appear to be purely technical and therefore simple, it has much wider social and economic implications. First, it implies a major change in the relations of force, a change from a batch production type organisation to something which is more like an assembly line, involving considerable changes in the hierarchy and skill differentials within the armed forces, themselves the historical reflection of complex class structures. While it is certainly the case that the growth of the professional and technical classes both within and outside the armed forces and the organisational experience of wars in Vietnam or Northern Ireland have created pressure for such changes, it is also the case that they are bitterly resisted by the traditional military hierarchy. Secondly, and perhaps more importantly, the PGM solution would have far-reaching implications for the arms industry and for the structure of the economy as a whole. It would imply the run-down of traditional arms manufacture and, without considerable government help, the demise of certain important companies in the defence-related sectors — a British example would be Vickers. It would have to be part of a general restructuring in which resources were shifted from slow-growing to fast-growing industrial sectors — something which could not take place without planning and state interference and, for that reason, let alone the vested interests in slow-growing sectors, would be opposed.

So it is that the dominant form of force in the capitalist world is approaching a crisis, one which can be explored both in military and economic terms, and one which could be viewed as part of wider crisis in the United States' world role. What are the implications of the crisis for the rest of the world, particularly the poorer nations?

The Third World

Figure 20.1 represents a model of the role of arms in the world capitalist economy. Down the centre are the various exchanges between industrialised countries and the Third World — aid, foreign investment, foreign military intervention, arms, luxuries, primary commodities, capital goods, repatriated profits and debts repayments; obviously, it is not a comprehensive list. The whole arrows show the direction of exchange; from left to right indicates a movement from industrialised to poor countries and vice versa. The left-hand side of the chart indicates the role of these exchanges in the economies of rich countries while the right-hand side indicates their role in the economies of poor countries. Evidently, the focus is on the latter. In what follows, we shall consider, first, the implications for exporting techniques of force for Third World countries, the right-hand side of the chart, and then consider what this implies for the changing form of force in rich countries.

Arms and Development or Underdevelopment

Views about the impact of arms on the economies of Third World countries differ according to different approaches towards the problem of development. One view which is held by more orthodox theorists might be termed the 'development' approach, while another, which is held by Marxists and neo-Marxists, might be termed the underdevelopment approach.

The orthodox theorists tend to treat the development process as ahistorical. Despite the use of such terms as pre-capitalist or feudal, change, in so far as it occurs, is treated as movement from one static situation, that of rural poverty, to another, that of urban wealth. This movement can be engineered by the ruling institutions, of which the military is one, and/or by external agents. The limited success of attempts to achieve development is explained by lack of resources or

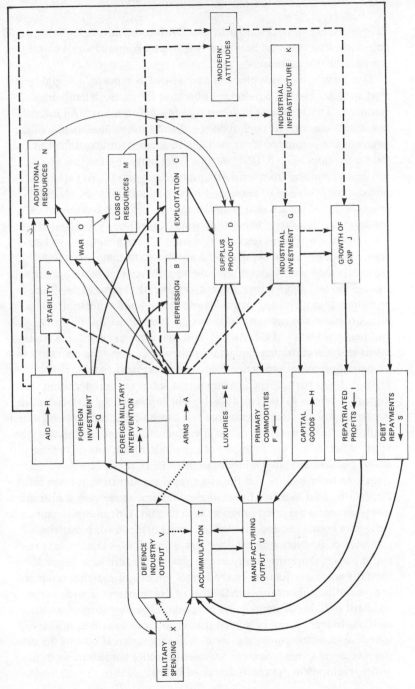

Figure 20.1

the persistence of backward attitudes. Within the development approach, however, can be found two strictly opposed views about the particular role of arms.

One view, which is typified in a series of UN reports,[13] would hold that arms are bad for development because they absorb badly needed resources. This argument is shown by the solid thin lines. Additional resources, acquired through foreign aid and foreign investment, which augment the surplus product available to society for investment in future development (R/QND on chart) are offset by the loss of resources resulting from arms expenditure and war (A/AO MD). No one disputes this line of reasoning. It is criticised, howver, on the grounds that it is partial. It is argued that it fails to take account of the resource-mobilising benefits of arms expenditure which might outweigh the effects of resource diversion. These benefits have been enumerated by Emile Benoît[14] and are shown in the broken lines. He argues that arms expenditure creates stability and therefore attracts foreign aid and foreign investment (APQ/R); that arms expenditure encourages 'modernising' attitudes and skills[15] and industrial infrastructure, contributing to industrial investment and to productivity and hence growth (ALGJ, AKGJ); and that arms expenditures tend to result in a less restrictive budgetary policy, increasing the demand for industrial products and hence industrial investment (AGJ). This argument was part of a general argument about the 'modernising' impact of armies in the Third World, which powerfully influenced the American military aid programme.[16] It can be criticised on two grounds. First there is no evidence for the growth-creating mechanisms described. While it is easy to find examples of the modernising role of the army, it is also possible to find counter-examples. Thus, it can be argued that arms lead to instability and therefore repel aid and foreign investment — Burma, the two Yemens, for example; that armies are very traditional and represent a brake on progress, as in certain African, Asian and Latin American countries; and that the increased demand for industrial products constitutes a demand for waste products — arms or luxuries — and does not therefore contribute to productive activities. Second, Benoit's argument focuses on the rate of growth of national product. It says nothing about other indicators of development — such as the standard of living of the poorest people and the provision of social services. Indeed, it can be argued that in so far as increased military spending leads to economic growth, it does so at great cost to the other goals of development. Such an argument is quite consistent with the underdevelopment approach described below.

According to the underdevelopment approach, the process of change in Third World countries is not a process of development, constrained by various factors, but a process of underdevelopment, which is inextricably linked to accumulation in rich countries. Arms are essential in maintaining an inequitable social structure in which this process can take place. This function can be explored by looking at three different models of the relationship of poor countries to rich countries, which are indicated by the solid thick lines on the chart.

The first is the pre-colonial model, in which local ruling classes import arms; this helps to absorb local economies into the international division of labour, with profound implications for domestic social structure. The French anthropologist, Emmanuel Terray, has described how this occurred in the Abron Kingdom of Guyaman in West Africa.[17] He shows how local ruling classes, in what were essentially kin-based societies with a certain amount of domestic slavery, imported guns which they used to capture slaves, who were used to produce gold for export. In exchange for the gold, the rulers received luxuries, which enhanced their prestige, and guns which they used to capture more slaves, to produce more gold, and so on. In other words, the import of arms enabled the rulers to introduce a new mode of production, namely slavery, which enabled them to increase exploitation, measured by the ratio between the output of labourers and their subsistence, and the surplus product, which was exported in exchange for arms and luxuries (ABCDE/F/A). The purchase of arms and luxuries and the sale of primary commodities increased manufacturing output in the industrial metropolis and, hence, accumulation (A/E/FUT).

The second model is the colonial model in which there is no international exchange of arms because there is no local ruling class. Foreign investment and foreign military intervention directly establish an exploitative system for producing primary commodities in exchange for manufactured imports (QC/YBC, D, E/F, UTQ).

The third model is the post-colonial model, which is associated with the early stages of industrialisation and in which the new ruling class is divided between an urban and a rural élite. Part of the surplus product is spent on industrial investment, which increases imports of capital goods and supports manufacturing output in the metropolis (DGHU), and which increases the rates of economic growth to the benefit of the urban élite (DGJ). Industrial investment may be augmented by foreign investment and aid, (GCDG, RNDG), but this is offset, at least in part, by repatriated profits (QCDGJI) and debt repayments (RS), both of which contribute directly to accumulation

in the metropolis. As in the pre-colonial model, arms play an essential
role in maintaining the rate of exploitation and, hence, ensuring
sufficient surplus product for industrial investment. Arms may also lead
to external war, in which victory could augment resources (A/OND) —
a form of foreign exploitation or sub-imperialism. Thus, for example,
India's victory against Pakistan in 1971 and the subsequent
independence of Bangladesh enabled India to capture Bangladesh's
world market for jute and Pakistan's market in Bangladesh fòr
manufactured goods. In other words, in the post-colonial model or the
industrial model, arms may contribute to urban-based economic
growth, as the 'modernisers' suggest, but not so much through its
effects on nation-building attitudes as through the use of force to
increase exploitation, through domestic repression or external war
(ABCD/AOND, E/F/A, GJHUT, GJIT). The result may be increased
poverty for rural producers.

In this process, the type of arms exported and the associated force
structure has important consequences for the political balance between
the rural and urban élite. In the pre-colonial model, where no urban
élite exists, the relations of force tend to reflect the predominant
relationships in society. The kings of Guyaman used retinue armies.
Today, the Bedouin levies owe military service to their leaders, the
sheikhs and kings of Arabia, in much the same way as feudal serfs
owed military service to their lords in the Middle Ages. The choice of
imported weapons is circumscribed by the relations of force. In some
cases, quite sophisticated weapons prove appropriate; the White Guard
of Saudi Arabia has, since 1963, made use of Vigilant man-portable
anti-tank missiles. In others, arms are designed in the metropolis
especially for their use, as with the ornate bayonets still manufactured
by Churchill's gun-makers in London (owned, incidentally, by the
American firm, Interarmco) for the use of Persian Gulf sheikhs. These
armies cannot make use of the major weapon-systems which might
whittle down their conservatism. This may be why, for example,
African armies have for so long opposed the introduction of tanks.
Thus the form of force does not necessarily involve capitalist relations
of force, but it is dependent on capitalist techniques and, in this, it
reflects the structure of pre-colonial societies, whose production is
orientated towards the capitalist world market although the methods
or relations of production are not necessarily capitalist.

As we have seen, with the introduction of the weapon system, the
possibilities for variation in the relations of force are much more limited.
With some qualification, the form of force thus becomes a reflection of

the form of force prevailing in the metropolis. The significance of this change in the form of force is primarily political, for it tends to orientate the army ideologically towards the urban élite. In that the form of force reflects the industrial structure of the metropolis, then soldiers tend to view the goals of industrialisation and growth favourably. The military importance of the weapon system is minor; for example, when direct repression is necessary, the industrial armies tend to revert to the methods of the pre-industrial armies or to the use of 'intermediate technology' weapons designed in the metropolis for the purpose. The primary function of the weapon system is not so much combat as political intervention. It is through the military *coup* that the army supports the political power of the urban élite. Thus in Libya, for example, it was the American-equipped regular armed forces that, through the military *coup,* initiated a bourgeois revolution against the rural-based élite led by the King, who had his own force of loyal Bedouin levies. The overthrow of Haile Selassie in Ethiopia can be interpreted in a similar way.

This argument about the significance of the form of force to the stage of development or underdevelopment and to the internal political balance of power has an interesting corollary. Since the weapons-system-based force structure reflects a decaying industrial structure in the metropolis, it is likely that soldiers will support the build-up of industries that are on the decline in the metropolis. Hence any economic growth achieved thorugh such investment is likely to be temporary and wasteful.

Empirical evidence, such as it is, about the role of arms spending in Third World economies would tend to support the underdevelopment approach. There are some countries in which high rates of economic growth are associated with high levels of military spending, measured as a share of GNP, but this association can also be correlated with foreign dependence and inequity.[18] The classic example is of course Brazil. Alfred Stepan, in a study undertaken for the Rand Corporation about military rule in Brazil, suggests that, despite the optimism of the modernisers, the huge financial and political American commitment to Brazil, and the high rates of economic growth, the demobilisation of 'all mass change-orientated movements, the inequitable fiscal stabilization policy, and the widespread use of torture has deeply inhibited social development.'[19]

Arms and Imperialism

If the analysis of arms and underdevelopment is correct, it then becomes possible to understand the function of arms exports in the international system and the consequences of arms exports for the economy as well as the form of force in the metropolis. One function is immediately obvious and is shown by the solid thick lines (AON/ABC/QC, D, A/E/F/GH/GJI, UT/T). This is the function of arms as an instrument of force to be used for domestic repression, war and political intervention.

In order to ensure the political conditions in which aid, trade and investment can take place, the key relationship is that between accumulation in rich countries and exploitation in poor countries, or between development in rich countries and underdevelopment in poor countries. This is generally known as the political or strategic function and it is in keeping with the classic theories of imperialism, such as those of Lenin and Bukharin. But there is another function of arms exports, which has excited some interest recently, and that is the direct function of arms in the international allocation of resources. Arms exports may directly support accumulation by increasing the output of the defence industry, as shown in the dotted lines (AVT), and by improving foreign exchange earnings. This is generally known as the economic or industrial function, and is consistent with under-consumptionist theories of imperialism, where waste production such as arms is considered necessary to maintain employment and where the push of military institutions results in an aggressive foreign policy. Versions of this theory can be found in the works of Rosa Luxembourg, Paul Baran and Paul Sweezy, as well as in the writings of the military-industrial-complex school.

Rather than viewing these two functions as mutually exclusive, one might argue that they represent successive phases of imperialism. In the early phase of imperialism, the most dynamic phase of capitalist development, a limited transfer of arms for repression, is sufficient to ensure the imperialist feedback. During this phase, it is possible to penetrate Third World economies primarily through trade; the task of exploitation can be largely delegated to local rulers and foreign rivals. Such was the situation of mid-nineteenth-century Great Britain, pre-1941 United States, and modern Germany and Japan. With the beginnings of economic decline, it becomes necessary to establish a monopoly political position in order to maintain or penetrate a dependent economy. The political function of arms exports becomes more important, as does direct foreign military intervention. Military aid and foreign military spending, however, represent a tax on the funds available for accumulation, offsetting the economic advantages of spheres of influence and exacerbating the process of decline. Part of this process is the momentum of the arms industry and the difficulties in employing military manufacturing capacity described in the first section. This phase characterises imperial Great Britain and France and post-1945 United States.

With the emergence of trade deficits and defence industry difficulties, the economic function of arms transfers becomes important. Arms are sold to save defence companies (for example, the Iranian purchase of F-14 fighters which saved the Grumman Aerospace Corporation), and to improve the balance of payments. This phase characterises Great Britain and France since the late 1950s and the United States since 1971. However, the economic function is not necessarily compatible with the political function. To be effective politically, it is necessary to be selective, to restrain as well as to promote arms, and to be able to eliminate competitors through the gift of arms, where necessary. The economic function requires unlimited promotion and full payment; it limits the political use of arms transfers and it encourages the diversification of sources of arms, that is penetration of new suppliers. The result is a decline in political power, the loss of monopoly political positions and a further retardation in accumulation.

The implication of this analysis is that the transfer of arms on a large scale, as in the two latter phases of imperialism, has negative consequences for the economies of both rich and poor countries. They support a decaying form of force and decaying industrial structure in the metropolis, what one might describe as overdevelopment, through an exploitative system of production in poor countries, namely underdevelopment. The successful developing capitalist economies, Germany and Japan, are low military spenders and low arms exporters.

In theory, underdeveloped countries could break this depressing feedback by reducing military spending and imports of weapon systems, by shifting economic policy from the goals of industrial growth to the goals of egalitarian development, and by reorganising the armed forces in a structure that is more in keeping with the goals of development. Such policies, if carried out, would have enormous impact on rich countries, inducing the crisis in military techniques and organisation which was described earlier. But like the apparent technical solution to that crisis, such a change in policy presupposes far-reaching changes in social structure. Current élites, including the armed forces, owe their existence to the present system. It is poor peasants, who constitute the majority of the world population, who would benefit primarily from a transformation of the system, and they have no power.

Notes

1. Alfred Wagts, *A History of Militarism: Civilian and Military* (New York, 1967).
2. See the description of British Government reports, particularly the Morley Report of 1887 and the Murray Report of 1906 in Philip Noel-Baker, *The Private Manufacture of Arms* (London, 1936), pp.58-9. See also the Annual Reports of American Aerospace Companies in 1946 and 1947.
3. See Lloyd J. Dumas, 'Payment Functions and the Productive Efficiency of Military Industrial Firms', *Journal of Economic Issues,* X (1976).
4. Quoted in Noel-Baker, *The Private Manufacture of Arms.*
5. See R. Smith, 'Military Expenditure and Capitalism', *Cambridge Journal of Economics,* I (1977).
6. See Organization for Economic Co-operation and Development, *Patterns of Resources devoted to Research and Experimental Development in the OECD Area, 1963-1971* (Paris, 1975).
7. Erick Janstch, *Technological Forecasting in Perspective* (OECD, Paris, 1967).
8. R.L. Perry, J.K. Smith, A.J. Harman and S. Henrichsen, *System Acquisition Strategies* (Rand Corporation, Santa Monica, California, 1971).
9. For other examples see Seymour Melman, *The Permanent War Economy: the Decline of American Capitalism* (New York, 1975).
10. Clive Trebilcock, ' "Spin-Off" in British Economic History: Armaments and Industry, 1960-1914', *Economic History Review,* XXII (1969), p.488.
11. For information on the precision-guided munitions (PGM) revolution see Jorma K. Miettinen, 'Can Conventional New Technologies and New Tactics replace Tactical Nuclear Weapons in Europe?', above, pp. 52-69; and James Digby, *Precision Guided Weapons* (International Institute for Strategic Studies, Adelphi Paper no.118, London, 1975).
12. During the first three weeks of the 1973 Middle East War, when PGMs were first applied on an extensive scale, an average of more than one aircraft and four tanks were lost every hour. See Stockholm International Peace Research Institute, *World Armaments and Disarmament: SIPRI Yearbook, 1974* (Stockholm, 1974), p.5.
13. See, for example, United Nations, *Economic and Social Consequences of the Arms Race and of Military Expenditure: Report of the Secretary General, Department of Political and Security Council Affairs,* A/8469/Rev.1, (New York, 1972); and *Disarmament and Development: Report of the Group of Experts on Social and Economic Consequence,* ST/ECA/174 (New York, 1972).
14. Emile Benoît, *Defense and Economic Growth in Developing Countries* (Lexington, Massachusetts, 1973).
15. These include 'following and transmitting precise instructions; living and working by the clock; noticing and reading signs; spending and saving money; using transportation (bicycles, motor cycles, autos, buses, boats, planes, etc.); – listening to radio'. Ibid.
16. The modernisers were very enthusiastic about the army's role in politics and development. For example, Manfred Halpern wrote:

    The more the army was modernised, the more its composition, organisation and spirit constituted a radical criticism of the existing political system.

Within the army, modern technology was eagerly welcomed and its usefulness and power appreciated. By contrast, the political system showed greater inertia, inefficiency, skepticism and greed in utilising the products of modern science. . .They have served as national standard bearers when others who claimed that role proved irresponsible and ineffective. They have supplied an education in modern technology when industry was too scant to provide it, a disciplined organisation without peer, a unity in the face of the corrupt and unprincipled competition of domestic interests and foreign imperialism.

Manfred Halpern, 'Middle Eastern Armies and the New Middle Class', in John J. Johnson, *The Role of the Military in Underdeveloped Countries* (Rand Corporation, Princeton, New Jersey, 1962).

17. Emmanuel Terray, 'Long Distance Exchange and the Formation of the State: the Case of the Abron Kingdom of Guyaman', *Economy and Society*, III (1974).

18. Benoît's data show a positive correlation between the military burden, the share of GNP spent on the military and high growth rates. But he also finds that, for most of the period, the high growth rates could also be explained by high bilateral aid. See Benoît, *Defense and Economic Growth*. This conclusion is supported by Philippe Schmitter, in a statistical survey of militarism in Latin America who finds 'the level of commercial and financial dependence on the United States' to be an important explanatory variable. He also finds that military rule tends to be associated with inequitable tax policies. See 'Military Intervention, Political Competitiveness and Public Policy in Latin America: 1950-67' in Morris Janowitz and Jacques van Doorn (eds.), *On Military Intervention* (Rotterdam, 1971). A crude examination of data on military and social spending and economic growth would also suggest that the high military spenders tend to be low social spenders. See Mary Kaldor, 'The Military in Development', *World Development*, IV (1976).

19. Alfred Stepan, *The Military in Politics: Changing Patterns in Brazil* (Rand Corporation, Princeton, New Jersey, 1971).

21 ECONOMIC AND TECHNOLOGICAL PREREQUISITES FOR ACHIEVING POLITICAL AND MILITARY STABILITY

Tom Stonier

Introduction

This paper begins with the proposition that an arms control agreement may well be counter-productive if the social climate is wrong. Following such an agreement, both sides spend more time worrying about the other side cheating than about implementing the agreements themselves. The SALT Agreements may be an example. Under other circumstances, there may be no formal agreement at all, but relations may work out very well because goodwill on both sides continuously reinforces positive peace signals. The futility of some agreements is epitomised by the Kellogg-Briand Pact and other agreements of the 1920s to limit naval armaments, agreements which turned out to be virtually useless in the 1930s. It is for this reason that arms controllers and those seeking universal disarmament should really concern themselves with the question of the social climate. It is towards this question that this chapter addresses itself by presenting a model of the global system as it exists today.

The recognition that political agreements are part of a broader system has practical implications for policy- and decision-makers. If we wish to curb the arms race, or better yet, achieve complete and universal disarmament, our social strategies will differ according to our assessment of the root causes of war. For example, if war is a part of human nature, as was believed by many nineteenth-century and twentieth-century evolutionists, then it may become necessary to change human nature. If, on the other hand, we are dealing with a society in which war is such an integral component that if you abolish war, you destroy the society as well, then we must have very fundamental changes in our society. Other views have it that wars are the product of historical forces, economic imperatives, or merely the quest for power. Among political scientists in the United States two views of the world dominate contemporary thinking. One view holds that the world is composed of about 150 independent actors, the nation-states, each striving to maximise their power and prestige. The other view holds that the world is composed of a global social system whose political organisation involves, at this point in history, about 150 *nation*-states.

The model presented here must be viewed as an effort to place the institution of war and its contemporary concomitant, the technological arms race, within a broader context of global social and economic forces which are part of an unfolding evolutionary historical process. In one way, this effort could be considered to be well within the philosophical tradition of Marx; in other ways, however, it is very different. In this connection I wish to acknowledge my intellectual indebtedness to four people in particular who have influenced my thinking profoundly: the anthropologist Robert Carneiro, the economist Fritz Machlup, the sociologist Daniel Bell, and the political scientist Johan Galtung.[1]

Macrohistory

To understand the world we live in, it is necessary to study macrohistory, and that will involve a look at Table 21.1. We are concerned primarily with three of the eras listed in the left-hand column, the 'agrarian', the 'mechanical' and the 'communicative' eras. In particular, we will consider the fate of three institutions listed in that third column opposite agrarian; namely war, slavery and the state. That is probably the order in which they appeared historically. In the third column, headed 'inventions, or other discontinuity', the reference is to both hardware and software, which can involve both physical and/or social technology. The agrarian society was founded primarily on the trinity of war, slavery and state. The mechanical era began about 1500 and was epitomised two centuries later by the Industrial Revolution. The communicative era, which has begun very recently, within the past twenty years, and only in some sectors of the world, is so close to us that it is very difficult to see. It is very difficult to perceive that we have made a transition, even though there is abundant evidence around us. It is like trying to explain to a fish what water is. We are swimming in a comparable cultural medium.

The basis for the communicative era is the Electronic Revolution. The difference between the Electronic Revolution and the Industrial Revolution is basically this: the Industrial Revolution involved the invention of devices which extended the human musculature. They were all devices which lifted things, transported things, crushed things, dug ditches and so on. In other words they were all physical operations. The Electronic Revolution produced devices which extended the human nervous syste. The telephone and radio: an extension of the ear. The film and television: an extension of the eye and ear. The computer:

Table 21.1: The Natural History of Humanity: Past, Present and Future

Type	Historical Period B.P. = Before Present P.P. = Post-Present	Invention or other Discontinuity	Major and New Energy Sources	Nature of Major Economic Activities	Percentage of Labour Force in Food Production
Hominid	$10^7 - 10^5$ B.P.	Weapons, hunting, food sharing, sex	Individual's own metabolic energy	Food gathering, hunting, sharing	100%
Paleolithic	$10^5 - 10^4$ B.P	Fire, language	as above	as above	100%
Neolithic	$10^4 - 10^3$ B.P.	Settlement, life agriculture	as above	Food production, barter	95%
Agrarian	$10^3 - 10^2$ B.P.	War, slavery, the state	Slaves, animals, wind, water	Agricultural production, money exchange	90%
Mechanical	$10^2 - 10^1$ B.P.	Industrial revolution	Steam, electric, petroleum	Industrial production, money and banking credit	10-90%
Communicative	10^1 B.P.-10^2 P.P.	Electronic revolution	Nuclear, solar, chemical, geothermal	Service economy, individual credit	5-10%
Cerebral	$10^2 -$ P.P.$-?$	Behavioural science revolution	Fusion, atmospheric, geologic, other?	Knowledge production, automated mass credit	<5%

Percentage of Labour Force in Knowledge Industry	Major and New Forms of Communication	Major and New Forms of Transportation	Nature of Group	Size of Group	Type of Group Organisation	Growth in (in addition to) Trans-generation Information Transmission Storage and Retrieval Systems
—	Face to face (visual signals and calls)	Foot	Primate troops	$10^0 - 10^2$	Hominid dominance hierarchy	DNA, protoculture
—	Face to face (calls, smoke)	Foot	Bands	$10^0 - 10^2$	Male-dominated egalitarianism	Culture (grandmothers)
—	Face to face	Foot, canoe	Villages	$10^1 - 10^3$	Male-dominated egalitarianism	Elaborate oral tradition, art, artefacts
1%	Messengers, despatches, signalling systems	Roads, animals, sail ships, post-chaise	Chiefdoms, kingdoms, city states, empires	$10^4 - 10^6$	Strong hierarchy, bureaucracy	Temples, records, monasteries, books, printing, universities
1-10%	Postal systems, newspapers, telegraph	Railways, steamships	Urbanised nation-states	$10^6 - 10^8$	Hierarchical group representation, increasing bureaucracy	Publishers, public education, extensive libraries, museums
10-50%	Telephone, TV computer	Motorways, jet planes, pipelines	Super-nations, regional economic associations	$10^8 - 10^9$	Participatory citizenship, male-female equality, automated organisations	Transnational information storage systems, film, records and tapes, TV, computers
>50%	Global holographic videophone network	Inter-planetary	Global association	10^{10}	Electronic egalitarianism? Technological anarchy?	Global information storage and retrieval systems available to all. Ultra-intelligent thinking machines. Brain computer junctions?

an extension of the brain. The social impact of this new technology is still not generally understood. In a sense, the Industrial Revolution created a bit of a Frankenstein's monster: enormous physical power, characterised in the 1950s by nuclear missiles, while retaining the mentality of a ten-year-old. The middle of the twentieth century was, if not a Stone Age culture, basically still an industrial culture.

In the fifth column, 'the nature of major economic activities', are listed some of the economic criteria for defining the eras. The chief economic function of agrarian society was the production of agricultural products such as wheat, olive oil, wine, leather and flax. There was some trade, of course, in metals, including rare metals, and an enormous trade in slaves. But basically the major function of agrarian economy involved agricultural products. The major economic activity of the mechanical era was industrial production, that is to say manufactured goods — textiles, steel, cars and so on. The communicative era was characterised by a shift to a service economy: more than 50 per cent of the GNP now went to services rather than to production. Probably the major economic function in the communicative society is in the production of organisation. That is to say, we are now in a society which is busy organising itself in terms of solving its various problems, including the production and distribution of resources.

Let us return to the origin and evolution of the state as an institution. We have to go back to the Neolithic|era in order to understand the origin of the state. The earliest traces of settlement life are about 14,000 years old. This doesn't mean that these are the oldest, but only the oldest found thus far. The Neolithic Revolution allowed an increase in the size of the primal group to many hundreds of people, organised into villages. And the villages, judging by present Neolithic cultures, tend to split once the village has reached the size of several hundred individuals. Very often they split because of the hostilities which develop within the villages: an aggrieved group picks up and goes off upstream into the jungle. This process still occurs in some remote parts of the world such as the headwaters of the Amazon. It is, however, very much the exception, because by and large, the world is fully occupied. In fact, the world probably has been largely occupied since the late Neolithic periods. The anthropologist Robert Carneiro has made a study of the various levels of social organisations in South America, and has come up with a very interesting theory: the theory of

Circumscription. Carneiro points out that within certain circumscribed areas, at some point late in Neolithic times, an increasing population must have run out of land. The process of village fissioning — moving further upstream into the jungle — could no longer take place. All the land had been taken up. He cites in particular the case of Peru, which is circumscribed by the Pacific to the west, the Andes to the east, and deserts to the north and south.

Institutionalised forms of conflict in Neolithic cultures, although lethal, tend to exhibit a very low lethality — it sometimes seems almost fun and games. In some instances it looks as though it might be functional as a population control device. In other instances the fighting centres around a scarce resource: women. A third type of Neolithic conflict involves grudge fights — acts of revenge. And sometimes fighting involves a simple jockeying for status. However, irrespective of the motivation, the lethality is, in general, relatively low. I believe one reason for the low lethality of Neolithic aggression is that normally the stakes are not very high. But as soon as, for example, land begins to run out, or some other resource becomes critical, then the stakes become high because the groups are now dealing with survival itself. Thus there must have come a time in which, as Carneiro points out, the most significant component in the environment of a society had become its enemies. And from this time on, for the next ten thousand years or so, we see most of the world engaged in a struggle for military power. Only cultures in remote places with stable populations could survive with a pacifist mode of life. In some instances, these proved totally pacifist, in which grown men never fought.

To understand the further evolution of the state, we must look at what became recorded history. Actually, recorded history did not come until much later. Recorded history began when there existed a civilisation sufficiently advanced to create records. Carneiro points out that in the span of a mere two millennia, there occurred a profound shift from village organisation to supra-village organisation. The chief who could effectively organise his village, make alliances, conquer other villages, and strengthen these by co-operative interactions began the processes leading to state formation. Those societies which could develop a more effective political centre of authority were militarily successful, because usually they were able to put a larger number of men into the field. The state originated in those circumscribed parts of the world where Neolithic villages were forced into new forms of social organisation as they began to run out of land. It was at this point that military efficiency became paramount. States able to put into the field large numbers of well-organised troops tended to win. Discipline became increasingly important. The phalanx probably was not known until later on. It seems to have been invented on more than one occasion. (For example, both the classical Greeks and the classical Mexica in central Mexico possessed it.) In any case, *organised warfare* became institutionalised and warriors became institutionalised. Carneiro envisions a rapid development of a three-layer society, with the top layers composed of those who were successful in war and returned with booty, including women and, later, slaves. The next layer were the freemen who were the kinsmen of the victorious villagers, but were not the warriors themselves; and then there were the slaves who became increasingly necessary (as we shall discuss in the origin of slavery) for developing and maintaining the economic infrastructure of this new development, the state.[2]

About 8,000 years later, in Western Europe, the state system had evolved into a system of feudal states. We are now speaking of a period which is possible to document historically. The state system of the late Middle Ages was beginning to show changes. A profound revolution had taken place in Northern and Western Europe in the ninth and tenth centuries. It led to an immense increase in agricultural productivity, followed by a steady pace of further technological advances. A commitant of these technological advances was a rapidly expanding trade system, so that the rise of mercantilism and capitalism began to transcend the much more limited economic activities of the feudal states. In due course the feudal states became economically non-viable. The process was accelerated by developments in military technology. Local barons were no longer safe behind their castles if they could not afford 'modern' armies, that is armies with artillery and mobile troops. The feudal state succumbed to the twin assaults of mercantilism and the new militarism. It became displaced by increasingly larger political units. By the middle of the seventeenth century, the Treaty of Westphalia had established political outlines in modern Europe which we still recognise today as having been the basis of the nation-state system. Able military leaders, such as King Gustavus Adolphus of Sweden, had reorganised armies along modern lines, with such branches as cavalry and artillery — armies which could only be matched by correspondingly armed and organised units. No feudal baron could resist such armies, while at the same time the larger towns could no longer survive on a trade limited to the local countryside.

We are at a similar juncture in history today. The traditional European nation-state is no longer a viable political unit. Nuclear missile technology has compromised the security of the national state. No longer can the state protect its people – not even the children. Thus the primary function of the state has become unmanageable among contemporary nation-states. Perhaps even more important is that the new technology has created a transnational web of interactions which is so extensive that the technologically advanced nation-states of Europe are no longer economically viable. Only the very large supernation states, such as the United States and the Soviet Union, do not suffer from that deficiency at this point in history. The obvious evidence which indicates that the technologically advanced sector of the world is beginning to see changes in the political organisation of the state system is the creation of the European Community.

The Abolition of Slavery

So much for macro-history. Now let us turn to a specific historical example: the abolition of an ancient institution – slavery. We do not know the origin of slavery, but in the light of what evidence is available, it probably originated as a by-product of warfare. The earliest slaves probably were women and children taken as prisoners. The successful capture of women was crucial to survival in a jungle surrounded by enemies. Their capture not only reduced the numbers of the enemies' future battalions, but at the same stroke increased one's own. Unwittingly this practice also brought new genes into isolated groups, and, most importantly, fostered cross-cultural fertilisation. This is vividly illustrated by comparing two Indian tribes along the tributaries of the Amazon: the Txukahamei and the Kreen-Akrore. The former take prisoners while the latter do not. Thus the Txukahamei learned to use, and even repair, the guns which they took in raids on whites, because the captured women taught them how. In contrast the Kreen-Akrore take no prisoners, but kill all instead. As a result, they have never learned how to use guns which they have captured from either the whites or other Indian tribes. Once warfare had become institutionalised in late Neolithic times, groups inclined to taking prisoners generally had a selective advantage over those which did not. Thus the practice must have spread through the more successful cultures and become a natural and accepted part of society. Limiting war prisoners to women and children, and enslaving these, continued as standard practice until the late high civilisations. This is illustrated by the Mexica of the early sixteenth century at the time of the Spanish conquests.

Mexica society had three kinds of slave groups *(tlacotli)*: slaves obtained in warfare, criminal slaves, and contracted slaves. The first, as discussed earlier, included only women and children; males, if not killed outright, were sacrificed to the insatiable Aztec gods. Criminal slaves were usually forced to serve their victim or his family. A man who had murdered another might thus be forced to serve his family in compensation. Crimes against the state could also be punished by committing the person to servitude. Lastly, individuals who could not pay a personal debt or a public tribute might sell themselves, or one of their children, into slavery. Slaves were used in the house and in the field, and were particularly important for the heavy work so crucial to an advanced civilisation which lacked draught animals. Considering the size and splendour of the palaces, temples, dams and other public structures, there must have been a lot of heavy work.

Forced labour was vital not only in the absence of draught animals. No great agrarian civilisation could produce its surpluses and its edifices, and also maintain a significant military and bureaucratic establishment, without coercing a lot of people into labouring well beyond their own needs. The evidence is clear about the importance of various forms of slavery in the other ancient cultures, such as China, India, Persia and Mesopotamia. In Western cultures we have been exposed to Egyptian relief figures showing slaves, while the Bible is filled with references to slavery (for example, Exodus and Deuteronomy) defining Jewish laws governing this institution, including the slave trade. Similarly, Greek and Latin literature attest to the fact that slavery was not only widespread, but taken for granted. Athens, the cradle of democracy, was also a centre for the slave trade. Thoughtful Greeks considered slaves to be absolutely necessary, for without them citizens would be unable to devote themselves to noble pursuits, including the services of the state. Slavery in Rome existed from early times but not until Rome became a military power did the number of slaves owned by Rome become very large. When it did, however, it did so with great efficiency. There are records which indicate that Caesar sold 53,000 slaves on one occasion. In the second century BC the Greek island of Delos was made a free port by the Romans and became a great slave trading centre, in which as many as 10,000 slaves might be sold in a single day. The slaves laboured on Roman estates, they worked in Roman households, and they built the public works for the Roman state.

Slave labour continued to play a prominent part throughout subsequent European history, although it took the form primarily of serfs and indentured servants. Similarly, from Africa through Asia and the Americas, all advanced forms of civilisation relied on slave labour to supply the economic surplus needed for the maintenance of the state.

Like tin (and other vital resources), slaves became an essential commodity and both sources and trade routes were fought over. The course of slavery in Africa is historically particularly well documented. The trade in African slaves dates back at least into Egyptian times. It continued through the Roman and Hellenic period. After the fall of the Roman Empire, the Arabs began their incursions. The East African coastal region was colonised as early as the eighth century AD. For the next millennium, like ripples from a stone dropped into a pond, the dreaded slavers caused mass dislocation and social disorganisation to spread across all of Africa. In the fifteenth century the Portuguese joined the Arabs on the East African coast in the thriving spice and slave trade. By the early sixteenth century the Portuguese conquered Zanzibar and the nearby coast. At the same time, in West Africa, Sir John Hawkins began the slave trade to the Americas in 1652. Actually the Portuguese had already established a hold on the West Coast in the fifteenth century, particularly in Ghana. By the end of the eighteenth century the West African coast was dotted with Portuguese, Spanish, French, Dutch, Danish and Swedish trading posts, all engaged in the slave trade.

It should become apparent that slave labour was endemic to virtually every post-Neolithic society until well into the eighteenth century. It was practically universal, confined to no one continent, race or civilisation. Yet after being such a prominent part of the social scene for millennia, slavery almost totally disappeared within the short span of about two centuries. Some time during the latter part of the eighteenth century, the climate of enlightened opinion changed. The first country to make a formal judicial decision was Great Britain in 1772, which for all practical purposes eliminated slavery in the home country, although not in the colonies.

As with any form of progress, it takes inspired individuals to translate an idea into reality. Such inspired individuals may arise from any class, and may initially have no connection, either with reformers or the objects of reform. Granville Sharp was such a man. Born in 1735 to the Archdeacon of Northumberland, the 12th of 14 children, he lost out on the education afforded some of his elder brothers. Nevertheless he pursued studies on his own while a minor civil servant. In 1765 Sharp chanced to encounter a slave named Strong, so savagely beaten by his master, David Lisle, that he was nearly blind and could hardly walk. Since he was of no further use to his master he had been turned out into the street. Sharp and his surgeon brother attended to Strong and had him treated until he was sufficiently well to be discharged.

The brothers found a job for him as an errand boy, and that seemed to be the end of the story.

Two years later, Lisle happened to see his former slave in the street. Realising that Strong had recovered his value, he sold him to a Jamaican planter named James Kerr. Kerr, to make sure of his property, kidnapped Strong and committed him to prison for safe keeping until the next ship for Jamaica. Out of this arose a complicated legal case, which initially looked as though it would cost Sharp at least £200 in damages. Sharp's lawyers advised him to settle out of court. They cited a series of earlier judicial decisions which judged that a master did not lose his property rights over a slave by residing in England, and that he could compel a slave to return to the plantation. Sharp, although he had no formal training in law, was not easily intimidated, not by his lawyers, not by Kerr's lawyers, and not even by a challenge to a duel by Lisle. For two years he worked on his defence, then he sent a lengthy memorandum on his case to eminent lawyers in London. His arguments were so devastating as to cause Lisle and Kerr's advisers to discontinue their suit, although ultimately the latter were fined triple costs for dropping it. It took another two years, however, before the critical test case arose. This related to a slave, James Somerset, and was the basis of a decision by Lord Chief Justice Mansfield in 1772: 'The state of slavery. . .is so odious that nothing can be suffered to support it but positive law. Whatever inconveniences therefore may follow from the decision. . .the black must be discharged.' This decision marked the turning point in the institution of chattel slavery throughout the Atlantic community, and ultimately the whole world. It is a tribute to Lord Mansfield, and particularly to Granville Sharp.

With the Somerset decision as background, the battle lines were drawn: on one side were the vested interests who pocketed handsome profits from slavery, or the slave trade, or both — on the other side were the humanitarians to whom slavery was a moral outrage. Throughout Britain, various individuals and groups began picking up the question of abolition. They tended to be individuals or groups already engaged in intellectual pursuits. The abolition campaign developed more rapidly in Britain than anywhere because, there existed at that time a public more liberal than in any other country, served by a complex network of newspapers, pamphlets, handbills, posters and other forms of printed media. The abolitionists learned to utilise the system for educating the public. Church leaders began to become increasingly concerned. Among these, John Wesley was among the most influential. The sum total of this type of activity led to one of the greatest propaganda movements of all time.

Such a propaganda movement is sterile if it cannot be translated into political action, and towards that end there arose the so-called Clapham Set, with its most articulate voice, William Wilberforce. Wilberforce became a leader in Parliament and the Clapham Set became the nerve centre of the propaganda movement, both inside Parliament as well as in the country at large. Wilberforce was born in 1759 into an old prosperous Yorkshire family. He was educated at Cambridge, where he formed a very close bond with William Pitt. When the younger Pitt became Prime Minister, it was Wilberforce who became his chief spokesman in Parliament. Wilberforce therefore was placed in an excellent position to engage in political activity. Interestingly enough, he was ready to leave Parliament altogether in consequence of a religious conversion, but was dissuaded by a clergyman, who first introduced him to some of the details of the slave trade. Before long, Wilberforce had come under the influence of other abolitionists, and from then on abolition became a form of Christian crusade which could allow him to utilise his political position for a constructive purpose. In 1787 Pitt suggested to Wilberforce that the latter introduce a motion in Parliament against the slave trade. Wilberforce did so, thereby initiating a struggle within that august body which was to last for almost four decades. Initially, the winds were with Pitt and Wilberforce. In the early 1790s the demise of the slave trade seemed close to hand. Only the House of Lords insisted on delaying it. Unfortunately, the excesses of the French Revolution brought about a shift in public opinion, so that Englishmen became more interested in hating Frenchmen than slave traders. By 1804 the matter seemed so hopeless that Wilberforce, discouraged, did not even bother to introduce the motions any more. Ironically, a mere three years later, in 1807, he produced a Bill which abolished the slave trade (followed by an amending act in 1811 to make the slave trade a felony). The struggle continued. Finally, at midnight on 31 July 1834, all slaves in the territories owing allegiance to the Crown became free. Wilberforce had died the year before. The British planters received compensation totalling £20,000,000. It should also be noted that the competition of sugar from East India and other parts of the world had caused the commercial and political power of the West Indian planters to decline. What had been considered an indispensable social system nearly half a century earlier had become irrelevant as the force of the Industrial Revolution continued to change the economic realities of the European-based world.

Both aboslute monarchy and slavery were noxious institutions by

present-day standards. However, both were probably vital to the
survival of older societies competing for limited resources: the former
to weld large, unwieldy social units into organised politics capable of
exercising both the economic and military tasks required for societal
survival (and, where possible, growth); the latter to provide the
economic infrastructure and assure the general productivity required
for the maintenance, and if possible the expansion, of such an agrarian
society. But the pressures were always there to rid society of either,
or both of these two institutions whenever it became practical to do
so. This occurred under a variety of circumstances throughout history;
what concerns us here is that the technological developments leading
to the Industrial Revolution provided the opportunity for eliminating
the institution of slavery. Given the fact that coercing people to work
for reasons other than their own interest has always been undesirable,
coupled with the cruelty and brutality frequently associated with the
institution of chattel slavery, the rise of industrial society was
characterised by three features which made the demise of slavery
virtually inevitable. First, the increasing productivity of agriculture
made available a large pool of cheap labour to compete with slave
labour. Secondly, the Industrial Revolution created the machines and
factory system to which this labour could be coupled, producing a
new economic unit of much greater versatility. During good times
machines manned by wage labour were highly productive. During
slumps, the wage labour could be fired, while the idle machines, unlike
idle slaves, required little expense in the way of maintenance. With
cheap 'free' labour available, capital was better invested in machines
than in bodies. Thirdly, associated with industrialisation was the further
rise of an industrious middle class competing for power with the
traditional, and increasingly non-functional, hereditary aristocracy —
an ideal climate for the rise of meritocratic egalitarianism. This ideology
was incompatible with the institution of slavery. Thus slavery tended to
disappear as the industrial system spread; furthermore, as the industrial
nations became the globe's most powerful, the abolition of slavery was
imposed on others.

The Abolition of War

What lessons for the abolition of war may be drawn from the abolition
of slavery? Both are social *institutions* which trace their origins back
to the time of transition from Neolithic to agrarian society. The great
ancient civilisations required both institutions for survival and
expansion. Those societies which failed to expand the economic

infrastructure on which their economic and military power depended ran the risk of being subjugated or destroyed by more powerful neighbours. On the other hand, those which could muster the necessary military strength conquered or at least plundered their neighbours, thereby enhancing their own prestige, and more importantly, extending their resources. That is the *primary* social motivation for war. (Secondary motives include defence, prestige and revenge.) The primary motivation for war has now been obviated by a new force — technological innovation — a new force which is leading to the demise of war as an institution in a manner very analogous to the demise of slavery.

The shift in the means of extending a society's resources reflects the enormous increase in productivity by technologically advanced nations. For example, in the north-east of England, Imperial Chemical Industries (ICI) is building a new petrochemical plant for the production of terylene fibres. The plant will cover two acres and will produce about £100 million worth of fibres per year. The total workforce is expected to involve 300 people. Not too long ago, entire cities couldn't produce as much as that one single plant produces with a total labour force of 300. That is the new reality: these are the new industries: that is the coming age.

In addition, the new production and marketing systems are associated with an enormous increase in transnational co-operation. The markets for that terylene are not going to be primarily in Great Britain. They are going to be elsewhere, and most of the raw material also comes from beyond British shores. The pressure favouring the formation of multinational enterprises have been reviewed by P.J. Buckley and M. Casson.[3] This transnational co-operation, coupled with economic, technical and cultural interdependence, leads to the decline of the nation-state, and the formation of transnational systems such as the European Economic Community.

The ascendancy of industrial economic power over military power is another feature of the communicative society. The classic case is Japan. Nobody questions Japan as a major power, yet its existing military force is smaller than that of its traditional enemy, South Korea. Both Koreas and Vietnam are significant military powers in the Western Pacific, but no one considers them on a par with Japan. Then there is the increasing tendency not to rely on military force: in 1973 the Arabs threatened to cut off the flow of oil to Western Europe. It was the first time in history in which minor military powers threatened a strategic resource of major military powers, and this threat not only failed to elicit military action, there was not even any public talk of military action at the time. (A year later the US Secretary of State, Henry Kissinger, waved a stick.) Instead, the technologically advanced nations began considering alternatives to oil. Two years later, Icelandic gunboats were harrassing British fishing boats. That Her Majesty's Government should tolerate such action would have been inconceivable even three decades earlier. Europe, the traditional centre of wars over the past two millennia, is now an island of peace.[4] Even when one looks at Northern Ireland, the total number of people killed over the last four or five years is about 1,200. As many people get killed from road accidents as do from revolutionary actions. Contrast the level of violence in Northern Ireland with that of Lebanon.

Countries moving into the post-industrial communicative society are characterised by economies which are primarily service-oriented and transnational. The major emerging industry is the knowledge industry. Traditional analyses, both Marxist and non-Marxist, are inadequate for analysing these emerging societies. One significant characteristic of these societies is the tendency to rely less and less on military solutions, exercising technological ingenuity instead. This applies, however, only to the technologically advanced nations, the ones moving from mechanical into communicative society.

Unfortunately, in the last quarter of the twentieth century, most of the world is still moving from agrarian into mechanical society. For the people in these countries, the prospects are much gloomier. The tendencies in these societies are towards increasing nationalism, increasing ethnic strife, and increasing militarism. Even within technologically advanced countries, there are frequently three levels of development — in a sense, three major subcultures. In Great Britain, for example, people at universities tend to be part of communicative society. Then there is still a large sector, such as older factory labour, which is in the mechanical society; and finally, in remote parts of the Scottish Highlands, there are some people who, for practical purposes, still live in agrarian life. The analysis is further complicated by a second phenomenon which one might call 'cultural lag'. Most of our political leaders suffer from this cultural lag. They were brought up in the mechanical era, and view the world in those terms. In fact, many of us carry with us this cultural lag — it is a problem of assimilation. Sometimes it is so obvious and so serious that we refer to it by the phrase coined by Alvin Toffler: 'future shock.'[5] It is a form of cultural shock — the older generation just does not understand what has happened to society. It is probably fair to state that in 1976 the American Secretary of State, in his view of the world, exhibited a cultural lag of about two decades, while his President exhibited four. This probably reflects the extent of the cultural lag characteristic of most of the world's leaders.

Conclusion

Technology changes reality. This is true not only of armaments, the arms race, and hence arms control, but it is even more true in determining the economic base of society. It is this changing economic base — highly specialised, transnational, interdependent — which is causing the decline of the institution of war, while at the same time causing the nation-state to become displaced by increasingly larger political units.

Continuing advances in military technology cause a spread, both horizontally and vertically, throughout the world, thereby increasing the possibility of a nuclear (or other) disaster. At the same time, technologisation of society descreases the tendency to resort to military solutions. The chief strategy of all concerned with securing global peace must be to shift the balance from the former to the latter. On the one hand, every effort must be made to slow the arms race and slow the spread of nuclear and other highly destructive weapons. On the other hand, every effort must be made to accelerate the process of social and cultural evolution throughout the world. We must increase global productivity, particularly in the Third World, and as part of that it behoves those from First and Second World countries to redirect the policies of the technologically advanced nations from massive military expenditure aimed at an East-West confrontation to massive expenditure aimed at increasing Third World productivity.

Notes

1. Robert Carneiro, 'A Theory of the Origin of the State', *Science,* CLXIX (1970), pp.733-8; Fritz Machlup, *The Production and Distribution of Knowledge in the United States* (Princeton, New Jersey, 1962); Daniel Bell, *The Coming of Post-Industrial Society* (New York, 1973); and Johan Galtung, *On the Future of the International System* (Peace Research Institute, Publication no.25-26, Oslo, 1967).
2. Carneiro, 'A Theory of the Origin of the State', loc.cit.
3. P.J. Buckley and M. Casson, *The Future of the Multinational Enterprise* (London, 1976).
4. See István Kende, '116 Wars in 30 Years', above, pp.303-21.
5. Alvin Toffler, *Future Shock* (New York, 1970).

CONTRIBUTORS

Steven J. Baker (US) is Assistant Professor in the Government Department at the University of Texas, Austin. He has also held research appointments at Cornell and Harvard Universities, He was awarded a Ph.D. at the University of California for a study of the Italian nuclear programme and political integration in Western Europe. He has contributed articles to *Foreign Policy* and to *Arms Control Today.*

J. Bowyer Bell (US) is Senior Research Associate at the Institute of War and Peace Studies, Columbia University. He has written six books and over thirty articles on war, revolution and political violence. He holds a Ph.D. degree from Duke University and has been been awarded, at various times, a Fulbright Fellowship, a Guggenheim Fellowship and a Ford Foundation Grant.

David Carlton (British) (co-editor) is Senior Lecturer in Diplomatic History at the Polytechnic of North London. He is author of *MacDonald versus Henderson: The Foreign Policy of the Second Labour Government* (Macmillan, London, 1970) and of numerous articles on problems of international politics in the twentieth century. He is co-editor of the two previous volumes in this series, *The Dynamics of the Arms Race* and *International Terrorism and World Security* (Croom Helm, London and John Wiley, New York, 1975).

William Epstein (Canadian), formerly Director of the Disarmament Division of the United Nations, is now a Special Fellow of the United Nations Institute for Training and Research, New York. He is also University Visiting Professor at the University of Victoria, British Columbia. He has written on many aspects of arms control and disarmament, his latest book being *The Last Chance: Nuclear Proliferation and Arms Control* (The Free Press, New York, 1976).

Thomas Halsted (US) is Executive Director of the Arms Control Association, Washington D.C. He is also Program Director (Arms Control) of the Carnegie Endowment for International Peace.

Mary Kaldor (British) is a Research Fellow at the Science Policy Research Unit of the University of Sussex. She was a co-author of *The Arms Trade with the Third World* (SIPRI, Stockholm, 1971).

István Kende (Hungarian) is Professor of International Relations at the

Karl Marx University of Economic Sciences, Budapest. He specialises in conflicts of the period after 1945 with particular reference to Asia and Africa. He has published widely in Hungarian and also in translation in French, English and Spanish.

Peter King (Australian) is Senior Lecturer in Government at the University of Sydney. He has published *The Strategy of Total Withholding* (Canberra Papers on Strategy and Defence, Australian National University Press, 1971) and has also contributed to *Pacific Affairs, Australian Outlook* and *International Journal.*

Herbert M. Levine (US) is Professor of Political Science at the University of Southwestern Louisiana, Lafayette, Louisiana. He specialises in international politics with a particular interest in American foreign policy.

Jorma K. Miettinen (Finnish) is Professor of Radiochemistry at the University of Helsinki. He has been active in the Pugwash Movement since 1970 and has published articles on chemical disarmament and on the role of tactical nuclear weapons in Europe.

Michail A. Milstein (Soviet) is a Chief of Section at the Institute of Canadian and US Studies of the Soviet Academy of Sciences. He has published, *inter alia,* in Russian (and in translation) a study of *Contemporary Bourgeois Military Science.* He is a retired General of the Soviet Union.

Hans J. Morgenthau (US) is Albert A. Michelson Distinguished Service Professor Emeritus of Political Science and Modern History at the University of Chicago; Leonard Davis Distinguished Professor Emeritus of Political Science, City College of the City University of New York; and University Professor of Political Science, New School for Social Research, New York. He has published innumerable books and articles .

Mario'n Mushkat (Israeli) is Director of the Institute for the Study of International Affairs, Tel Aviv, and Professor of International Law at the University of Tel Aviv.

Michael Nacht (US) is Assistant Director of the Program for Science and International Affairs and Lecturer in Government at Harvard University. He is a consultant to the Ford Foundation in international security and arms control. He has written for *Foreign Affairs, Foreign Policy* and *Survival.* He is also editor of a new quarterly journal, *International Security.*

Robert A. Nalewajek (US) is a student of International Relations with the University of Southern California. He is at present on assignment with American NATO forces in Federal Germany.

Bert Röling (Dutch) is Professor of International Law and Polemology at the University of Groningen. He is also Director of that University's Polemological Institute. He was a Judge on the International Military Tribunal for the Far East, 1946-8, and a member of the Netherlands' delegation to the General Assembly of the United Nations, 1950-7. He has published widely in the field of international law.

Carlo Schaerf (Italian) (co-editor) is Professor of Physics at the University of Rome. He was formerly a Research Associate at Stanford University and on the staff of the Italian Atomic Energy Commission. With Professor Eduardo Amaldi he founded in 1966 The International School on Disarmament and Research on Conflicts (ISODARCO). He was appointed Director of ISODARCO in 1970. He is co-editor of the previous volumes in the series, *The Dynamics of the Arms Race* and *International Terrorism and World Security* (Croom Helm, London and John Wiley, New York, 1975).

Enid C.B. Schoettle (US) is Program Officer of European and International Affairs, the Ford Foundation, New York. She was formerly Assistant Professor in the Department of Political Science at the University of Minnesota. Her article in the present volume will in due course be expanded for publication under the auspices of the Stockholm International Peace Research Institute.

Herbert Scoville Jr. (US) is a consultant and writer on security affairs and disarmament. He served in the US Government from 1948 to 1969. He has been a Technical Director in the Department of Defense; an Assistant and a Deputy Director in the Central Intelligence Agency; and an Assistant Director in the Arms Control and Disarmament Agency. He has contributed to *Foreign Affairs, Scientific American, Foreign Policy* and *Survival.* His Book, *Missile Madness,* was published by Houghton-Mifflin.

Tom Stonier (US) is Professor of Science and Society, University of Bradford, Great Britain. He was formerly Professor of Biology and Director of the Peace Studies Program, Manhattan College, New York. He is author of *Nuclear Disaster* (Penguin, 1964).

Kosta Tsipis (US) is a Professor at the Center for International Studies at Massachusetts Institute of Technology. He has also been associated with the Stockholm International Peace Research Institute. He has written widely on arms control.

Herbert F. York (US) is Professor of Physics at the University of San Diego. He was one of the nuclear scientists who developed the atomic bomb. He subsequently served in the Department of Defense under both Presidents Eisenhower and Kennedy. His most recent works are *Race to Oblivion: A Participant's View of the Arms Race* (Simon and Schuster, New York, 1970); and *The Advisers: Oppenheimer, Teller and the Superbomb* (W.H. Freeman, San Francisco, 1976).

LIST OF COURSE PARTICIPANTS
Nemi, 22 June — 7 July 1976

Adebisi, Adebiyi (Nigerian) Student in Peace and Conflict Studies, School of Peace Studies, Bradford University, Bradford, Great Britain.

Ali, Shamsher (Bangladesh) Director, Atomic Energy Centre, P.O. Box 164, Dacca-2, Bangladesh.

Aupers, Gerard (Dutch) Staff Member, Polemological Institute, Rijkstraatweg, 76, Haren, Groningen, The Netherlands.

Baker, Steven J. (US) Assistant Professor in Government, University of Texas, Austin, Texas, United States.

Batzella, Franco (Italian) Military operational researcher in Italian, Ministry of Defence, Via Pineta Sacchetti 438, 00165 Roma, Italy.

Behar, Nansen (Bulgarian) Scientific Research Worker, Institute of Economics, 1000 Sofia, ul. Aksakov 3, Bulgaria.

Bell, J. Bowyer (US) Senior Research Associate, Institute of War and Peace Studies, Columbia University, New York, NY 10027, United States.

Biesiot, Wouter (Dutch) Graduate Student, Laboratorium voor Algemene Natuurkunde, Westersingel 34, Groningen, The Netherlands.

Bilandzic, Vladimir (Yugoslav) Research Assistant, Institute of International Politics and Economics, Makedonska 25, 11000 Belgrade, Yugoslavia.

Calogero, Francesco (Italian) Professor of Theoretical Physics, Istituto di Fiscia, Università di Roma, Piazzale della Scienze 5, 00185 Roma, Italy.

Carlton, David (British) Senior Lecturer in Diplomatic History, Polytechnic of North London, Prince of Wales Road, London, N.W.5., Great Britain.

Cavallaro, Evaldo (Italian) Expert on Economics of Developing Countries, SIOI, Piazza S. Marco 51, Roma, Italy.

Corradi, Sofia (Italian) Professor of Education, Università di Roma, Piazzale delle Scienze 5, 00185 Roma, Italy.

Drago, Antonino (Italian) Professor of Physics, Istituto di Fiscia Teorica, Mostra d'Oltremare, Pad.19, Napoli, Italy.

Dumas, Lloyd J. (US) Associate Professor, Department of Industrial

and Management Engineering, Columbia University, New York, N.Y.
10027, United States.

Eide, Asbjørn (Norwegian) International Peace Research Institute,
Oslo 1, Radhusgt.4, Norway.

Epstein, William (Canadian) Special Fellow, Institute for UN Training
and Research, 801 UN Plaza, New York, NY 10017, United States.

Eriksson, Lars (Swedish) Swedish Defence Staff, Stockholm 11323,
Halsingegatan 3, Sweden.

Fabiyi, Edwin O. (Nigerian) Student, Nice University, Nice, France.

Feeg, Peter (Austrian) Student, Austrian UN Association, 1010 Wien,
Josephsplatz 6, Austria.

Frankel, Giorgio (Italian) Industrial Adviser, Via Bligny 8, 10122
Torino, Italy.

Freeman, John P. (British) Student, Department of War Studies, King's
College, Strand, London W.C.2., Great Britain.

Gliksman, Alex (US) Lecturer, Graduate School, University of Southern
California, Tegernseerlandstr. 227/2, 8 Munich 90, Federal Germany.

Grodzinska, Zofia (Finnish) Student, Kilonrinne 10 A 21, 02610
ESPOO 61, Finland.

Gueye, Amadou Mactar (Senegalese) Journalist, Centre d'Études
Internationales des Tensions du Monde Moderne 4, Bd. de Courcelles,
Paris 17ᵉ, France.

Gyarmati, Istvan (Hungarian) Journalist, 1136 Budapest, Sallai 1. 24,
Hungary.

Halsted, Thomas A. (US) Executive Director, Arms Control Association,
11 Dupont Circle N.W., Washington D.C. 20036, United States.

Heiskanen, Ilkka (Finnish) Attaché, Ministry for Foreign Affairs,
Aleksanterink 3 D, 00170 Helsinki, Finland.

Huq, Khondaker Muzammel (Bangladesh) Research Student, Worcester
College, Oxford, Great Britain.

Jacchia, Enrico (Italian) Hon. Director General of the EEC, Piazza
dell'Orologio 7, Roma, Italia.

Jacob, Kurt (West German) Research Assistant, Stiftung Wissenschaft
und Politik, D-8026 Ebenhausen, Federal Germany.

Joublanc, Luciano (Mexican) Diplomat, Mexican Embassy, 9 Rue de
Longchamp, 75116 Paris, France.

Kaldor, Mary (British) Science Policy Research Unit, University of
Sussex, Mantell Building, Falmer, Brighton, Sussex, Great Britain.

Kaplan, Martin (US) Director General, Pugwash Conferences on Science
and World Affairs, Chemin de Marley Collonge, Bellerive, 1245
Geneva, Switzerland.

Karpan, Leonid (Soviet) Diplomat, Soviet Embassy, Via Gaeta 5, Roma, Italy.

Kende, István (Hungarian) Professor of International Relations, Karl Marx University of Economic Sciences, Budapest, Hungary.

King, Peter (Australian) Senior Lecturer, Department of Government, University of Sydney, Australia.

Lapter, Karol (Polish) Professor, Swedish Institute of International Politics, 23 Lilla Nygatan, 11128 Stockholm, Sweden.

Letterie, Jacobus W. (Dutch) Post-doctoral Researcher in Economics, Jekerstraat 28 II, Amsterdam, The Netherlands.

Levine, Herbert M. (US) Professor of Political Science, University of Southwestern Louisiana, Box 4-1492 USL Sta., Lafayette, Louisiana 70504, United States.

Massai, Alessandro (Italian) Research Assistant, Istituto di Diritto Internazionale, Università di Pisa, Via S. Maria 32, 56100 Pisa, Italy.

Miettinen, Jorma K. (Finnish) Professor of Radiochemistry, University of Helsinki, Unioninkatu 35, Helsinki 17, Finland.

Milstein, Michail (Soviet) Chief of Section, Institute of Canadian and US Studies, Soviet Academy of Sciences, Khlebny per 2/3, Moscow 121069, Soviet Union.

Moussa, Abou (Chad) Student, Centre d'Études Internationales des Tensions du Monde Moderne 4, Bd. de Courcelles, 75017 Paris, France.

Mushkat, Mario'n (Israeli) Director, Institute for the Study of International Affairs, P.O.B. 17027, Tel Aviv 61170, Israel.

Myjer, Eric P.J. (Dutch) Student, Department of War Studies, King's College, Strand, London W.C.2., Great Britain.

Nacht, Michael (US) Assistant Director, Program for Science and International Affairs, Harvard University, 9 Divinity Avenue, Cambridge, Mass. 02138, United States.

Nakai, Yoko (Japanese) C/O USIS, American Embassy, 2 Aoi-cho, Minato-ku, Tokyo, Japan.

Nalewajek, Robert A. (US) Platen Strasse 22/7 B-3, 6000 Frankfurt/Main, Federal Germany.

Nitti, Gianfranco (Italian) Researcher in International Affairs, Università di Bari, Bari, Italy.

Ooms, A. Jack (Dutch) Director, Chemical Laboratory, Organization for Applied Sciences, P.O.B. 45, Rijkwijk 2100, The Netherlands.

Pascolino, Allessandro (Italian) Institute of Physics, Università di Padova, Padua, Italy.

Peeters, Chris (Dutch) Staff Manager, Peace Research Centre,

van Schaeck Mathonsingel 4, Nijmegen, The Netherlands.
Perry Robinson, Julian (British) Science Policy Research Unit,
University of Sussex, Mantell Building, Falmer, Brighton, Sussex,
Great Britain.
Pfeifenberger, Werner (Austrian) Professor of International Relations,
von-Esmarch-Str. 157, D-44 Münster, Federal Germany.
Prosser, Richard (British) 6 Southview Drive, Worthing, Sussex,
Great Britain.
Röling, Bert (Dutch) Professor, Polemological Institute, Rijksuniversiteit
Groningen, Riksstraatweg 76, Haren, Groningen, The Netherlands.
Sandole, Dennis J.D. (US) Lecturer, University of Southern California
School of International Relations, Sioli Strasse, 6000 Frankfurt/
Main, Federal Germany.
Schaerf, Carlo (Italian) Professor of Physics, Istituto di Fisica,
Università degli Studi di Roma, Piazzale delle Scienze 5, Roma, Italy.
Scheelen, Willem (Dutch) Arms Control and Disarmament Office,
Ministry of National Defence, Plein 4, The Hague, The Netherlands.
Schoettle, Enid C.B. (US) Program Officer, Office of European and
International Affairs, The Ford Foundation, 320 East 43rd Street,
New York, New York 10017, United States.
Schütz, Hans-Joachim (Austrian) Research Associate, Institute for
International Law, University of Kiel, 23 Kronshagen, Heischberg 2
VI, Federal Germany.
Scoville, Herbert Jr. (US) Arms Control Association, 6400 Georgetown
Pike, McLean, Virginia 22101, United States.
Segal, Jack D. (US) Candidate US Foreign Service Officer, 6374
Steinbach, Niederhöchstädtsterstr. 18, Federal Germany
Slovo, Gillian (British) Research Assistant, Science Faculty, Open
University, Walton Hall, Milton Keynes, Great Britain.
Stonier, Thomas (US) Professor, School of Science and Society,
University of Bradford, Bradford, Great Britain.
Tsipis, Kosta (US) Professor, Center for International Studies,
Massachusetts Institute of Technology, 77 Massachusetts Avenue,
Cambridge, Mass., United States.
Vaghi, Sergio (Italian) Astronomer, Astronomical Observatory,
Torino, Italy.
Van der Meer, Frans-Bauke (Dutch) Research Assistant, Science and
Society Group, Technical University of Twente, Enschedé, The
Netherlands.
Vetschera, Heinz (Austrian) Research Assistant, Institut für
militärstrategische Grundlagenforschung, Stiftsgasse 2a,

A-1070 Wien, Austria.

York, Herbert F. (US) Professor of Physics, University of California, San Diego, La Jolla, California 92037, United States.

Ziai, Iradj (Iranian) Student in Political Science, 148 Av. Arya-Mehr, Machad, Iran.

N.B. One author of a paper was unfortunately unable to attend the course, namely Professor Hans J. Morgenthau.